Innovations and Contemporary Trends in Business & Economics

Cemil Şenel / Mücahit Burak Ünlüönen /
Muhammed Veysel Kaya (eds.)

Innovations and Contemporary Trends in Business & Economics

PETER LANG
Berlin - Bruxelles - Chennai - Lausanne - New York - Oxford

Bibliographic Information published by the Deutsche Nationalbibliothek
The Deutsche Nationalbibliothek lists this publication in the Deutsche Nationalbibliografie; detailed bibliographic data is available in the internet at http://dnb.d-nb.de.

Library of Congress Cataloging-in-Publication Data
A CIP catalog record for this book has been applied for at the Library of Congress.

ISBN 978-3-631-91957-6 (Print)
E-ISBN 978-3-631-92391-7 (E-PDF)
E-ISBN 978-3-631-92392-4 (E-PUB)
DOI 10.3726/b22148

Published by Peter Lang GmbH, Berlin, Deutschland

info@peterlang.com - www.peterlang.com

This publication has been peer reviewed.
www.peterlang.com

Foreword

Our book called "Innovations and Contemporary Trends in Business & Economics" consists of 24 chapters. 62 authors have contributed to our book. This book contains trends and innovations in the field of economy and business. The target audience of this book is researchers, students and academics interested in business and economics. We think that it is a book in which you can find various topics and read with pleasure. We would like to express our gratitude to our publisher PETER LANG for the care they have taken in the preparation of the book.

Table of Contents

List of Contributers

Entela Abdul
Luarasi University, Faculty of Law, Tiranë, Albania

Turaev Abdurakhim Nortojiyevich
Tashkent State University of Economics, Uzbekistan

Tarlan Ahmadov
Tallinn University of Technology, Tallinn, Estonia

Elshod Alimardonov
PhD, Associate Professor, Department of International Finance and Credit, Tashkent State University of Economics, Tashkent, Uzbekistan.

Ilkhom Alimardonov
Tashkent State University of Economics, Tashkent, Uzbekistan

Plarent Anamali
Member of National Lawyer Association of Republic of Albania

Daniela Antonescu
Center of Mountain Economy, Vatra Dornei, Suceava, Romania

Pedro Fernandes da Anunciação
Setúbal Polytechnic University, School of Business, Setúbal, Portugal

Jasurbek Ataniyazov

Tashkent State University of Economics, Tashkent, Uzbekistan

Nigora Ravshanovna Bazarova
Associate Professor, Tashkent State University of Economics, Faculty of Business Administration. Tashkent . Uzbekistan

Tulkin Bobakulov
Tashkent State University of Economics, Tashkent, Uzbekistan

António Juan Briones Peñalver
Polytechnic University of Cartagena, Cartagena, Spain

Francisco José Videira Cachatra
Setúbal Polytechnic University, School of Business, Setúbal, Portugal

Jessica Cristina Caeiro José
Setúbal Polytechnic University, School of Business, Setúbal, Portugal

Constantinos Challoumis
N.K.U.A. (National and Kapodistrian University of Athens), Athens, Greece

Cátia Cristina Ferro Guégués
Setúbal Polytechnic University, School of Business, Setúbal, Portugal

Yi Ding
Central University of Finance and Economics, Center for China Fiscal Development, Beijing, China

Francisco Joaquim Madeira Esteves
Setúbal Polytechnic University, School of Business, Setúbal, Portugal

Wolfgang Gerstlberger
Tallinn University of Technology, Tallinn, Estonia

Fernando Miguel do Couto Gonçalves
Setúbal Polytechnic University, School of Business, Setúbal, Portugal

Hélder Miguel da Graça Alexandre
Setúbal Polytechnic University, School of Business, Setúbal, Portugal

Aníbal Júdice Guerreiro Cabanita Vieira
Setúbal Polytechnic University, School of Business, Setúbal, Portugal

Marija Ham
Faculty of Economics in Osijek, Croatia

Akrom Ishnazarov
Tashkent State University of Economics, Uzbekistan

Shoh-Jakhon Khamdamov
Ph.D., Associate professor, Tashkent State University of Economics, Faculty of Finance and accounting, Tashkent, Uzbekistan

Salman Kimiagari
Thompson Rivers University, Gaglardi School of Business and Economics, Kamloops, BC, Canada

Dorota Kuchta
Wroclaw University of Science and Technology, Faculty of Management, Wroclaw, Poland

Nigora Nematovna Kurbonova
Tashkent State University of Economics, Tashkent, Uzbekistan

Filipe António de Lemos
Setúbal Polytechnic University, School of Business, Setúbal, Portugal

Rossella Locatelli
University of Insubria, Department of Economics, Varese, Italy

Hailton Lopes da Silva
Setúbal Polytechnic University, School of Business, Setúbal, Portugal

Elira Luli
"Luarasi" University, Faculty of Law, Tirana, Albania

Mohammad Mahbobi
Thompson Rivers University, Gaglardi School of Business and Economics, Kamloops, BC, Canada.

Muxlisa Mahmudova
Ph.D., Head of Department of Commercialization of Scientific and Innovative Developments, Tashkent State University of Economics, Tashkent, Uzbekistan

Samariddin Makhmudov
Ph.D., Associate professor, Tashkent State University of Economics, Faculty of Finance and accounting, Tashkent, Uzbekistan

Zokir Mamadiyarov
Professor, Head of the Department of Financial market and insurance, Tashkent State University of Economics, Tashkent, Uzbekistan

Qamariddin Qo`ldoshev Mansurovich
Tashkent State University of Economics, Uzbekistan

Ewa Marchwicka
Wroclaw University of Science and Technology, Faculty of Management, Wroclaw, Poland

Tymon Marchwicki
Wroclaw University of Science and Technology, Faculty of Management, Wroclaw, Poland

Mirela Metushaj
"Aleksander Moisiu" University of Faculty of Political Science and Law, Tirana, Albania

Khurram Ali Mubasher
Iqra university, Department of Business Administration, Karachi, Pakistan

Agha Amad Nabi
Government College University Hyderabad, Faculty of Business Administration, Hyderabad, Pakistan

Badar un Nisa
COTHM College, Lahore, Pakistan

Saira Noor
Independent Researcher, Pakistan

Nuno Duarte Pereira
ESGT, Polytechnic of Santarém, Amibússola, Santarém, Portugal

Mário Joaquim Pereira
Setúbal Polytechnic University, School of Business, Setúbal, Portugal

Farhat Rasul
University of Management and Technology, Lahore, Pakistan

Humberto Nuno Rito Ribeiro
GOVCOPP; ESTGA, University of Aveiro, Aveiro, Portugal

Anvar Saidmakhmudovich Usmanov
Professor, Head of the Sector of the Research Centre, Tashkent State University of Economics, Tashkent, Uzbekistan

Umida Salikhodjaeva
Tashkent State University of Economics, Uzbekistan

Makhmudov Samariddin
Tashkent State University of Economics, Faculty of Finance and accounting, Tashkent, Uzbekistan

Joana Ribeiro dos Santos
Setúbal Polytechnic University, School of Business, Setúbal, Portugal

Nasiba Sattorova
Senior Lecturer of Banking and Investment Department, Tashkent State University of Economics, Tashkent, Uzbekistan

Cristiana Schena
University of Insubria, Department of Economics, Varese, Italy

Waqas Shair
Minhaj University Lahore, Pakistan

Khamdamov Shoh-Jakhon
Tashkent State University of Economics, Faculty of Finance and accounting, Tashkent, Uzbekistan

Marta Sofia dos Santos Simões Vasques Matos
Setúbal Polytechnic University, School of Business, Setúbal, Portugal

Alessandra Tanda
University of Pavia, Department of Economics and Management, Pavia, Italy

Rusudan Tsiskaridze
Tallinn University of Technology, Tallinn, Estonia

Fayaz Hussain Tunio
Shaheed Zulfiqar Ali Bhutto University of Law, Faculty of Law, Karachi, Pakistan

Hayati Yusof
Universiti Tunku Abdul Rahman, Malaysia

Jurabek Yusufovich Boltayev
Ph.D., Associate professor, Tashkent State University of Economics, Faculty of Finance and Accounting, Tashkent, Uzbekistan

Lucia Zbihlejová
Faculty of Management and Business, University of Prešov in Prešov, Slovakia

Zulnurhaini Zolkaply
Universiti Tunku Abdul Rahman, Malaysia

Ong Hock Siong
Universiti Tunku Abdul Rahman, Malaysia

Yee Chew Fong
Universiti Tunku Abdul Rahman, Malaysia

Mohamad Fared Mohamad Makmor
Universiti Tunku Abdul Rahman, Malaysia

Lee Weng Onn
Universiti Tunku Abdul Rahman, Malaysia

Rizwan Ul Hassan
The Lahore ALMA, Lahore, Pakistan.

List of Figures and Graphs

List of Tables

Constantinos Challoumis

Approach on Arm's Length Principle and Fix Length Principle Mathematical Representations

1. Introduction

The arm's length principle is about the differences which are determined between two enterprises in their financial and commercial relations in the case of controlled transactions, with the case of uncontrolled transactions. Should be mentioned that to reach the arm's length principle a company that participates in controlled transactions should preliminarily comply with two conditions. Thereupon, a company that is a tested party should reach the best method rule. The best method rule is about the method that should choose the company as the procedure for its tax business plan policy. The next preliminary obligation is about the comparability analysis. There the company of controlled transactions should make a series of comparisons to establish that meet the goals of the arm's length principle. Finally, is the check of the company that participates in controlled transactions that satisfy the arm's length principle. Then, in this step tax authorities will receive the decision if the submitted data complies with the goals of the arm's length principle. The fixed length principle which follows in the next section is about a new principle that tackles the unbalances caused by the arm's length principle by the best method rule and the comparability analysis. Additionally, should refer that the estimations of the arm's length principle and the fixed length principle are done using the Karush-Kuhn-Tucker method.

The fixed length principle is about an additional tax obligation of companies identified by tax authorities as enterprises that participate in controlled transactions. The authorities should have low tax rates for the companies which participate in uncontrolled transactions, and high tax rates for the companies which participate in controlled transactions. But, should notify that is not plausible to have two different tax rates. Thence, the result is that the authorities should have constant additional taxes for the companies that participate in controlled transactions activities. This is the basis for the fixed length principle. In that way is plausible to discourage the enterprises of controlled transactions from following the uncontrolled transactions, because the taxes would be lower. Consequently, the global tax rates would be increased.

The arm's length principle stands on the thought that the identification of differences between the controlled transactions with the case of the uncontrolled transactions could reveal the truth about the international business activities of the companies (Challoumis, 2018b, 2018d, 2019a, 2019c, 2022a, 2023i, 2023e, 2023a, 2023h, 2023b). The issue is that the companies that participate in those activities have the advantage of the best method rule. This means that these enterprises are able through the comparability analysis to tackle the efficient diversion between the controlled and the uncontrolled transactions (Al-Ubaydli et al., 2021; Arbel et al., 2019; Bento, 2009; Bourdin & Nadou, 2018; Cai, 2017; Cruce & Quinn, 2019; Dancygier & Laitin, 2014; Giglio et al., 2021; Jensen, 2020; Lal et al., 2018; Nicoleta Dospinescu, 2019; Noland, 2020; Peres et al., 2020). Therefore the three criteria of transfer pricing which are the best method rule, the comparability analysis, and the arm's length principle can avoid the antiquate taxation of the tested parties (Challoumis, 2021b, 2024m). On the other hand, the fixed length principle separately or in combination with the arm's length principle can tackle controlled transactions, because is more friendly to uncontrolled transactions, and simultaneously more restrictive to controlled transactions. In the analysis of the arm's length principle, the data have a central role in the comparison between the controlled transactions with the uncontrolled transactions (Baldwin et al., 2011; Béland, 2017; Hausman et al., 2016; Michener & Brower, 2020; Mueller, 2020; Ng, 2018; Omrani et al., 2021; Penchev, 2014; Schwartz, 2019; Torres Salcido et al., 2015; van den Bergh, 2022). Therefore, the critical points for the data of the arm's length principle are those:

- The first issue about the data is the adequacy of the offered information to the companies that participate in controlled transactions.
- One more crucial thing is the reliability of the data. In many cases, the data come from sources that cannot be trusted or should be identified if they are a proper source of information.

The prior two factors for the data are crucial for the business tax plan of the enterprises that participate in controlled transaction activities (Challoumis, 2020c, 2023g, 2023c, 2023f, 2024c). Therefore, if the companies have the appropriate data can clarify their business in such a way as to have comparability analysis results that comply with the arm's length principle. But, in that case, the tax authorities would not have accurate information about the business activities of the companies which participate in controlled transactions and therefore will have losses to their tax income, from the global economic view. It is mentioned in the global economic view because the tax heavens have some tax income, but the reality is that the real taxation is lost, and then from an international economic view are noticed tax losses.

The fixed length principle could be used in two ways. Then, there are two cases for the fixed length principle:

- The first method of the fixed length principle is the case of the direct method. This case is about the immediate application of the fixed-length method. Thence, the step of the comparability analysis and the step of the arm's length principle are avoided. One tax is higher for the companies identified for their participation in controlled transactions (Bergquist et al., 2020; Buonomo et al., 2020; Campos, 2015; Engström et al., 2020; Erickson, 2016; Kanthak & Spies, 2018; Khan & Liu, 2019; Leimbach et al., 2017; Miailhe, 2017; Miljand, 2020; Nowlin et al., 2020; Schram, 2018).
- The second approach of the fixed length principle is the case of the indirect method. In that case, it follows the schedule of the transfer pricing criteria. Forasmuch as, there are four steps, the best method rule, the comparability analysis, the arm's length principle, and the fixed length principle. Hence, in the indirect method of the fixed length principle, there are two taxations, the basic one and that which is caused by the fact that there is a case of transfer pricing (smaller additional tax).

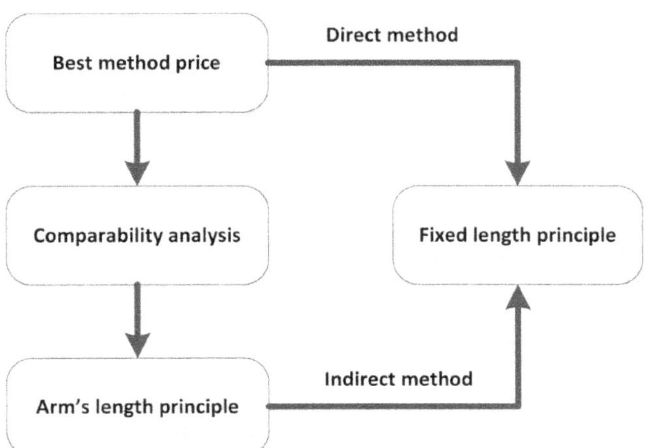

Figure 1. Direct and indirect method of the fixed length principle

The prior scheme illustrated the two axes of application of the fixed length principle. One case refers to the direct application of the fixed length principle and the other case refers to the indirect application of the fixed length principle which was analyzed before.

2. Literature Review

The impact factor of tax revenues of countries which are tax heaves, ***s*** (or otherwise global tax revenue) according to the "Methods of controlled transactions and identifications of tax avoidance" is determined as that:

$$\mathbf{s}=\frac{\mathbf{k}+\mathbf{l}}{\mathbf{r}+\mathbf{c}+\mathbf{t}+\mathbf{i}} \tag{1}$$

Therefore, some countries receive the products that are taxed in different countries. This allocation of profits between profits and losses permits the enterprises that participate in controlled transactions of the transfer pricing activities to maximize their utility. But contemporaneously the tax revenue from a global view is declined. Then, the loss of tax income from some countries is more than the profits that make the countries that are tax havens (Challoumis, 2019a). Thereupon, the symbol of ***s*** is the impact factor of tax revenue from a global view, and there are some coefficients which are ***k***, ***l***, ***r***, ***t***, *i* and ***c*** (Challoumis, 2023d, 2024b, 2024f, 2024a, 2024e, 2024d, 2024j, 2024l, 2024i, 2024k). Thus, the symbol of ***k*** is about the impact factor of capital, ***l*** is the impact factor about the liability of the authorities on the tax system. The interpretation of the liability is about how unbalanced it is the tax system. The parameter of r is about the risk, the t is about how trustworthy is the tax system (bureaucracy). The symbol of ***i*** examines the case of intangibles (the intangibles charged to the subsidiaries) of the tax system (Bergh, 2009; Bourdin & Nadou, 2018; Challoumis, 2020a; 2020b; Ortun et al., 2017; Tuter, 2020; Van de Vijver et al., 2020; Woody & Viney, 2017; Zamudio & Cama, 2020; Παπακωνσταντίνου et al., 2013). Additionally, the symbol of c is about the cost of enterprises. The symbols with the "~" are accordingly the same thing but from the view of the uncontrolled transactions. Thus, the numerator is proportional to the income of taxes, as the investments and the stable tax environments, with liability enhance the tax income (Challoumis, 2018c, 2019b, 2019c, 2019d, 2020d, 2021a, 2021c, 2022b). On the other hand, the denominator is inverted and proportional to the tax income, as the risk, the cost, and the unbalance of taxation cause less tax income:

$$\tilde{s} = \frac{\tilde{k} + \tilde{l}}{\tilde{r} + \tilde{c} + \tilde{t} + \tilde{i}} \tag{2}$$

Inasmuch the Eq. (3) is determined the aggregate impact factor of tax revenues, which is symbolized by $\hat{s}$, and is defined by the next equation:

$$\breve{s} = s + \tilde{s} \tag{3}$$

Based on the prior equations it is plausible to proceed to the identification of the behavior of the impact factors of tax revenues in the case of tax heavens and the case of the non-tax heavens. Consequently, using the prior equations is plausible to examine the controlled and the uncontrolled transactions (Challoumis, 2018a). Then, ***s*** is a factor which allows the comparison between the controlled with the uncontrolled transactions (Androniceanu et al., 2019; Bhuiyan & Farazmand, 2020; Farah, 2011; Jeon et al., 2020; Moreno-Jiménez et al., 2014; Ng, 2018; Shamah-Levy et al., 2019; Silva et al., 2020; Snow, 1988; Sultana, et al., 2020; Torres & Riaño-Casallas, 2018). Thence is able to have a standalone behavior analysis of controlled transactions and a combined behavior analysis between the controlled transactions with the uncontrolled transactions. The next section analyzes the impact factor of tax revenues with the rest impact factors.

For the global tax revenue:

- The bureaucracy reduces the global tax revenue in the case that this impact factor is avoided. The companies of controlled transactions are reduced in the case that there is no bureaucracy.
- The liability of the tax system increases the global tax system. This means that the tax system which does not have a lot of disturbances and changes in their law offers better conditions for the incensement of global tax revenue. Companies that don't participate in controlled transactions are increased in the case that there exists a liable tax system.
- The charged intangibles of the tax system decrease the global tax revenue. This shows that as more tools have the companies that participate in controlled transactions for allocation of their profits and losses, then more is the decrease of global tax revenue. When there are intangibles the companies of controlled transactions increase because they use them for better allocation of their profits and losses.

- The absence of risks of enterprises in the tax system causes an increase in global tax revenue. Moreover, the number of companies that participate in controlled transactions is increased in the case that there are risks. The reason is that the risks are connected with the existence of the companies or in other words with their willingness to participate in controlled transactions activities. Then as safer is the tax system, the more the income from taxes is a global view.
- The capital invested in the companies increases the global tax revenue. But, for the companies, many times the requirements for enlarging their capital at the same time make them more hesitant to reduce their business activities.
- The absence of costs in the tax system increases the global tax revenue. Thereupon, the enterprises that participate in controlled transactions of transfer pricing with costs are more than in the case where there are no costs. The interpretation is that the costs make the enterprises increase their business activities. As a more commercially active company, this means that increases its spending.

From the previous points, it is determined the general behavior of the global tax revenue with a series of impact factors (AICPA, 2017; Limberg, 2020; Martin & Freeland, 2021; Noland, 2020; Ortún et al., 2016; Rashid et al., 2020; Tvaronavičienė et al., 2018; Wright et al., 2017). It has concluded that the more helpful the rules and the economic environment for uncontrolled transactions the more the global tax revenue. Then, this situation is enhanced in the case that there are more restricted conditions for the controlled transactions of transfer pricing.

After the prior clarifications should be notified that reliable and adequate data are very critical in the decisions that a company could make. If the data are not appropriate it is plausible for a company to make wrong decisions, not because the analysis is wrong, but because the data gives a wrong orientation to the business plan and the taxation analysis (Bernasconi & Espinosa-Cristia, 2020; Campos, 2015; Dancygier & Laitin, 2014; Delgado Rodríguez & de Lucas Santos, 2018; Fan et al., 2020; Howlett, 2020; Johnston & Ballard, 2016; Kalambokidis, 2014; Khan & Liu, 2019; Liu et al., 2018; Marume, 2016; Muñoz & Flores, 2020; Prestianawati et al., 2020). Thereupon, the data are the base of any analysis from the companies that participate in controlled transactions. Therefore, companies should have the appropriate knowledge of their activities to make the right decisions, because otherwise will not be able to tackle the data of the controlled transactions and the uncontrolled transactions. Consequently, the conclusions will not be right, and therefore no adjustments could be made. The production of goods or services creates profits and costs for the companies:

$$\mathbf{u} = \mathbf{s}\left(\mathbf{zf} + \tilde{\mathbf{z}}\mathbf{d}\right) \tag{4}$$

$$\mathbf{z} = \left|\tilde{\mathbf{z}} - 1\right| \tag{5}$$

The symbol $\boldsymbol{u}$ is about the impact factor of the comparability analysis which has any method to the $\boldsymbol{u}$. The symbol z is a coefficient which takes values between 0 and 1. What value could be received is determined by the influence of the method (using the best method rule) on the $\boldsymbol{s}$. The symbol of $\boldsymbol{f}$ is about the cost which comes up from the production of goods, and the symbol of $\boldsymbol{d}$ is about the cost which comes from the distribution of the goods.

3. Methodology and Data

According to Eq. (1) – (5) is plausible to determine the following equations:

$$\mathbf{u}_{\mathrm{c}} = \mathbf{zf} + \tilde{\mathbf{z}}\mathbf{d} \tag{6}$$

$$\mathrm{b} = \left(\mathrm{p} - \mathbf{u}_{\mathrm{c}}\right) * \mathbf{j}_{1} \tag{7}$$

The symbol of $\boldsymbol{b}$ in the prior equation is about the amount of taxes that should be paid to the companies of controlled transactions in the application of the arm's length principle. The $\boldsymbol{u}_c$ is the amount of tax obligations that can be avoided through the allocations of profits and losses. Moreover, $\boldsymbol{j}_1$ is a coefficient for the rate of taxes. Then, the Eq. (7) shows the case of the arm's length principle. In the case of the fixed length principle:

$$\mathrm{b} = \left(\mathrm{p} - \mathbf{u}_{\mathrm{c}}\right) * \mathbf{j}_{1}, \left\{\mathbf{u}_{\mathrm{c}} = 0, \text{and } \mathbf{j}_{1} \rightarrow \mathbf{j}_{2}, \mathrm{b} \rightarrow \mathbf{v}\right\} \tag{8}$$

$$\mathbf{v} = \mathrm{p}^{*}\mathbf{j}_{2} \tag{9}$$

The symbol of $\boldsymbol{v}$ in the previous equation shows the taxes that should be paid to the enterprises of controlled transactions in the application of the fixed length principle. Then, $\boldsymbol{j}_2$ is a coefficient for the rate of taxes in the case of the fixed length principle:

$$\mathbf{v} \geq \mathbf{b} \tag{10}$$

The tax for the companies that participate in controlled transactions of transfer pricing in the case of the fixed length principle is higher or at least equal to that of the case of the arm's length principle. At the same time, the tax is lower for companies with uncontrolled transactions. According to that way, it is plausible to have higher global tax revenue and less controlled transactions according to the prior theory.

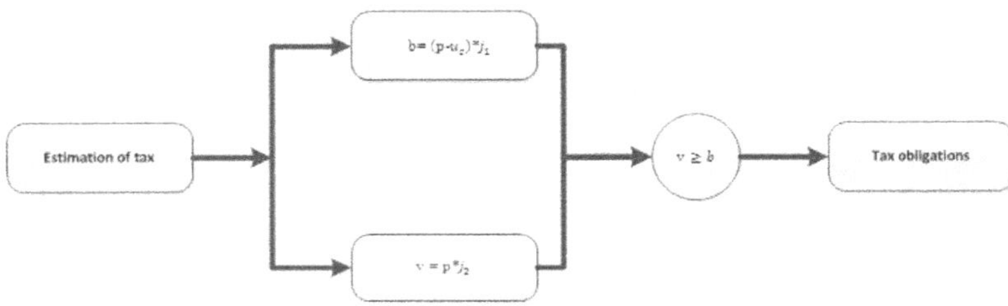

Figure 2. Tax policy according to the fixed length principle in combination with the arm's length principle

Figure 2 illustrates the application of the fixed length principle after the comparison with the arm's length principle.

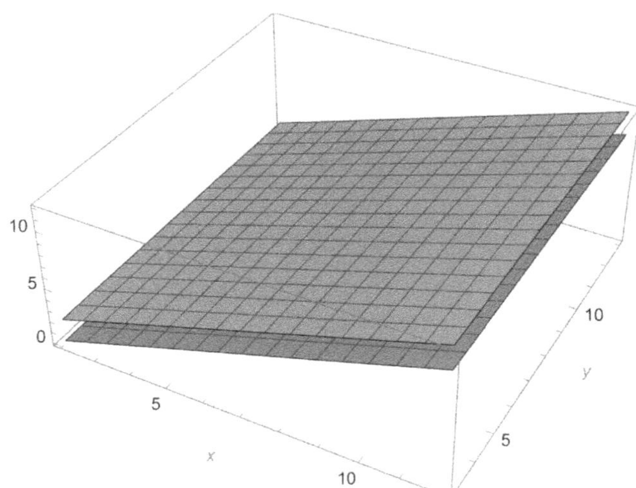

Figure 3. The brown color is the fixed length principle revenue and with blue color is the arm's length principle

4. Research Results and Comments

The tax obligations of companies that are tested parties are higher and then the authorities face the transfer pricing caused by the flexibility which allows the enterprises to choose the method that they wish and to adjust their data in the comparability analysis. Afterward, it was applied the Karush-Kuhn-Tucker method:

$$\left\{ s = \frac{k+1}{r+c+t}, b = \left(p - u_c\right) * j_1 \text{ and } v = p * j_2 \right\} \quad (11)$$

$$\mathcal{L} = s - \lambda \left[\left(p - \frac{u}{s} \right) * j_1 - b \right] - \kappa \left(p * j_2 - v \right)) \quad (12)$$

Thus:

$$\frac{d\mathcal{L}}{ds} = 0 \Rightarrow 1 - \lambda \frac{u}{s^2} * j_1 - 0 \Rightarrow \lambda \frac{u}{s^2} * j_1 = 1 \Rightarrow \lambda = \frac{s^2}{j_1 * u} \quad (13)$$

$$\frac{d\mathcal{L}}{dj_1} = 0 \Rightarrow -\lambda \left(p - \frac{u}{s} \right) * j_1 = 0 \Rightarrow u_c = \frac{u}{s} = p, \text{or, } u = s * p \quad (14)$$

$$\frac{d\mathcal{L}}{dj_2} = 0 \Rightarrow p = 0 \quad (15)$$

From the prior results, a visual representation could be presented by the following figure:

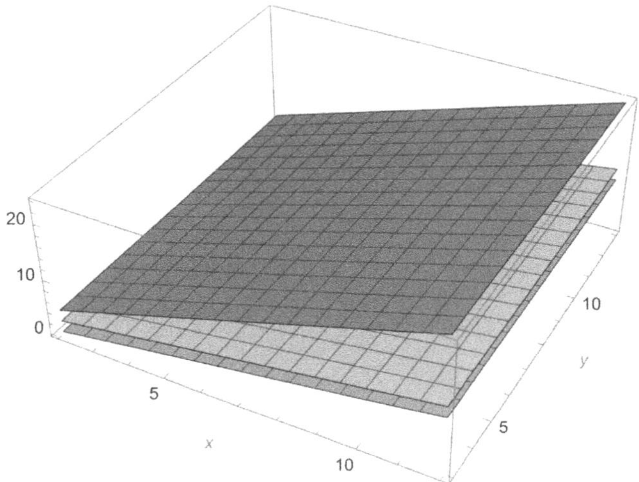

Figure 4. With the green color is the marginal revenue

It is concluded as was expected that the less tax in the arm's length principle is that which the companies which participate in controlled transactions achieve to maximize their allocation of profits and losses. In contradiction with the arm's length principle in the fixed length principle the companies which participate in controlled transactions are not able to make any allocation of profits and losses and the only way to have the minimum tax is the ideal case of no tax obligation at all (Challoumis, 2018b, 2019c, 2021b, 2022a, 2023i, 2023e, 2023a, 2023h, 2024h, 2024g). Then, it is obvious that the enterprises that are tested parties prefer the arm's length principle because they have the flexibility to choose the method they want and adjust their data at the comparison level and pay in that way fewer taxes.

5. Conclusion

The taxation of small and medium-sized enterprises reduces the competitiveness of the economy and leads to quasi-monopolies or oligopolies, thus burdening the economies of countries. The money cycle is maintained where there is a greater dispersion of money, i.e. small, and medium-sized businesses and freelancers. In large companies, there is more added value, but it does not replace smaller companies.

Based on this analysis, it would be advisable for government policies to be based on the concept of the Fix Length Principle (F.L.P.), instead of the Arm's Length Principle (A.L.P.), i.e. international companies, which use legal tax avoidance practices, should not choose the method by which to present their finances. but in any case, if they are judged to be subject to companies substituting smaller ones, they should be subject to additional tax to prevent the substitution of smaller enterprises.

References

AICPA. (2017). Guiding principles of good tax policy: A framework for evaluating tax proposals. *American Institute of Certified Public Accountants*, 2017(March 2001).

Al-ubaydli, O., Lee, M. S., List, J. A., Mackevicius, C. L., & Suskind, D. (2021). How can experiments play a greater role in public policy? Twelve proposals from an economic model of scaling. *Behavioural Public Policy*, 5(1). Retrieved from https://doi.org/10.1017/bpp.2020.17

Androniceanu, A., Gherghina, R., & Ciobănaşu, M. (2019). The interdependence between fiscal public policies and tax evasion. *Administratie Si Management Public*, 2019(32).

Arbel, Y., Fialkoff, C., & Kerner, A. (2019). Public policy for reducing tax evasion: implications of the Yule–Simpson paradox. *Applied Economics Letters*, 26(13). Retrieved from https://doi.org/10.1080/13504851.2018.1537471

Baldwin, R., Forslid, R., Martin, P., Ottaviano, G., & Robert-Nicoud, F. (2011). *Economic geography and public policy. Economic geography and public policy*. Retrieved from https://doi.org/10.1093/jnlecg/lbh045

Béland, D. (2017). Identity, politics, and public policy. *Critical Policy Studies*, 11(1). Retrieved from https://doi.org/10.1080/19460171.2016.1159140

Bento, A. (2009). Biofuels: Economic and public policy considerations. In R. W. Howarth & S. Bringezu (Eds.), *Biofuels: Environmental consequences and implications of changing land use* (September 2008).

Bergh, J. C. J. M. va. den. (2009). The GDP paradox. *Journal of Economic Psychology*, 30(2). Retrieved from https://doi.org/10.1016/j.joep.2008.12.001

Bergquist, P., Mildenberger, M., & Stokes, L. C. (2020). Combining climate, economic, and social policy builds public support for climate action in the US. *Environmental Research Letters*, 15(5). Retrieved from https://doi.org/10.1088/1748-9326/ab81c1

Bernasconi, O., & Espinosa-Cristia, J. F. (2020). No politics, no society: Questioning the justification of entrepreneurship in chilean public policies. *RAE Revista de Administracao de Empresas*, 60(2). Retrieved from https://doi.org/10.1590/S0034-759020200206

Bhuiyan, S., & Farazmand, A. (2020). Society and public policy in the Middle East and North Africa. *International Journal of Public Administration*. Retrieved from https://doi.org/10.1080/01900692.2019.1707353

Bourdin, S., & Nadou, F. (2018). French tech: A new form of territorial mobilization to face up to global competition? *Annales de Geographie*, 2018, 723–724.

Buonomo, I., Benevene, P., Barbieri, B., & Cortini, M. (2020). Intangible assets and performance in nonprofit organizations: A systematic literature review. *Frontiers in Psychology*, 11. Retrieved from https://doi.org/https://doi.org/10.3389/fpsyg.2020.00729

Cai, Y. (2017). Nonlinear analysis of economic growth, public debt and policy tools. *Asian Economic and Financial Review*, 7(1). Retrieved from https://doi.org/10.18488/journal.aefr/2017.7.1/102.1.99.108

Campos, J. N. B. (2015). Paradigms and public policies on drought in Northeast Brazil: A historical perspective. *Environmental Management*, 55(5). Retrieved from https://doi.org/10.1007/s00267-015-0444-x

Challoumis, C. (2018a). Identification of significant economic risks to the international controlled transactions. *Economics and Applied Informatics*, 2018(3), 149–153. Retrieved from https://doi.org/https://doi.org/10.26397/eai1584040927

Challoumis, C. (2018b). Methods of controlled transactions and the behavior of companies according to the public and tax policy. *Economics*, 6(1), 33–43. Retrieved from https://doi.org/10.2478/eoik-2018-0003

Challoumis, C. (2018c). The Keynesian theory and the theory of cycle of money. *Hyperion Economic Journal*, 6(3), 3–8. Retrieved from https://hej.hyperion.ro/articles/3(6)_2018/HEJ nr3(6)_2018_A1Challoumis.pdf

Challoumis, C. (2018d). The role of risk to the international controlled transactions. *Economics and Applied Informatics*, 2018(3), 57–64. Retrieved from https://doi.org/10.26397/eai1584040917

Challoumis, C. (2019a). The arm's length principle and the fixed length principle economic analysis. *World Scientific News*, 115(2019), 207–217. Retrieved 21 April 2021 from https://doi.org/10.2139/ssrn.1986387

Challoumis, C. (2019b). The issue of utility of cycle of money. *Journal Association SEPIKE*, 2019(25), 12–21. Retrieved from https://5b925ea6-3d4e-400b-b5f3-32dc681218ff.filesusr.com/ugd/b199e2_dd29716b8bec48ca8fe7fbcfd47cdd2e.pdf

Challoumis, C. (2019c). The R.B.Q. (Rational, Behavioral and Quantified) model. *Ekonomika*, 98(1), 6–18. Retrieved from https://doi.org/10.15388/ekon.2019.1.1

Challoumis, C. (2019d). Transfer pricing methods for services and the policy of fixed length principle. *Economics and Business*, 33(1), 222–232. Retrieved from https://doi.org/https://doi.org/10.2478/eb-2019-0016

Challoumis, C. (2020a). Analysis of the theory of cycle of money. *Acta Universitatis Bohemiae Meridionalis*, 23(2), 13–29. Retrieved from https://doi.org/https://doi.org/10.2478/acta-2020-0004

Challoumis, C. (2020b). Impact factor of capital to the economy and tax system. *Complex System Research Centre*, 2020, 195–200. Retrieved from https://www.researchgate.net/publication/350385990_Impact_Factor_of_Capital_to_the_Economy_and_Tax_System

Challoumis, C. (2020c). The Impact Factor of Costs to the Tax System. *Journal of Entrepreneurship, Business and Economics*, 8(1), 1–14. Retrieved from http://scientificia.com/index.php/JEBE/article/view/126

Challoumis, C. (2020d). The Impact Factor of Education on the Public Sector – The Case of the U.S. *International Journal of Business and Economic Sciences Applied Research*, 13(1), 69–78. Retrieved from https://doi.org/10.25103/ijbesar.131.07

Challoumis, C. (2021a). Index of the cycle of money – The case of Latvia. *Economics and Culture*, 17(2), 5–12. Retrieved from https://doi.org/10.2478/jec-2020-0015

Challoumis, C. (2021b). Index of the cycle of money – The case of Bulgaria. *Economic Alternatives*, 27(2), 225–234. Retrieved from https://www.unwe.bg/doi/eajournal/2021.2/EA.2021.2.04.pdf

Challoumis, C. (2021c). *The cycle of money with and without the enforcement savings*. Complex System Research Centre.

Challoumis, C. (2022a). Conditions of the CM (Cycle of Money). In *Social and economic studies within the framework of emerging global developments, Volume -1, V. Kaya* (pp. 13–24). Retrieved from https://doi.org/10.3726/b19907

Challoumis, C. (2022b). Impact factor of the rest rewarding taxes. In *Complex System Research Centre*. Retrieved from https://doi.org/10.2139/ssrn.3154753

Challoumis, C. (2023a). A comparison of the velocities of minimum escaped savings and financial liquidity. In *Social and economic studies within the framework of emerging global developments, Volume – 4, V. Kaya* (pp. 41–56). Retrieved from https://doi.org/10.3726/b21202

Challoumis, C. (2023b). Comparisons of the cycle of money with and without the mixed savings. *Economics & Law*. Retrieved from http://el.swu.bg/ikonomika/

Challoumis, C. (2023c). From savings to escape and enforcement savings. *Cogito*, XV(4), 206–216.

Challoumis, C. (2023d). G7 – Global minimum corporate tax rate of 15%. *International Journal of Multicultural and Multireligious Understanding (IJMMU)*, 10(7).

Challoumis, C. (2023e). Impact factor of liability of tax system according to the theory of cycle of money. In *Social and economic studies within the framework of emerging global developments volume 3, V. Kaya* (Vol. 3, pp. 31–42). Retrieved from https://doi.org/10.3726/b20968

Challoumis, C. (2023f). Index of the cycle of money: The case of Costa Rica. *Sapienza*, 4(3), 1–11. Retrieved from https://journals.sapienzaeditorial.com/index.php/SIJIS

Challoumis, C. (2023g). Index of the cycle of money – The case of Canada. *Journal of Entrepreneurship, Business and Economics*, 11(1), 102–133. Retrieved from http://scientificia.com/index.php/JEBE/article/view/203

Challoumis, C. (2023h). Risk on the tax system of the E.U. from 2016 to 2022. *Economics*, 11(2).

Challoumis, C. (2023i). Utility of cycle of money without the escaping savings (Protection of the Economy). In *Social and economic studies within the framework of emerging global developments volume 2, V. Kaya* (pp. 53–64). Retrieved from https://doi.org/10.3726/b20509

Challoumis, C. (2024a). Estimations of the cycle of money without escape savings. *International Journal of Multicultural and Multireligious Understanding*, 11(3).

Challoumis, C. (2024b). From axiomatics method to multiple axiomatics method – Q.E. (Quantification of Everything) method. *International Journal of Multicultural and Multireligious Understanding.*

Challoumis, C. (2024c). From economics to economic engineering (The Cycle of Money): The case of Romania. *Cogito*, XVII(2).

Challoumis, C. (2024d). Impact factor of capital using the sensitivity method. *International Journal of Multicultural and Multireligious Understanding.*

Challoumis, C. (2024e). Impact factor of cost using the sensitivity method. *International Journal of Multicultural and Multireligious Understanding.*

Challoumis, C. (2024f). Impact factors of global tax revenue – Theory of cycle of money. *International Journal of Multicultural and Multireligious Understanding*, 11(1).

Challoumis, C. (2024g). Index of the cycle of money – The case of Switzerland. *The Index of the Cycle of Money: The Case of Switzerland. J. Risk Financial Manag. 2024, 17, 135.* https://Doi.Org/10.3390/Jrfm17040135, 17(4), 1–24. Retrieved from https://doi.org/https://doi.org/10.3390/jrfm17040135

Challoumis, C. (2024h). *Rewarding taxes on the cycle of money. Social and Economic Studies within the Framework of Emerging Global Developments* (Vol. 5).

Challoumis, C. (2024i). Rewarding taxes on the economy (The theory of cycle of money). *International Journal of Multicultural and Multireligious Understanding (IJMMU)*, 11(3).

Challoumis, C. (2024j). Synopsis of principles for the authorities and controlled transactions. *International Journal of Multicultural and Multireligious Understanding.*

Challoumis, C. (2024k). The cycle of money – Escape savings and the minimum financial liquidity. *International Journal of Multicultural and Multireligious Understanding (IJMMU)*, 11(4).

Challoumis, C. (2024l). The cycle of money – Minimum escape savings and financial liquidity. *International Journal of Multicultural and Multireligious Understanding (IJMMU)*, 11(5).

Challoumis, C. (2024m). The impact factor of Tangibles and Intangibles of controlled transactions on economic performance. *Economic Alternatives.*

Cruce, J. R., & Quinn, J. C. (2019). Economic viability of multiple algal biorefining pathways and the impact of public policies. *Applied Energy*, 233–234. Retrieved from https://doi.org/10.1016/j.apenergy.2018.10.046

Dancygier, R. M., & Laitin, D. D. (2014). Immigration into Europe: Economic discrimination, violence, and public policy. *Annual Review of Political Science*, 17. Retrieved from https://doi.org/10.1146/annurev-polisci-082012-115925

Delgado Rodríguez, M. J., & de Lucas Santos, S. (2018). Speed of economic convergence and EU public policy. *Cuadernos de Economia*, 41(115). Retrieved from https://doi.org/10.1016/j.cesjef.2017.01.001

Engström, G., Gars, J., Jaakkola, N., Lindahl, T., Spiro, D., & van Benthem, A. A. (2020). What policies address both the coronavirus crisis and the climate crisis? *Environmental and Resource Economics*, 76(4). Retrieved from https://doi.org/10.1007/s10640-020-00451-y

Erickson, K. (2016). Defining the public domain in economic terms – Approaches and consequences for policy. *Etikk i Praksis*. Retrieved from https://doi.org/10.5324/eip.v10i1.1951

Fan, Y., Yang, S., & Jia, P. (2020). Preferential tax policies: An invisible hand behind preparedness for public health emergencies. *International Journal of Health Policy and Management*. Retrieved from https://doi.org/10.34172/ijhpm.2020.139

Farah, M. F. S. (2011). Public policy and public administration. *Revista de Administracao Publica*, 45(3).

Giglio, C., Musmanno, R., & Palmieri, R. (2021). Cycle logistics projects in Europe: Intertwining bike-related success factors and region-specific public policies with economic results. *Applied Sciences (Switzerland)*, 11(4). Retrieved from https://doi.org/10.3390/app11041578

Hausman, D., McPherson, M., & Satz, D. (2016). *Economic analysis, moral philosophy, and public policy. Economic analysis, moral philosophy, and public policy*. Retrieved from https://doi.org/10.1017/9781316663011

Howlett, M. (2020). Challenges in applying design thinking to public policy: Dealing with the varieties of policy formulation and their vicissitudes. *Policy and Politics*, 48(1). Retrieved from https://doi.org/10.1332/030557319X15613699681219

Jensen, P. H. (2020). Experiments and evaluation of public policies: Methods, implementation, and challenges. *Australian Journal of Public Administration*, 79(2). Retrieved from https://doi.org/10.1111/1467-8500.12406

Jeon, J., Kim, S., & Kwon, S. M. (2020). The effects of urban containment policies on public health. *International Journal of Environmental Research and Public Health*, 17(9). Retrieved from https://doi.org/10.3390/ijerph17093275

Johnston, C. D., & Ballard, A. O. (2016). Economists and public opinion: Expert consensus and economic policy judgments. *Journal of Politics*, 78(2). Retrieved from https://doi.org/10.1086/684629

Kalambokidis, L. (2014). Creating public value with tax and spending policies: The view from public economics. *Public Administration Review*, 74(4). Retrieved from https://doi.org/10.1111/puar.12162

Kanthak, L., & Spies, D. C. (2018). Public support for European Union economic policies. *European Union Politics*, 19(1). Retrieved from https://doi.org/10.1177/1465116517740638

Khan, S., & Liu, G. (2019). Socioeconomic and public policy impacts of China Pakistan economic corridor on Khyber Pakhtunkhwa. *Environmental Management and Sustainable Development*, 8(1). Retrieved from https://doi.org/10.5296/emsd.v8i1.13758

Lal, A., Moodie, M., Peeters, A., & Carter, R. (2018). Inclusion of equity in economic analyses of public health policies: Systematic review and future directions. *Australian and New Zealand Journal of Public Health*. Retrieved from https://doi.org/10.1111/1753-6405.12709

Leimbach, M., Kriegler, E., Roming, N., & Schwanitz, J. (2017). Future growth patterns of world regions – A GDP scenario approach. *Global Environmental Change*, 42. Retrieved from https://doi.org/10.1016/j.gloenvcha.2015.02.005

Limberg, J. (2020). What's fair? Preferences for tax progressivity in the wake of the financial crisis. *Journal of Public Policy*. Retrieved from https://doi.org/10.1017/S0143814X18000430

Liu, N., Liu, R., Huang, J., & Chen, L. (2018). Pollution, happiness and willingness to pay taxes: The value effect of public environmental policies. *Problemy Ekorozwoju*, 13(1).

Martin, A. S., & Freeland, S. (2021). The advent of Artificial Intelligence in space activities: New legal challenges. *Space Policy*, 55. Retrieved from https://doi.org/10.1016/j.spacepol.2020.101408

Marume, S. B. M. (2016). Public policy and factors influencing public policy. *International Journal of Engineering Science Invention*, 5(6).

Miailhe, N. (2017). Economic, social and public policy opportunities enabled by automation. *Field Actions Science Reports. The Journal of Field Actions*, (Special Issue 17).

Michener, J., & Brower, M. T. (2020). What's policy got to do with it? Race, gender & economic inequality in the United States. *Daedalus*, 149(1). Retrieved from https://doi.org/10.1162/DAED_a_01776

Miljand, M. (2020). Using systematic review methods to evaluate environmental public policy: Methodological challenges and potential usefulness. *Environmental Science and Policy, 105*. Retrieved from https://doi.org/10.1016/j.envsci.2019.12.008

Moreno-Jiménez, J. M., Pérez-Espés, C., & Velázquez, M. (2014). E-Cognocracy and the design of public policies. *Government Information Quarterly*, 31(1). Retrieved from https://doi.org/10.1016/j.giq.2013.09.004

Mueller, B. (2020). Why public policies fail: Policymaking under complexity. *EconomiA*, 21(2). Retrieved from https://doi.org/10.1016/j.econ.2019.11.002

Muñoz, O. G., & Flores, M. C. (2020). Basic principles of economic policy and public decision in the 21st century. *Journal of Social Sciences (COES&RJ-JSS)*, 9(1). Retrieved from https://doi.org/10.25255/jss.2020.9.1.21.31

Ng, Y. K. (2018). Ten rules for public economic policy. *Economic Analysis and Policy*, 58. Retrieved from https://doi.org/10.1016/j.eap.2018.01.002

Nicoleta Dospinescu, O. D. (2019). A profitability regression model in financial communication of romanian stock exchange's companies. *Asociația de Cooperare Cultural-Educațională Suceava, 1*(8).

Noland, M. (2020). Protectionism under Trump: The China Shock, Deplorables, and the First White President. *Asian Economic Policy Review*. Retrieved from https://doi.org/10.1111/aepr.12274

Nowlin, M. C., Gupta, K., & Ripberger, J. T. (2020). Revenue use and public support for a carbon tax. *Environmental Research Letters*, 15(8). Retrieved from https://doi.org/10.1088/1748-9326/ab92c3

Omrani, H., Modroiu, M., Lenzi, J., Omrani, B., Said, Z., Suhrcke, M., … Parmentier, B. (2021). COVID-19 in Europe: Dataset at a sub-national level. *Data in Brief*, 35. Retrieved from https://doi.org/10.1016/j.dib.2021.106939

Ortún, V., Lopez-Valcarcel, B. G., & Pinilla, J. (2017). Tax on sugar sweetened beverages in Spain. *SSRN Electronic Journal*. Retrieved from https://doi.org/10.2139/ssrn.3004464

Ortún, V., López-Valcárcel, B. G., & Pinilla, J. (2016). El impuesto sobre bebidas azucaradas en España. *Revista Espanola de Salud Publica*, 90.

Penchev, P. (2014). The "Alternative" socialism of professor Alexander Tsankov. *Economic Alternatives*, 2(2014), 61–75.

Peres, M. F. P., Oliveira, A. B., Sarmento, E. M., Rocha-Filho, P. S., Peixoto, P. M., Kowacs, F., … Benseñor, I. M. (2020). Public policies in headache disorders: Needs and possibilities. *Arquivos de Neuro-Psiquiatria*, 78(1). Retrieved from https://doi.org/10.1590/0004-282X20190144

Prestianawati, S. A., Mulyaningsih, S., Manzilati, A., & Ashar, K. (2020). Rethinking tax leakage: Is it the impact of public policy failure? Retrieved from https://doi.org/10.2991/aebmr.k.200606.024

Rashid, H., Warsame, H., & Khan, S. (2020). The differential impact of democracy on tax revenues in developing and developed countries. *International Journal of Public Administration*. Retrieved from https://doi.org/10.1080/01900692.2020.1741616

Schram, A. (2018). When evidence isn't enough: Ideological, institutional, and interest-based constraints on achieving trade and health policy coherence. *Global Social Policy*, 18(1). Retrieved from https://doi.org/10.1177/1468018117744153

Schwartz, M. (2019). Social and economic public policy goals and their impact on defense acquisition – A 2019 update. *Defense Acquisition Research Journal*, 26(3).

Shamah-Levy, T., Romero-Martínez, M., Cuevas-Nasu, L., Gómez-Humaran, I. M., Avila-Arcos, M. A., & Rivera-Dommarco, J. A. (2019). The Mexican national health and nutrition survey as a basis for public policy planning: Overweight and obesity. *Nutrients*, 11(8). Retrieved from https://doi.org/10.3390/nu11081727

Silva, S. E., Venâncio, A., Silva, J. R., & Gonçalves, C. A. (2020). Open innovation in science parks: The role of public policies. *Technological Forecasting and Social Change*, 151. Retrieved from https://doi.org/10.1016/j.techfore.2019.119844

Snow, M. S. (1988). Telecommunications literature. A critical review of the economic, technological and public policy issues. *Telecommunications Policy*, 12(2). Retrieved from https://doi.org/10.1016/0308-5961(88)90007-9

Sultana, A., Or Rashid, M. H., Akter Eva, S., & Sultana, A. (2020). Assessment of relationship among regional economic development policy, urban development policy and public policy. *Sumerianz Journal of Economics and Finance*, (310). Retrieved from https://doi.org/10.47752/sjef.310.171.177

Torres, S. H. Á., & Riaño-Casallas, M. I. (2018). Public policy for safety and health at the worksite: The Colombian case. *Revista Gerencia y Politicas de Salud*. Retrieved from https://doi.org/10.11144/Javeriana.rgps17-35.ppss

Torres Salcido, G., del Roble Pensado Leglise, M., & Smolski, A. (2015). Food distribution's socio-economic relationships and public policy: Mexico City's municipal public markets. *Development in Practice*, 25(3). Retrieved from https://doi.org/10.1080/09614524.2015.1016481

Tuter, C. (2020). Persepsi Masyarakat Terhadap Isu Pajak Lingkungan Di Kabupaten Kepulauan Siau Tagulandang Biaro (SITARO). *Jurnal Ekonomi Dan Bisnis Airlangga*, 30(1). Retrieved from https://doi.org/10.20473/jeba.v30i12020.1-13

Tvaronavičienė, M., Tarkhanova, E., & Durglishvili, N. (2018). Sustainable economic growth and innovative development of educational systems. *Journal of International Studies*, *11*(1). Retrieved from https://doi.org/10.14254/2071-8330.2018/11-1/19

Van de Vijver, A., Cassimon, D., & Engelen, P. J. (2020). A real option approach to sustainable corporate tax behavior. *Sustainability (Switzerland)*, 12(13). Retrieved from https://doi.org/10.3390/su12135406

van den Bergh, J. C. J. M. (2022). A procedure for globally institutionalizing a 'beyond-GDP' metric. *Ecological Economics*, 192. Retrieved from https://doi.org/10.1016/j.ecolecon.2021.107257

Woody, W. D., & Viney, W. (2017). *A history of psychology: The emergence of science and applications* (6th ed., pp. 1–599).

Wright, A., Smith, K. E., & Hellowell, M. (2017). Policy lessons from health taxes: A systematic review of empirical studies. *BMC Public Health*. Retrieved from https://doi.org/10.1186/s12889-017-4497-z

Zamudio, A. R., & Cama, J. L. N. (2020). Assessment of fiscal effort and voluntary tax compliance in Peru. *Revista Finanzas y Politica Economica*, 12(1).

Retrieved from https://doi.org/10.14718/REVFINANZPOLITECON.V12.N1.2020.3121

Παπακωνσταντίνου, Α., Κανάββας, Λ., & Ντόκας, Ι. (2013). Οικονομία & μικρές επιχειρήσεις. In *Ινστιτούτο μικρών επιχειρήσεων* (pp. 1–208).

Dorota Kuchta, Ewa Marchwicka, Tymon Marchwicki

Estimation of Risks in a Development Team of a Global Software Project Based on Fuzzy Information and Credibility Assessment

1. Introduction

The popularity of global software development projects has been growing rapidly for several years (Beecham, 2021), along with the dynamic development of tools enabling such a model. Functionalities offered by modern videoconference and information sharing tools make project remote communication easier than ever. The recent pandemic accelerated this trend and today project managers can run projects using Scrum methodology and organize Scrum events in a team that is located in several different countries.

Some researchers already proved that scaled-Agile practices used in global software development (GSD) projects allow to handle and mitigate many of the risks (Beecham, 2021). But these practices are considered at the project-level (not Sprint level) and are disconnected from Scrum events, like Sprint planning.

Classical Scrum planning ignores explicit risk information that is available to the Development Team. Instead, an implicit risk management is handled in Scrum in several ways, for example by using increased estimations (Prater et al., 2019; Ghazali et al., 2018) during Sprint Planning or by using short development cycles (Georgiev & Stefanova, 2014). The few existing attempts of introducing explicit risk management to Scrum (Hammad & Inayat, 2018), (Tomanek & Juricek, 2015; Chourch et al., 2019; Hossain et al., 2009) have not been validated in practice yet and remain in the conceptual phase. At the same time, the list of standard risks that can endanger the realization of global software development projects is extensive and can be considered in several different dimensions, like importance and level of control (Beecham, 2021). The literature indicates that risk management is a very important aspect of global software development, including projects that are realized using Scrum. Implicit risk management specific for Scrum teams may not be enough to properly control GSD risks that can affect the realization of Sprint commitment. On the other hand, managing risks can be easily extended from the project-level (like in the scaled Agile approach) to the Sprint-level (e.g. adaptive Sprint planning). The latter approach makes the Scrum Development Team aware of risks that impact Sprint realization.

Managing Sprint-level risks allows to better adapt to the predicted and materialized risks, which protects the realization of Sprint commitment.

The motivation of this research is to address risks in Scrum-based global software development projects at the Sprint-level. The objective of the paper is developing the estimation algorithm for the risks in global software development projects that can be used for adaptive Sprint planning.

In this work an approach that extends Scrum with explicit risk estimations related to global software development is proposed. The approach is based on imprecise linguistic information gathered from the Development Team. Input risk information is linguistic, so that it can be used by every Scrum Team member (and not risk experts or project managers only). For this reason, the risks are modelled as fuzzy numbers. The estimation algorithm that is suggested allows to quantify Sprint risks. The quantification is performed using elementary operations on fuzzy numbers, like addition and multiplication. To the best knowledge of the authors, the algorithm is novel in several ways: e.g., it combines group estimations (each Scrum Team member is involved in the estimation), different consensus strategies (determining group decision based on individual estimations), self-credibility, optimistic/pessimistic credibility adjustments applied at the team-level, and it is based on linguistic representation of risks. Additionally, the algorithm uses multi-level representation of global software development risks. The high-level difference between the estimation algorithm that has been suggested and the estimation algorithms that are used in standard Scrum is that the algorithm suggested in this paper allows to manage risks separately from the backlog items and assumes the information can be updated during Sprint realization (and utilized in the adaptive Sprint planning).

2. Literature Review

This section contains literature review related to the estimation techniques that are used in Scrum as well as the review of quantitative risk management methods and a review of project risks in global software development (GSD) projects.

2.1. Estimation Techniques for IT and Scrum

There are some standard estimation techniques that can be used in IT projects, e.g.: Bottom Up, Expert Judgement, Questioning, Analogy, Reference Class, AACE, Two Estimates or Risk-Based (Prater et al., 2019). The last-mentioned approach includes risks in estimations. Many Scrum projects implement Scrum-Poker (Delphi) estimation approach (Alsaadi et al., 2021), which is not risk-based. However, the standard Scrum-poker can be extended and incorporate risk information, as an estimation described in (Ghazali et al., 2018). For all the approaches mentioned above that are risk-based it is assumed that the risk estimation is fixed after Sprint planning and cannot be updated during the Sprint.

2.2. Selected Risk Management Methods

There are several risk management methods that are described in the literature. The standard risk-management approach has been popularized in (PMBoK, 2021), which suggests using probability and impact matrix for risk analysis. Three points estimation is listed as one of the techniques in (Hulett, 2011), but this approach does not allow to include probability in the analysis. A better approach, called Risk Driver Method, is presented and recommended by the Author.

2.3. Risks in Global Software Development Projects

The first step of risk management is the identification process (PMBoK, 2021). Risks related to GSD can be identified after project is started, but there are some standard GSD risk catalogues that can be found in the literature. These catalogues can help to select a predefined list of possible risks that can occur. They often contain some mitigation practices or strategies to reduce the effect of risks to the project. For example, (Hossain, 2009) presents a conceptual framework with 7 risks identified, 13 strategies and 46 practices to handle them, (Verner et al., 2014) presents a catalogue of 85 risks in 12 categories and more than 70 mitigation strategies, (Shameem et al., 2020) contains a catalogue of 22 risks factors (called there the barriers) in 5 categories. Finally, (Beecham et al., 2021) presents a catalogue of 63 risks in 4 categories.

3. Materials and Method

This section presents the core part of the research, including research design, use case description, observations, inputs identification, the algorithm and the idea of quality assessment.

3.1. Research Design

The research presented in the paper is based on the GSD use case. One of the authors of this article participated in two GSD projects. Participant observations of risks were made, that included listing common threats, identifying different levels of risk sources and analyzing the consequences of risks. The observations were then supported by the literature review. Based on the observations and on the methods available in the existing literature, a fuzzy-based risk estimation algorithm is suggested as a result of conceptual work: its inputs are identified, the estimation algorithm is proposed, together with its quality assessment overview.

3.2. Fuzzy Numbers

Trapezoidal fuzzy numbers (TrFN) are used for modeling risks. A fuzzy number $\tilde{A} = (a, b, c, d)$ is a trapezoidal fuzzy number if the membership function is defined as in Equation 1.

$$\mu_{\tilde{A}}(x) = \begin{cases} 0, x < a \\ \dfrac{x-a}{b-a}, a \le x \le b \\ 1, b \le x \le c \\ \dfrac{d-x}{d-c}, c \le x \le d \\ 0, x > d \end{cases} \quad (1)$$

The degree of fuzziness is defined by the length of support, i.e., $|d - a|$. Some basic arithmetic operations (addition, subtraction, multiplication, scalar multiplication) on trapezoidal fuzzy numbers can be defined (Elsayed et al., 2022).

3.3. Use Case Description

Global software development project under research is a Scrum-based project, with several sub-teams distributed in two different countries and four different locations (Table 1). The first location is where some part of the code is being developed (external supplier), the second location is where project is being managed (Product Manager and Product Owner) and where requirements are defined. Development Team is two other locations. Because the project is part of the program, some cross-cutting project components are also developed by the Cross-Cutting Team, which includes architects from three different locations. Although different teams are in different locations, they collaborate in Scrum events using popular videoconference and information sharing tools.

Table 1. Global software project basic characteristics

ID	Sub-Team	Country	Location
1	External supplier	*A*	*1*
2	Product Manager	*A*	*2*
3	Product Owner	*A*	*2*
4	Requirements Team	*A*	*2*
5	Cross-Cutting Team	*A, B*	*2* and *3* and *4*
6	Scrum Development Team	*B*	*3* and *4*

Source: Own elaboration

3.4. Observations on Risks in the Global Project

Based on the use case presented, observations about risks were made. Some observations are supported by the literature, some are original and cannot be found in the existing literature.

Table 2. Observations used for the development of the algorithm

ID	Observation	Source	Comment
1	There are three levels of GSD risks	Authors analysis, based on project specifics	Risks related to external-supplier development, cross-cutting development, Scrum team development (compare: Table 1).
2	Risks from different levels are independent	Authors analysis, based on project specifics	There is no correlation between the risks on each level.
3	Only one (dominant) risk can be selected for each level	Authors simplification to simplify data collection	However, non-dominant risks can also be included (see Table 3, Ids 3, 4).
4	A predefined list of risks is used	GSD risks from (Beecham et al., 2021), filtered by the authors (only most appropriate risks for the project)	The risks from the literature are mapped to the tree risk levels (listed for Id 1).
5	Impact of risks is multiplicative	Assumption from (Hulett, 2011)	Risk-Driver method from (Hulett, 2011) uses the same assumption.
6	Individual risks consequences assessments can use linguistic expressions	Authors analysis, suitable for the Development Team, not risks experts	Consequences of individual risks cannot be directly measured and are based on the intuition.

(continued on next page)

Table 3. Continued

ID	Observation	Source	Comment
7	Total consequences of risks can be expressed as fuzzy numbers	Approach used in (Marchwicka & Kuchta, 2022)	Fits the Scrum context, where risk-related delays (post-factum) are relative and cannot be measured directly but only in relation to other tasks (i.e., are measured in Story Points, not days).
8	All risk-related assessments are Scrum-Team assessments	Authors assumptions, based on Scrum context	All Scrum-related decisions are group decisions, made using consensus strategy.
9	Credibility assessment (based on Z-fuzzy numbers) is needed to adjust the estimations	Approach used in (Marchwicka & Kuchta, 2022)	Group estimations of the whole team can be biased and need adjustments (e.g. can be too optimistic).
10	Self-credibility assessment is needed	Authors analysis, based on the fact that not every developer has the same knowledge about the risks that occurred.	Post-factum risks assessments are more precise for developers of the given Sprint item.

Source: own elaboration

3.5. Inputs Identification

Based on the observations, the following input information is required to perform the estimation: dominant risk names for each of the three risk-levels, dominant risk consequences assessment for each of the three risk-levels, additional risk name (compare Table 2/Id 3), additional risk consequences, self-credibility assessment. Additionally, each Scrum Development Team member was asked to define *LOW*, *MEDIUM*, *HIGH*. The inputs are summarized in Table 3.

Table 3. List of inputs for *N* backlog items and *M* team members

ID	Input	Possible values	Can be empty	Input size
1	Levels 1–3 dominant risk name	predefined list (most common risks)	YES	$3 \times N \times M$
2	Levels 1–3 dominant risk consequences linguistic assessment	$\in$ {*LOW*, *MEDIUM*, *HIGH*}	YES	$3 \times N \times M$

Table 3. Continued

ID	Input	Possible values	Can be empty	Input size
3	Additional risk name	User-given name (free text)	YES	$N x M$
4	Additional risk consequence linguistic assessment	∈ {*LOW, MEDIUM, HIGH*}	YES	$N x M$
5	Self-credibility assessment	∈ {*LOW, MEDIUM, HIGH*}	NO	$N x M$
6	$LOW, MEDIUM, HIGH$ definitions	Intervals [from %; to %] defining *LOW, MEDIUM, HIGH* consequence of a risk as a percentage added to the original risk duration	NO	$3 x M$
7	Post-factum total risk consequence assessment	$\in [0;100], i.e.,$ % of risks in total duration	NO	$N x M$

Source: own elaboration

3.6. Fuzzy Estimation Algorithm

The algorithm that is suggested in this paper uses fuzzy modeling of risks (Figure 1).

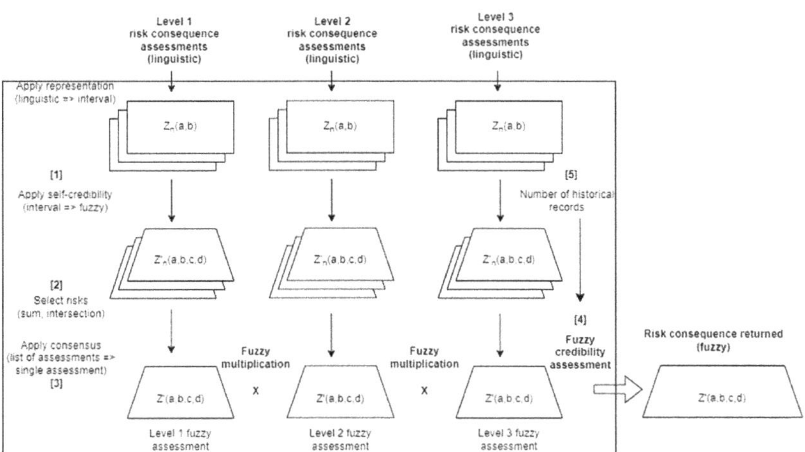

Figure 1. Risk-estimation fuzzy algorithm

Source: Own elaboration

The algorithm is based on the multiplication of fuzzy numbers. Linguistic risks from three levels of global software are converted to fuzzy numbers first and then multiplied. Multiple rectangles or trapezes represent multiple individual estimations. Algorithm parameters are enumerated from [1] to [5]. The output is represented as the trapeze on the right side of Figure 1.

The algorithm is executed several times during the Sprint, when information about risks is updated (adaptive Sprint planning). The algorithm is applied for each Sprint item with potential risks:

(1) Each team member selects one dominant risk for each level, based on the predefined list of risks and assigns consequences to it using linguistic expression (*LOW, MEDIUM, HIGH*). Eventually, if no predefined risk is suitable, team members can name the risk and assign consequences to it (described in Table 2/Id 3).
(2) Linguistic input is converted to the interval, based on the definitions of *LOW*, *MEDIUM* and *HIGH* consequences (each team member can differently define these values). The intervals define how much each risk prolongs given Sprint activity and are defined in %, e.g., *LOW* = [10%, 20%]. This is the first row in Figure 2.
(3) Interval is converted to a fuzzy number, based on the self-credibility assessment of a team member. Detailed conversion process can be arbitrary defined and can be parametrized (parameter [1]). The less credibility team member declares, the higher degree of fuzziness the converted number possesses. This is the second row in Figure 2.
(4) One dominant risk is selected for each level, based on the selection strategy (parameter [2]) and final assessment of the consequences is determined, based on the consensus strategy (determining group assessment, according to individual assessments – parameter [3]). This is the third row in Figure 2.
(5) Fuzzy numbers from Step 4 are multiplied (fuzzy product) and the output is produced as a fuzzy number defining how much all three risks (from each level) prolong given Sprint item.
(6) Last step is the application of group-credibility strategy (parameter [5]), based on the given number of historical records (parameter [4]), which adjusts the fuzzy number, according to the existing history of outputs and post-factum total risk consequences assessments.

3.7. Quality Assessment

The quality of the algorithm can be assessed by comparing algorithm's outputs (based on input data that was collected) with post-factum risk consequence assessments. This can be done for different combinations of algorithm parameters.

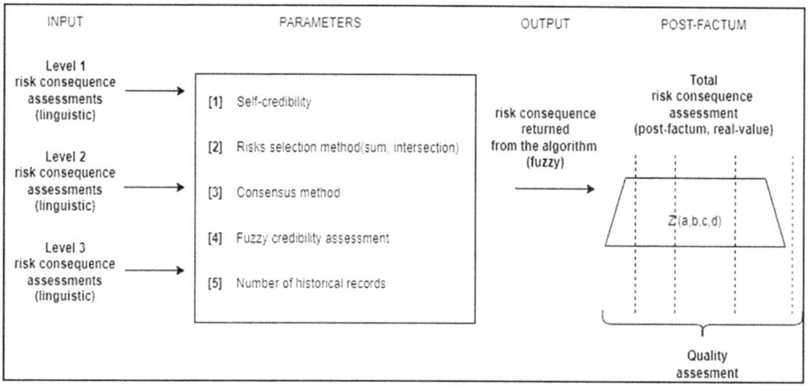

Figure 2. Quality assessment overview
Source: Own elaboration

The output of the algorithm is a fuzzy number representing possible risks consequences. This fuzzy output can be compared with total risk-consequences assessed post-factum by the Development Team and converted to a fuzzy number.

4. Results and Discussion

This section presents an illustrative example of the estimation algorithm. The results that are obtained are then discussed.

Two sample records (used for illustration purposes) are presented below in Table 4. Risk names come from (Beecham et al., 2021).

Table 4. Two sample records used for illustration

	Person 1-record	**Person 2-record**
Backlog item	Item1	Item1
Level 1 dominant risk	3.4 High level of tech. complexity	-
Level 1 risk assessment	*MEDIUM*	-
Level 2 dominant risk	3.1 Team unfamiliar with development tools	-
Level 2 risk assessment	*LOW*	-

(*continued on next page*)

Table 4. Continued

	Person 1-record	**Person 2-record**
Level 3 dominant risk	2.8 Unclear system requirements	2.6 Incorrect system requirements
Level 3 risk assessment	*MEDIUM*	*LOW*
LOW definition	[+5 %; +50 %]	[+5 %; +40 %]
MEDIUM definition	[+20 %; +100 %]	[+40 %; +60 %]
HIGH definition	[+150 %; +200 %]	[+60 %; +200 %]
Self-credibility	*HIGH*	*MEDIUM*
Post-factum assessment (risk-percentage)	*50 %*	*30 %*

Source: Own elaboration

The first step is to represent the inputs using self-credibility. For *Person 1* (credibility *HIGH*) we could use crisp intervals *I*. But because *Person 1* defined overlapped *LOW* and *MEDIUM*, those two also need to be fuzzy, i.e. $LOW = I[1.05,\ 1.5] => Z_{LOW}(a,b,c,d) = (1.05,\ 1.05,\ 1.2,\ 1.5)$, $MEDIUM = I[1.2,\ 2.0] => Z_{MEDIUM}(a,b,c,d) = (1.2,\ 1.5,\ 2.0,\ 2.0)$, $HIGH = I[2.5,\ 3.0] => Z_{HIGH}(a,b,c,d) = (2.5,\ 2.5,\ 3.0,\ 3.0)$. For *Person 2* the credibility is lower, which means all intervals should be fuzzified (e.g. by *±10 %*), i.e. $LOW = I[1.05,\ 1.4] => Z_{LOW}(a,b,c,d) = (1.05,\ 1.05,\ 1.3,\ 1.5)$, $MEDIUM = I[1.4,\ 1.6] => Z_{MEDIUM}(a,b,c,d) = (1.3,\ 1.5,\ 1.5,\ 1.6)$, $HIGH = I[1.6,\ 3.0] => Z_{HIGH}(a,b,c,d) = (1.5,\ 1.6,\ 3.0,\ 3.0)$. $Z_{LOW}(a,b,c,d)$, $Z_{MEDIUM}(a,b,c,d)$ *and* $Z_{HIGH}(a,b,c,d)$ are trapezoidal fuzzy numbers.

The next step is to apply risk selection strategy. Let us use the sum of risks (a maximum set of risks), which is this case means all 3 level risks appear. In Level 3 we have an inconsistency in a dominant risk, but a risk selected by the person which higher certainty was finally agreed. After this operation the following risks are selected: *3.4* for Level 1, *3.1* for Level 2, *2.8* for Level 3.

The next step is to apply a consensus method and determine the result. Before doing this, *Person 2* has re-estimated risks that were selected above: *LOW* was selected for all 3 levels. Consensus method that is used is the arithmetic average of the fuzzy numbers obtained after multiplying risks from levels 1–3. *Person 1* result is $Z_{MEDIUM} \times Z_{LOW} \times Z_{HIGH} = (1.2,\ 1.5,\ 2.0,\ 2.0) \times (1.05,\ 1.05,\ 1.2,\ 1.5) \times (2.5,\ 2.5,\ 3.0,\ 3.0) = (3.2,\ 3.9,\ 7.2,\ 9.0)$, where $\times$ is the fuzzy multiplication operator. *Person 2* result is $Z_{LOW} \times Z_{LOW} \times Z_{LOW} = (1.05,\ 1.05,\ 1.3,\ 1.5) \times (1.05,\ 1.05,\ 1.3,\ 1.5) \times (1.05,\ 1.05,\ 1.3,\ 1.5) = (1.16,\ 1.16,\ 2.2,\ 3.4)$. The arithmetic average is *(2.2, 2.5, 4.7, 6.2)*, using fuzzy sum operator and scalar multiplication to determine the average. Changing the representation to risk ratio, the following fuzzy number is obtained: $\tilde{A} = (0.55, 0.6, 0.79, 0.84)$. This is the initial output of the algorithm.

The fourth step (fuzzy credibility assessment) can be done for available historical records and post-factum risk assessments. There is only one historical record (obtained in the step above). Post-factum assessment $\tilde{R}$ is the interval = *[0.3, 0.5]*, but based on the self-credibility of *Person 2*, it can also be fuzzified, e.g., $\tilde{R} = (0.2, 0.4, 0.5, 0.5)$. The $\tilde{Z}$ representing the credibility can be now determined using the following formula (Marchwicka & Kuchta, 2022): $\tilde{Z} = \left(\frac{1}{1-\frac{0.2-0.55}{0.55}}, \frac{1}{1-\frac{0.4-0.6}{0.6}}, \frac{1}{1-\frac{0.5-0.79}{0.79}}, \frac{1}{1-\frac{0.5-0.84}{0.84}} \right)$ = (0.6, 0.8, 0.7, 0.7). The number of historical records used equals one.

5. Conclusion

In this paper a fuzzy risk estimation algorithm has been suggested. The algorithm is applicable for global software development (GSD) Scrum-based projects with different sub teams and risks that can be considered on different project levels. Three risk levels presented in the algorithm are based on the GSD use case with three different sub-teams. A simple computational example has been suggested that shows how to apply the algorithm.

The algorithm is novel as it combines group estimations (each Scrum Team Member is involved in the estimation), different consensus strategies (determining group decision based on individual estimations), self-credibility, optimistic/pessimistic credibility adjustments applied at the team-level, and it is based on linguistic representation of risks.

The algorithm can be used in different configurations. In this simple example a Scrum team with two people has been presented. Self-credibility has been applied for the fuzzy representation of linguistic inputs, a sum of risks has been used as risk selection strategy, arithmetic average of individual estimations as a consensus strategy and credibility method from (Marchwicka & Kuchta, 2022) has been demonstrated on one historical record.

The suggested approach allows to control GSD risks at the Sprint-level. It enables Scrum Team to track and adapt to the risks and increases chances of successfully realizing the Sprint commitment.

An overview of the quality assessment method for the algorithm has been also presented. Testing the suggested algorithm on multiple GSD project risk records in different configurations of input parameters (Figure 2) and selecting the best configuration is planned as the future research.

Funding: National Science Centre (Poland), grant number 394311, 2017/27/B/HS4/01881 Grant title: Selected methods supporting project management, taking into consideration various stakeholder groups and using type-2 fuzzy numbers.

References

Alsaadi, B., Alsaadi, B., Alfhaid, M., Alghamdi, A., Almuallim, N., & Fakieh, B. (2021). Scrum poker estimator: A planning poker tool for accurate story point estimation. *International Journal of Computer Information Systems and Industrial Management Applications*.

Beecham, S., Clear, T., Lal, R., & Noll, J. (2021). Do scaling agile frameworks address global software development risks? An empirical study. *The Journal of Systems and Software* 171, 1–30.

Chaouch, S., Mejri, A., & Ghannouchi S. A. (2019). A framework for risk management in Scrum development process. *Procedia Computer Science,* 164, 187–192.

Elsayed, A., Ahmad, N., & Malkawi, G. (2022). Solving arbitrary coupled trapezoidal fully fuzzy sylvester matrix equation with necessary arithmetic multiplication operations. *Fuzzy Information and Engineering*, 425–455.

Georgiev, V., & Stefanova, K. (2014). Software development methodologies for reducing project risks. *Economic Alternatives*, 104–113.

Ghazali, S. N., Salim, S. S., Inayat, I., & Hamid, S. H. (2018). A risk poker-based testing model for Scrum. *Computer Systems Science and Engineering*, 33.

Hammad, M., & Inayat, I. (2018). Integrating risk management in Scrum framework. *Conference: Frontiers of Information Technology At: Islamabad Pakistan*.

Hossain, E., Babar, M. A., Paik, H., & Verner J. (2009). Risk identification and mitigation processes for using Scrum in global software development: A conceptual framework. *16th Asia-Pacific Software Engineering Conference.*

Hulett, D. (2011). *Integrated cost-schedule risk analysis* (pp. 97–99). Gower Publishing.

Marchwicka, E., & Kuchta, D. (2022). Critical path for projects with activity durations modelled as Z-Fuzzy numbers. *Journal of Mult.-Valued Logic & Soft Computing,* 39, 539–559.

Prater, J. B., Kirytopoulos, K., & Ma, T. (2019). An investigation of estimation techniques for information technology projects. In *International Conference on Industrial Engineering and Engineering Management (IEEM)*, Macao.

Project Management Institute. (2021). *A guide to the project management body of knowledge and the standard for project management* (7th ed.). Pennsylvania: PMI.

Shameem, M., Kumar, R. R., Nadeem, M., & Khan, A. A. (2020) Taxonomical classification of barriers for scaling agile methods in global software development environment using fuzzy analytic hierarchy process. *Applied Soft Computing Journal*, 90.

Tomanek, M., & Juricek, J. (2015). Project risk management model based on PRINCE2 and Scrum frameworks. *International Journal of Software Engineering & Applications*, 6(1), 81–88.

Verner, J. M., Brereton, O. P., Kitchenham, B. A., Turner, M., & Niazi, M. (2014). Risks and risk mitigation in global software development: A tertiary study. *Information and Software Technology*, 56, 54–78.

Mohammad Mahbobi, Salman Kimiagari

An Integrated Classification Approach in Predicting Daily Stock Market Fluctuations: Implications for the Aftermath of COVID-19

1. Introduction

The prediction of daily upward and downward movements of the stock market in general and the market indices have been an interesting task for many financial institutions, public sector analysts, central banks, and agents. Graphical and statistical methods applied to predict market movements are frequently utilized by market players (Beattle, 2011). Classification models to learn algorithms, reduce errors, and enhance prediction accuracy are frequently applied to define patterns, recognize problems, and collect, prepare, and preprocess data (Unica Technologies Inc., 1997). The effective use of data mining and pattern recognition is likely to result in more efficient investment decisions about the stock market (Palace, 1996). Data mining tools can also simplify the understanding of stock market activities and overcome most stock market predictions (Nawawi, 2013). Data mining techniques such as artificial neural networks (ANNs), support vector machines (SVMs), K-nearest neighbors (KNN), and naïve Bayes (NB) classification models, can be applied and used in the classification of stock market movements. Considering a scenario under the efficient market hypothesis, the flow of information will enable the market to absorb the information and move upward or downward depending on the availability of information and the degree to which the market will absorb it. If the information reflects positive changes, such as the expected earnings of companies, a large acquisition deal, and the negotiation of a free trade deal, it will move the market upwards. If the information causes uncertainty stemming from geopolitical uncertainty, war, global conflict, or a similar phenomenon, it will move the market downwards. These upward and downward movements of the market can be converted into a binary classification problem. For instance, the upward movement can be assigned a value of 1, and the downward movement can be assigned a value of 0. As most of the market interest lies in daily market movements, classification techniques can easily be applied to predict the directional changes in such daily movements. In this study, such binary variables were applied to this problem.

In this study, we developed a methodology using machine learning and data mining techniques, such as ANNs, KNNs, NB, and SVMs, as well as undersampling and oversampling strategies to predict daily upward and downward fluctuations in both the S&P/TSX Composite and S&P 500 indices. Oztekin et al. (2016) proposed an integrated method applying K-fold cross-validation and three classification models, namely, the adaptive neuro-fuzzy inference system (ANFIS), an ANN, and an SVM, and compared their accuracy, sensitivity, and specificity. This study was motivated by Oztekin et al. (2016) and attempts to study the effect of data mining techniques on these indices. The use of undersampling and oversampling strategies can aid in overcoming the imbalanced dataset problem, which is a highly recurring problem in financial datasets, particularly with stock market daily returns. To understand the accuracy of the predictions, additional performance measures, such as balanced accuracy, G-mean, F1 measures, and the area under the receiver operating characteristic (ROC) curve, have also been implemented. In addition to using classifications, ensemble learning techniques such as voting and bagging have been implemented to enhance model accuracy.

The main objective of this paper is to introduce a new integrated classification technique using data mining procedures. Specifically, this technique increases the accuracy of predicting the fluctuation in daily stock returns for the TSX and S&P 500 indices. This study expects that the proposed integrated approach will further aid financial institutions, investors, and stock market traders in making superior and reliable predictions for stock market returns. The remainder of this paper is organized as follows. Section 2 provides a detailed literature review and highlights gaps in the literature. Section 3 describes the methodology and the estimation phases. Section 4 describes the data compilation and preprocessing, Section 5 presents the empirical results, and Section 6 presents the concluding remarks, implications, contributions of this paper, and future research.

2. Methodology and the Estimation Phases

In this study, we built our process by employing a classical multilayer perceptron (MLP) artificial neural network (Hastie et al., 2009). The methodology used in this study is based on the cross-industry data standard process for data mining (CRISP-DM) proposed by Shearer (2000). When the dataset was preprocessed, it was passed through sampling techniques such as SMOTE and random undersampling (RUS), which are prominent resampling techniques used in imbalanced datasets. In the next stage, the data was cross-validated using stratified K-fold and walk-forward cross-validations, also known as rolling window methods. The cross-validations were applied to fix the potential challenges that may result from overfitting. A commonly accepted technique to fix this potential problem and minimize the bias associated with the training and test data is to split the original dataset into two distinct subsets: training and test subsets. We used the same technique proposed by Desai et al. (1996) and Oztekin et al. (2016). This approach approximates the performance of our model on the new dataset. This will likely prevent overfitting in the stratified K-fold validation process. For the walk-forward method, we split the data into 80 % for training and the remaining 20 % for testing.

In this study, four different classification models were used: ANN, SVM, NB, and KNN. They were selected based on the literature review, as they have exhibited the highest accuracy for the prediction problem in numerous studies (Liu & Zhou, 2010; Dhaoui et al., 2015; Qiu & Song, 2016; Oztekin et al., 2016; Chen & Hao, 2017; Soni et al., 2018; Henrique et al., 2018; Shastri, et al., 2019; Jiang et al., 2019). Of all the fitted models, compared to Oztekin et al. (2016), we selected the top two of the best-performing classification models based on their accuracies, areas under the curve (AUCs), root mean square errors (RMSEs), and log loss functions. With respect to the complexity of the model and to be consistent with the literature review, datasets with smaller features and data points have been observed to exhibit better accuracy with the base classifiers than advanced models such as the deep neural network and adaptive neural fuzzy inference system (Oztekin et al., 2016).

To evaluate the classification models on imbalanced datasets and to avoid both the risk of overoptimism and overfitting in predicting the labels, we adopted the approach introduced by Santos et al. (2018). In this approach, cross-validation techniques such as K-fold and walk-forward, also known as rolling window, methods were implemented on the training set during random oversampling and undersampling. In the stratified 10-fold, the data were divided into ten mutually exclusive data folds using stratified cross-validation. The folds were stratified to ensure that the class distribution in each fold was approximately the same as that in the initial data; He and Ma (2013) stated that for class imbalances, the use of stratified 10-fold cross-validation maintains the original distribution in the same order as the proportion of positive to negative labels. Ładyżyński et al. (2013) demonstrated that by implementing walk-forward cross-validation, the out-of-sample (real market) performance was more solid compared with alternative cross-validations. Based on Inoue et al. (2017), this study incorporated the walk-forward cross-validation estimator, which is a local constant estimator with a truncated kernel that assigns weights between 0 and 1 to the data points. Pesaran et al. (2013) described the optimization of these kernel weights.

In this study, we used both 10-Fold stratified and rolling window cross-validations under both oversampling and undersampling strategies. A flowchart of the proposed methodology is presented in Figure 1.

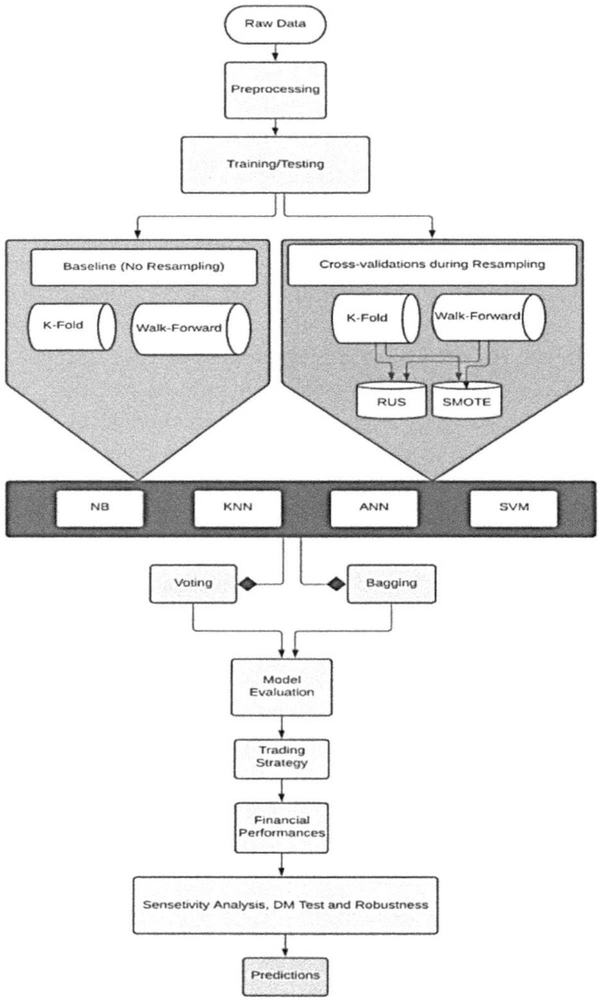

Figure 1. Overall steps of the proposed algorithm

The next section outlines the seven main phases of the estimation process.

Phase 1: Raw data

In this study, daily data from March 15, 2010, to March 12, 2021, of the S&P/TSX Composite and S&P 500 indices were considered. The data used in this study were extracted from Yahoo Finance and Investing.com servers. The features in the models were selected based on their relative importance to the daily fluctuations of both indices. For TSX, the five relative important market cap stocks returns such as TD, Scotia bank, BMO, Brookfield Assets, and TC-Energy- a network of natural gas, crude oil pipelines, along with other power facilities- were observed to be relatively more important than other stock returns. For S&P 500, Visa, MasterCard, Microsoft, Johnson & Johnson, Apple, and Berkshire Assets were also selected based on the proposed automated search process, also known as GETS.

Phase 2: Preprocessing

All data points were checked for any potential error, missing, not available, etc., and the entire dataset underwent the auto search process to identify variables using a general unrestricted model (GUM). To reduce the complexity of the fitted models, Sucarrat and Escribano (2012) applied a multi-path known as GETS modeling to reduce the complexity associated with financial models. They introduced a more flexible method that automates financial multipath GETS modeling. This algorithm reconstructs the work of Hoover and Perez (1999). In each step of this algorithm, the result is checked against a set of diagnostic tests such as the Ljung–Box test, also known as Q-statistic test on the residuals at the specified significance and number of lags, and the Lagrange multiplier test at $\alpha=0.05$. This algorithm splits the entire dataset into different blocks, each with its own GUM, with a subset of search features. The algorithm operates through each block separately, and then combines the selected variables from each block into a new GUM and runs one more time. The insignificant variable is then removed, and if the diagnostic tests fail after the removal of a variable, that variable is placed back into the model. The process stops when no more insignificant variables remain. The final models are compared based on information criteria such as the Akaike and Bayesian information criteria. Finally, the best model is identified using the selected significant set of features. These selected features are then used in the remainder of the estimation, classification, cross-validation, and resampling processes.

Phase 3: Defining the sampling technique method: SMOTE and RUS

Two main sampling techniques, SMOTE and RUS, were selected to improve accuracy. In the oversampling technique, the samples were generated synthetically, and the majority class was reduced to match the minority class using two nearest neighbors.

Phase 4: Cross-validations to eliminate bias in the training period

Sampling techniques can often result in the overfitting of models. This study utilized two cross-validations: stratified K-fold and walk-forward. To control the bias in the training stage, a stratified 10-fold cross-validation technique was implemented. The records were divided randomly into ten disjoint sets of equal size to minimize bias and variance. Each of the four classifiers was trained. This typically improves the generalization of errors (Duda et al., 2001). The model performance measurements were obtained from the average of *K* performances (Olson & Delen, 2008). To maintain the original distribution in the same order as the proportion of positive to negative labels, walk-forward cross-validation was also applied under two scenarios.

Phase 5: Classification models

In this study, five classification algorithms were implemented for binary models: KNN, ANN, NB, SVM, and voting.

Phase 5.1. Artificial neural network

This is the most common classification model in machine learning in a financial market. When designing a neural network, selecting the correct number of layers and neurons is necessary. A more complicated network may overfit the training data. The architecture of the neural network used in this study was inspired by Oztekin et al. (2016) and consisted of four layers: one input layer, one output layer, and two hidden layers. The input layer consisted of neurons that were equal to the number of input variables in the dataset. The input layer contained seven neurons as there were seven input variables in the dataset. The last layer in the neural network was the output layer, which consisted of neurons equal to the number of outputs expected from the model. In this study, because the problem at hand converts the forecasting study into a classification problem, the last layer consisted of one neuron to provide us with the output. No specific study has been conducted to determine the optimized number of neurons for the hidden layers, as it completely depends on the dataset, the number of hidden layers, and other parameters, such as epochs, learning rate, and momentum. To determine the optimized number of neurons for the hidden layers, beginning from 10 in both the hidden layers, we implemented incremental neurons and tested the models for best performance measures, i.e., accuracy and AUC score. The prediction accuracy of the neural network model increased as we increased the number of neurons in the hidden layers and achieved the highest accuracy and AUC score with 140 neurons in both hidden layers. In this study, the number of epochs, learning rate, and momentum were fixed at 500, 0.001, and 0.9, respectively. The output layer consisted of a log-sigmoid function for the results.

Phase 5.2. K-nearest neighbors

The KNN algorithm is a nonparametric classification, but also a relatively simple clustering method in supervised machine learning. In implementing the KNN, the threshold k would be required. To determine the optimum k for this dataset, the same incremental approach was used and tested for k =2.

Phase 5.3. Naive Bayes

The NB algorithm operates based on probability theory and has been used in various fields. The Bayesian theorem exhibits high accuracy for large amounts of data, and the main condition is the independence of a feature in each class. Despite the efficiency and simplicity of this model, its performance is not as high as that of other classification models; thus, its performance should be enhanced through other approaches (Ko, 2017), such as the voting technique applied in this study.

Phase 5.4. Support vector machines

SVM models are widely used in classification problems, particularly in binary classification. They are known to reduce risks and errors while training the dataset. The functional form of the SVM parameters and default values used in this study was linked to the radial basis function (RBF) (Khemakhem & Boujelbene, 2017).

Kernel-based algorithms, known as SVMs, have become considerably popular within the machine learning community. They are easier to implement and perform better than other algorithms. Compared with ANNs, SVMs have fewer parameters, as they are only kernel-based algorithms. Some of the major kernels used in the classification problem are RBF, sigmoid, and polynomial kernels. In this study, we used an RBF kernel. SVMs with the RBF kernel were employed with 10-fold and walk-forward cross-validations.

Phase 6: Performance of improving techniques

Phase 6.1. Voting technique

The voting technique can be used to analyze the overall effect of models on the features and to understand the potential increase in the performance measures by using a combination of models. A preconceived approach in this study was to simultaneously use all four classification models in a hybrid form based on the objective of the voting system, whereby votes are selected for the selection of the sample class label, and each one of them predicts the label, whereas the most votes select the output label.

In some scenarios, the accuracy of the model prediction can be increased. In this study, a soft voting approach was used, enabling equal weights to be given to all the models. The voting approach is an ensemble learning approach that can be used to learn the overall effect of the features and understand the potential increase in the performance measures using the selected models.

Phase 6.2. Bagging technique

Another technique that might result in an improved upshot is bootstrap aggregation, also known as bagging. The concept of this approach is to integrate the classification of randomly generated training sets. Two different random samples result in different results because of the tracking noise resulting from a nonparametric regression in overfitting. To overcome this problem, we can bootstrap and average them together. This study used the bagging technique to integrate the classification of randomly generated training sets. Of the four classification models, the two top-performing models based on accuracy were selected to evaluate their performance for the dataset and features used in this study.

Phase 7. Evaluation of the classification models

The evaluation of the classification models can be either a task to select among the fitted models by tuning the parameters and their features or the performance of the models for the testing period. Evaluation metrics can also be used to demonstrate the performance of the fitted models. When the models were trained and tested, the input features were then tested for their relative importance using sensitivity analysis, and we used the DM test to identify better performance between each pair of the predicted values. In this study, major performance criteria were used. The calculation of these criteria was based on true positive, false negative, false positive, and true negative values. The accuracy indicates the precision in predicting the correct trend, whereas sensitivity and specificity indicate the precision in predicting a bullish and bearish trend. Another set of performance criteria consists of determining the balanced accuracy, geometric mean, F1 measure, and AUC or ROC for the models.

Phase 7.3.2. Statistical significance test

To understand the difference between the predicted upward and downward daily movements outlaid by the models and to highlight which models performed significantly better, this study employed the DM (1995) test, with the modifications suggested by Harvey et al. (1997).

In assessing forecasting accuracy, these two studies are the benchmark tests available for understanding the significance of the forecasting completed by different methodologies or models, as studied in this paper. The quality of the forecast can be based on the errors produced by the forecasting models. The original DM (1995) test statistic followed a standard normal distribution, whereas the modified version suggested by Harvey et al. (1997) follows a student's t distribution with n-1 degrees of freedom. In this study, the test was conducted in the last iteration of the stratified 10-fold cross-validation for each model under both sampling techniques, and the corresponding p-values were reported to compare them with the confidence intervals of 95 % and 99 %.

3. Data Compilation and Preprocessing

For this research, the S&P/TSX Composite Index daily data from March 15, 2010 to March 12, 2021, were considered. All information used in this study was extracted from Yahoo Finance and Investing.com. The features in the models were selected based on a combination of the companies' index activities. This study tested CAD/USD and CAD/EUR foreign exchange rates, along with a proxy of the Canadian equity market, i.e., the Canadian Universe Bond Index, and the West Texas Intermediate (WTI) oil price. After the blank data, noise, and outliers were removed, 2769 and 2760 records remained for the US and Canadian markets respectively.

The list of the non-component features used by Oztekin et al. (2016) and the selected components of the market cap features for both markets were tested and used in this study are as follows:

- The percentage change of the S&P/TSX Composite Index was obtained between its closing value on day t_{-1} and the next morning's opening value at t_0.
- The percentage change of the S&P 500 Index was obtained between its closing value on day t_{-1} and the next morning's opening value at t_0.
- The percentage change of the NASDAQ Composite Index was obtained between its closing value on day t_{-2} and its closing value on t_{-1}.
- The gold price (XAU) data were used to obtain the percentage change in gold prices in USD between the closing value on day the day t_{-2} and the closing value on t_{-1}.
- The percentage change in WTI oil prices were obtained between the closing oil price on day t_{-2} and the closing value on t_{-1}.

- The percentage change of the daily returns of TD, Scotia bank, BMO, Brookfield Assets, and TC-Energy obtained between its closing value on day t_{-1} and the next morning's opening value at t_0.
- The percentage change of the daily returns of Visa, MasterCard, Microsoft, Johnson & Johnson, Apple, and Berkshire Assets obtained between its closing value on day t_{-1} and the next morning's opening value at t_0.

Imbalanced learning is a challenging and active research topic in the artificial intelligence, machine learning, data mining and many related research areas (Haibo & Garcia, 2009). In particular, the imbalanced classification problem is when there is skewed data in the training set. Under this circumstance, the learner tends to classify new observations as belonging to the majority class because of the inherit bias when the imbalance is high (Rivera & Xanthopoulos, 2016). This imposes a higher cost of misclassifying the minority class. The ultimate goal of the proposed approach is to improve the performance of the proposed learning algorithm in predicting the daily returns of S&P/TSX Composite and S&P 500 indices. The imbalance feature of the distribution may affect the selected prediction approach when it completely ignores the minority class of the upward movement of the daily stock returns, where such minority class is often the class that financial agents and professionals are interested in. Figures 2 and 3 show the two classes of the daily returns of the S&P/TSX Composite and S&P 500 indices. In this paper, we defined upward and downward daily fluctuations of the S&P/TSX Composite and S&P 500 indices returns built on Nevasalmi (2020). The directional prediction of the binary dependent variable is then created consistent

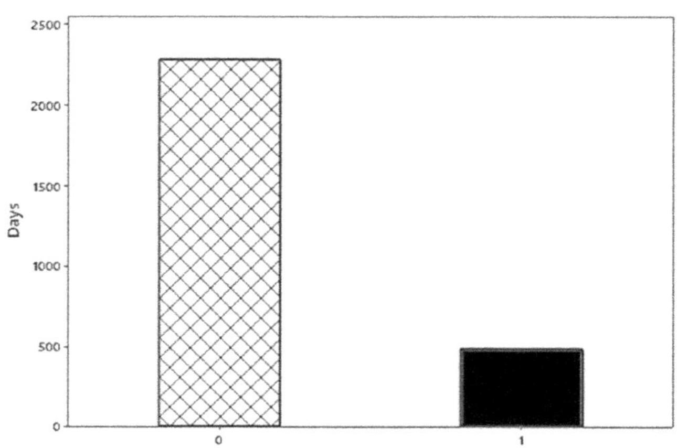

Figure 2. Class distribution of TSX Daily upwards (1) and downwards (0)

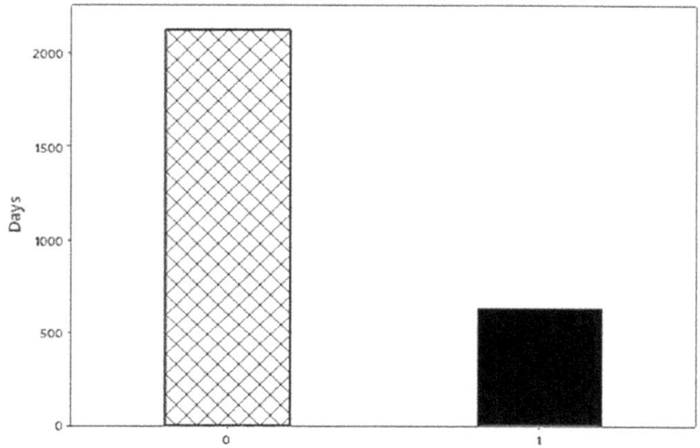

Figure 3. Class distribution of S&P 500 Daily upwards (1) and downwards (0)

with the upper quartile of each returns[1]. The daily movement was defined as the adjusted closing values subtracted from the opening values. This movement reflected downward and coded 0, whereas daily upwards coded as 1.

3.1. Sampling Techniques: SMOTE and RUS

When the dataset was preprocessed, the records were divided into two classes: an upward class with 605 records and a downward class with 2,405 records. As class division results in an unbalanced dataset, we applied under-sampling and oversampling techniques to increase the accuracy. SMOTE and RUS were selected for the oversampling and undersampling techniques, respectively. SMOTE was first proposed by Chawla et al. (2002); since then, it has become a widely used sampling technique for imbalanced datasets. SMOTE is a standard benchmark for learning from imbalanced data (Fernandez et al., 2018). To apply SMOTE, the nearest neighbors should be selected. The five nearest neighbors are practical. The aim is to increase the upward class records to a number almost equal to that of the downward class records. Throughout the SMOTE process, the number of instances assigned to the majority class did not decrease.

1 The complete descriptive statistics of both indices are presented in Appendix A.

3.2. Performance Criteria

Classification models are evaluated based on their accuracy in predicting a target variable. The major performance criteria used in this study were accuracy, sensitivity, and specificity. The computation of these criteria can be summarized from Olson and Delen (2008). The accuracy indicates the precision of a model in predicting the correct trend, whereas sensitivity and specificity indicate the precision of the model in predicting a bullish and bearish trend. Sensitivity also aids in the model precision in predicting a positive change, whereas specificity aids in predicting a negative change. Because the dataset used in this study was imbalanced, sampling techniques were used to balance the dataset. Hence, to make an accurate decision on the performance of the model, we used several other performance criteria as measurements. The second set of performance criteria consisted of determining the balanced accuracy, G-mean, F1 measure, and AUC or receiver operating characteristics ROC for the models.

3.2.1. Cross Entropy Loss (Log Loss)

The RMSE is widely used in predictive analytics. An alternative measure for the RMSE in binary classification is the cross-entropy loss or log loss. The log loss function for binary classification is determined as follows (Murphy, 2012), Eq. (1):

$$LL = -\frac{1}{N}\sum_{i=1}^{N}[y_i \log(p_i) + (1 - y_i)\log(1 - p_i)] \tag{1}$$

Here, y_i indicates the true values, and p_i indicates the predicted values. The higher the deviation from the true values, the higher the log loss values, and the lower the log loss values, the better the prediction and accuracy.

4. Results

The daily movements of stock market indices are influenced by many exogenous factors. In this study, the ma-jor components of both TSX and S&P 500, which indicate the performance of the companies, also known as market capitalizations, were considered. Consistent with the influence of the financial performance of these companies, daily upward and downward movements occur because of the absorption of information on the market indices, i.e., TSX and S&P 500. Several experiments were conducted to determine the relative importance of these input features. These experiments, along with the implementation of GETS search modeling, aided us in identifying the more influential features for each of the two markets. The models were selected with varying parameters and attributes, which resulted in maximum accuracy and an ROC score for each model. The binary classes of the final dataset were imbalanced; hence, oversampling and undersampling techniques were the appropriate sampling strategies. To avoid overfitting problem, 10-Fold stratified and walk-forward cross-validations on each of the models were employed. The results of the best performance measures and the classification models are shown in Tables 4 and 5. The SMOTE and RUS resampling techniques under the two scenarios are shown for both indices. Under the first scenario (baseline), no resampling technique was selected. The second scenario included both the SMOTE and RUS resampling strategies under alternative classifications and cross-validations.

Under both scenarios, the KNN classification mode outperformed all the other models in terms of accuracy, whereas under the undersampling technique, voting performed better in terms of accuracy. In terms of ROC, the voting technique performed better in providing a higher ROC score. The closest accuracy score obtained by the KNN model was that of the ANN and the voting techniques, while the lowest scores were obtained through the NB and SVM techniques, which are not reported here.

Table 6 and Table 7 provide accuracy measurements of the classification models under the two Scenarios with the ensemble machine learning algorithm called Bootstrap Aggregation or Bagging. Under both SMOTE and RUS, in terms of accuracy, the Bagging technique has not increased sensitivities and ROC scores, indicating that the Bag-ging technique could not help the classification models in accurately predicting positive changes in the stock mar-kets. Both results presented in Appendix B.

In a direct comparison with the models implemented by Oztekin et al. (2016), our models outperformed them in most performance measures. The performance measures of our models, particularly for KNN and ANN, can be considered as the best in accurately predicting stock markets, with an accuracy of above 80 % for both models. This indicates that both the KNN and ANN are better at detecting positive changes than negative changes. The results were opposite for the undersampling technique. In comparing their specificity and sensitivity measures of the ANN and KNN, under the RUS resampling, we observed a lower specificity, while the SMOTE indicated an in-crease in their specificity measure. This indicated that, under all conditions, irrespective of the sample dataset used in training, the KNN models can detect positive changes more accurately it can than negative changes. This study added an alternative predictive power to analyze the daily market fluctuations which would further help financial agents, stockbrokers, and public sector policy makers in analyzing these two top vital North American financial market stock indices.

Table 1. Accuracy measurements of the classification models under two scenarios (TSX Index)

Classification, Cross-Validation, and Sampling Methods / Accuracy Measurements	Baseline (no sampling)				Cross-validation during sampling							
	10-fold		walk-forward		10-fold during SMOTE		10-fold during RUS		Walk-forward during SMOTE		Walk-forward during RUS	
	KNN	ANN	KNN	Voting	KNN	Voting	ANN	Voting	KNN	Voting	ANN	Voting
Accuracy	0.898	0.862	**0.920**	0.888	0.994	0.848	0.756	0.811	**0.997**	0.865	0.862	0.869
Specificity	0.999	0.974	0.999	0.983	0.999	0.860	0.753	0.824	0.999	0.878	0.857	0.864
Sensitivity	0.417	0.332	0.654	0.429	0.964	0.817	0.773	0.748	0.980	0.802	0.886	0.889
Balanced accuracy	0.709	0.653	0.827	0.706	0.982	0.838	0.763	0.789	0.990	0.865	0.871	0.879
Geometric mean	0.646	0.569	0.809	0.650	0.982	0.838	0.763	0.759	0.990	0.865	0.871	0.862
Precision	0.999	0.727	0.999	0.843	0.999	0.553	0.398	0.474	0.999	0.573	0.589	0.876
Recall	0.417	0.332	0.654	0.429	0.945	0.817	0.773	0.748	0.989	0.867	0.885	0.889
F1	0.589	0.456	0.791	0.569	0.982	0.659	0.526	0.581	0.990	0.690	0.708	0.718
AUC	0.709	0.653	0.827	0.706	0.982	0.850	0.763	0.787	0.995	0.865	0.919	0.906
Mean of log loss function	0.145	0.337	**0.095**	0.253	0.121	0.319	0.553	0.457	**0.094**	0.306	0.795	0.298
S.D. of log loss function	0.003	0.059	0.022	0.068	0.026	0.074	0.100	0.073	0.024	0.068	0.463	0.119
RMSE	0.101	0.139	0.079	0.112	0.006	0.152	0.347	0.201	0.004	0.135	0.147	0.142

Table 2. Accuracy measurements of the classification models under two scenarios (S&P 500 Index)

Classification, Cross-Validation, and Sampling Methods / Accuracy Measurements	Baseline (no sampling)				Cross-validation during sampling							
	10-fold		walk-forward		10-fold during SMOTE		10-fold during RUS		Walk-forward during SMOTE		Walk-forward during RUS	
	KNN	**ANN**	**KNN**	**Voting**	**KNN**	**Voting**	**ANN**	**Voting**	**KNN**	**Voting**	**ANN**	**Voting**
Accuracy	0.898	0.862	**0.920**	0.888	0.994	0.848	0.756	0.811	**0.997**	0.865	0.862	0.869
Specificity	0.999	0.974	0.999	0.983	0.999	0.860	0.753	0.824	0.999	0.878	0.857	0.864
Sensitivity	0.417	0.332	0.654	0.429	0.964	0.817	0.773	0.748	0.980	0.802	0.886	0.889
Balanced accuracy	0.709	0.653	0.827	0.706	0.982	0.838	0.763	0.789	0.990	0.865	0.871	0.879
Geometric mean	0.646	0.569	0.809	0.650	0.982	0.838	0.763	0.759	0.990	0.865	0.871	0.862
Precision	0.999	0.727	0.999	0.843	0.999	0.553	0.398	0.474	0.999	0.573	0.589	0.876
Recall	0.417	0.332	0.654	0.429	0.945	0.817	0.773	0.748	0.989	0.867	0.885	0.889
F1	0.589	0.456	0.791	0.569	0.982	0.659	0.526	0.581	0.990	0.690	0.708	0.718
AUC	0.709	0.653	0.827	0.706	0.982	0.850	0.763	0.787	0.995	0.865	0.919	0.906
Mean of log loss function	0.145	0.337	**0.095**	0.253	0.121	0.319	0.553	0.457	**0.094**	0.306	0.795	0.298
S.D. of log loss function	0.003	0.059	0.022	0.068	0.026	0.074	0.100	0.073	0.024	0.068	0.463	0.119
RMSE	0.101	0.139	0.079	0.112	0.006	0.152	0.347	0.201	0.004	0.135	0.147	0.142

The accuracy rate measured the overall performance of the model, but since the implementation of balancing techniques required further validation of the models, several other parameters were also measured for all the models. In terms of balanced accuracy, geometric mean, and the F1 measure, KNN with the SMOTE technique outperformed the other models in the oversampling technique. In terms of ROC, which is a measure of a real-life classifier, the resampling technique boosted the ROC score to 0.99 for TSX and 0.98 for S&P 500, whereas under the no resampling technique, KNN achieved an ROC score of 0.83 for TSX and 0.84 for S&P 500.

To better understand the contribution of this study to the selected classification algorithm, we ran the models without any sampling technique as a benchmark model for the Canadian market (Tables 1 and 2). We compared the best two algorithms with the benchmark method for the Canadian stock market. The KNN, along with cross-validation during SMOTE, was identified as the dominant method compared with the ANN. In comparing all models, we used the log loss cost function. The results presented in Tables 4 and 5 clearly indicate that the best selected model was KNN using walk-forward cross-validation, regardless of the selected resampling method. We can conclude that our proposed algorithm identified the KNN as the superior classification model when walk-forward cross-validation is used during SMOTE. None of the performances of the other fitted models under RUS and the benchmark were considered for predicting TSX and S&P 500 daily stock returns. The oversampling and KNN classification model increased the average accuracy rate by 8.4 % for TSX and 7.1 % for S&P 500 compared with the benchmark model. The optimization process was also tested under alternative parameter settings for annual, quarterly, and monthly steps. The best results were obtained for a longer period of step, i.e., annual compared with quarterly and monthly steps. These results were consistent for both the TSX and S&P 500 datasets.

To confirm the performance and robustness of the proposed algorithm, a similar dataset from the US market was used as a means of cross-examining. This aided in verifying the performance of the model in a similar market and compared it with the Canadian dataset. Tables 4 and 5 present the performance measures of the models observed for both TSX and S&P 500. The KNN algorithm, under the SMOTE sampling technique, outperformed the other models used in this study, which indicated its robustness in the forecasting technique implemented in this study. This further confirmed that the models used in this study can be further implemented to forecast stock market returns in different markets. To further understand the robustness of the models used in this study, the RMSE was used for forecasting evaluation. The RMSE values for both the Canadian and US stock markets were calculated.

When the best classification models are selected based on the closest value of the log loss function to zero, the predictive power of each classification model is tested. The Diebold-Mariano (1995) test is used to understand the statistical significance of each pair of the selected classification models under both over-sampling and undersampling methods, with or without cross-validation methods. The null hypothesis under the DM test assumes that the forecasting accuracies of the different models tested in the h-step ahead prediction when h= 1 are not different. Table 6 shows the test statistic and associated p-values calculated for each pair of the models for the TSX index. Under the baseline, the KNN model when cross-validation is performed during the SMOTE technique was significantly different from that of voting, whereas the ANN was not significantly different from the voting classification model under the walk-forward approach. The results obtained for S&P 500 under walk-forward during SMOTE indicated that KNN and ANN provide significantly different predictions. The performance of the KNN and voting models under the baseline approach was insignificant.

Table 3. Results of the DM test for all classification models (TSX)

Baseline/ walk-forward			
Test statistic [p-value]	**KNN**	**ANN**	**Voting**
KNN		−4.705 [0.000]	−4.982 [0.000]
ANN			−0.674 [0.500**]
Walk-forward during SMOTE			
KNN		−0.309 [0.757**]	−3.521 [0.000]
ANN			−5.305 [0.000]

Table 4. The results of the DM test for all classification models (S&P 500)

Baseline/ walk-forward			
Classification models	**KNN**	**ANN**	**Voting**
KNN		−5.201 [0.000]	−1.451 [0.147**]
ANN			−5.959 [0.000]

(continued on next page)

Table 4. Continued

Walk-forward during SMOTE			
KNN		−5.269 [0.000]	5.807 [0.000]
ANN			−0.703 [0.482**]

(*) indicates that we failed to reject the hypothesis at a 5 % level of confidence, i.e. there is no difference between the accuracy of the two forecasting models.
(**) indicates that we failed to reject the hypothesis at a 10 % level of confidence.

In assessing the importance of the included features for the prediction models, the relative variable importance of the features was computed and are pre-sented in Figures 4 and 5. The relative variable importance of the selected features from the GETS approach is presented in the score ranking order, which indicates the relative influence of each feature on the performance of each index returns.

A significant downfall in one or more of the components of an index, closely related commodities, and other influential factors may have significant positive or negative impacts on their daily movements. In further determining the relative importance of the selected market components of the daily percentage changes of the S&P/TSX composite index, this paper applied the relative variable importance process. The outcome for the TSX index is presented in Figure 4. The highest-ranked feature is the bank of Nova Scotia daily stock returns, and the lowest relative importance is the interaction between the COVID-19 dummy variable and the same returns. In the case of the S&P 500 daily returns, as

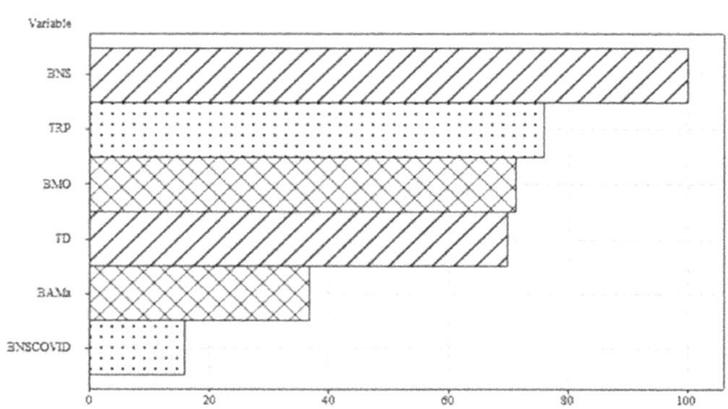

Figure 4. Relative variable importance (in %) for TSX returns

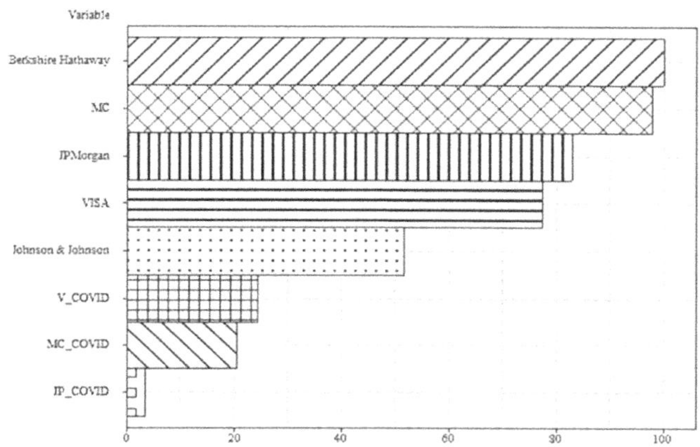

Figure 5. Relative variable importance (in %) for S&P 500 returns

depicted in Figure 5, we found that the COVID-19 factors along with more of the components of the US market index contributed in the predictions of its daily fluctuations.

5. Trading Strategy

The general expectation from classification models together with resampling methods is a higher accuracy rate that can be translated into a more accurate prediction of daily upward and downward fluctuations. However, better classification and resampling accuracy may not always result in better financial performance. Built on Enke and Thawornwong (2005), a two-stage trading strategy was used to examine the financial performance of the best-fitted classification models. In the first stage, the investor fully invests in the stock or maintains and receives the expected returns if the actual return for the period is positive. Under a negative daily return scenario, and when the classification consistently predicts downward returns, the investor will expect to receive government-issued bond/T-bill yields, ignoring potential dividends and all other transaction costs. In the second stage, the daily outcomes of this comparison will generate a series of predicted returns under the two scenarios, i.e., the baseline and cross-validation during the SMOTE sampling approach. To directly com-pare the performances of the two scenarios under the post-COVID period for both TSX and S&P 500, the Sharpe ratio and maximum drawdown were calculated against the actual returns and are presented in Tables 8 and 9.

Table 5. Financial metrics of TSX under alternative scenarios (March 15, 2010–March 12, 2021)

Financial Metrics	Actual	Post COVID-19 performance with classification	
		Baseline/KNN/ walk-forward	SMOTE/KNN/ walk-forward
Average returns	0.485 %	0.998 %	1.390 %
Standard deviation (volatility)	3.821 %	10.030 %	9.867 %
Market rate (US 10-year T-Bill yield)	0.055 %	0.055 %	0.055 %
Sharpe ratio	0.113	0.094	0.135
Maximum drawdown	−0.339	−0.917	−0.917
Sortino ratio	0.0293	0.0322	0.0471
Downward deviation	14.83 %	29.29 %	28.33 %

The outcomes of the trading strategy using walk-forward cross-validation during the SMOTE resampling approach indicated improvements in both markets for the post-COVID-19 pandemic. Specifically, for the Canadian stock market, the post-COVID-19 Sharpe ratio was slightly elevated above the current rate. However, the same ratio for the post-COVID-19 era had a more promising performance for the S&P 500.

6. Conclusión

The aim of this research was to introduce an integrated predictive architecture in providing more accurate predictions for the directional changes in the daily returns of both Toronto Stock Exchange (TSX) and NYSE S&P 500 indices. This study aimed to fill the literature gap related to balancing techniques in an imbalanced dataset to improve the prediction accuracy when employing alternative classification techniques. The implementation of automated multi-path specification search of financial models to reduce the complexity of the original statistical models introduced by Sucarrat and Escribano (2012) General-to-specific modeling- GETS- was employed to identify the significant set of features along with the relative variable importance analysis. In cross-examining the outcomes of the proposed algorithm, it was also applied to predicting the daily movements of the S&P 500.

The methodology used in this paper utilized the application of imbalance resampling techniques such as SMOTE and RUS and presented multiple performance measurements. The techniques used in this paper have achieved better results in terms of accuracy, ROC scores, and other performance measures than previous studies conducted within the prediction of the daily fluctuations of stock market domain. It has been observed that the proposed models and resampling techniques have outperformed the accuracy measures reported by Oztekin et al. (2016) and Kara et al. (2011). The level of accuracy reported in our study is in line with recent literature on sign predictability of daily returns (Krauss & Huck, 2017; Zhong & Enke, 2019). In addition, our accuracy is higher than Gyamerah, Ngare, and Ikpe (2019). Compared with Jiang et al. (2019), our accuracy sensitivity, specificity, F-score, and AUC are higher, and we did not use the kappa index. The analyzes presented in this study suggest that periodically updating the SVM model reduces the RMSE compared to using a rigid model without periodic updating. This result contrasts with Hsu et al. (2016), who did not achieve better performance when using a sliding window on the training data, and Henrique et al. (2018), who used SVR (Support Vector Regression).

The major contribution of this paper compared with the prior studies are the use of SMOTE and RUS resampling techniques and more appropriate stratified K-Fold and Walk-forward cross validations. Existing of imbalanced date in financial markets is common and challenging task due to the fact that the minority class may not always receive appropriate weight in the classification and forecasting process. This study used SMOTE and RUS imbalanced techniques to resolve this issue.

The ANN and KNN classification models showed substantially superior performances to the SVM and NB models. Other classification techniques employed in this paper presented a distinctive methodology in understanding the daily movements of both markets. This approach will help the investor, traders, and bankers to predict the market's future movements with higher accuracy. Additionally, this study also filled the existing gap in the literature in reducing the complexity of the estimated statistical models by identifying relative variable importance using GETS approach.

Expanding on Oztekin et al. (2016) methodology, this study contributed to the prediction of the daily market fluctuations by adding an alternative predictive power to further help the analysts, financial agents, stockbrokers, and public sector policy makers in analyzing these two top vital North American financial market stock indices. The features used in this study can be easily expanded or modified, consistent with the environment of the stock market from both developing and emerging economies.

Further research can focus on utilizing the proposed architecture combined with decision trees, Bayesian networks, and clustering techniques. Future research can focus on using this approach in both Canadian and the US stock markets, on closely related commodity markets by identifying macroeconomic variables regarding the recent shifts towards a high-tech/financial service-based economies and the incorporation of the cryptocurrencies. Finally, future research can also be extended by applying more optimization such as expanded windows, and other alternative walks.

Appendix A

Table A1. Descriptive statistics for S&P 500 returns and all the tested and used features

Features and Label	Count	Mean	Variance	St. Dev	Minimum	Sum	Q1	Median	Q3	Maximum	IQR	Skewness	Kurtosis
VISA	2769	0.0010	0.0003	0.0163	−0.1355	2.6320	−0.0070	0.0013	0.0089	0.1498	0.0159	0.1700	11.0900
Master Card	2769	0.0011	0.0003	0.0178	−0.1273	3.1697	−0.0070	0.0017	0.0091	0.1661	0.0161	0.4000	10.3000
Johnson & Johnson	2769	0.0004	0.0001	0.0108	−0.1004	1.0697	−0.0044	0.0003	0.0057	0.0800	0.0101	−0.2400	10.2900
JPMorgan Chase	2769	0.0006	0.0003	0.0182	−0.1496	1.7321	−0.0077	0.0004	0.0090	0.1801	0.0167	0.2300	10.5600
Berkshire Hathaway	2769	0.0005	0.0001	0.0121	−0.0855	1.3629	−0.0054	0.0003	0.0063	0.1129	0.0117	0.1400	9.1500
S&P500	2769	0.0005	0.0001	0.0110	−0.1198	1.4005	−0.0035	0.0007	0.0054	0.0938	0.0089	−0.5700	15.1100
Label	2769	0.2308	0.1776	0.4214	0.0000	639	0.0000	0.0000	0.0000	1.0000	0.0000	1.2800	−0.3700

Table A2. Descriptive statistics for TSX returns and all the tested and used features

Features and Label	Count	Mean	St. Dev	Variance	Minimum	Sum	Q1	Median	Q3	Maximum	IQR	Skewness	Kurtosis
TD-Toronto Dominions	2760	0.0004	0.0116	0.0001	−0.1233	1.0008	−0.004	0.0007	0.0054	0.1788	0.0097	0.8500	38.2200
BNS- Bank of Nova Scoria	2760	0.0002	0.0118	0.0001	−0.1337	0.6618	−0.004	0.0005	0.0053	0.1684	0.0098	0.3100	34.2300
BMO- Bank of Montreal	2760	0.0003	0.0123	0.0002	−0.1641	0.8220	−0.003	0.0007	0.0052	0.1698	0.0091	−0.3800	44.1200
TRP-TC Energy	2760	0.0003	0.0140	0.0002	−0.2186	0.7345	−0.005	0.0004	0.0066	0.1995	0.0121	−0.2500	46.2500
BAMa-Brookfield Asset Management	2760	0.0007	0.0149	0.0002	−0.1396	1.9358	−0.006	0.0007	0.0078	0.1679	0.0143	0.0300	18.9900
TSX	2760	0.0002	0.0095	0.0001	−0.1234	0.5795	−0.003	0.0007	0.0045	0.1196	0.0082	−0.9700	34.8300
Label	2760	0.1746	0.3797	0.1442	0.0000	482	0.0000	0.0000	0.0000	1.0000	0.0000	1.7100	0.9400

Acknowledgments

The authors would like to thank Marriappan Vasudevan for his supports throughout this research work.

References

Bai, Y., Wang, H., Wu, J., Zhang, Y., Jiang, J., & Long, G. (2016). Evolutionary lazy learning for Naive Bayes classification. International Joint Conference on Neural Networks (IJCNN). *IEEE*, 3124–3129.

Beattle, A. (2011). *The basics of business forecasting*. Available at: http://www.investopedia.com/articles/financial-theory/11/basicsbusiness-forcasting.asp. Accessed 01 March 2014.

Chawla, N. V., Bowyer, K. W., Hall, L. O., W., & Kegelmeyer, P. (2002). SMOTE: Synthetic minority over-sampling technique. *Journal of Artificial Intelligence Research*, 16, 321–357.

Chen, Y., & Hao, Y. (2017). A feature weighted support vector machine and K-nearest neighbor algorithm for stock market indices prediction. *Expert Systems with Applications*, 80, 340–355.

Desai, V. S., Crook, J. N., & Overstreet, G. A. (1996). A comparison of neural networks and linear scoring models in the credit union environment. *European Journal of Operational Research*, *95*(1), 24–37. https://doi.org/10.1016/0377-2217(95)00246-4

Dhaoui, A., Aydi, M., & Ben Ali, R. O. Ahmed. (2015). Revisiting empirical linkages between direction of Canadian stock price index movement and oil supply and demand shocks: Artificial neural netweoks and support vector machines approaches. *Journal of Academic Research in Economics*, 7(3), 319.

Diebold, F. X., & Mariano, R. S. (1995). Comparing predictive accuracy. *Journal of Business & Economic Statistics*, 13(3), 253.

Duda, Richard. O., Hart, P. E., & Stork, D. G. (2001). *Pattern classification* (2nd ed.). Wiley.

Enke, D, & Thawornwong, S. (2005). The use of data mining and neural networks for forecasting stock market returns. *Expert Systems with Applications*, 29, 927–940.

Fernandez, A. Garcia, S., Herrera, F., & Chawla, N. V. (2018). SMOTE for learning from imbalanced data: Progress and challenges, marking the 15-year anniversary. *Journal of Artifial Intelligence Research*, 61, 863–905.

Gyamerah, S. A., Ngare, P., & Ikpe, D. (2019). On stock market movement prediction via stacking ensemble learning method. In *2019 IEEE Conference on*

Computational Intelligence for Financial Engineering & Economics (CIFEr), Computational Intelligence for Financial Engineering & Economics (CIFEr), 2019 IEEE Conference On, 1–8

Haibo, He, & Garcia, E. A. (2009). Learning from imbalanced data. *IEEE Transactions on Knowledge and Data Engineering*, 21(9), 1263–1284.

Harvey, D., Leybourne, S., & Newbold, P. (1997). Testing the equality of prediction mean squared errors. *International Journal of Forecasting*, 13(2), 281–291.

Hastie, T., Tibshirani, R., & Friedman, J. (2009). *The elements of statistical learning: Data mining, inference, and prediction*. Springer Science & Business Media.

He, H., & Ma, Y. (2013). *Imbalanced learning: Foundations, algorithms, and applications*. Wiley-IEEE Press. ISBN-13: 978–1118074626.

Henrique, B. M., Sobreiro, V. A., & Kimura, H. (2018). Stock price prediction using support vector regression on daily and up to the minute prices. *The Journal of Finance and Data Science*, 4(3), 183–201.

Hoover, K. D., & Perez, S. J. (1999). Data mining reconsidered: Encompassing and the general-to-specific approach to specification search. *The Econometrics Journal*, 2(2), 167–191.

Hsu, M. W., Lessmann, S., Sung, M. C., Ma, T., & Johnson, J. E. (2016). Bridging the divide in financial market forecasting: Machine learners vs. financial economists. *Expert Systems with Applications*, 61, 215–234.

Inoue, A., Jin, L., & Rossi, B. (2017). Rolling window selection for out-of-sample forecasting with time-varying parameters. *Journal of Econometrics*, *196*(1), 55–67. https://doi.org/10.1016/j.jeconom.2016.03.006

Jiang, M. Q., Liu, J. P., & Zhang, L. (2019). An improved stacking framework for predicting stock price index direction. *Economic Computation & Economic Cybernetics Studies & Research*, 53(3).

Kara, Y., Boyacioglu, M. A., & Baykan, Ö. K. (2011). Predicting direction of stock price index movement using artificial neural networks and support vector machines: The sample of the Istanbul stock exchange. *Expert Systems with Applications*, 38(5), 5311–5319.

Khemakhem, S., & Boujelbene, Y. (2017). Artificial intelligence for credit risk assessment: Artificial neural network and support vector machines. *ACRN Oxford Journal of Finance and Risk Perspectives*, 6(2), 1–17.

Ko, Y. (2017). How to use negative class information for Naive Bayes classification. *Information Processing and Management*, 53, 1255–1268.

Krauss, C., Do, X. A., & Huck, N. (2017). Deep neural networks, gradient-boosted trees, random forests: Statistical arbitrage on the S&P 500. *European Journal of Operational Research*, 259(2), 689–702.

: Ladyzynski, P., Zbikowski, K., & Grzegorzewski, P. (2013). Stock Trading with Random Forests, Trend Detection Tests and Force Index Volume Indicators. *International Conference on Artificial Intelligence and Soft Computing.*

Liu, S. H, & Zhou, F. (2010). On stock prediction based on KNN-ANN algorithm. In *2010 IEEE Fifth International Conference on Bio-Inspired Computing: Theories and Applications (BIC-TA), Bio-Inspired Computing: Theories and Applications (BIC-TA), 2010 IEEE Fifth International Conference On* (pp. 310–312).

Murphy, Kevin P. (2012). *Machine learning: A probabilistic perspective*. The MIT Press. Illustrated edition, ISBN 978-0262018029.

Nawawi, A. (2013). Stock market tip: Use Google Trends. *The Conversation*, 26 April. Available at: http://theconversation.com/stockmarkettipusegoogletrends13745. Accessed: 1 April 2014.

Nevasalmi, L. (2020). Forecasting multinomial stock returns using machine learning methods. *The Journal of Finance and Data Science*, 6, 86–106.

Olson, David L., & Delen, Dursun. (2008). *Advanced data mining techniques* (1st ed., p. 138) Springer (1 February, 2008), ISBN 3-540-76916-1.

Oztekin, A., Kizilaslan, R., Freund, S., & Iseri, A. (2016). A data analytic approach to forecasting daily stock returns in an emerging market. *European Journal of Operational Research*. https://doi.org/10.1016/j.ejor.2016.02.056.

Palace, B. (1996). *Data mining*. Available at: http://www.anderson.ucla.edu/faculty/jason.frand/teacher/technologies/palace/datamining.htm. Accessed 3 March 2014.

Pesaran, M. H., Pick, A., & Pranovich, M. (2013). Optimal forecasts in the presence of structural breaks. *Journal of Econometrics*, 177(2), 134–152.

Qiu, M., & Song, Y. (2016). Predicting the direction of stock market index movement using an optimized artificial neural network model. *PLoS One*, 11(5), 1.

Rivera, W. A., & Xanthopoulos, P. (2016). A priori synthetic over-sampling methods for increasing classification sensitivity in imbalanced data sets. *Expert Systems with Applications*, 66, 124–135.

Santos, M. S., Soares, J. P., Abreu, P. H., et al. (2018). Cross-validation for imbalanced datasets: Avoiding overoptimistic and overfitting approaches [research frontier]. *IEEE Comp. Int. Mag.*, 13(4):59–76.

Shastri, M., Roy, S., & Mittal, M. (2019). Stock Price Prediction using Artificial Neural Model: An application of big data. *EAI Endorsed Transactions on Scalable Information Systems*, 6(20), 1.

Shearer, C. (2000). The CRISP-DM model: The new blueprint for data mining. *Journal of Data Warehousing*, 5(4), 13–22.

Soni, D., Agarwal, S., Agarwel, T., Arora, P., & Gupta, K. (2018). Optimised prediction model for stock market trend analysis. In *2018 Eleventh International Conference on Contemporary Computing (IC3), Contemporary Computing (IC3), 2018 Eleventh International Conference On*, 1–3.

Sucarrat, G., & Escribano, A. (2012). Automated model selection in finance: General-to-specific modelling of the mean and volatility specifications. *Oxford Bulletin of Economics and Statistics*, 74(5), 716–735.

Unica Technologies Inc. (1997). *Solving data mining problems using pattern recognition software with Cdrom.* NJ, USA: Prentice-Hall PTR Upper Saddle River.

Zhong, X., & Enke, D. (2019). Predicting the daily return direction of the stock market using hybrid machine learning algorithms. *Financial Innovation*, 5(1), 2024 (5).

Humberto Nuno Rito Ribeiro, Nuno Duarte Pereira

The Importance of Financial Literacy for Investment Decisions: The Financial Leverage Revisited

1. Introduction

Despite mankind living a new age of information, the reality is that the current dominance of social media, artificial intelligence, together with other technological phenomena, are bringing confusing elements to people's and corporation's lives. In this new world where facts are competing with fake news, literacy becomes critical, being financial literacy key for businesses. Being financial literacy the ability to understand and correctly apply financial skills, becomes obvious its importance for proper management decisions, from investing budgeting (vid. e.g. Çera et al., 2020, 2021)

Throughout the life of a company, it faces several adversities and it is responsibility of the management team to assume a set of decisions. No matter how diversified the decisions are, they can be grouped into two groups: operational and strategic decisions.

Investment decisions fall into the second group above, as they produce medium and long-term effects, have a greater impact on the value of the company, and therefore require greater care in their analysis.

In the analysis of investment decisions, it is useful to differentiate between economic and financial value. The economic value is directly related to the economic activity of the company while the financial value is directly related to the form of financing, in other words, with its financial structure.

At the core of the understanding of the difference between the results obtained in the economic and financial evaluation of investments is the financial leverage effect. In this paper we will highlight the usefulness of the financial leverage formula in anticipating and understanding the effect of debt on the following evaluation criteria: net present value and internal rate of return.

Common sense generally views debt as a necessary evil, due to the fact that the financial expenses incurred have a negative effect on net income. Plenty of literature have been discussing the pros and cons of debt, and its effects on economies and economic agents (vid. e.g. Ribeiro et al., 2012; Ribeiro & Pereira, 2021).

Regarding literature on this topic, it is well known, and strongly suggested that, although excessive indebtedness has a negative effect on net income, it does not necessarily mean that the return on capital invested by partners or shareholders is lower.

2. Financial Literacy, Profitability and Risk

The economic and financial concepts are often associated with studies related to profitability and risk analysis, as well as in investment appraisal (vid. e.g. Götze et al., 2008; Ross et al., 2022). Regarding the study of profitability, Fairfield and Yohn (2001) refer to three aspects: operating margin ratio, economic return on assets and return on equity. These authors note that, despite most textbooks advocating the disaggregation of profitability into profit margin and asset turnover, while developing financial analysis, its usefulness is not necessarily guaranteed, particularly when forecasting is a goal.

Like Fairfield and Yohn (2001), in this research some prominent techniques, duly described in well-known textbooks, are challenged, as it is believed that they are examined in a more exhaustive way, which is believed to be more accurate as well, therefore contributing to increase the overall financial literacy from individuals and corporations.

The goal of this approach is not to revolutionize the existing practice and knowledge, but to improve it, by presenting alternative views, while using the same mainstream theoretical background, as follows.

The purpose of operating margin ratio is to determine the portion of operating income (sales) that has generated operating results, i.e., operating margin ratio is obtained by the quotient between operating results and operating income.

$$Operating\,margin\,ratio = \frac{Operating\,Results}{Operating\,Income} \tag{1}$$

By calculating the economic return on investments, the aim is to measure the relationship between the net economic results and all the means used by the company to achieve these results. In these terms, this measure of profitability is obtained by the ratio between net economic results and total net assets.

$$Return\,on\,assets = \frac{Net\ Economic\ Result}{Total\,net\,assets} \tag{2}$$

Return on equity measures the efficiency with which companies use the capital that the partners/shareholders have put into the company. It is determined by the quotient between net income and equity.

$$Return\ on\ equity = \frac{Net\ Income}{Equity} \quad (3)$$

In the same order of ideas, Bodie et al. (2022) refer to the study of profitability presenting the same terms, essentially supported on the Dupont system for profitability analysis created by electrical engineer F. Donaldson Brown in 1914 (vid. Flesher and Previts, 2013).

Doron and Penman (2003) also present a set of profitability indicators, among which are return on assets and financial profitability. Although with slightly different designations, they coincide in their content with the designations presented by the previous authors. Therefore, the economic return on investments is to the return on assets just as the return on equity is to the financial return.

Similarly to Doron and Penman (2003), other literature, as Penman (2013), Damodaran (2001), or Bodnar et al. (2019), while examining risk, make remarks on the economic degree of leverage and the financial degree of leverage, once again highlighting the importance of the difference between the economic and financial concepts.

Both degrees of economic and financial leverage are calculated based on an income statement that disaggregates fixed and variable costs, as follows:

$$Degree\ of\ Operating\ Leverage = \frac{Gross\ Margin}{Earnings\ Before\ Interest\ and\ Taxes} \quad (4)$$

and,

$$Degree\ of\ Financial\ Leverage = \frac{Earnings\ Before\ Interest\ and\ Taxes}{Earnings\ Before\ Taxes} \quad (5)$$

We can easily observe, through all these indicators, that the difference between the economic and financial ratios only occurs when there is debt. In fact, the essence of the difference between economic and financial profitability lies in explaining the financial leverage effect.

The financial leverage can be expressed by calculating the financial profitability that shows the financial structure. Menezes (1993) besides presenting the formula, explains its origin by deducing it in the following terms:

$$NI = EBIT - I - T$$

$$NI = \left(\frac{EBIT}{A}.A - i.D \right).(1-T)$$

$$NI = \left[ROA.(E+D) - i.D \right].(1-T)$$

$$NI = \left[(ROA.E) + (ROA - i).D \right].(1-T)$$

$$ROE = \frac{\left[(ROA.E) + (ROA - i).D \right].(1-T)}{E}$$

$$ROE = \left[.(ROA - i) + ROA \right].(1-T) \tag{6}$$

In which each of the abbreviations has the following meaning:

NI – Net income;
EBIT – Earnings before interest and taxes;
I – Interest;
T – Taxes;
A – Net Assets;
E – Equity;
D – Debt;
ROA – Return on assets (before taxes);
ROE – Return on equity (after taxes);
i – Debt weighted effective cost rate before taxes
t – Taxes;
λ – Debt to equity ratio (D/E).

It was based on this deduction that Pereira (2006), rewrote the formula presenting all elements of profitability after taxes, eliminating the (1-T) portion of the formula and highlighting two portions that make it easier for us to understand.

$$\underbrace{R_{fin} = R_{econ}}_{1.^{a}\ Part} + \underbrace{\frac{D}{E}.(R_{econ} - i)}_{2.^{a}\ Part} \tag{7}$$

We prefer to use other acronyms and, in some cases, other designations that in no way differ from their content, but that facilitate congruence throughout this paper.

R_{fin} – Financial return after taxes;

R_{econ} – Economic return after taxes;
D/E – Debt to equity ratio
i – Cost of debt after tax.

As we can observe, the formula was divided into two parts to facilitate its understanding. In the first part we have equality between financial and economic return after taxes, which is verified when the second part of the formula is equal to zero, that is, when there is no debt or when the cost, of debt after taxes is equal to economic return after taxes.

The effect will be positive when, if there is debt, economic return exceeds the cost of debt after tax. The effect will be negative when, in the presence of debt, economic return is lower than the after-tax cost of debt.

All these indicators, presented so far, are ratios and, to a large extent, their calculation is obtained from the income statement. In the evaluation of investments, the evaluation criteria must be supported in the previous calculation of cash flow.

Several authors, as Habib (2011), justify the prevalence of criteria based on cash flow to the detriment of criteria based on results, as is the case of the ratios presented above. Cash flow is an objective, clearly defined concept that can be unambiguously recorded. Net income depends on bookkeeping procedures which, through different methods of valuing inventories or the method of recording depreciations and amortizations, can give them a subjective character.

Furthermore, in what concerns cash flow, we can determine it for economic or financial evaluation purposes. Literature often classifies cash flow from the project's perspective and from the investor's perspective, having the same correspondence with cash flow for economic and financial evaluation purposes, respectively (vid. e.g. Brush et al., 2010). To evaluate the project from the project's perspective is to evaluate it in itself regardless of the form of financing, while evaluating the project from the investor's perspective, as the name implies, is to evaluate the project based on the estimate of capital inflows and outflows from the investor's point of view.

Regardless of the type of evaluation (economic or financial) it is usual to classify cash flow as investment cash flow, operating cash flow, and net cash flow, the latter corresponding to the sum of the first two, always representing cash inflows or outflows.

According to Barros (1999), the investment cash flow for economic evaluation purposes comprises the investment in fixed capital and working capital and, in the last year of useful life, with a positive sign, their respective terminal values.

Thus, representing each variable with its respective sign, positive for cash inflows and negative for cash outflows, we have:

$$Investment\ cash\ flow = -Investment + Terminal\,value \tag{8}$$

In calculating the operating cash flow, Barros (1999) defines it as the value of net receipts of payments associated with the operation of the project, presenting the following formula:

$$Operating\ Cash\ flow = NI + D - Imp + I \tag{9}$$

Where each of the acronyms has the following meaning:

NI – Net operating income;
D – Depreciation
Imp- Impairments
I – Interest.

Although we consider the definition to be perfect, the formula does not meet it. First, the negative sign associated with impairments is probably an editing error, since it should be positive, since these expenses are not disbursable and, as such, if they negatively influenced the net income, they should be added. On the other hand, if the formula starts from the net operating result, it means that this is not influenced by debt and, therefore, the financial charges (Interest) should not be added or, if by hypothesis the net operating result should be the net result, then it would make sense in the formula to consider the addition of financial charges but, even so, corrected for the tax effect, because if they were not considered, the result before taxes would be higher, as well as the respective tax.

Therefore, for the formula to meet the definition, in our view it should be:

$$\text{Operating}\ Cash\ flow = NI + D + Imp + I(1-T) \tag{10}$$

Soares et al. (2006), suggested another formula whose result converges with ours:

$$Operating\ Cash\ flow = EBIT(1-t) + D + Imp \tag{11}$$

Instead of starting from the net results, it starts from the EBIT, before the financial function that after multiplied by (1-T) represents the net economic result to which the same variables are added.

As far as financial evaluation is concerned, Barros (1994) defines investment cash flow as the amount of equity that goes into the project, that is, the formula will come in these terms:

$$Investment\ Cash\ flow = -Equity + Terminal\ value \tag{12}$$

Although Barros (1994) does not make reference to residual value, underlying the explanation about the evaluation from the investor's point of view is the need to consider.

In our opinion, when the author refers to equity, this should be understood in a broader form than its strict meaning, for it should include any cash inflows from the project promoters (partners, shareholders, etc.) even if they do not fall under the accounting heading of equity, such as loans from partners.

In the same scope of assessment, Barros (1994) defines operating cash flow as the flow after financial charges and debt amortization, that is,

$$Operating\ Cash\ flow = NI + D + Imp - Amortization \tag{13}$$

To measure the effect of the financial structure on the return on capital invested by the partners/shareholders we can determine several evaluation criteria, such as the net present value and the internal rate of return.

The calculation of the internal rate of return only requires the estimation of cash flows while the net present value calculation still needs the estimation of the discount rate.

3. Measuring the Effect of Indebtedness on Profitability of Owners

3.1. Based on Ratios

Despite the limitation of ratios in the valuation of investments, they constitute a good starting point for understanding the financial leverage effect and, consequently, an interesting basis to explain the difference between economic and financial valuation when elaborated through the calculation of the internal rate of return and net present value.

Based on the example below we will try to demonstrate its usefulness. Consider a company that intends to make an investment of 100,000 euros and estimates the following operating values:

Table 1. Income statement (euros)

Sales	500,000
Variable costs	350,000
Gross margin	**150,000**
Fixed costs	100,000
Depreciation	25,000
Earnings before interest and taxes (EBIT)	**25,000**

Source: Authors

In this paper we consider three hypotheses for financing the investment:

Table 2. Financing hypotheses

Hypothesis 1		**Hypothesis 2**		**Hypothesis 3**	
Equity	100 %	Equity	75 %	Equity	50 %
Debt	0 %	Debt	25 %	Debt	50 %

Source: Authors

In either circumstance, the cost of borrowed capital (before taxes), by assumption, is 5 %/year. Let's further consider a tax rate on profits of 20 %.

Let's now look at the development of income statement for each financial structure hypothesis and the respective economic and financial rates of return.

3.1.1. Hypothesis One

Table 3. Net income, hypothesis 1 (euros)

Earning before interest and taxes (EBIT)	**25,000**
Interest	0
Earning before taxes (EBT)	25,000
Taxes	5,000
Net income	20,000

Source: Authors

Assuming this financing structure, the economic and financial profitability, after taxes, is estimated at 20 %, obtained by the ratio between the means made available (denominator) and the expected result from the availability of those same means (numerator).

Since there is no debt, there is no difference between economic and financial profitability.

3.1.2. *Hypothesis Two*

Table 4. Net income, hypothesis 2 (euros)

Earnings before interest and taxes (EBIT)	**25,000**
Interest	1,250
Earnings before taxes (EBT)	23,750
Taxes	4,750
Net income	19,000

Source: Authors

Assuming this financing structure the economic profitability, after taxes, is estimated at 20 %. This does not change in relation to the previous hypothesis, since there is no change in economic terms.

As for financial profitability, this is determined by the quotient between net income (19,000) and invested capital (75,000), i.e. 25.3(3)%.

3.1.3. *Hypothesis Three*

Table 5. Net income, hypothesis 3 (euros)

Earning before interest and taxes (EBIT)	**25,000**
Interest	2,500
Earning before taxes (EBT)	22,500
Taxes	4,500
Net income	18,000

Source: Authors

As explained earlier, the estimate of economic profitability, after taxes, remains at 20 %.

As far as financial profitability is concerned, this is determined in the same way, although now the net results show a value of 18,000 and an invested capital of 50,000, i.e. the financial profitability obtained is 36 %.

As we can observe, in this example, through indebtedness (financial leverage) the partners or shareholders are able to increase the expectation of financial profitability, that is, of their invested capital.

Similarly, within the same example, a circumstance is presented in which indebtedness favors the return on invested equity. This is not always the case. The effect of debt can be positive, negative or zero. We recall the financial leverage formula [7].

To what extent this formula and its application can help us interpret the results obtained with the net present value calculation and the internal rate of return?

Although these criteria are determined based on cash flows, the formula will still help us anticipate the effect of debt on the return on invested capital as well as interpret the results obtained.

3.2. Based on Cash Flows

We will try to be enlightening about the usefulness of the financial leverage formula based on our previous example, although now, adding some more variables to it. Let's consider the same investment amount, i.e. 100,000 Euros with an estimated useful life of 4 years. The projected operating plan remains the same throughout its useful life:

Table 6. Partial income statements: Years 1–4 (euros)

Sales	500,000
Variable costs	350,000
Gross margin	**150,000**
Fixed costs	100,000
Depreciation	25,000
Earnings before interest and taxes (EBIT)	**25,000**

Source: Authors

We will only analyze a financing structure, corresponding to our hypothesis 2 of the previous example, that is, 75 % equity and 25 % borrowed capital, which will be repaid in 4 continuous instalments of principal and interest, subject to an interest rate of 5 %/year.

In these terms, the loan repayment table will present the following values (euros):

Table 7. Loan repayment (euros)

Period	**Beginning Balance**	**Interest**	**Principal**	**Total Payment**	**Ending Balance**
0	–	–	–	–	25,000
1	25,000	1,250	5,800	7,050	19,200
2	19,200	960	6,090	7,050	13,110
3	13,110	655	6,395	7,050	6,715
4	6,715	335	6,715	7,050	0

Source: Authors

In this way, we are able to proceed to the realization of the income statement for the 4 years of useful life, as presented:

Table 8. Income statements (euros)

	Year 1	Year 2	Year 3	Year 4
Sales	500,000	500,000	500,000	500,000
Variable costs	350,000	350,000	350,000	350,000
Gross margin	**150,000**	**150,000**	**150,000**	**150,000**
Fixed costs	100,000	100,000	100,000	100,000
Depreciation	25,000	25,000	25,000	25,000
Earnings before interest and taxes	**25,000**	**25,000**	**25,000**	**25,000**
Interest	1,250	960	655	335
Earnings before taxes (EBT)	23,750	24,040	24,345	24,665
Taxes	4,750	4,808	4,869	4,933
Net income	19,000	19,232	19,476	19,732

Source: Authors

Now, based on this, we will determine the cash flows, first for economic valuation purposes and then for financial valuation purposes.

For economic valuation purposes, the investment cash flow is the investment itself and the operating cash flow is the net economic result earnings before interest and taxes x (1 – tax rate) plus depreciation. Accordingly, we will have:

Table 9. Net cash flows for economic evaluation (euros)

	Year 0	Year 1	Year 2	Year 3	Year 4
Investment cash flow *Operating Cash flow*	–100,000	45,000	45,000	45,000	45,000
Net Cash flow	–100,000	45,000	45,000	45,000	45,000

Source: Authors

For financial evaluation purposes, the investment cash flow refers to the amount invested by the promoters, i.e., the capital inflows. The operating cash flow corresponds to the flow generated by the company that, after paying the financial charges and debt service, is available to the owners. Thus, it can be determined by adding the net income with the depreciation expenses minus the debt amortization.

It was on these terms that we determined the following cash flows for financial valuation purposes.

Table 10. Net cash flows for financial evaluation (euros)

	Year 0	Year 1	Year 2	Year 3	Year 4
Investment cash flow *Operating Cash flow*	−75,000	38,200	38,142	38,081	38,017
Net Cash flow	−75,000	38,200	38,142	38,081	38,017

Source: Authors

We are now able to determine the net present value, considering a discount rate of 7.75 %, and the internal rate of return for economic and financial valuation purposes that we will summarize in the following Table 11.

Table 11. Result of NPV and IRR

	Economic Evaluation	Financial Evaluation	Variation
Net present value (7,75 %)	49,879€	51,058€	1,179€
Internal rate of return	28,5 %	36 %	7,5 %

Source: Authors

4. Justification of the Indebtedness Effect on the Promoters' Profitability

Starting by analysing the internal rate of return criterion which, as the name indicates, represents the expected profitability, we verify that the use of debt favors the project's promoters since the financial profitability exceeds the economic one by 7.5 %. Note that, even before performing the calculations, understanding the formula presented above for the financial leverage effect allowed us to anticipate this effect.

Let's remember the financial leverage formula [7] Instead of financial profitability, once determined by a ratio, it now corresponds to the internal rate of return for financial valuation purposes. Instead of economic profitability, once determined by a ratio, it now corresponds to the internal rate of return for economic valuation purposes. Then, the effect will be zero when there is no debt (2nd tranche of the formula equals zero) or when the after-tax economic return (internal rate of return) equals the after-tax cost of debt.

Since the after-tax economic return (28.5 %) is greater than the after-tax cost of borrowed capital (4 %) the effect is positive, and the higher the degree of debt, the greater the effect would be. If the cost of borrowed capital after tax were 28.5 % the two internal rates of return would be equal to 28.5 % and if, hypothetically, the cost of borrowed capital after tax were higher than 28.5 % the effect would be negative. The formula allows us to conclude all this without doing any calculations. It does not allow us to go further in determining the value of the internal rate of return for financial valuation purposes because this formula was derived on the basis of one economic period and the internal rate of return is calculated on the basis of cash flows, taking into account various economic periods in which the debt ratio changes.

It will be more difficult to fit this formula for net present value calculation purposes, since this criterion provides a result in monetary terms. Instead of financial profitability, once determined by a ratio, it now corresponds to the net present value for financial valuation purposes. Instead of economic profitability, once determined by a ratio, it now corresponds to the net present value for economic valuation purposes. Therefore, the effect will be zero when there is no debt (2nd part of the formula equals zero) or when the after-tax economic return equals the after-tax cost of debt. It is in this part of the formula that the difficulty arises because in this part of the formula our economic return cannot be the net present value. It would make no sense for us to compare an absolute value with a relative value. Accordingly, on can question what is being considered in this part of the formula when we calculate the net present value for financial valuation purposes? How can we anticipate the effect when there is recourse to debt?

As we will have the opportunity to demonstrate in the net present value calculation for financial valuation purposes we are considering as economic return the minimum desired return, i.e. the discount rate.

To assist our arguing, we will resort to the concept of adjusted net present value (ANPV) presented by Brealey et al. (2023). The added utility of the ANPV is that it separates the economic value from the financial value in its calculation. If we use the same discount rate, the ANPV corresponds to the net present value for financial valuation purposes. If we consider efficient markets, as Brealey et al. (2023) do, the discount rate should be the loan's own interest rate and, in this case, the present value of the financing decision will correspond to the present value of the tax savings of the financial charges.

Analysing the respective formula:

$$ANPV = NPV_{\text{Economic Evaluation}} + PV_{\text{Financing Decision}} \tag{14}$$

Only the last part of the formula needs explanation. It is precisely this part of the formula that concerns the effect of debt. If the present value (PV) of the financing decision is positive the effect will be positive. If the present value (PV) of the financing decision is negative the effect will be negative. If the present value (PV) of the financing decision is zero the effect will be zero. Note that this can be anticipated by the financial leverage formula explained earlier. Calculating the present value of the financing decision has the added benefit of knowing how positive or negative it will be.

To determine the present value of the financing decision we first need to calculate the cash flows inherent to the debt, i.e., the value of the debt with a positive sign, reflecting its receipt, and then, with a negative sign, when the debt is repaid, the value of the repayments and respective interest adjusted for the tax effect.

Thus, in a first analysis, we will demonstrate that the net present value for financial valuation purposes is necessarily equal to the adjusted net present value as long as the same discount rate is used.

Let's remember how to determine the cash flow for economic valuation purposes. When the investment is made we have:

$$Investment\ Cash\ flow = -Investment \tag{15}$$

Assuming there is no terminal value, all that remains is to consider the periodic flow of exploitation, i.e. [10]:

$$\text{Operating}\ Cash\ flow = NI + D + Imp + I(1-T)$$

Let's also remember which flows come from debt. When the debt is contracted, to finance the investment we have:

$$+Debt \tag{16}$$

Periodically, we also have the flow related to the payment of the debt and the respective interest corrected of the fiscal effect, that is:

$$-Amortization - I(1-T) \tag{17}$$

Now, if we add the cash flows for economic valuation purposes with the cash flows inherent to the debt, in the respective time periods, we get the cash flows for financial valuation purposes, as we easily demonstrate below:

In year 0:

$$\begin{array}{l} -Investment \\ \underline{+Debt} \\ \boldsymbol{-Equity} \end{array} \tag{18}$$

That is, we obtain the investment cash flow for financial valuation purposes, assuming zero terminal value [13].

Periodically:

$$\begin{array}{c} NI + D + Imp + I(1-T) \\ \underline{-Amortization - I(1-T)} \\ \boldsymbol{NI + D + Imp - Amortization} \end{array} \tag{19}$$

I.e., we obtain the operating cash flow for financial valuation purposes.

Therefore, the adjusted net present value necessarily corresponds to the sum of the net present value for economic valuation purposes and the present value of the financing decision, when using the same discount rate.

Let's take our example again. Based on this example we will calculate the cash flows associated with the debt:

Table 12. Loan repayment cash flow (euros)

Period	Beginning Balance	Interest	Principal	Total Payment	Ending Balance	Cash flow
0					25,000	+25,000
1	25,000	1,250	5,800	7,050	19,200	−6,800
2	19,200	960	6,090	7,050	13,110	−6,858
3	13,110	655	6,395	7,050	6,715	−6,919
4	6,715	335	6,715	7,050	0	−6,983

Source: Authors

To determine the present value of the financing decision, all that remains is to update the cash flows at a rate of 7.75 %. Having done the math, we obtain a value of 1,179 euros, exactly identical to the difference between the net present values obtained previously.

It is also interesting to note that, although it is simpler to determine the cost of debt after taxes this way [5 %*(1–20 %) = 4 %], it can also be obtained by calculating the “internal rate of return” based on the cash flows determined, obtaining the same 4 %.

This last form of calculation has the benefit of understanding the effect through the discounting process of the cash flows.

If we use the after-tax cost of debt rate as the discount rate, the present value of the financing decision will be zero. If we use a rate below 4 % the relative weight of negative cash flows at time zero exceeds the value of the loan, making the effect negative. If, on the other hand, we use a rate above 4 %, as is the case of 7 %, the effect is positive because the relative weight of negative flows at time zero is lower than the value of the loan.

In order to show the benefit of this understanding, let’s resume our example, now with a single change, replacing the discount rate of 7.75 % by 3 %.

Our internal rate of return results would not change at all. The effect of debt would remain positive. However, if we were to calculate the net present value we would contradict ourselves. The net present value for economic valuation purposes would be higher than the net present value for financial valuation purposes, respectively 67,629 euros and 66,666 euros (VA -603 euros).

This contradiction is ultimately understood by the financial leverage formula and the NPV calculation of the financing decision.

In fact, when through the internal rate of return we say that the effect would be positive, we are considering that our economic return is the maximum expected, i.e., 28.5 %.

On the other hand, reading through the net present value, we conclude that the effect would be negative, and it would be so if we have an economic return equal to the minimum desired (3 %) or even higher, as long as it is below 4 % (cost of debt after taxes). In fact, even without recourse to mathematics, it is easy to understand that if the money costs us 4 % and we can only make it profitable at 3 %, the higher the debt, the greater the negative effect.

However, we cannot forget the limitations of this calculation. When we determine the NPV we are estimating the creation of wealth, which is a function of cash flows and also of the discount rate which represents the cost of money over time. Therefore, how can it be justified that the cost of debt after taxes would be 4 % and the discount rate 3 %? Certainly, the discount rate will also be a function of the cost of debt and the degree of debt.

No doubt the question is quite pertinent and will be our starting point to refine our model using the concept of weighted average cost of capital.

It is legitimate to think in these terms: if debt has a cost of 4 % and if, by hypothesis, the investment was financed 100 % through debt, then the discount rate should be 4 %, assuming no associated guarantees. The following reasoning is also legitimate: if equity has a cost of 6 %, and if by hypothesis the investment were financed 100 % through equity, then the discount rate should be 6 %. Finally, it is also legitimate to think in the following way: if, by hypothesis, the investment was financed 50 % through debt and 50 % through equity, then the discount rate should be its weighted average, i.e. 5 % (4 % × 0.5 + 6 % × 0.5).

Taking our example again to show the application of the weighted average cost of capital for the purpose of calculating the NPV in the financial appraisal of projects and its relationship with the adjusted net present value.

In this sense, we will introduce some additional variables that explain the discount rate based on the CAPM (Capital Asset Pricing Model). Thus, the opportunity cost of capital for a debt-free capital structure was considered to be 7.75 % [8 % + 1.1(7.5 %–5 %)], based on the following information:

- ✓ Risk-free return on assets (R_f)= 5 %;
- ✓ Beta (β_E) of equity = 1,2;
- ✓ Average market return (Rm) = 7.5 %;
- ✓ Cost of equity (R_E) = 8 % [5 % + 1.2(7.5 %–5 %)];
- ✓ Cost of debt capital (R_D) = 7 %;
- ✓ Beta (β_D) of debt capital = 0.8 [(7 %–5 %)/(7.5 %–5 %)];
- ✓ Beta (β_u) of assets = 1.1 (For a capital structure with 25 % debt and 75 % equity [1.2 x 75 % + 0.8*25 %)]

Thus, considering the net cash flows we used previously for the economic valuation, now updated to the weighted average cost of capital [8 % × 0.75 + 7 % × (1–0.2) × 0.25], we obtain an NPV(7.4 %) = 51,058 representing the financial valuation by adjusting the discount rate.

In this calculation, however, we are considering that the capital structure remains constant over the life of the project, i.e., 75 % equity and 25 % debt. Therefore, the debt service map previously considered no longer makes sense, which is why we present the following table with the cash flows, asset value and borrowed capital:

Table 13. Capital structure (euros)

	Year 0	**Year 1**	**Year 2**	**Year 3**	**Year 4**
Net Cash flow	–100,000	45,000	45,000	45,000	45,000
Assets*	151,058	117,236	80,912	41,899	–
Debt (25 %)	37,765	29,309	20,228	10,475	–

**Determined by the present value of future cash flows.*
*In year 0 it is equal to the investment plus NPV*Source: Authors

Thus, the interest you get is equal to 7 % of the debt amount, i.e:

Table 14. Interests (euros)

	Year 0	Year 1	Year 2	Year 3	Year 4
Interests	–	2,643	2,052	1,416	733

Source: Authors

This way, we can also calculate the ANPV in which the disaggregation of the economic and financial value of the project is expressed. Now, to determine the present value of the financing decision, it is enough to update the profit tax savings that derive from finance charges (interest):

Table 15. Tax savings on interests (euros)

	Year 0	Year 1	Year 2	Year 3	Year 4
Tax savings on interests	–	529	410	283	147

Source: Authors

Having done the calculation, we get a PV (7.75 %) of 1,179. Added to the 49,879, we get 51,058 identical to the NPV determined using the weighted average cost of capital. The same value would be obtained if we ascertained the cash flows for financial valuation purposes and updated them at the 8 % rate (R_E). Otherwise, observe the following section.

Let's start by recalculating the net income based on the new assumptions (constant capital structure over the life of the project):

Table 16. Net income with a constant capital structure (euros)

Earnings before interest and taxes (EBIT)	**25,000**	**25,000**	**25,000**	**25,000**
Interest	2,644	2,052	1,416	733
Earnings before taxes (EBT)	22,356	22,948	23,584	24,267
Taxes	4,471	4,590	4,717	4,853
Net income	17,885	18,359	18,867	19,413

Source: Authors

It is also possible to calculate the cash flows from the investor's point of view:

Table 17. Net cash flows for financial evaluation (euros)

	Year 0	Year 1	Year 2	Year 3	Year 4
Net Cash flow	–62,235	34,430	34,278	34,114	33,939

Source: Authors

Finally, one can determine the NPV considering the cost of equity (R_E = 8 %). Once the math is done, we can confirm that the same value is obtained, i.e. 51,058 euros.

5. Conclusion

The formula that explains the financial leverage effect, despite not being able to quantify the effect of debt (unless it is zero) on financial profitability, through the net present value and internal rate of return criteria, is extremely useful as it allows us to anticipate the effect (positive or negative) and makes it easier to understand it within certain assumptions.

Through this formulation it became easier to understand the adjusted net present value criterion and, with it, demonstrate that net present value for financial valuation purposes assumes that the economic return is the minimum desired while the internal rate of return considers that the economic return is the maximum expected.

This formula also helps us conclude that in calculating the adjusted net present value we should not adjust the discount rate of the financing structure. If we did, then the result of the present value of the financing decision, independently interpreted, would no longer make sense.

On the other hand, our study made it easier to understand the usefulness of the weighted average cost of capital, what are its assumptions, and how to apply it in calculating the net present value for financial valuation purposes. Furthermore, this way it was possible to determine the adjusted net present value, disaggregating the economic value from the financial value.

Finally, it should also be mentioned that the internal rate of return is not influenced by the cost of capital and, therefore, a higher internal rate of return (financial) does not necessarily imply a higher value creation because, associated to that rate of return, there is also a higher financial risk.

This paper offers a relevant contribution for knowledge, while promoting financial literacy, by the means of a better understanding of key concepts related to investments appraisal, as indebtedness and risk; or planning and budgeting. In the current information era, it is critical to deliver suitable management decisions, duly grounded by data and information produced with quality and accuracy. As discussed and demonstrated in this paper, this requires proper skills and techniques on the financial field, which need to cover a broad number of significant possibilities, which, in turn, may determine the possibilities of financial success for businesses and individuals.

References

Barros, C. (1994). *Decisões de Investimento e Financiamento de Projectos* (3rd ed.). Lisbon, Portugal: Edições Sílabo.

Barros, C. (1999). *Avaliação Financeira de Projectos de Investimento*. Lisbon, Portugal: Editora Vulgata.

Bodie, Z., Kane, A., & Marcus, A. J. (2022). *Essentials of investments* (12th ed.). New York, NY: McGraw-Hill.

Bodnar, G., Giambona, E, Graham, J., & Harvey, C. (2019). A view inside corporate risk management. *Management Science*, 65(11), 5001–5026.

Brealey, R., Myers, S., Allen, F., & Edmans, A. (2023). *Principles of corporate finance* (14th ed.). New York, NY: McGraw-Hill.

Brush, T. H., Bromley, P., & Hendricks, M. (2010). The free cash flows hypothesis for sales growth and firm performance. *Strategic Management Journal*, 11(22), 455–472.

Çera, G., Khan, K. A., Rowland, Z., & Ribeiro, H. (2021). Financial advice, literacy, inclusion and risk tolerance: The moderating effect of uncertainty avoidance. *E&M Economics and Management*, 24(4), 105–123.

Damodaran, A. (2001). *Corporate finance: Theory and practice* (2nd ed.). New York, NY: John Wiley & Sons.

Doron, N., & Penman, S. (2003). Financial Statement Analysis of Leverage and how it Informs about Profitability and Price-to-Book Ratios. *Review of Accounting Studies*, 8, 531–560.

Fairfield, P. M., & Yohn, T. L. (2001). Using asset turnover and profit margin to forecast changes in profitability. *Review of Accounting Studies*, 6, 371–385.

Flesher, D., & Previts, G. (2013). Donaldson Brown (1885-1965): The power of an individual and his ideas over time. Accounting Historians Journal, 40(1), 51-78.

Götze, U., Northcott, D., & Schuster, P. (2008). *Investment appraisal: Methods and models*. Heidelberg, Germany: Springer-Verlag Berlin.

Habib, A. (2011). Growth opportunities, earnings permanence and the valuation of free cash flow. *Australian Accounting Business and Finance Journal*, 5(4), 101–122.

Menezes, C. (1993). *Princípios de Gestão Financeira* (4th ed.). Lisbon, Portugal: Editorial Presença.

Penman, S. (2013). *Financial statement analysis and security valuation* (5th ed.). New York, NY: McGraw-Hill.

Pereira, N. (2006). *Manual de Avaliação Financeira de Projectos.* Santarém, Portugal: Amibússola.

Ribeiro, H., & Pereira, B. (2021, November). A new millennium of crises and public debt for the European Union countries. In A. Silva, L. Luic & A. Nechad (Eds.), *Proceedings of the 74th International Scientific Conference on Economic and Social Development* (pp. 224–234). Lisbon, Portugal: Vadea and University North.

Ribeiro, H., Vaicekauskas, T., & Lakštutienė, A. (2012). The effect of public debt and other determinants on the economic growth of selected European countries. *Economics and Management Journal*, 17(3), 914–921.

Ross, S., Westerfield, R., & Jordan, B. (2022). *Essentials of corporate finance* (11th ed.). New York, NY: McGraw-Hill.

Soares, J., Fernandes, A., Março, A., & Marques, J. (2006). *Avaliação de Projectos de Investimento na Óptica Empresarial* (2nd ed.). Lisbon, Portugal: Edições Sílabo.

Daniela Antonescu

Analysis SWOT at Regional Level. Case Study: Economy of Dornelor Basin, Suceava County, Romania

1. Introduction

The SWOT analysis is important in the formulation and selection of existing objec-tives and directions in territorial development strategies, being considered a viable instrument, a guide, which helps the decision-making factors and actors involved in local development (authorities, population, universities, companies of research and development, innovative clusters, NGOs, etc.) to strengthen policies, correct weak-nesses and protect against internal problems and external threats. Also, through the SWOT analysis, the general context in which the actions are proposed is addressed, as well as the recognition and exploitation of new opportunities. Based on this, the Territorial Development Strategy is drawn up (local, county, regional, national, etc.).

This paper aims to sketch a SWOT analysis related to the main fields of activity that take place in the Dornelor Basin (composed of 12 TAUs – territorial administrative units). Thus, the chapter proposes and tests the development of a spatial analysis based on official statistical indicators (National Institute of Statistics – NIS), highlighting the strengths, weaknesses, opportunities and threats of a complex territorial system, characterized by multiple and exceptional values, as Dornelor basin is.

The innovative value of the research comes not only from the integrated methodological approach, based on the combination of spatial analysis with indicator systems and traditional SWOT analysis, but also from the contextual characteristics of the investigated area. Moreover, the integrated framework proposed in the study has an important practical significance, due to the possibility of replicating the methodological approach in other spatial contexts (mountain areas).

2. Literature Review

Territorial planning is the process by which a certain area (county, city, commune, etc.) is managed, ensuring the fair, rational, efficient and responsible use of resources (natural, human, infrastructural facilities, etc.). It also consists of a

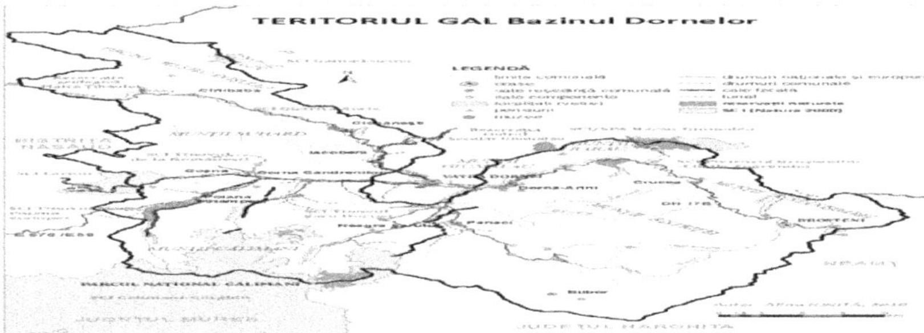

Figure 1. Dornelor mountain basin
Source: https://galbazinuldornelor.ro/teritoriu-2/

set of methods used by the public sector to rationally and efficiently organize the territory it manages.

Within the territorial planning process, there are development strategies, policies and programs whose object of activity is the territory, and which aim at the balanced and sustainable development of local communities, calling on a series of necessary financial resources (Law no. 350/2001 regarding land use and urban planning).

Territorial planning is also an integrative and participatory decision-making process, which addresses competing interests, being correlated with a common vision and a set of development strategies (national, regional and local); this is a basic component of the new paradigm of good governance, which promotes local democracy, participation, inclusion, transparency and accountability, in order to ensure sustainable and quality development (Antonescu, 2003).

Territorial planning is based on a series of principles, as follows:

1. it applies appropriate standards associated with good living and working conditions for local communities, present and future;
2. it ensures a fair distribution of costs, opportunities and territorial benefits;
3. it promotes social inclusion and cohesion.

Territorial planning is a powerful decision-making mechanism that can ensure sustained economic growth, social development, sustainability, aiming to promote better connectivity at all spatial levels.

In the framework of territorial planning, different forms of government must cooperate with each other as follows (Ianos, 2001):

- ✓ to support the development of the area, through the appropriate grouping of supporting elements (sectors of economic activity, public sectors, NGOs, etc.) to promote specialization, complementarity, synergies and economies of scale, cultural heritage and the diversity of local communities;
- ✓ for the creation of dynamic partnerships, including with the private sector, to ensure that territorial planning coordinates the spatial location and distribution of economic activities, building on economies of scale, agglomeration, proximity and connectivity, thus contributing to increased productivity, competitiveness and prosperity;
- ✓ for supporting cooperation to ensure optimal and sustainable mobilization of resources and preventing unhealthy competition between local actors;
- ✓ for the support of a local economic development and an adequate policy framework that integrates key concepts of the local economy (encouragement of private initiative, expansion or regeneration of the local economy, employment, etc.).

Local authorities, together with various relevant partners in territorial planning, have the following tasks (Cianga, 2007; Surd, 2005):

(a) to acknowledge the major role of citizens in making decisions about development directions;
(b) to ensure that planning contributes to the equitable access of all citizens to quality services;
(c) to include in territorial planning a clear and detailed component of local investments;
(d) to be based on progressive zoning associated with regulations or performance- based zoning;
(e) to support local economic development, in particular by generating jobs, by supporting local organizations, cooperatives, small and medium-sized enterprises etc.
(f) to ensure adequate security of citizens, creating a safe, comfortable and efficient environment, enabling a high degree of connectivity.

The main characteristics of the land development process are:

- it has a global and integrated character;
- is functional in nature (takes into account the natural and built environment based on cultural values and shared interests);
- has a prospective character;
- it must be democratic (wide participation of all stakeholders).

350/2001 on territorial planning and urban planning (updated by Law 151/ 2019) stipulates that territory management is a mandatory, continuous and forward-looking activity that takes into account the interest of local communities. According to the law, the central and local public administration authorities are responsible for the territory planning activity. Among other things, they must ensure the participation of the population in this process, ensuring that the options and opinions of citizens are taken into account.

3. Characteristics of Dornelor Basin

The Dornelor Basin area includes the municipality of Vatra Dornei, the town of Broşteni and the localities: Cârlibaba, Ciocăneşti, Iacobeni, Dorna Arini, Crucea, Dorna Cândrenilor, Coşna, Poiana Stampei, Panaci and Şaru Dornei. Bioaria is a component part of Suceava County, a county that is part of the North East development region (NUTS 2 region – according to the EU territorial nomenclature).

The Dornelor Depression is surrounded by mountains, as follows: to the North by the Suhard Mountains, to the Northeast by the Giumalău Mountains, to the E-SE by the Bistriţei Mountains, to the South by the Călimani Mountains, and to the West by the Bârgău Mountains. It presents a clear depression aspect, although tracing the southern and western limits is quite difficult, because the peaks, detached from the Călimani and Bârgău mountains and delimited by the tributaries of the two main arteries (Dorna and Neagra Şarului), pass in slopes towards the bottom of the depression, so that the frame of the depression is trenched only in the northern and eastern parts. Thus, the asymmetric profile of the depression is highlighted, also accentuated by the considerable development of the terraces on the right side of Bistriţa River.

Methodology

The applied methodology is based on the SWOT analysis. This analysis evaluates the internal specificity of the Dornelor Basin territorial entity, its strengths and weaknesses. In the process of developing a SWOT analysis, strengths and weaknesses will always be determined before identifying opportunities and threats. Different elements of the SWOT analysis are grouped in order of their importance and significance. The SWOT analysis is drawn up in the form of a table related to each field analyzed and is based on the analysis of the specific indicators of each field separately.

The SWOT analysis is based on elaborated research on the evolution of some economic and social indicators that provide information on the profile of the mountain area. The statistical data used were provided by the National Institute of Statistics, the analysis was carried out using Excel computer program. The collected data belong to the 12 TAUs located in the Dornelor Basin.

Types of information and reasons why such information should be collected and analyzed for a local economy assessment:

- Economic information will provide an understanding of the structure, characteristics and nature of the local economy of Dornelor Basin.
- The breakdown of local economic information by industrial sector can provide an insight into how the local economy is performing, is interlinked, which sectors are prospering, which are declining, where business development opportunities exist, and the aggregate value of local productive chains.
- Collecting labor market information can provide a workforce profile that highlights skills levels, shortages, skills in decline and LED trends. It can be used to identify labor market deficiencies, barriers to labor market entry and employment take-up and potential workforce programs, as well as identify industrial sectors that can be assisted and encouraged to locate in the area.

4. Economic Development

4.1. Labour Resources

The analysis of labor resources is one of the strengths of a local development strategy. A good demographic potential ensures the continuity and support of the local labor market. The general level of economic development of an area can be analyzed with the help of the labor market and its problems. It should also be noted that, at the national level, there is a significant shortage of labor resources in almost all areas of economic activity, with firms and companies having to adopt strategies to stop the emigration of the labor force.

Labor resources include those categories of the population that have all the physical and intellectual capacities that allow them to carry out useful work in an economic activity, within the national system.

In 2022, the Dornelor Basin had a total of 9,948 people in the category of labor resources, down from 11,718 people (2014), by -15.1 %.

The analysis was carried out on the basis of the official age groups that could fit into the labor market. Thus, in 2022, the age category of labor resources between 30–54 years old held 65.7 % of the total labor resources (people born before 1990). This category has increased its weight compared to 2014, when it recorded the value of 57.4 %. Also, there is a decrease in labor resources in the 20–24 year old category (from 8.99 % to 7.5 %) and those in the 25–29 year old category (from 11.56 % to 7,1 %). At the same time, there is an increase in labor resources in the 50–54 age group (from 9.28 % to 16.1 % of total resources).

This aspect shows that, in the next period, labor resources will no longer be able to be restored to the same level, nor will they be able to provide the labor market with adequate resources, thus identifying an important deficit in this sector.

In terms of dynamics, the analysis of labor resources in bioareas shows that significant reductions were recorded in the age groups 25–29 years (−48.2 %), 55–59 years (−29.8 %) and 35–39 of years (-24.1 %). At the same time, there was an important upward trend in the 50–54 age group (decree generation) (Table 1).

Table 1. The evolution of labor resources in the Dornelor Basin (no. of people, %)

;Groups of age	*2014*	*2014 (%)*	*2022*	*2022 (%)*	*Dynamics (2022 vs. 2014)*
20–24	1053	8.99	746	7.5	−29.2
25–29	1355	11.,56	702	7.1	−48.2
30–34	1224	10.45	1112	11.2	−9.2
35–39	1478	12.61	1122	11.3	−24.1
40–44	1415	12.08	1326	13.3	−6.3
45–49	1479	12.62	1377	13.8	−6.9
50–54	1088	9.28	1597	16.1	46.8
55–59	1351	11.53	948	9.5	−29.8
60–64	1275	10.88	1,018	10.2	−20.2
Total ***Bornelor Basin***	*11,718*	*100.00*	*9,948*	*100.0*	*−15.1*

Source: Author computations.

In 2022, the total labor resources consisted of 9,948 people, of which 4,827 were male (48.5 %) and 5,121 were female (51.5 %). There is a tendency to reduce the male population by -16.13 % and the female population by −14.12 % (Figure 61). An aspect considered a weak point is the fact that the registered gross activity rate (or general activity rate) in the Bazinul Dornelor bioarea. Thus, in 2022, it had a value of 21.89 %, down from 2014, when it recorded a value of 24.47 % (−2.58 p.p.).

4.2. Work-Force

The labor force is analyzed using the average number of employees active on the labor market. At the level of the Dornelor Basin, in 2021, 7,002 employees were reported, 4.45 % less than in 2014 (7,335 employees). Compared to Suceava County, the average number of employees of the bioarea is in a process of decrease, from 8 % to 6.65 % (2014 vs. 2022).

At the UAT level, the biggest decreases were recorded in Dorna Candrenilor (−65.2 %), Iacobeni (−52.86 %) and Crucea (−47.34 %). There were also increases in the average number of employees in Dorna Arini (+157.98 %), Panaci (+ 141.11 %), Şaru Dornei (+126.57 %). The municipality of Vatra Dornei recorded the lowest rate of only 0.29 % (Table 2).

Table 2. The evolution of the average number of employees in the Dornelor Basin and at the UAT level (no. pers.)

	2014	*2015*	*2016*	*2017*	*2018*	*2019*	*2020*	*2021*	*Dynamics (%)*
VATRA DORNEI	3,507	3,542	3,687	3,845	3,957	4,071	3,526	3,517	0.29
BROŞTENI	521	526	510	532	547	563	578	590	13.24
CÂRLIBABA	207	209	178	186	191	196	192	185	−10.63
CIOCANESTI	176	178	97	101	104	107	157	153	−13.07
COŞNA	71	72	56	58	60	62	131	152	114.08
CRUCEA	714	721	457	477	491	505	469	376	−47.34
DORNA CANDRENILOR	1,089	1,100	1,007	1,050	1,081	1,112	409	379	−65,20
DORNA-ARINI	119	120	232	242	249	256	287	307	157.98
IACOBENI	367	371	451	470	484	498	216	173	−52.86
PANACI	180	182	142	148	152	156	425	434	141.11
POIANA STAMPEI	177	179	129	135	139	143	248	267	50.85
ŞARU DORNEI	207	209	134	140	144	148	424	469	126.57
Dornelor Basin	**7,335**	**7,409**	**7,080**	**7,384**	**7,599**	**7,817**	**7,062**	**7,002**	**-4.54**
% in total Suceava County	*8.00*	*8.00*	*7.34*	*7.34*	*7.34*	*7.34*	*6.89*	*6.65*	

Source: Author computations.

Relative to the active population, the employment rate (employees/active population) increased from 62.6 % to 70.39 %. This value is above the value recorded at the national level (in 2022, the employment rate of the population aged 20–64 years old was 68.5 %, increasing compared to the previous year by 1.4 percentage points).

The analysis of the structure by UATs shows that the highest proportion of employees is in the municipality of Vatra Dornei (50.23 % of the total), followed by a long distance from Broşteni (8.43 %) and Şaru Dornei (+6.70) . The fewest employees are in the localities of Crucea (2.17 %), Ciocăneşti (2.19 %) and Iacobeni (2.47 %).

The registered unemployed represent the able-bodied persons who cannot be employed due to the lack of available jobs and who have registered with the Territorial Employment Agency.

In July 2023, in the Dornelor Basin, a number of 311 unemployed people were registered in the records of the Suceava County Employment Agency, with a downward trend compared to July 2014 of -64 % (864 unemployed). At the level of Suceava County, in July 2023, 9,911 unemployed were registered, 38.6 % less than in 2014 (July). The share of the unemployed in the total county represents 55.56 %, showing a downward trend compared to the same month of 2014, when it had a value of 59.35 %.

At the level of UATs, in July 2023, the most unemployed are reported in the city of Broşteni (25.4 %), followed by the municipality of Vatra Dornei (16.4 %), Dorna Arini (9.65 %) and Poiana Stampei (9.32 %). In Ciocăneşti and Coşna, no unemployed were reported in July 2021 (Table 3). Compared to the same month of 2014, it can be seen that Vatra Dornei municipality ranked first in the total number of unemployed (with 28.94 % of the total), followed by the city of Broşteni (15.97 %).

Table 3. The evolution of the number of unemployed in the Dornelor Basin and at the level of UAT (number of people, %)

	2014 (July) No.pers.	%	**2023 (July) No.pers.**	%
MUNICIPALITY VATRA DORNEI	250	28.94	51	16.40
City BROŞTENI	138	15.97	79	25.40
CÂLIBABA	37	4.28	20	6.43
CIOCĂNEŞTI	34	3.94	0	0,00
COŞNA	23	2.66	0	0,00
CRUCEA	28	3.24	15	4.82
DORNA CANDRENILOR	49	5.67	25	8.04
DORNA-ARINI	66	7.64	30	9.65
IACOBENI	59	6,83	23	7.40
PANACI	45	5.21	14	4.50
POIANA STAMPEI	61	7.06	29	9.32

	2014 (July) No.pers.	%	2023 (July) No.pers.	%
ŞARU DORNEI	74	8.56	25	8.04
Total	864	100.00	311	100.00

Source: Author computations.

Of the total number of unemployed registered in July 2023, 160 were men (51.4 %) and 151 were women (48.6 %). Compared to 2014 (July), there is a decrease in male unemployed (from 53.1 %) and an increase in female unemployed (from 46.9 %).

In Suceava County, it can be observed that the value of the nominal average monthly salary is lower than that recorded at the national level. The workforce in the county is paid 20 % less than the national average. By gender, men are paid 21.7 % less and women 18.19 % less. Also, at the county level, it is found that women are paid less than men (3,004 lei compared to 3,078 lei) (Table 4).

Table 4. Average monthly net nominal salary gain in Suceava County (Lei, %)

		2014	*2015*	*2016*	*2017*	*2018*	*2019*	*2020*	*2021*	*2022*
Total	TOTAL Dornelor Basin	1,697	1,859	2,046	2,338	2,642	2,986	3,217	3,416	3,801
-	Suceava County	1,352	1,489	1,593	1,876	2,118	2,445	2,646	2,737	3,042
	% in county	−20.3	−19.9	−22.1	−19.8	−19.8	−18.1	−17.7	−19,9	−20.0
Male	TOTAL Dornelor Basin	1,761	1,928	2,116	2,383	2,666	3,057	3,283	3,493	3,920
-	Suceava County	1,306	1,449	1,592	1,839	2,046	2,370	2,597	2,702	3,078
	% in county	−25.84	−24.84	−24.76	−22.83	−23.26	−22.47	−20.90	−22.65	−21.48
Female	TOTAL Dornelor Basin	1,627	1,783	1,968	2,288	2,615	2,908	3,144	3,331	3,672
-	Suceava County	1,406	1,534	1,593	1,917	2,200	2,530	2,699	2,775	3,004
	% in county	−13.58	−13.97	−19.05	−16.22	−15.87	−13.00	−14.15	−16.69	−18.19

Source: Author computations.

4.3. Active Local Companies

At the level of the Dornelor Basin, there are 621 active companies in the urban area (55.2 % of the total) (Vatra Dornei and Broşteni) and 504 active companies in rural mountain localities (44.8 %), with a total of 1,125 companies.

In the urban area, active companies operate mainly in the Retail Trade sector (22.87 %), followed by those in the hotel/accommodation sector (7.41 %), building construction (7.25 %), wood processing (6.44 %), restored (5.31 %), land transport (5.15 %), wholesale trade (4.99 %).

So the entrepreneurial profile of the Dornelor Basin is based on services, which, *in general, do not have high added value and, in many cases, are seasonal and highly dependent on the demand for tourist services, a demand that is becoming more and more complex in the conditions of a very rich offer at national or global level.*

Table 5. Active companies in the urban area of Dornelor Basin (no. of active companies, %)

	Vatra Dornei	Broşteni	Total	% in total
Agriculture, hunting and related services	1		1	0.16
Forestry	5	23	28	4.51
Fishing and aquaculture	4		4	0.64
Extraction of metallic ores	2		2	0.32
Food industry	6	2	8	1.29
Manufacture of beverages	2		2	0.32
Garment manufacturing	1	1	2	0.32
Wood processing, manufacture of wood and cork products, except for furniture; manufacturing articles from straw and other woven plant materials	***22***	***18***	***40***	***6.44***
Printing and reproduction on media of records	3		3	0.48
Manufacture of other products from non-metallic minerals	1		1	0.16
The industry of metal constructions and metal products, exclusive of machines, equipment and installations	1	2	3	0.48
Manufacture of road transport vehicles, trailers and semi-trailers	1		1	0.16
Furniture manufacturing	5		5	0.81

(continued on next page)

Table 5. Continued

	Vatra Dornei	Broşteni	Total	% in total
Other industrial activities n.e.c.	**1**	**1**	2	0.32
Collection, treatment and disposal of waste; recovery activities of recyclable materials	**3**		3	0.48
Construction of buildings	***37***	***8***	***45***	***7.25***
Special construction	**16**		16	2.58
Wholesale and retail trade, maintenance and repair of motor vehicles and motorcycles	**19**	**7**	26	4.19
Wholesale trade except trade in motor vehicles and motorcycles	**27**	**4**	31	4.99
Retail trade, except motor vehicles and motorcycles	***112***	***30***	***142***	***22.87***
Land transport and pipeline transport	**27**	**5**	32	5.15
Storage and auxiliary activities for transport	**2**		2	0.32
Postal and courier activities	**6**		6	0.97
Hotels and other accommodation facilities	***44***	***2***	***46***	***7.41***
Restaurants and other food service activities	***28***	***5***	***33***	***5.31***
Editing activities	**3**		3	0.48
Cinematographic, video and television program production activities; audio recordings and music editing activities	**3**		3	0.48
Broadcasting and program transmission activities	**2**		2	0,32
Telecommunications	**1**		1	0,16
Service activities in information technology	**4**		4	0,64
IT services activities	**1**		1	0,16
Auxiliary activities for financial intermediation, insurance activities and pension funds	**5**		5	0,81
Real estate transactions	7	**2**	9	1,45
Legal and accounting activities	**6**		6	0,97
Activities of the directorates (headquarters), centralized administrative offices; management and management consulting activities	7		7	1,13
Architecture and engineering activities; testing activities and technical analysis	**5**	**3**	8	1,29
Advertising and market research activities	**4**		4	0,64
Other professional, scientific and technical activities	**10**		10	1,61
Veterinary activities	**3**		3	0.48
Rental and leasing activities	**4**		4	0.64

Table 5. Continued

	Vatra Dornei	Broşteni	Total	% in total
Workforce service activities	**3**		3	0.48
Activities of tourist agencies and tour operators; other reservation services and tourist assistance	**6**		6	0.97
Landscaping activities and services for buildings	**2**		2	0.32
Secretarial activities, support services and other service activities provided mainly to businesses	**1**		1	0.16
Education	**4**		4	0.64
Activities related to human health	**20**		20	3.22
Creative activities and artistic interpretation	**1**		1	0.16
Gambling and betting activities	**1**		1	0.16
Sports, recreational and fun activities	**5**	**3**	8	1.29
Repairs of computers, personal and household items	**1**		1	0.16
Other service activities	**19**	**1**	20	3.22
	504	**117**	621	100.00
Total urban area	**621**			

Source: Author computations.

According to the INS, 504 active companies were identified in the rural area of Baznul Dornelor, most of them being located in Şaru Dornei (17.7 %), followed by Dorna Arini (15.9 %), Poiana Stampei and Panaci (each with 10.1 %).

The entrepreneurial profile of the UATs in the Dornelor basin is as follows:

- Silviculture and logging, retail trade and land transport predominate in Cârlibaba;
- In Coşna: land transport, wood processing and retail trade;
- In Crucea: retail trade and forestry;
- In Dorna Candrenilor: forestry and logging, retail trade and transport;
- Iacobeni: restaurants and food services, retail and transport;
- Poina Stampei: wood processing, retail trade;
- Ciocăneşti: retail trade, wood processing, hotels and transports;
- Dorna Arini: wood processing, hotels, retail, construction;
- Panaci: retail trade, land transport, forestry and logging.

Table 6. Swot analysis – Workforce

Strenght	**Weakness**
• there is an important share of labor resources in the 30–54 age category (65.7 % of the total), but with an obvious tendency to decrease as a result of the aging of the population; • employment rate higher than the national one (employees compared to the active population); • decrease in the number of registered unemployed; • greater decrease in the number of unemployed compared to the trend at the county level;	– reducing the volume of labor resources (−15.1 %); – increasing the share in the labor resources of the population aged 50–54; – an aging process of labor resources at Basin level; – trend of greater decrease of the male population in the labor resources of the bioarea; – decrease in the number of employees (−4.5 %); – reducing the proportion of employees from bioarea in the total county; – large number of employees in Vatra Dornei municipality (50.23 %); – high concentration of unemployed in the urban of the bioarea; – at the county level, the net average salary is lower than at the national level; women have lower wages than men; – the profile of active companies is based on the service sector and wood exploitation.
OPORTUNITIS	**RISKS**
– important funding sources (Regional Operational Programe North East region, FEADR, Resilience and Recovery Plan); – increased demand for some tourist services specific to the area; – means of promotion on the national, European and international market; – organization of national and international tourism fairs; – the existence of certification systems for ecotourism and agrotourism guesthouses (ANTREC, ECO-ROMANIA).	– competition at regional and national level – Economic crisis; – rural tourism is oversized in Europe; – political and geo-political instability; – legislative instability in the field – heavy crediting of the business sector in tourism; – the lack of predictability of the legislative framework for business – lack of financial resources for small producers (SMEs) for production diversification and superior technology.

5. Conclusions

Territorial planning, through its specific activities, regulates the management processes of a territory, following their evolutionary dynamics, including the effects and impact on some communities. It is considered a functional tool for analysis and evaluation of the impact that the actions of the various factors involved can have on an area/territory (for example, regulating the exploitation of natural resources, promoting economic growth, etc.). A main tool of territorial planning is the SWOT analysis. This paper intended to capture the main elements of the SWOT analysis related to some fields of activity – demographic, economic, social, infrastructure – characteristic of the Dornelor Basin.

Based on the results presented by the SWOT analysis, we can draw some major territorial development directions for Dornelor Basin, as follows:

DMI 1. Agriculture and mountain rural development: The purpose of this intervention is the development of competitive agriculture in the mountain area based on knowledge and private initiative, the use of specific techniques and the establishment of systems for adaptability to climatic conditions, the establishment of zootechnical farms and points for processing and collection of the resulting resources, the profitability of agricultural practices in order to increase the productivity of works applied on agricultural lands.

DMI 2. Infrastructure and the environment: The purpose of this intervention is to improve the quality of the infrastructure and the surrounding environment by modernizing or expanding roads, utility networks (water, sewerage, gas), fitting out existing buildings, public lighting by investing in the promotion and use of renewable energies for mitigating the effects of climate change, collecting household and industrial waste, protecting the community from natural risks, as well as activities to raise awareness among residents about the importance of preserving the environment where they live.

DMI 3. Mountain economy and business environment: The purpose of the intervention is to contribute to the economic development of the mountain area, by creating the conditions for the emergence of a prosperous and healthy business environment, based on competition and meeting the real market requirements. A special accent will be placed on attracting the financial resources necessary to support and implement some projects of major importance for the economic development of the commune and the creation of an institutional framework to stimulate investments, in which to activate human resources with a high degree of training and information. To improve the local business investment climate, an assessment of the local business enabling environment can be undertaken to determine the performance and effectiveness of the Vatra Dornei municipality in those aspects of the investment climate that it has control over. The municipality should aim to become responsive to the needs of business and put in place, procedures and regulations that improve the functioning of local businesses. In doing so, the municipality should include projects that simplify burdensome and bureaucratic procedures and rules of starting, owning, operating and managing a business. Such projects should be publicly accountable and transparent, and be initiated in conjunction and collaboration with local businesses and local business associations.

DMI 4. Supporting and promoting mountain tourism: The purpose of the intervention is to protect the natural, cultural and historical heritage of the mountain biodiversity, as well as a better valorization of the tourist heritage through the restoration and valorization of the historical and cultural heritage, the development of accommodation and leisure services and activities to promote the tourist potential of the area.

DMI 5. Education, culture and sport: The aim of this intervention is to contribute to increasing the attractiveness of the mountain area for its inhabitants, especially for young people, by organizing educa-tional, cultural and sports activities adapted to the target groups. A particularly im-portant aspect is the need to capitalize on the existing material base and stimulate the involvement of parents in the educational process, training and transmission of tradi-tional practices to future generations. An indirect effect would be that of reducing the risk of dropping out of school and the crime rate among young people, as well as the settling of young people in the area.

The development strategy of the Dornelor Basin must be a complex document, containing a package of measures and projects necessary to support the communities of the 12 UATs and increase the atractiveness for company and workforce.

References

Antonescu, D. (2003). *Romanian regional development policy in context of European Union structure*, MPRA Paper 57728. Germany: University Library of Munich. Revised 01 Jun 2014. https://ideas.repec.org/p/pra/mprapa/57728.html.

Ciangă, N. D. (2007). *Strategia de amenajare turistică*. Cluj –Napoca: Presa Universitară Clujeană.

Elaborarea Strategiilor de Dezvoltare Regională. Îndrumar Metodologic, 2012.

Ianoş, I. (2001). *Sisteme teritoriale*, Ed. Tehnică. ISBN: 973-31-1482-0, Bucharest.

Surd, V., coord. (2005). *Amenajarea teritoriului și infrastructuri tehnice*, ed. Cluj –Napoca: Presa Universitară Clujeană.

Tălângă, C. (2015). *Planificare teritorială strategică*, Editura Universitară, ISBN 978-606-28-0365-0, Bucharest.

Legea nr. 350/2001 privind amenajarea teritoriului şi urbanismului.

National Plan of Recovery and Resilience.

Regional Operational Programme.

https://www.nature.org/content/dam/tnc/nature/en/documents/Territorial%20Planning%20-%20Executive%20Summary%20-%20English.pdf

https://www.emerald.com/insight/content/doi/10.1108/S1871-317320180000015011/full/html

https://www.oar-bucuresti.ro/glosar/termen/planificare-teritoriala

https://galbazinuldornelor.ro/strategia-de-dezvoltare-2014-2020/

https://www.business-academy.ro/bazei-de-cunostinte/marketing/analiza-swot

https://taradornelor.ro/arii-protejate/

https://taradornelor.ro/parcul-national-calimani/

https://www.visitvatradornei.ro/activitati-outdoor/#pescuit

https://www.madr.ro/docs/dezvoltare-rurala/memorandum/Anexa-Memorandum-zona-montana-defavorizata-2014-2020.pdf

https://azm.gov.ro/despre-anzm/

http://intermaster.geo.unibuc.ro/wp-content/uploads/2014/10/18.dumitrache.pdf

https://agro-tv.ro/bazinul-dornelor-atrage-fonduri-europene/

Tarlan Ahmadov, Rusudan Tsiskaridze, Wolfgang Gerstlberger

Exploring the Roots of Sustainable HR Practices in Estonian Firms

1. Introduction

In response to the grand societal challenges outlined in the United Nations' Sustainable Development Goals (SDGs) (United Nations, 2022), organizations worldwide are increasingly recognized as critical contributors to sustainable development. Management scholars, emphasizing the design of business models and management practices, have explored avenues to align organizational strategies with these sustainability goals (George et al., 2016). Within this landscape, human resource management (HRM) has emerged as a focal point, offering the potential to drive organizations towards sustainability objectives (Stahl et al., 2020; Taylor et al., 2012). The evolution of "green HRM" (Jackson et al., 2011; Ren et al., 2023) and the broader concept of sustainable HRM (Aust et al., 2020; Kramar, 2014, 2022) underline a strategic assumption that well-crafted HRM practices contribute to organizational sustainability (Ren & Jackson, 2020).

Within the specific context of Estonian organizations, this study aims to address a significant gap in comprehending the role of HR professionals in driving sustainability initiatives. As Estonia implement various actions towards sustainability goals (Ahmadov, 2023; Ahmadov et al., 2022; Gerstlberger et al., 2023), organizations face the challenge of navigating a paradigm shift towards sustainability. Despite the acknowledged importance of HR in the sustainability discourse, there is a notable gap in understanding the specific contributions, particularly within the Estonian business landscape.

This research responds to a call from the literature (Ren et al., 2023) and seeks to investigate the motives driving sustainability initiatives, with a specific focus on the role of HR practitioners. By exploring the nuanced aspects of HR's involvement, the study aims to contribute a deeper understanding of current strategies, HR practices, and their sources within Estonian organizations. The research question, "What are the underlying motives for engaging with the sustainability agenda?" reflects this call from the literature and underscores the need for an in-depth exploration of the motivations propelling HR practitioners towards sustainable practices. Through an examination of the experiences and practices of HR professionals, this research aspires to offer valuable insights to academia and provoke discussions on the pivotal role of HR in fostering sustainability and catalysing transformative organizational change.

The chapter unfolds as follows: Section 2 provides comprehensive background, delving into existing literature relevant to the research topic. In Section 3, the methodology employed in the study is detailed. Section 4 unfolds the study's results, while Section 5 discusses the findings and concludes the chapter, addressing limitations, and outlining potential avenues for future research.

2. Literature Background

The rise of Green HRM in the 21st century is a response to environmental incidents and the excessive consumption of natural resources by industries (Ahmad, 2015). Alkhateeb et al. (2018) argues that Green HRM is effective in reducing pollution and environmental degradation, aligning with the broader goal of conservation.

Green HRM, defined as the planned alignment of HR practices with organizational environmental goals (Jabbour, 2013), represents a form of process innovation. This involves adopting environmentally friendly technologies and initiatives, including carpooling, job-sharing, online training, and telecommuting. These practices contribute to increased employee awareness and commitment to environmental sustainability (Mishra et al., 2014).

The integration of green HRM practices for the sustainability of the organization has become imperative in contemporary organizational settings. Human resource professionals play a pivotal role in garnering employee support for environmentally friendly initiatives, emphasizing the critical intersection between HRM and environmental management.

Performance management emerges as a key HR practice for fostering environmental behavior and sustainable development (Gholami et al., 2016). Green performance appraisal, as advocated by Gholami et al., adds value by incorporating green behaviors into the assessment, thereby enhancing their perceived importance and encouraging compliance. Aligning compensation and reward systems with green behaviors is another crucial aspect (Berrone & Gomez-Mejia, 2009). Research indicates that CEOs of environmentally friendly firms are often financially rewarded, reinforcing the potential of a green compensation and reward system to drive sustainable practices.

Despite gaining attention, Green HRM is still considered a relatively new concept (Ren et al., 2018). Limited factors influencing its adoption have been identified to date, indicating a need for further exploration. The literature suggests that the adoption of Green HRM is essential for environmental sustainability and provides organizations with a competitive advantage (Ren et al., 2018). This is reinforced by the resource-based perspective, which highlights that an organization's competitive advantage depends on the efficient utilization of its resources, including a high-quality and motivated workforce (Barney, 1991; Wright & McMahan, 1992). Strategic Human Resource Management (SHRM) is positioned as a critical player in fostering a culture of sustainable growth within an organization (Wright & McMahan, 1992).

3. Methodology

This research adopts an exploratory qualitative approach to deeply investigate the pivotal role of HR as a driver of sustainability within organizations. Recognizing the necessity for reliable and valid evidence, the study employs a focus group discussion and analysis methodology, following the principles outlined by O. Nyumba et al. (2018).

The discussion, lasting approximately one and a half hours, aims to reach a consensus on sustainable HR practices and the origin of motivations. A designed discussion guide covers all major aspects relevant to the research objectives. Throughout the discussion, the defined protocol is followed for data collection, analysis, consensus building, and moderation (Grudens-Schuck et al., 2004). This ensures a structured and rigorous approach, adhering to the principles of qualitative methodology.

3.1. Data Sample

The focus group, comprising 8 carefully selected HR professionals, aligns with the recommended group size for a robust discussion (Grudens-Schuck et al., 2004). The data sample for this study comprises professionals from diverse industries, including transportation and storage, manufacturing, financial and insurance activities, and education. Participants hold key positions such as HR Manager, Sustainability Manager, and Chief Happiness Officer, providing a comprehensive representation of roles within the HR domain. The sample encompasses mostly large corporations and a smaller entity, offering insights into sustainability practices across different organizational scales. Table 1 summarizes the characteristics of the organizations.

Table 1. Characterization of the organisations

Organisation #	Industry	Year founded	Company size (*)	Interviewee	Year of experience
# 1	Transportation and Storage	1969	Large	HR Manager	10
# 2	Transportation and Storage	1976	Large	HR and Sustainability Manager	14
# 3	Transportation and Storage	1989	Large	HR Specialist	6
# 4	Manufacturing	1876	Large	Head of People Function	9
# 5	Financial and insurance activities	1972	Large	Head of HR	2
# 6	Transportation and Storage	1998	Small	Chief Happiness Officer	16
# 7	Education	1918	Large	Head of HR	17
# 8	Manufacturing	1947	Large	HR Partner	2

* – micro enterprises: fewer than 10 persons employed; small enterprises: 10 to 49 persons employed; medium-sized enterprises: 50 to 249 persons employed; large enterprises: 250 or more person.

3.2. Data Analysis

The analysis process commenced with the transcription of focus group discussions, utilizing recorded materials for accuracy. Thematic analysis, following Braun and Clarke's (2006) approach, is employed to derive meaningful patterns and themes from the transcribed discussions. Categories and themes emerged organically, rooted in observed patterns within the data. Through an iterative process, internally convergent categories and themes were pinpointed, aligning them with the study objectives. This phase involved data reduction, focusing on pertinent views and eliminating irrelevant information. Thematic analysis was then conducted, assigning titles (codes) to major categories under each theme, providing a comprehensive overview of related data for interpretative purposes. Subsequently, the organized and coded data underwent multiple reviews to establish coherence and identify interconnections. The final analysis was performed in alignment with the pre-defined themes, contributing to a nuanced understanding of the study objectives. The ensuing section discusses the identified themes in detail.

4. Findings and Discussion

The findings section begin with an exploration of the diverse landscape of sustainability strategies adopted by organizations. This initial inquiry reveals a spectrum of approaches, from openly declared sustainability strategies to varied practices without formalization. The spotlight then shifts to the realm of Sustainable HR Practices, where the study navigates the nuanced strategies employed by HRs in embracing sustainability, particularly in hybrid work, work-related mobility, and the deployment of digital tools. As the exploration continues, the focus expands to decipher the origins and motivations behind sustainability initiatives.

4.1. Sustainability Strategies

The first inquiry into the existence of sustainability strategies reveals a heterogeneous landscape among the organizations within the focus group. Only four out of the discussed organizations have openly declared and published sustainability strategies. These strategies exhibit significant diversity, covering aspects ranging from diversity, social support, and charity to carbon neutrality and environmental innovation.

In-depth examination of these strategies exposes a noteworthy pattern. Two of the organizations with established sustainability strategies boast specialized units dedicated to implementation, delving into areas such as supply chain, product portfolio, energy efficiency, and employee awareness raising. However, the involvement of HR professionals in these organizations is circumscribed, primarily limited to awareness-raising activities. The existence of separate units, responsible for training on sustainability and corporate social responsibility, diminishes the direct involvement of HR professionals in the core strategy implementation.

Conversely, the remaining four organizations without formal sustainability strategies still exhibit various practices supporting sustainability. Nevertheless, the role of HR professionals in these organizations is conspicuously absent from the implementation phase. In the case of Organization 3, which produces sustainability reports with a limited focus on the environmental dimension, parallels can be drawn with the missions of Organizations 6 and 7.

The standout case is Organization 8, which takes a distinctive approach. Despite lacking a formal sustainability strategy, this organization operates a specialized unit that spans all pillars of sustainability – sustainability for clients, environmental excellence in operations, responsible leadership, and societal impact. Notably, sustainability practices are intricately woven into recruitment processes, incorporating diversity, inclusion policies, and employee awareness initiatives. This unique case challenges conventional norms by engraving sustainability into HR practices without a formal strategy in place.

4.2. Sustainable HR Practices

As organizations grapple with the imperatives of sustainability, the landscape of HR practices becomes a critical arena for transformation. The exploration of existing practices within the focus group discussion sheds light on the nuanced strategies employed by organizations in embracing sustainability, particularly concerning hybrid work, work-related mobility, and the deployment of digital tools.

Hybrid work, an amalgamation of office and home-based working, emerges as a practical solution to the evolving work landscape. Organization 5 exhibits proactive initiatives, including guidelines, technical support, and the provision of necessary equipment. However, the commitment to hybrid work is not uniform across all participants; for instance, Organization 1 embraces hybridity by making it an option for their employees while maintaining an office-centric culture. This duality within organizations underscores the complex interplay between sustainability and ingrained workplace practices.

Work-related mobility, a critical facet of organizational sustainability, unfolds through diverse initiatives. Organization 2 encourages sustainable commuting options, such as bicycling during the summer, without offering tangible rewards. In contrast, Organization 4 actively engages with local municipalities to facilitate green mobility, ranging from electric scooters to electric car charging stations. The nexus between sustainability, employee mobility, and infrastructure development underscores a holistic approach to corporate responsibility.

In the digital age, the adoption of technology stands out as a pivotal enabler of sustainability in HR practices. Organizations like 2, 4, and 5 embrace paperless processes, e-learning platforms, and augmented reality to streamline operations. The use of digital tools extends beyond convenience; it becomes a strategic lever for fostering transparent communication, self-service functionalities, and knowledge sharing. The alignment of digital platforms with sustainability goals signifies a synergy between technological innovation and environmental responsibility.

While sustainability practices are evident, challenges persist. The partial adoption of hybrid work models and variations in support reflect the tug-of-war between traditional workplace norms and emerging sustainability imperatives. Similarly, despite notable strides in sustainable mobility, a uniform commitment across all organizations remains elusive.

4.3. Origins and Motivations behind Sustainability Initiatives by HRMs

The quest to understand the origins and motivations behind sustainability initiatives unveils a multifaceted landscape. Environmental knowledge, employee skills, and a green culture serve as fundamental pillars driving organizations towards environmentally friendly HR practices. However, a critical examination of the sources provides deeper insights.

The influence of organizational culture is unmistakable. In several organizations, sustainability initiatives are not merely strategic maneuvers; they are deeply embedded in the cultural fabric. This cultural integration is particularly evident in organizations with long-standing commitments to sustainability (Org. 1, Org. 2, Org. 5). The sustained existence of initiatives speaks to the institutionalization of sustainability within these organizational cultures.

Leadership, especially the attitudes of top management, board members, and influential executives, emerges as a primary driver of sustainability initiatives across organizations. The motivation often trickles down from the top, shaping the organizational agenda and fostering a commitment to sustainability. Individual motivations, both from leaders and employees, play a pivotal role in steering organizations towards sustainable practices.

External factors exert a substantial influence on sustainability initiatives. Customer demands, highlighted by organizations like Org. 4, Org. 5, and Org. 8, drive the development and promotion of products and services aligned with sustainability goals. Legal requirements also emerge as a significant catalyst, influencing the sustainability landscape for organizations like Org. 5, Org. 7, and Org. 8. These external pressures, coupled with industry-driven sustainability initiatives, shape the organizational response to sustainability challenges.

Several organizations emphasize the importance of internal collaboration and knowledge exchange. Initiatives are fueled by engagement within organizational units, local forums, and central sustainability teams. Training programs, workshops, and feedback mechanisms further facilitate knowledge exchange and contribute to the development of corporate sustainability.

Global initiatives, such as HR conferences (Org. 1), and mission-driven approaches (Org. 7) that aim to educate and facilitate a transition to green practices, reflect a broader perspective on sustainability. State-level expectations also play a role in steering organizations towards environmental responsibility.

5. Discussion and Conclusion

One key aspect highlighted in our study is the nuanced nature of HR professionals' involvement in sustainability initiatives. Existing literature often acknowledges the evolving role of HR in embracing sustainability, emphasizing the need for a strategic approach. The diversity we observed in sustainability strategies aligns with prior research that emphasizes the importance of tailoring initiatives to fit the unique organizational context (Jackson et al., 2011; Renwick et al., 2013). This aligns with the argument that a one-size-fits-all approach to sustainable HR practices may not be effective, considering the organizational variations in culture, leadership, and industry dynamics.

The study's emphasis on the delicate balance between organizational norms and environmental responsibility resonates with literature discussing the challenges of integrating sustainability into established organizational structures. Scholars like Bansal and Roth (2000) have highlighted the difficulties in reconciling economic and environmental goals within organizations. Our findings reinforce the idea that sustainable HR practices require a strategic alignment that respects existing organizational norms while driving positive environmental outcomes.

The recognition of sustainability initiatives as multifaceted, stemming from a confluence of internal and external factors, aligns with research emphasizing the influence of organizational culture, leadership, and external pressures on sustainability efforts (Aguinis & Glavas, 2012; Ahmadov et al., 2023; Martinez, 2022). This supports the argument that sustainable HR practices cannot be isolated from broader organizational dynamics and should be integrated into overall strategic goals.

The practical insights derived from our study, such as advocating for hybrid work models and fostering a green organizational culture, align with recent literature discussing the role of HR in shaping sustainable work practices (Bag et al., 2021; Claus, 2019). This underlines the importance of HR professionals in championing sustainability initiatives, acting as change agents within organizations.

In conclusion, this chapter delves into the multifaceted landscape of sustainability practices within Estonian organizations, with a specific focus on the pivotal role of HR professionals. The exploration reveals a diverse array of sustainability strategies, ranging from explicit, formalized approaches to implicit practices, emphasizing the complexity and variability within the organizational landscape. Notably, the study highlights a distinctive case where sustainability is intricately embedded in HR practices without a formal strategy, challenging conventional norms.

The investigation of sustainable HR practices underscores the intricate balance between established workplace norms and emerging environmental imperatives. The challenges in adopting hybrid work models and achieving uniform commitment across organizations reflect the ongoing tug-of-war between tradition and sustainability.

The origins and motivations behind sustainability initiatives further unveil a complex web of influences, emphasizing the intertwining roles of organizational culture, leadership, external pressures, and internal collaboration. This in-depth exploration contributes valuable insights into the current strategies, HR practices, and their underlying motivations, providing a nuanced understanding within the unique context of Estonian organizations.

5.1. Limitations and Future Research Directions

However, a limitation of this study lies in its focus on organizations within a specific geographical context, Estonia. While providing valuable insights into sustainability practices in this region, generalizability to a broader international context may be constrained by unique cultural, legal, and economic factors in Estonia. To overcome this limitation, future research could adopt a comparative approach, exploring sustainability practices across diverse regions and cultures. Such an analysis would deepen the understanding of how contextual factors influence the adoption of sustainable HR practices. Additionally, investigating the impact of government policies, digitalization, artificial intelligence, and industry-specific influences on HR sustainability practices would contribute to a more comprehensive understanding of the factors shaping organizational sustainability initiatives globally.

Acknowledgments

This work was supported by the Estonian Ministry of Education and Research through the Centre of Excellence in Circular Economy for Strategic Minerals and Carbon Resources (01.01.2024–31.12.2030, TK228), and the authors express gratitude to the participants of the group interview for their cooperation and valuable input.

Research Ethics and Consent

This study strictly adhered to ethical guidelines, prioritizing participant confidentiality and anonymity. Informed consent was diligently obtained from all participants before initiating the research process.

References

Aguinis, H., & Glavas, A. (2012). What we know and don't know about corporate social responsibility: A review and research agenda. *Journal of Management*, 38(4), 932–968. https://doi.org/10.1177/0149206311436079

Ahmad, S. (2015). Green human resource management: Policies and practices. *Cogent Business & Management*, 2(1), 1030817. https://doi.org/10.1080/23311975.2015.1030817

Ahmadov, T. (2023). Innovation for circular economy : Overview of estonian enterprises' transition journey. In Muhammed Veysel Kaya (Ed.), *Social and economic studies within the framework of emerging global developments* (3rd ed., pp. 103–116). Peter Lang. https://doi.org/10.3726/b20968

Ahmadov, T., Durst, S., Gerstlberger, W., & Kraut, E. (2023). SMEs on the way to a circular economy: Insights from a multi-perspective review. In *Management Review Quarterly* (Issue 0123456789). Springer International Publishing. https://doi.org/10.1007/s11301-023-00380-2

Ahmadov, T., Gerstlberger, W., & Prause, G. K. (2022). *Fiscal incentives for circular economy: Insights from the Baltic States BT – Business models for the circular economy: A European perspective* (pp. 219–239). V. Prokop, J. Stejskal, J. Horbach, & W. Gerstlberger (Eds.). Springer International Publishing. https://doi.org/10.1007/978-3-031-08313-6_9

Alkhateeb, T. T. Y., Alkahtani, N. S., & Mahmood, H. (2018). Green human resource management, financial markets and pollution nexus in Saudi Arabia. *International Journal of Energy Economics and Policy*, 8(3), 33–36.

Aust, I., Matthews, B., & Muller-Camen, M. (2020). Common Good HRM: A paradigm shift in sustainable HRM? *Human Resource Management Review*, 30(3), 100705. https://doi.org/https://doi.org/10.1016/j.hrmr.2019.100705

Bag, S., Pretorius, J. H. C., Gupta, S., & Dwivedi, Y. K. (2021). Role of institutional pressures and resources in the adoption of big data analytics powered artificial intelligence, sustainable manufacturing practices and circular economy capabilities. *Technological Forecasting and Social Change*, 163(November 2020), 120420. https://doi.org/10.1016/j.techfore.2020.120420

Bansal, P., & Roth, K. (2000). Why companies go green: A model of ecological responsiveness. *The Academy of Management Journal*, 43(4), 717–736. https://doi.org/10.2307/1556363.

Barney, J. (1991). Firm resources and sustained competitive advantage. *Journal of Management*, 17(1), 99–120. https://doi.org/10.1177/014920639101700108

Berrone, P., & Gomez-Mejia, L. R. (2009). Environmental performance and executive compensation: An integrated agency-institutional perspective. *The*

Academy of Management Journal, 52(1), 103–126. http://www.jstor.org/stable/40390278

Braun, V., & Clarke, V. (2006). Using thematic analysis in psychology. Qualitative Research in Psychology, 3(2), 77–101. https://doi.org/10.1191/1478088706qp063oa

Claus, L. (2019). HR disruption-time already to reinvent talent management. *Brq-Business Research Quarterly*, 22(3), 207–215. https://doi.org/10.1016/j.brq.2019.04.002 WE – Social Science Citation Index (SSCI)

George, G., Howard-Grenville, J., Joshi, A., & Tihanyi, L. (2016). Understanding and tackling societal grand challenges through management research. *Academy of Management Journal*, 59(6), 1880–1895. https://doi.org/10.5465/amj.2016.4007

Gerstlberger, W. D., Ahmadov, T., & Tuisk, T. (2023). *Enablers and barriers in circular economy : The case of estonia enablers and barriers in circular economy : The Case of Estonia Merle Küttim Wolfgang Gerstlberger Ulrika Hurt Arseni Kotov Margit Kull Tarvo Niine Tarlan Ahmadov Tarmo Tuisk* *. July.

Gholami, H., Rezaei, G., Saman, M. Z. M., Sharif, S., & Zakuan, N. (2016). State-of-the-art Green HRM System: Sustainability in the sports center in Malaysia using a multi-methods approach and opportunities for future research. *Journal of Cleaner Production*, 124, 142–163. https://doi.org/https://doi.org/10.1016/j.jclepro.2016.02.105

Grudens-Schuck, N., Allen, B. L., & Larson, K. (2004). *Focus group fundamentals* (pp. 1–6). Methodology Brief IOWA State University, University Extension.

Jabbour, C. J. C. (2013). Environmental training in organisations: From a literature review to a framework for future research. *Resources, Conservation and Recycling*, 74, 144–155. https://doi.org/https://doi.org/10.1016/j.resconrec.2012.12.017

Jackson, S. E., Renwick, D. W. S., Jabbour, C. J. C., & Muller-Camen, M. (2011). State-of-the-art and future directions for green human resource management: Introduction to the special issue. *German Journal of Human Resource Management*, 25(2), 99–116. https://doi.org/10.1177/239700221102500203

Kramar, R. (2014). Beyond strategic human resource management: Is sustainable human resource management the next approach? *The International Journal of Human Resource Management*, 25(8), 1069–1089. https://doi.org/10.1080/09585192.2013.816863

Kramar, R. (2022). Sustainable human resource management: Six defining characteristics. *Asia Pacific Journal of Human Resources*, 60(1), 146–170. https://doi.org/https://doi.org/10.1111/1744-7941.12321

Martinez, F. (2022). Organizational change in response to environmental complexity: Insights from the business model innovation literature. *Business Strategy and the Environment*, 31(5), 2299–2314. https://doi.org/10.1002/bse.3022

Mishra, R. K., Sarkar, S., & Kiranmai, J. (2014). Green HRM: Innovative approach in Indian public enterprises. *World Review of Science, Technology and Sustainable Development*, 11(1), 26–42. https://doi.org/10.1504/WRSTSD.2014.062374

O. Nyumba, T., Wilson, K., Derrick, C. J., & Mukherjee, N. (2018). The use of focus group discussion methodology: Insights from two decades of application in conservation. *Methods in Ecology and Evolution*, 9(1), 20–32. https://doi.org/10.1111/2041-210X.12860

Ren, S., Cooke, F. L., Stahl, G. K., Fan, D., & Timming, A. R. (2023). Advancing the sustainability agenda through strategic human resource management: Insights and suggestions for future research. *Human Resource Management*, 62(3), 251–265. https://doi.org/https://doi.org/10.1002/hrm.22169

Ren, S., & Jackson, S. E. (2020). HRM institutional entrepreneurship for sustainable business organizations. *Human Resource Management Review*, 30(3), 100691. https://doi.org/https://doi.org/10.1016/j.hrmr.2019.100691

Ren, S., Tang, G., & Jackson, S. E. (2018). Green human resource management research in emergence: A review and future directions. *Asia Pacific Journal of Management*, 35(3), 769–803. https://doi.org/10.1007/s10490-017-9532-1

Renwick, D. W. S., Redman, T., & Maguire, S. (2013). Green human resource management: A review and research agenda. *International Journal of Management Reviews*, 15(1), 1–14. https://doi.org/https://doi.org/10.1111/j.1468-2370.2011.00328.x

Stahl, G. K., Brewster, C. J., Collings, D. G., & Hajro, A. (2020). Enhancing the role of human resource management in corporate sustainability and social responsibility: A multi-stakeholder, multidimensional approach to HRM. *Human Resource Management Review*, 30(3), 100708. https://doi.org/https://doi.org/10.1016/j.hrmr.2019.100708

Taylor, S., Osland, J., & Egri, C. P. (2012). Guest editors' introduction: Introduction to HRM's role in sustainability: Systems, strategies, and practices. *Human Resource Management*, 51(6), 789–798. https://doi.org/https://doi.org/10.1002/hrm.21509

United Nations. (2022). *The sustainable development goals 2022*. United Nations.

Wright, P. M., & McMahan, G. C. (1992). Theoretical perspectives for strategic human resource management. *Journal of Management*, 18(2), 295–320. https://doi.org/10.1177/014920639201800205

Pedro Fernandes da Anunciação, Filipe António de Lemos, Hailton Lopes da Silva, Mário Joaquim Pereira

Digital Asset Governance and Competitive Intelligence: The Case of a Media Company

1. Introduction

Information is an economic and social asset of high value. In the humanity evolution, each of its evolutionary phases, demonstrate the generation of additional amounts of knowledge (Oliveira, 2022). The current time is marked by information Overload, ubiquity of access, processing speed, availability, and ease of use (Anunciação & Zorrinho, 2006). The devices incorporate intelligence characteristics and are connected in a myriad of networks, through which data and information are shared. The expression of Big Data shows this exponentiation of data as a result of the connection of the various technological devices integrated in production chains and services, challenging information governance (Esteves & Anunciação, 2023) and information systems (IS) (ceGSI, 2019).

Although the production of data/information is overwhelming, it is not always possible to safely assess the quality and veracity of some sources. The strategic focus has been more on technology than information. However, the attention of management should be more focused on information, as this is a strategic asset in the competitiveness and economic sustainability of organizations, although the potential that technologies offer in the extraction of data/information value should also be considered. It is information that allows access to knowledge and, this, to intelligence. Since the mission of information systems is the production of information, it becomes obvious the need of an IS that allows to provide, quickly and safely, this asset (Oliveira, 2023).

Although the valuation of information should have an objective, utilitarian and context character, which provides the increase of knowledge and the generation of intelligence (Briones-Peñalver et al., 2021), this should be assessed by availability, quality, and opportunity. In addition, its management should consider other dimensions, such as the life cycle, risk management, organizational functions and processes, the strategic plan for information or the plan for Asset management. In a simpler perspective, there are three dimensions that should be the basis of their valuation, namely, the ability to use in a timely manner (access), knowing how to act (competence) and knowing in what direction to act (strategy). The availability of reliable and timely information on significant business variables tends to be a critical success factor, assuming information management a key strategic role (Anunciação & Zorrinho, 2006).

Information and IS should be managed like other business (Oliveira, 2019), since there is no economy or society without information, that there are no economic organizations without IS and that there is no management without information. Dobbs, Manyika and Woetzel (2015) highlight the existence of much less predictable and controllable dynamics of information in the current economy. These conditions make emerge the dimension of governance in information and IS (Esteves & Anunciação, 2021), to reach knowledge and intelligence. Information governance, in relation to information systems and information ans communication technologies (IS/ICT), should ensure appropriate formats and timings for the viability of opportunities and the achievement of competitive advantages, interconnecting the objectives of the business model with the information resources, providing the understanding of the nature of the activities, the identification of the boundaries of the various business areas and the integration and sharing of information between the different organizational levels (Esteves & Anunciação, 2023).

These are important conditions in the generation of intelligence, which can be developed at two levels: competitive and organizational. Competitive intelligence corresponds to the ability of the organization to listen to its surroundings, diagnosing opportunities and threats but also identifying, qualifying, and quantifying risk, objectives, and the establishment of short, medium, and long-term action strategies. Organizational intelligence, in turn, must support a systemic view of the organization that integrates organizational functions as well as their systems and information technologies, to be able to implement new dynamics and monitor performance. Both aim to print adaptive behaviors to the organization, in the objectives, structure, products and services, in response to the demands of the environment (Zambon & Anunciação, 2014). The great revolution associated with this challenge lies in the opportunity given to economic agents, through knowledge and learning, to generate intelligence allowing to develop new skills, capabilities and dynamics of evolution, development, and sustainability (Zambon & Anunciação, 2014).

2. Digital Asset Management

Organizations are currently facing the challenge of organizing, distributing, and providing controlled stakeholder access to their assets (Fine & Johnson, 2005).

With the recent development of digital technologies, namely streaming and social networks, in sectors such as the media, there has been a challenge of digital asset management (DAM) and urbanism (Anunciação & Zorrinho, 2006) as systems need to be integrated with other existing software such as account management, customer records and planning systems to maximize operational benefits (Austerberry, 2012, 2005).

The concept of digital assets should be considered in two aspects: the asset side, which means that it is an economic asset to which a certain value can be attributed, and a certain profitability may be associated, and the digital side, which means that their nature is not conditioned by the form or limitations of matter. Thus, digital assets correspond to the digital elements or resources that appear to be central in the economic activity carried out by an enterprise, to which value is associated and which must be managed in the sense of its profitability. Its management can be supported by digital asset management systems (DAMS) that correspond to a set of components integrated in a technological infrastructure used to capture, catalog, store and manage digital assets and expose them to creative tools to produce video, audio, web and print content. These systems allow to view digital content assets and the associated metadata allows their identification; group individual assets to form collections or asset packages; index, browse, transform, reuse, package and publish a wide range of digital formats, protecting the integrity of original assets; develop business services such as integrated library systems, web portals and course management systems; among others (Mauthe & Thomas, 2004).

In the DAMS the following elements stand out: essence, which corresponds to the program material, represented by images, sound, text, video, etc.; and, metadata, essential to the description of the real Essence and its different manifestations. Metadata may be related to the content, if it provides a description of the actual content or subject; material, if it describes available formats, encoding parameters and recording specific information; and, location, if it describes location and number of copies, condition of carriers, etc.

Now, knowing that the amount of data that is part of the collection of an organization has been increasing significantly, its valuation requires management capacity and identification, or calculation associated with its use (profitability). To this end, it is important to consider several key features additional to the processes: the typology of the organization; the operational context; the constraints of the organization (financial and regulatory); the needs of the organization and the stakeholders involved (Cecconi et al., 2020). The expected benefits are, for example, more efficiency and effectiveness, reduced uncertainty, increased reliability, etc.

This relevance has given rise to investments in ICT to facilitate the aggregation, organization and distribution of content and enhancement through access to these information assets.

3. Objectives and Methodology

This study aimed to analyze the importance of information governance as a determining factor for the creation of organizational and competitive intelligence associated with digital assets. It was chosen a media company that integrates a television station and a popular radio station located in the capital of the state of Goiás (Brazil). Its activity, along with a collection of over 12 radios and consolidated presence in social networks, has constituted a pillar of multifaceted regional communication. Throughout its two and a half decades of existence, the group has acted as a cultural catalyst and as a driving agent of information and entertainment, demonstrating resilience and relevance in the dynamic scenario of the media.

The Focus group of work was identified to study the intelligence requirements to optimize the economic and commercial value related to the interest in the acquisition of a technological solution for the management of digital assets in the company. This team adopted the brainstorming technique, having held a number of meetings necessary to reach a consensus on the more specific objectives defined for their work, in particular the identification of the life cycle in the management of digital content, the identification of the phases for the management of the investment in a technological solution for the management of digital assets, and the definition of a set of Key Performance Indicators (KPIs) for organizational and competitive intelligence generation. Focus group integrated all internal managers whose area of responsibility could be directly related to digital assets, from content management to infrastructure management. In the end, a proof of concept was carried out to analyze the potential of adopting a solution meeting the needs and expectations of the company.

4. Analysis of the Results

The first objective of the Focus group was to identify the life cycle for digital content management. In this context, the following phases were identified:

- research – identification of subjects, topics, and keywords relevant to the target audience and creation of an editorial calendar/schedule.

- analysis and monitoring of competitors – benchmarking to map themes and opportunities for building a strategy that leads the content to achieve the expected results.
- preparation of the content grids – affect the visual contents to the planned schedule and prepare the elements of dissemination/promotion focused on the needs and interests of the target audience.
- content review and editing – ensuring the quality and accuracy of the content, as well as adequacy to editorial guidelines.
- Results monitoring – monitor the performance of programs/contents and check the performance regarding the time of views.

Regarding the second objective, five phases were identified, namely planning, implementation, testing, migration, and maintenance. It was also assumed that investing in a DAMS solution would have the potential to generate customer-centric organizational and competitive intelligence. Regarding planning, it was clear the need to define the business objectives to be achieved with the investment in the software and the expected results, namely, at the competitive level, such as increasing the efficiency and effectiveness of content management, meeting customer needs, the feasibility of incorporating organizational intelligence at the process level. This evaluation should include the identification of specific goals to be achieved, such as:

- improvement of the organization and management of digital assets – through the using of machine learning algorithms to analyze user behavior patterns and automatically suggest tags relevant to digital assets.
- facilitating access and distribution of digital assets – through the development of a customized interface that uses predictive analytics to anticipate user needs, offering relevant asset suggestions based on their history of interactions.
- protection of digital assets – through the implementation of intelligent access controls, using biometric or behavioral authentication to ensure the security of assets, while facilitating authorized and personalized access.
- reduction of storage and management costs – through the using of advanced compression algorithms and optimization techniques to minimize storage requirements while maintaining the quality and accessibility of essential assets for the audience.
- definition of a paradigm for organizational intelligence – through automatic analysis of the volume and type of digital assets used under the prism of popularity and consequent identification of promotion strategies.

The technology solution should adopt or integrate smart features to boost audience, such as the ability to analyze user behavior data to optimize content delivery.

Regarding the second phase, implementation, software installation in a test environment and parameter configuration to optimize system intelligence should be considered. Should also be transposed the conceptual guidelines outlined in the planning phase for a practical implementation in DAMS. In this context, we highlight the following aspects to consider:

- installation of the software – through the incorporation of machine learning algorithms, intended for the semantic analysis of content, such as the application of natural language processing techniques for the autonomous extraction of topics and feelings of media assets, promoting a more refined categorization.
- configuration of parameters – through the intrinsic optimization of system intelligence, allowing the possibility of automatic adjustments in the recommendations of digital assets, based on dynamic patterns of user behavior, flexibly adapting to changes in preferences.
- migration of analog and digital assets – through the incorporation of intelligence to increase the quality of search and retrieval, such as the implementation of an OCR (Optical Character Recognition) image recognition system for the automatic categorization of photographs that facilitates an effective search through the use of visual markers and capture by means of analog tape readers for digital files.
- user awareness (testing team), for the use of smart features – through recommendation algorithms to encourage users to explore and understand personalized suggestions.

The analysis of intelligence in processes, during implementation, transcends technical efficiency, and should be focused on the user experience. As an example, the customization of the user interface, anchored in past interaction patterns, allows a more intuitive navigation and relevant to each user. The implementation should also address pragmatic considerations such as the choice between on-premises installation and the adoption of cloud-based solutions, considering the impact on the scalability and accessibility of intelligent resources.

As regards the testing phase, third phase, the team considered that a systematic evaluation of the effectiveness and coherence of the DAMS should be carried out in accordance with the defined targets. This phase is critical in that it must confirm the adherence of the solution to organizational requirements. During the testing phase, KPIs should be defined to measure DAMS' ability to deliver the most personalized and relevant digital asset recommendations to users according to historical behavior patterns, such as the location time of the materials, the length of stay in suggested assets and/or filter rejection rates, among others. Thus, it will be possible to assess whether the implementation of intelligence can result from more motivating user experiences and, consequently, contributes to a measurable increase in the audience.

In addition, the test phase should also verify the robustness and reliability of the DAMS solution in different scenarios, considering variations in data volume, competing offers and potential anomalies. This should ensure that embedded intelligence in processes maintains expected performance under variable conditions, ensuring operational consistency. The test phase should also allow confirmation of the assumptions defined at the planning stage.

Regarding the migration and customization phase, the fourth phase, the transition from the chosen DAMS to the operational environment. This stage aims at the effective integration of the solution in the organizational context, contemplating the intelligent functionalities previously tested, to optimize and potentiate the increase of the audience. The migration of digital assets should allow a data analysis to identify the preferences of the audience and analyze the feasibility of the implementation of intelligence in the processes identified in the planning phase, through the pragmatic insertion of advanced algorithms and the customization of the user experience to optimize the audience. At this stage, the solution should be disclosed to end users to maximize its acceptance and use. In this context, several communication strategies can be developed, such as the preparation of information material, workshops, and training sessions to present the new features and ensure the generation of value. In addition, it is crucial to establish processes for continuous monitoring of the performance of the solution, such as the adoption rate of intelligent functionalities over time, allowing a continuous assessment of the impact of these characteristics on the user experience. Still at this stage, it is also necessary to ensure the achievement of the results obtained during the tests, highlighting the controlled and monitored implementation of the solution in a real context. The final objective will be the evaluation of the audience's leverage potential through the application of the built-in smart features.

The maintenance phase, the last specified phase, was a crucial step to ensure operational continuity and dynamic adaptation to the evolving needs of the organizational and economic environment. It shall ensure the continuous efficiency of the DAMS, including the integration of software updates, the correction of any failures and the resolution of operational challenges, ensuring that updates are made, compatibility with existing infrastructure or bug fixes, resulting, for example, from inconsistencies in the search engine that impact the accuracy of the results. This maintenance phase is intrinsically associated with sustainability and the continuous adaptation of technological systems, as updating, correction and problem solving are imperative to preserve the effectiveness and relevance of the DAMS over time.

5. Importance of Key Performance Indicators

Performance indicators can be important elements in the assessment of digital asset governance and competitive intelligence indexes. Thus, some examples of indicators considered as relevant in this evaluation may be the following:

- Efficiency rate in the search for video content – evaluates the effectiveness of the file management system when calculating, for example, the percentage of searches completed in each period of time.
- Metadata cataloging accuracy rate – evaluates the accuracy of the system by verifying, for example, the number of searches that resulted in relevant information in relation to the metadata provided.
- Reduction in average research time – shows the percentage reduction in average search time after implementation of the system compared to the previous period.
- System adoption rate by users – measures the proportion of team users who are actively using the file management system.
- Rate of occurrence of repeated searches – indicates how often users need to repeat a search, possibly due to challenges in using the system or cataloging metadata.
- Utilization rate of recovered assets – evaluates the effectiveness of DAMS by measuring the percentage of recovered assets that were used by the team.
- Critical metadata update accuracy – measures the accuracy of DAMS in maintaining vital information by accurately updating critical metadata.
- Average response time to support requests – indicates the average time needed to meet support requests, reflecting efficiency in troubleshooting.
- Adoption of new functionalities by department – measures the specific acceptance of new functionalities in departments, allowing more granular insights on adoption.
- Post-deployment user satisfaction index – reflects overall user satisfaction after DAMS deployment, providing a qualitative assessment of perceived success.

6. Proof of Concept Results

Regarding the proof of concept, which aimed to analyze the potential success of the solution adoption, some indicators were identified, and the benefits associated with this paradigm shift in the management of the company's digital assets were estimated. Thus, the following estimates were obtained:

- Search time – average reduction from 120 minutes to 10 minutes of the time required to search for content. This estimated gain is the result of the development potential of a more accurate and comprehensive cataloging, enriched by metadata, and that will enable an agile and effective recovery of the desired contents, resulting in a considerable optimization of internal processes.
- Effectiveness in search – increase in about 90 % of the searched content in less than 10 minutes.
- Cataloging accuracy – 80 % accuracy in cataloging metadata.
- Average search time – 91.67 % reduction in average search time, which will represent substantial improvements in customer attractiveness.
- Repeated searches – occurrence of repeated searches in only 10 % of cases, which corroborates the reliability and effectiveness of the system, considerably reducing the need for repetition of queries.
- System adoption rate – it is estimated the reach of 90 % in the system adhesion by users. Such adherence is essential to ensure the continuous effectiveness of the system and its successful integration into daily operations.

7. Discussion of Results and Conclusion

The adoption and implementation of a DAMS may represent a significant advance in the administration of digital assets, insofar as, if well executed, can mark a new era in which intelligence plays a crucial role in the circulation of information between various organizational areas (organizational intelligence) and contribute, in the case study, for the development of strategies that result in increased audience and the opening of new media channels (competitive intelligence). Information governance and information systems governance are two critical success factors not only for management but, above all, for the governance of digital assets. This investment will allow a new look at the management of digital assets.

This case study serves not only as a valuable benchmark for the analyzed company, but also for other economic organizations that want to optimize their operations through innovation in digital asset management. Investment in advanced technologies should not only increase productivity, but also improve the satisfaction of users and customers, consolidating the competitive position in the market.

References

Anunciação, P. F., & Zorrinho, C. (2006). *Organizational Urbanism – How to manage technological shock*. Lisboa: Sílabo Publishing *(In Portuguese)*.

Austerberry, D. (2005). The components of a digital asset management system. *Journal of Digital Asset Management*, 1(2), 131–145.

Austerberry, D. (2012). *Digital asset management*. Routledge.

Briones-Peñalver, A. J. B., Fonseca, G. L., & Anunciação, P. F. (2021). Organizational intelligence: A technological reference only? In F. J. M. Esteves, & P. F. Anunciação, (Eds.), *Information systems – Paradigms and solutions for management* (pp. 72–79). Plátano Publishing *(In Portuguese)*.

Cecconi, F. R., Dejaco, M. C.,Moretti, N., Mannino, A., & Cadena, J. D. B. (2020). Digital asset management. In B. Daniotti, M. Gianinetto, & S. Della Torre (Eds.), *Digital transformation of the design, construction and management processes of the built environment* (pp. 243–253). Springer Open.

ceGSI. (2019). *Information Systems Governance – Concepts, good practices, and case studies, Information Systems Governance European Club (ceGSI-Portugal)*. Chiado Publishing *(In Portuguese)*.

Fine, D., & Johnson, T. (2005). Digital asset management in the public sector. *Journal of Digital Asset Management*, 1, 25–31.

Dobbs, R., Manyika, J., & Woetzel, J. (2015). *No ordinary disruption. The four global forces breaking all the trends*. New York: Public Affairs.

Esteves, F. J. M., & Anunciação, P. F. (2021). Architecture - Essential dimension in information systems; . In *Information systems - Paradigms and solutions for management*, (pp. 9-36), Plátano Publishing *(In Portuguese)*.

Esteves, F. J. M., & Anunciação, P. F. (2023). Information systems governance: Some dimensions to management. In Muhammed Veysel Kaya (Ed.), *Social and economic studies within the framework of emerging global developments* (Vol. 1, pp. 139–152). Peter Lang Publishing.

Mauthe, A., & Thomas, P. (2004). *Professional content management systems – Handling digital media assets*. Wiley.

Oliveira, A. (2019). *Is Governance – Why?, Information Systems Governance – Concepts, good practices and case studies, Information Systems Governance European Club (ceGSI-Portugal)* (pp. 189–201). Chiado Publishing, *(In Portuguese)*.

Oliveira, A. (2022). *Information & management – Two sides of the same coin.* Sílabo Publishing *(In Portuguese).*

Oliveira, A. (2023). *Journey through the brave world of business sciences.* Sílabo Publishing *(In Portuguese).*

Zambon, A., & Anunciação, P. F. (2014). Competitive intelligence. Perceptions of value in the jewelry sector. *Portuguese and Brazilian Management Journal,* 13(2), April/June 2014 *(In Portuguese).*

Joana Ribeiro dos Santos, Francisco Joaquim Madeira Esteves,
Pedro Fernandes da Anunciação, Fernando Miguel
do Couto Gonçalves

Big Data, Business Intelligence and Business Competitiveness

1. Introduction

In a complex market, decision-making agility becomes critical. This is a noble but critical function of management in any organization. The quality of decisions has a significant impact on the success of a business if they are based on knowledge, experience, and logic (Chen et al., 2015). However, any type of decision is based on information. In fact, privileged ownership of information at a given time and place is a key differentiating factor for any business or organization. However, the current exponentiation of the amount of data in companies and the economy makes the decision process more difficult and complicated. This reality led to the emergence of the concept of Big Data and Big Data Analytics, which expresses a volume of information that goes beyond the capacity of analysis and human processing. The reality of Big Data Analytics, expresses the possibility of extracting valuable information from large amounts of data with capabilities to technologies, including structured, semi-structured and unstructured data.

As companies began to accumulate large amounts of data and given the evolution of information and communication technologies (ICT), decision support systems began to evolve into Business Intelligence (BI) systems. BI expresses the ability to make significant use of data resulting from daily operations (Ram et al., 2016), promoting the provision of strategic information, business analysis and business profitability (Williams, 2016; Ziora, 2015; Negash, 2004). BI integrates an analytical process supported by technology that gathers and transforms fragmented data from companies and markets into information or knowledge (Ossimitz, 2015), constituting an aggregating element of decision-making (Muntean et al., 2014; Kimball & Ross, 2013). These systems contribute to the improvement and transparency of information flows, due to the control of profitability and expenses, and allow to discover anomalies and fraud (Olszak & Ziemba, 2007). In BI solutions, some important components stand out. The Data Warehouse (DW) are data repositories to support queries, analysis, modeling the organization's business and reporting (Turban et al., 2008). These DW integrate the data sources; the processes of extraction, transformation, and loading (ETL); the data repositories; and the mechanisms of information analysis (Sá, 2010). Data sources can originate from different Information Systems (IS) (Watson, 2009), internal or external to the organization (Ong et al., 2011). The ETL process consists of data preprocessing and includes the phases of data extraction, transformation, and loading (Niu et al., 2009), to improve their quality (Watson, 2009). A repository can correspond to an organizational data Warehouse, independent data marts, or dependent data marts. Although there are several access and query options, such as ad-hoc querying tools or as complex and sophisticated as data Mining or process simulation/modelling systems, most users access the data through analytical and reporting applications that contain a set of predefined indicators by the creators of the DW and Metadata repository (Kimball & Ross, 2013). Finally, the information visualization and analysis mechanisms integrate a set of analysis tools that allow access to the data stored in the repository to obtain useful information made available through reports, Customer Relationship Management, dashboards, among others (Sá, 2010; Santos & Ramos, 2006).

We live in a data-driven world (Grus, 2015). All «clicks» that we make on websites are being registered, the smartphone itself is constantly recording our location, and usage data of applications and gadgets such as smartwatches record all our steps, exercise habits and even sleep patterns, among other examples. The Internet represents an endless source of data, and it is in this context that the term big data arises. Big data thus corresponds to the exponential growth of data as a result of the intense use of smartphones, websites, social networks, transactions, sensors and the use of cloud storage (Institute, 2011), characterized by high volumes (McAfee & Brynjolfsson, 2012)variability (McAfee & Brynjolfsson, 2012) (Chan, 2013), speed (Gandomi & Haider, 2015) and complexity, which requires advanced technologies and techniques for their collection, treatment, analysis and availability TechAmerica Foundation's Federal Big data Commission (International Data Corporation, 2012) (Gartner, 2022a). To these characteristics, the literature also adds the value (International Data Corporation, 2012) and the veracity (Ozkose et al., 2015).

The immensity of data does not create value for the business by itself. It is necessary to have the ability to process, collect, analyze, and convert them into relevant insights, able to help in the decision-making process. Thus arises the concept of data Analytics, as a term characteristic of the ability to analyze the data to realize this realization of value (Gartner, 2022b). Data Analytics is defined as the application of advanced analytical techniques on a huge and diverse set of structured, semi-structured and unstructured data from different sources, with various sizes (IBM, 2022; Gandomi & Haider, 2015).

2. Investment Impact in Business Intelligence

Richards et al. (2019) and Bronzo et al. (2013) consider that the effective implementation of a BI system influences positively and significantly management practices and has a positive impact on organizational performance. Changes the way companies are managed, the execution of tasks and decisions are made, saving time, providing quality information, improving processes, and supporting the achievement of strategic objectives (Sherman, 2015). BI solutions also allow a financial valuation of data, known as monetization, which involves the possibility of sale, sharing or use to boost decision making and the creation of new products or services (Côrte-Real, 2022). This monetization strategy is most evident in the ease of customer segmentation, optimizing prices and products, monitoring performance, or discovering new monetization opportunities, among other examples. These benefits are important elements in the assessment of the return on investment since this assessment should not correspond to an intuitive process. Even if the benefits of projects, tangible and intangible, are often difficult to assess financially, given the increased complexity, the ROI calculation should be performed. The complexity of the calculation is associated with the fact that the return-on-investment projects in BI solutions does not only translate into increased organizational efficiency or optimization of working times, but rather by the evident return in the decision-making process. Better decisions correspond to saving resources or increasing revenues, which would be more difficult to obtain without these tools (Kasabian, 2009).

3. Objectives and Methodology

The overall objective of the study was to highlight the functional, economic, and competitive benefits of an investment in a BI solution. To this end, we sought to show how the definition and adoption of Key Performence Indicators (KPIs) relevant to the organization can be reflected in an efficiency (operational improvement), effectiveness (functional) and competitiveness (economic) for the company studied. The methodology adopted was the case study (Yin, 2010) and the technique applied to semi-structured interviews, to facilitate and evaluate information and more complete and enriching elements of reflection. Interviews were conducted with the CEO of the company and those responsible for the various existing functional areas, to obtain a global vision of the business and the various functional perspectives.

The company studied is part of a business group with several and distinct business areas, from specialized retail to financial services, and is part of food retail. In the area of food retail, the company has several coffee shops that can be divided into three main groups: integrated coffee shops, which integrate those found inside the hypermarket space; adjacent coffee shops, which integrate those that are in the shopping gallery, near the hypermarket; and autonomous coffee shops, which integrate those that function independently of the hypermarket. Currently, this company has more than 140 coffee shops, aiming to expand, in six more by the end of 2023.

The choice of the case study results from the difficulties in accessing management information since it is dispersed in various formats and with very time-consuming and costly access. Latency in data access can differ between 20 seconds and 2 minutes or more, depending on the state of the technology infrastructure. To access organizational information, it is necessary to create pivot Tables in Excel that interact with the company's databases. Also, this process is usually quite time consuming because, given the huge volume of data stored on the company's servers, a frequent refresh to the pivot's tables must be performed. In addition, the filtering process that the team needs to perform until they find the data, they need is also complex, as they have access to several business units/ companies and not only to the business unit/ company of the coffee shop.

In this sense, in addition to a roadmap proposal necessary for an evolution to a new BI system to support the management decision, a proof of concept will be made from the definition of a set of KPIs, which shows the estimated gains associated with this evolution.

4. Case Study Analysis

The group companies have three data sources: *Enterprise Resource Planning* (ERP), P*oint of sale (POS)* and external data, derived for example from the *WinRest* system. As a data repository there is an organizational Data Warehouse that coexists with other dependent Data Marts that are fed synchronously with the organizational Data Warehouse. Finally, there is a set of analysis tools that allow access to the data stored in the repository. This reality has systematically impaired the company in its decision-making capacity and consequent adaptation to the challenges of the market where it operates. There is awareness on the part of the management of existing problems, synthesized in the following aspects: existence of information with poor quality, difficulties in the opportunity associated with decision making, difficulties in commercial reaction to the commercial and economic time-to-market demanded by consumers, loss of competitiveness; excessive human and technical involvement and cost associated with the processes of generating information management, inefficiency and inefficiency in internal and external operations.

Faced with this reality, there is a sensitivity of management to make an investment in a technological solution within the BI. In this context, it was validated with the various organizational leaders, involved in this analysis, the need to define a roadmap necessary to achieve the desired state (To Be) having as a starting point the current state of the company (As Is). The proposed and agreed phases were as follows:

- Identification of data sources to support the solution, which in the case under analysis result from the company's ERP, the POS of the integrated stores and external data sources from WinRest, which are related to autonomous coffee shops.
- Data extraction/integration for the Power BI software, considering the Data Warehouse as a centralized data warehouse, as well as the techniques of extraction and integration of data from the various sources that allow the loading to this nuclear repository.
- Data preparation, enabled by the Power Query component of Power BI, step also responsible for data processing and preparation, activities that cover data cleaning, transformation, and loading. This stage aims to correct all the anomalies given us (incomplete data, errors…), becoming homogeneous for subsequent transformation.
- Data model design, in which the data should be associated through a model that relates the main data entities necessary for the intended objectives. It is at this stage that the various dimensions that allow to understand more about the data to be measured for an adequate answer to the business questions are constructed.
- Definition of measures to support KPIs and their validation, at which stage it should be possible to perform some calculations and perform comparative analysis.
- Development of dashboards, corresponding to data visualizations to make the identification of opportunities easier to understand and, later, make it possible to share with other users. Thus, at this stage it will be possible to generate dashboards consisting of data panels, charts and maps that help users to visualize behaviors and trends.

Subsequently, the most relevant KPIs were identified to support the management of the various processes and activities related to the coffee shops. To this end, we identified the critical processes/activities, as well as the main problems/

difficulties in the management of resources. The following situations were identified to improve time spent on daily updating of the various files in Excel format, decisions made based on the experience/ intuition of cafeteria managers, information dispersed in various formats. The KPIs identified were as follows:

- Sales
  - o Systems – ERP, Winrest.
  - o Description – quantity (units) and the value (€) of products that are purchased in each period by a customer.
  - o «To-Be» – connection of the company's central data sources to Power BI and update according to periodicity.
  - o Expected benefits – assess progress of sales goals, allowing you to adjust strategies faster for better results.
  - o Beneficiary organizational units/functions – Head of Coffee Shop, Commercial department, CEO, Financial department, Business Analyst, Marketing department.
  - o Periodicity – daily.
- Product breaks
  - o Systems – ERP, Winrest.
  - o Description – financial losses of food waste that exist in stores resulting from non-sales and can also be calculated in value (€) or percentage (%).
  - o «To-Be» – connection of the company's central data sources to Power BI and update according to periodicity.
  - o Expected benefits – daily information on breaks, optimization of stock planning and production.
  - o Beneficiary organizational units/beneficiary – Head of Coffee Shop, Commercial department, CEO, Financial department, Business Analyst.
  - o Periodicity – daily.
- Profit margem (*Front Office*)
  - o Systems – ERP, Winrest.
  - o Description – financial measure representing the difference between the sale price and the cost price of a product, and which can be calculated in value (€) or in percentage (%).
  - o «To-Be» – connection of the company's central data sources to Power BI and update according to periodicity.
  - o Expected benefits – daily information on revenue evolution, optimization of purchase planning, bet on products that release greater margin value.

- Beneficiary organizational units/beneficiary – Head of Coffee Shop, Commercial department, CEO, Financial department, Business Analyst.
- Periodicity – daily.

- Average order
  - Systems – ERP, Winrest.
  - Description – average order is a preponderant performance indicator that provides the average sale value per customer.
  - «To-Be» – connection of the company's central data sources to Power BI and update according to periodicity.
  - Expected benefits – daily information on potential customers, improvement of promotion channels, personalized promotion, effectiveness of campaigns.
  - Beneficiary organizational units/beneficiary – Head of Coffee Shop, Commercial department, CEO, Business Analyst, Marketing department.
  - Periodicity – weekly.

- Number of transactions
  - Systems – ERP, Winrest.
  - Description – amount of financial movements that are made in store and can become in number of customers.
  - «To-Be» – connection of the company's central data sources to Power BI and update according to periodicity.
  - Expected benefits – daily information on financial movements performed by store.
  - Beneficiary organizational units/beneficiary – Head of Coffee Shop, Commercial department, CEO, Business Analyst, Marketing department.
  - Periodicity – weekly.

- Stocks
  - Systems – ERP, Winrest.
  - Description – quantity of products that the company has and is analyzed in the various Excel files that exist.
  - «To-Be» – Connection of the company's central data sources to Power BI and update according to periodicity.
  - Expected benefits – daily stock information, optimization of stock management, optimization of store production planning, as well as suppliers, avoiding disruption in both parties.

- o Beneficiary organizational units/beneficiary – Head of Coffee Shop, Commercial department, CEO, Business Analyst, Stock management department.
- o Periodicity – daily.

- Budgetary value
  - o Systems – ERP.
  - o Description – Budgetary amounts made by the Financial Department.
  - o «To-Be» – Loading Excel into Power BI for update according to frequency.
  - o Expected benefits – budgetary value information(s) to support the overall activity of the company and each department area.
  - o Beneficiary organizational units/beneficiary – CEO, Commercial department, Head of Cpffee Shop.
  - o Periodicity – monthly and anual.

5. Conclusion and Expected Results

The objective of this study was to support the investment decision in a BI solution to help decision making. The implementation of a BI system can bring several significant benefits and returns to the organization, such as:

- more informed decision making – BI allows the organization to have access to relevant and updated information quickly and easily.
- Holistic view of the business – BI brings together data from multiple company sources and areas, providing an integrated and comprehensive view of overall business performance. This allows you to identify cause and effect relationships between different aspects of the business.
- Identifying opportunities and threats – With BI, you can identify growth opportunities, new potential markets, and emerging trends. In addition, it also helps identify threats and potential problems, allowing the company to take preventive or corrective measures.
- Reducing risks and uncertainties – By basing decisions on concrete data, the organization reduces the risks associated with mistaken or uninformed decisions, becoming more resilient to changes and uncertainties in the market.
- Advanced Analytics – Offers advanced analytical capabilities including predictive analytics and machine learning integration. Enables organizations to gain insight into future trends, identify anomalies and make data-driven forecasts.

In the opinion of the company's management, both the operational team and the top, there were several benefits in this implementation. The biggest benefit was the fact that with these metrics the team was able to understand in a much more complete way what is happening in each store at an operational level and its evolution. This allows the coffee shop managers to be calm, or not, with the performance of stores, products, stocks, know where to intervene to improve, and helps top management to assess the viability of these indicators. For example, if in a certain store the number of regular customers starts to decrease regularly, it can lead to the perception that the store is not viable in future terms and that something must be done to change this downward path.

Another benefit of this implementation is the updates. In Excel to update a Gigabyte media file can take several minutes, while in Power BI it takes seconds. These factors, added to the advantages listed above, explain the decision on the tool chosen for the BI solution.

With the dashboards in Power BI, it is possible to better understand the indicators and their evolution in coffee stores and understand why they are evolving positively or negatively, easily compare stores, products and draw conclusions about this behavior. This is possible due to the high decomposition of this Dashboard that has become quite useful was to confirm previous perceptions of top management or operational management, to deny them.

Power BI can be a tool undoubtedly more scalable, fast, user-friendly, visual, simple to work with than current systems and will allow greater ease of access to information, allowing the company to design initiatives, make sales forecasts and create customer retention programs to improve results.

References

Bronzo, M., Resende, P. T., Oliveira, M. P., McCormack, K. P., Sousa, P. R., & Ferreira, R. L. (2013). Improving performance aligning business analytics with process orientation. *International Journal of Information Management*, 300–307.

Chan, J. (2013). *An architecture for big data analytics*. Communications of the International Information Management.

Chen, W.-J., Kamath, R., Kelly, A., Lopez, H. D., Roberts, M., & Yheng, Y. P. (2015). *Systems of insight for digital transformation: Using IBM operational decision manager advanced and predictive analytics*. IBM Redbooks.

Côrte-Real, N. (2022). *Big data and analytics: Power to transform data into intelligence and impact on business competitiveness*. Lisbon: Influence. Penguin Random House Editorial Portuguese Grup *(In Portuguese)*.

Gandomi, A., & Haider, M. (2015). *Beyond the hype: Big data concepts, methods, and analytics*.

Gartner. (2022a). *Information technology gartner glossary: Big data*. Retrieved October 23, 2023, from https://www.gartner.com/en/information-technology/glossary/big-data

Gartner. (2022b). *Information technology gartner glossary: Analytics*. Retrieved October 23, 2023, from https://www.gartner.com/en/information-technology/glossary/analytics

Grus, J. (2015). *Data science from scratch*. U.S.A: O'Reilly.

IBM. (2022). *What is big data analytics*?, ibm.com: https://www.ibm.com/analytics/hadoop/big-data-analytics

Institute, M. G. (2011). *Big data: The next frontier for innovation, competition, and productivity*. Mckinsey&Company. Retrieved June 21, 2023, from https://www.mckinsey.com/~/media/mckinsey/business%20functions/mckinsey%20digital/our%20insights/big%20data%20the%20next%20frontier%20for%20innovation/mgi_big_data_exec_summary.pdf

International Data Corporation. (2012). Retrieved October 23, 2023, from https://www.idc.com/about

Kasabian, D. (2009). *Funding for BI: It's all about, ROI*. IBM.

Kimball, R., & Ross, M. (2013). *The data warehouse toolkit – The definitive guide to dimensional modeling* (2nd ed., 3ª ed.). Indianapolis: John Wiley & Sons, Inc.

McAfee, A., & Brynjolfsson, E. (2012). *Big data. The management revolution*. Harvard Buiness Review.

Muntean, M., Cabau, L. G., & Rinciog, V. (2014). *Social business intelligence: A new perspective for decision makers*. Elsevier. Last Updated: 1 April 2023, from https://www.sciencedirect.com/science/article/pii/S1877042814020680

Negash, S. (2004). *Business intelligence. Kennesaw State University: Communications of the association for information system*. Retrieved June 2, 2023, from https://www.researchgate.net/publication/220890856_Business_Intelligence

Niu, L., Lu, J., & Zhang, G. (2009). *Cognition-driven decision support for business intelligence*. Berlim: Springer.

Olszak, C., & Ziemba, E. (2007). Approach to building and implementing bussiness intelligence systems, 2, pp. 135–148.

Ong, I., Siew, P., & Wong, S. (2011). A five-layered Business Intelligence architecture. *Communications of the IBIMA*. Retrieved on 23 April 2023, from https://doi.org/10.5171/2011.695619

Ossimitz, M.-L. (2015). The impact of Business Intelligence on the quality of decision making – A mediation model. *Procedia Computer Science*. Retrieved May 29, 2023, from https://www.researchgate.net/publication/283170779_The_Impact_of_Business_Intelligence_on_the_Quality_of_Decision_Making_-_A_Mediation_Model

Ozkose, H., Ari, E. S., & Gencer, C. (2015). Yesterday, today and tomorrow of *Big data. Procedira –Social and Behavioral Sciences*. Retrieved on 23 April 2023, from https://www.sciencedirect.com/science/article/pii/S1877042815036265

Ram, J., Zhang, C.-l., & Koronios, &. A. (2016). *The implications of Big data analytics on business intelligence: A qualitative study in China*. ELSEVIER. Retrieved June 2, 2023, from https://www.sciencedirect.com/science/article/pii/S1877050916304914?via%3Dihub

Richards, G., Yeoh, W., Chong, A. Y., & Popovic, A. (2019). Business Intelligence effectiveness and corporate performance management: An empirical analysis. *Journal of Computer Information Systems*, 188–196.

Sá, J. (2010). *Methodology of data warehouse systems*. Doctoral Thesis, Minho University.

Santos, M. Y., & Ramos, I. (2006). *Business intelligence: Information technologies in knowledge management*. FCA – Informatics Publishing *(In Portuguese)*.

Sherman, R. (2015). *Business Intelligence guidebook – From data integration to analytics*. ELSEVIER. Retrieved 23 April 2023, from https://www.sciencedirect.com/book/9780124114616/business-intelligence-guidebook?via=ihub=

Turban, E., Sharda, R., Aronson, J., & King, D. (2008). *Business intelligence: A managerial approach*. Prentice Hall.

Watson, H. J. (2009). Tutorial: Business Intelligence – Past, present, and future. *Communications of the Association for Information Systems*. Retrieved on 23 April 2023, from https://doi.org/10.17705/1CAIS.02539

Williams, S. (2016). Business Intelligence strategy and *Big data* analytics. *ScienceDirect*. Retrieved June 3, 2023, from https://www.sciencedirect.com/book/9780128091982/business-intelligence-strategy-and-big-data-analytics

Yin, R. K. (2010). *Case study: Planning and methods*. São Paulo: Bookman *(In Portuguese)*.

Ziora, L. (2015). The application of Business Intelligence systems in the support of decision processes in the application of Business Intelligence. *Recent Advances in Computer Science*. Retrieved 5 April 2023, from https://www.inase.org/library/2015/zakynthos/bypaper/COMPUTERS/COMPUTERS-18.pdf

Marta Sofia dos Santos Simões Vasques Matos, Francisco José Videira Cachatra, Pedro Fernandes da Anunciação, Aníbal Júdice Guerreiro Cabanita Vieira

Integration of Information Systems: Critical Success Factors for User Satisfaction

1. Introduction

The current society or networked economy highlights the importance of integration between information systems (IS) (Esteves et al., 2021). Smart Cities, at society level (Anunciação & Petiz, 2023) and industry 4.0 at the economic level (Anunciação et al., 2023), are two current and pragmatic examples of the centrality of the integration of IS as a factor of sustainability of the functioning of these realities. The relevance of related Information systems (IS) highlights the respective complexity (Madni & Sievers, 2014), as it is common to coexist multiple systems (Simon et al., 2014). Information systems and information and communication technologies (IS/ICT) as well as information are at the heart of a new network dynamics, which is only possible with the integration of the various Information systems (IS) of the different stakeholders. Information sharing is the basis of its operation, only possible if IS/ICT is integrated.

In the Industry 4.0 environment, in particular, interconnected computers, intelligent materials or intelligent machines that communicate with each other, interact with the environment, and make decisions with minimal human involvement, awaken us to the importance of digital connectivity. Integration is the true power of Industry 4.0 (Ghobakhloo, 2020). In a networked economic framework, information sharing has become a greater challenge, as it presupposes an urbanistic vision of the economy and organizations (Anunciação & Zorrinho, 2006), in which it requires a Governance perspective on IS (Oliveira & Anunciação, 2023; Oliveira, 2019) and should enable a joint capacity for generating and sharing information to the stakeholders involved.

The evolution of the needs of society, economy, and business in general lead to the need for integration of IS (He & Xu, 2012; Madni & Sievers, 2014), which should result in advantages for organizations, for example, in improving information flows, efficiency and effectiveness and added value creation. The information is the aggregating element of integration at the IS level (Francisco, 2011; Anunciação & Zorrinho, 2006), because only the information allows obtaining additional amounts of knowledge (Oliveira, 2022).

The need for IS integration derives from the evolution of organizations, markets, and technology, being interoperability a requirement for integration in a distributed environment. The concepts of integration and interoperability are often misinterpreted or even confused (Tomicic-Pupek et al., 2012). Integration is the ability of two or more systems or components to exchange information and use the information exchanged. While interoperability is the ability of disparate and diverse organizations to interact towards mutually beneficial and agreed common objectives involving the sharing of information and knowledge between organizations, through the business processes they support, through the exchange of data between their ICT systems (EIF, 2017). Integrated IS transformation is not always complete to create unique visions. "Legacy systems" are often difficult obstacles to overcome in the path of integration. The problem associated with legacy systems corresponds to the fact that, for many years, the IS have been developed in an isolated way, without integration and without overview, having been adopted middleware solutions for software integration, allowing the exchange of information. The integration of IS in complex organizations, for example, should consider the following characteristics (Tomicic-Pupek et al., 2012): modularity, coherence, vertical interoperability, horizontal interoperability, integrity, transparency, availability, functionality, reliability, usability, efficiency, sustainability, and portability.

Integrated systems are a very important pillar in organizations (Spathis, 2006). The constant needs for access and sharing of information, constitute a strong argument for the integration and implementation of IS transformation projects in economic organizations. The IS should constitute itself as a 'digital nervous system' and, in this sense, cover all economic and organizational operations, focus the opportunity in making decisions, facilitate the definition of strategies and optimize learning. In this sense, the strategy should be holistic (Gaspar, 2015). In this holistic view, the integration of IS is vital, as it contributes to competitiveness and economic sustainability. Failed IS integration projects cost economic organizations half a million euros a year (Opensoft, 2021), hence the importance of interoperability solutions that promote data access, quality, and security. For this reason, it becomes necessary to follow the critical factors of the business and the architecture of the IS (Fonseca et al., 2019).

2. Objectives and Methodology

The general objective of this work was to study the contribution of IS integration to organizational satisfaction. Based on the concept of IS integration, which includes interoperability between systems, data, or functionalities, with a view to communication and interaction, regardless of the technological support approach, systems, and people, we sought, first, analyze how the integration of IS can result in advantages in an organization, and, secondly, identify which factors, considering a process of IS integration, influence people's satisfaction. It was taken as a reference the model of Delone and Mclean (2003) that identifies six dimensions to evaluate the success of IS: system quality, information quality, system utility, user satisfaction, individual impact, and organizational impact. Moreira (2014) proposes some net benefits that can be obtained, such as, for example, the optimization of decision making, increased productivity, cost reduction, increased competitiveness, increased profits, increased performance, increased job satisfaction, etc.

Similarly, factors that impact user satisfaction (Bergensen, 2004) were considered, such as the appreciation of user needs and expectations, effectiveness of communication in the organization, the ability to provide support to the user, the perceived ease of use, perceived benefits, user participation and involvement in the IS design and development process, as well as the organization's attitude in terms of user support/training for effective use of the system.

In the first phase of the study, we used the Focus Group technique. He integrated two directors of IS two industrial companies, two Chief Executive Officer (CEO) of two software-house, and a commercial and logistics director with responsibilities for IS in the respective organization. In the first phase of the study, it was sought that the Focus group discuss the relevance of the theme and identify the dimensions to be included in the survey. In the second phase, information was collected through an investigation. The questionnaire comprised two sections: the first corresponding to the definition of the respondent's profile and the second tending to identify the influencing factors of organizational satisfaction. A Likert scale was used to evaluate each parameter. The questionnaire was developed on the Microsoft Forms platform and disclosed by several social networks, using the SPSS program, version 25.0, for its treatment.

3. Presentation and Discussion of Results

Regarding the first phase, it was possible to identify the relevant aspects associated with each of the dimensions analyzed. Thus, regarding the benefits in IS integration, it was highlighted:

- integration of systems by legal provision; minimization of fines and compliance with legal standards; and functional adjustments of IS in companies (Legal requirements).

- ensure adequate monitoring of data integration in security, systems integration to add value to the organization and economic activity; uniform language in all organizational areas; greater agility in organizational functioning and greater cohesion in teamwork (Functional requirements).
- training plan appropriate to the needs of employees, facilitates the management of change and the development of the spirit of belonging to the new project (Cultural requirements).
- increased productivity; reduction of errors; improved response time in decision making; availability of reliable and timely indicators (KPIs) for management; contributes to competitiveness, efficiency, effectiveness, and personal satisfaction (Result requirements).

As regards the limitations in IS integration, it was stressed:

- customization and change costs; investment in cybersecurity (Legal requirements).
- lack of technical resources; difficulty mapping data between systems (Functional requirements).
- nature data of each entity may condition the predisposition to its sharing (Cultural requirements).
- integration risk is not done correctly if there is no stakeholder involvement; SI should provide agility, efficiency, effectiveness, and value (Result requirements).

As regards the risks in IS integration, it was stressed:

- possibility of compromising the security of systems and data breaches and exposure; possibility of improper access may result in a cyber-attack (Legal requirements).
- integration failure may bring business stoppage; survey of needs made from organizational models already pre-existing in consultants and not by actual survey and analysis of the organization's operations; inability to specify the nature of the data may lead to poor data quality (Functional requirements).
- lack of interest of the organization or employees causes a failure in communication producing obstacles in the implementation of systems; lack of training of people in the operation of the IS (Cultural requirements).
- unavailability of data due to lack of security causes business continuity problems; assume that the technology generates, by itself, competitiveness not considering that it is a continuous project (Result requirements).

Regarding the second part of the study, we proceeded to the statistical analysis of the data obtained from the surveys to assess whether the integration of IS can contribute to organizational satisfaction. 274 observations were obtained, 54.4 % male and 45.6 % female. Most respondents (44.5 %) are in the age group between 41 and 50 years and 22.6 % between 51 and 60 years. Thus, it is found that most respondents are active and have professional maturity. Most respondents (49.3 %) have a degree and 3.6 % a doctorate, that is, a high degree of knowledge on the topics covered and a more real awareness of the relevance of the subject under study. The majority (52.9 %) belong to the public sector and, regarding the economic sector where they perform their professional functions, 39.4 % work in the Security/Defense sector, 14.6 % in Informatics and the rest in sectors such as Industry, Commerce and Services (9.9 %), Education (6.9 %), Training (6.6 %), Real Estate Activities (2.2 %) and 20.4 % in «Other».

It should also be noted that 79.9 % work in a large company and that, in total, 60.6 % has been in the current company for more than 10 years. In the universe of respondents, 97.4 % use IS in their professional activities and, of these, 59.1 % work with the same IS for more than a decade. Most respondents (52.6 %) consider that the IS has all the necessary features. However, 47.4 % mention the non-integration of all the features they need in the IS used.

Regarding the factors that influence organizational satisfaction, the majority (61.8 %) of respondents are globally satisfied or very satisfied with the level of integration of IS. Analyzing each of the dimensions considered, we have:

- 64.7 % say they are satisfied or very satisfied about the adequacy of the IS to the legal provisions (Legal requirements).
- satisfaction higher than 60 % regarding indicators, technological maturity, and types of integration (functional requirements).
- levels of satisfaction were identified in the items: personal contribution to the improvement of IS functionalities, the relationship between integrated IS and the perception of bond, previous training, and continuous training in the IS to perform tasks. Globally, the answers show people's satisfaction with their IS. The indicator where users are less satisfied is related to training (Cultural requirements);
- globally, the answers show that people are satisfied with their organizations (Result requirements).

It should be noted that, in some questions, the percentage of answers «does not know/does not answer» is significant, in some cases exceeding 30 %. This expressiveness is an opportunity for the development of the study to understand the reason associated with this reality. Does it represent an ignorance of reality or a desire not to speak out? It will correspond to a lack of participation in the development and improvement projects of the IS itself.

Overall, the level of satisfaction with the indicators that facilitate their tasks/decision making is the dimension that registers a lower expressiveness.

4. Main Conclusions

Information integration is the key to information management, inviting the evolution of business processes and strategies. Integration must result in interoperability between systems, being an absolutely structuring foundation for increasing the quality of decisions and increasing competitiveness through IS. The guarantee of good quality information, relevant, reliable, objective, in adequate quantity and at the right time, strengthens a more competitive behavior in the market.

Of the numerous advantages in the integration of IS, stand out, namely in the production and consultation of information in real time, access to relevant information that influence or validate decision making, generation of added value to the business, increase process efficiency and improve information quality. On the other hand, it facilitates organizational expansion, security, and data integrity, improves operational project management and adaptability of business processes, provides internal/external communication, and has a greater capacity in imposing regulation.

However, the management perspective on IS should be holistic. Without the existence of adequate human resource management policies, strategic and operational management, work environments that favor collaboration, communication, commitment, risk acceptance and tolerance to error, may not be met the objectives of the IS and represent a heavy financial burden for organizations.

People and organizational culture are a crucial factor and should be considered as critical to the success of IS integration projects. In this context, are success factors for a good integration of IS, among others, the commitment of top management, compliance with legislation, management of effective organizational changes, adequate training, good leadership, and effective communication. In this sense, any IS should help employees of an organization to perform their activity fully.

In this study, the model presented by Delone and Mclean (2003) was followed, which is based on a model of evaluation of the success of IS and its interdependent relationships. It is a very useful tool in IS evaluation processes, considering its multiple dimensions. In this sense, there are several advantages for organizations with the integration of IS, namely, reduction of fines and consequent mitigation of lawsuits, optimization of resources, efficiency of business processes, greater cohesion in teamwork, increased productivity, reduced errors and improved customer experience. However, the limitations of IS are many and exist at all stages of its life, from the design and architecture of the IS to the end of its life. The integration of IS in an organization requires a careful architecture, involving a detailed knowledge of both the organization and its activity.

On the other hand, there are risks identified in the Focus Group, namely the creation of organizational information silos, failures in the IS for reasons of poor design and information security. A good integration of IS, prepares and enhances the paths of the future evolution of an organization, freeing people for nobler tasks and better living and working conditions, translating naturally into personal satisfaction. In this context, it was possible to conclude that in general people (61.8 %) are satisfied with the integration process in their organizations. The factors influencing satisfaction in the IS integration process are:

- updates based on new legal frameworks, in which 64.7 % of the total respondents say they are satisfied/ very satisfied in their organizations (Legal requirements).
- technological maturity and types of integration, which leads us to a scenario of "satisfaction" higher than 60 % (Functional requirements).
- bond and training, generally showing the perception that people in their organizations are satisfied (Cultural requirements).
- indicators of efficiency, competitiveness, professional performance, and decision-making support, which also show satisfaction of respondents regarding their institutions (Result requirements).

The existence of reciprocal influence between the overall level of satisfaction associated with IS integration and the indicators foreseen in this study, recommended by the revised model of Delone and McLean (2003). Using the Spearman correlation, a statistically significant relationship between the variable organizational satisfaction and the respective indicators was confirmed, establishing a strong positive correlation regarding the indicator's competitiveness, bond, and professional performance.

Regarding the levels of agreement that influence the satisfaction of people in an organization, in the process of integration of an IS, there was a generalized agreement regarding the indicators legal provision, technological maturity, types of integration, link, training, efficiency, competitiveness, professional performance and decision-making support. The issues that presented the highest level of agreement perceived by IS users, belong to indicators whose content is about training, support for decision making and the link.

It is thus confirmed that the existence of IS integration in an organization can have a significant impact on the organization and play a key role in organizational satisfaction.

5. Limitations and Future Works

In carrying out this research were identified some limitations. Due to the technicity of the subject, it was not possible to study in an exhaustive way some factors considered with potential to reinforce the conclusions obtained, namely regarding the answers associated with the option "I do not know/ Not applicable". On the other hand, the impossibility of free answers conditioned a possible greater clarification of the respondents and may also lose the opportunity to collect relevant data.

The study was limited to professional organizations within the range of contacts of the authors, as can be seen in the percentage previously referenced (39.4 % work in the Security/ Defense sector) these may already be more aware of the issues associated with the integration of IS or even possibly distort the sampling, not ensuring more comprehensive results of an economic reality that was intended to be extended. However, this situation allowed the reduction of time in data collection, research, and response control as well as the speed in the treatment of the collected data.

As part of the contribution to knowledge, there are naturally several issues of a wider scope which, due to time and scope constraints, have not been deepened, for example, to understand how critical success factors contribution to organizational satisfaction, against the background of IS integration.

With this work we sought to show that users/ professionals are the first element of change, and they are ultimately built, adapt, or reject the changes introduced in organizations. By promoting the benefits of good IS integration, organizations are more likely to achieve high levels of satisfaction among their employees and gain competitive advantages.

Regarding future lines of research, it is suggested the continuation of research in this theme, highlighting the usefulness of carrying out a similar study in a larger number of organizations. It is also recommended the interest of carrying out a more concrete and in-depth study of a case study in an organization, in order to monitor the management of change, namely with the decision-making process of the evolution of the IS, the decisions of the integrations carried out or to be carried out, as well as the selection of integration strategies to be used in order to minimize the impact of challenges to the integration of identified systems, culminating in the benefits perceived by people.

It is undeniable that IS integration can play an essential role in organizational satisfaction, providing added value in the context of economic organizations, with a direct impact on their stakeholders. For this, it will be pertinent to evaluate impacts and benefits, ensuring the support of management, management and other employees, valuing training according to the IS to implement.

References

Anunciação, P. F., Dinis, V., Peñalver, A. B., & Esteves, F. J. M. (2023). Main dimensions of management preventive maintenance in the industry 4.0 context. In Muhammed Veysel. Kaya (Ed.), *Social and economic studies within the framework of emerging global developments* (Vol. 3, p. 219).

Anunciação, P. F., & Petiz, R. A. P. (2023). Governance to digital transformation in portuguese public local authorities. In Muhammed Veysel. Kaya (Ed.), *Social and economic studies within the framework of emerging global developments* (Vol. 3, p. 181). Peter Lang Publishing.

Anunciação, P. F., & Zorrinho, C. (2006). *Organizational urbanism – How to manage technological shock*. Sílabo Publishing. *(In Portuguese)*

Bergersen, B. M. (2004). User satisfaction and influencing issues. *Network and System Administration Research Surveys*, 1(1), 5–26.

DeLone, W. H., & McLean, E. R. (2003). The DeLone and McLean model of information systems success: A ten-year update. *Journal of Management Information Systems*, 19(4), 9–30. Retrieved December 28, 2023, from http://www.jstor.org/stable/40398604.

EIF-European Interoperability Framework. (2017). ISA² – Interoperability solutions for public administrations, businesses and citizens. *The New European Interoperability Framework*. Retrieved: December 15, 2023, from https://ec.europa.eu/isa2/eif_en/.

Esteves, F. J. M., Santos, J. C. E. R., & Anunciação, P. F. (2021). Information systems requirements for organizational sustainability in the information society. In F. J. M. Esteves, & P. F. Anunciação (Eds.), *Information systems – Paradigm and solutions for management* (pp. 63–71). Plátano Publhising. *(In Portuguese)*

Fonseca, P., Souza, D., Santos, E., & Miranda, M. (2019). *Critical success factors in the implementation of information systems from the perception of users: An experience in the public sector*. Retrieved: February 25, 2023, from https://www.dre.vanderbilt.edu/~schmidt/PDF/bookchapter-final.pdf *(In Portuguese)*.

Francisco, F. (2011). Understanding heterogeneous information systems integration architecture and its relationship with business architecture – A case study in Portugal. Retrieved: January 14, 2023, from https://www.repository.utl.pt/handle/10400.5/4528. *(In Portuguese)*

Gaspar, A. (2015). *Challenges to information systems integration: A case study in the Banking Sector*. MSc Thesis, Lisbon School of Economics & Management. Retrieved: February 7, 2023, from https://www.repository.utl.pt/handle/10400.5/10495.

Ghobakhloo, M. (2020). Industry 4.0, digitization, and opportunities for sustainability. *Journal of Cleaner Production*, 252, 119869. https://doi.org/10.1016/j.jclepro.2019.119869

He, W., & Xu. (2012). Integration of distributed enterprise applications: A survey. *IEEE Transactions on Industrial Informatics*, 10(1), 35–42. Retrieved: December 13, 2023, from. https://ieeexplore.ieee.org/abstract/document/6165353

Madni, A. M., & Sievers, M. (2014). Systems integration: Key perspectives, experiences, and challenges. *Systems Engineering*, 17(1), 37–51. Retrieved: January 19, 2023, from http://doi.wiley.com/10.1002/sys.21249.

Moreira, R. (2014). *User Satisfaction of Information and Documentation Systems Nursing in Electronic Support: A Study at the São João Hospital Center*. Nursing School of Porto. Master in Direction and Management of Services nursing. «Retrived: November, 1, 2022, from http://hdl.handle.net/10400.26/9732.pdf.»

Oliveira, A. (2019). *Manifesto of ceGSI, Information Systems Governance European Club – Portugal, Information Systems Governance – Concepts, good practices and case studies*. Chiado-Books Publishing. *(In Portuguese)*

Oliveira, A. (2022). *Information & management – Two sides of the same coin*. Sílabo Publishing. *(In Portuguese)*

Oliveira, A., & Anunciação, P. F. (2023). Information systems governance: Some dimensions to management. In Muhammed Veysel Kaya (Ed.), *Social and economic studies within the framework of emerging global developments* (Vol. 1, pp. 139–152). Peter Lang Publishing.

Opensoft. (2021). *Five advantages of system integration*. Retrieved: May 20, 2023, from https://www.opensoft.pt/5-vantagens-da-integracao-de-sistemas/. *(In Portuguese)*

Simon, A., Yaya, L. H., Karapetrovic, S., & Casadesus, M. (2014). Can integration difficulties affect innovation and satisfaction? *Industrial Management & Data Systems*, 114(2),183–202. Retrieved: December 10, 2023, from http://www.emeraldinsight.com/doi/abs/10.1108/IMDS-03-2013-0148.

Spathis, C. (2006). Enterprise system implementation and accounting benefits. *Journal of Enterprise Information Management*, 19(1), 67–82.

Tomicic-Pupek, K., Dobrovic, Z., & Tomicic Furjan, M. (2012). Strategies for information systems integration. In *Proceedings of the ITI 2012 34th International Conference on Information Technology Interfaces* (pp. 311–316.), Cavtat, Croatia, 2012. https://doi.org/10.2498/iti.2012.04.

Jessica Cristina Caeiro José, Pedro Fernandes da Anunciação, Dorota Kuchta, António Juan Briones Peñalver

Potential of Virtual Reality in Tourism in Portugal

1. Introduction

The Covid-19 Pandemic has significantly changed the paradigm of economic activities. This was a virus that changed the world, the economy and society. Conditioned the mobility of people, economic operations, and social relations. Among the various economic areas, the tourism and hospitality industry were drastically affected by the strong limitations or even impossibility of making trips (Chang et al., 2020; Chandrasekaran & Dhanalakshmi, 2020). The limitations associated with confinement have stimulated many organizations to reinvent their economic activities and to seek, in the digital context, solutions for their sustainability.

Faced with this need for digital transformation, some organizations followed a logic of transformation and others a logic of complementarity. In the first, companies took the opportunity to change the business model according to digital platforms. In the second, the companies carried out a strategy of complementarity through innovation and value addition compared to the current services. The extreme difficulties served, as well, as «Wake-up calls» for the various stakeholders to prepare and develop strategies and firm responses to existing problems.

Tourism has found in technological innovation the lever for value creation in the stages of the value chain (Buhalis, 2008), having provided, for example, new paradigms in information research, in the evaluation of tourist alternatives, ease of purchase decision or post-purchase interaction (Neuhofer et al., 2015, 2014). In this context, knowing that virtual reality (VR) has been a technological domain of taken potential and considering the opportunity to experience virtually a monument or destination, how this opportunity can be a useful and competitive lever in the tourism industry.

2. Covid-19 Pandemic and the Opportunity to Rethink Tourist Activities

The recent Covid-19 Pandemic forced companies to rethink their economic activities. The impossibility of reaching customers or the impossibility of carrying out their economic operations in a face-to-face way stimulated, in many cases, creativity as a factor of sustainability. Those who have failed to reinvent their business and activities have either disappeared or experienced serious survival difficulties. The tourist consumer has become more independent, dynamic, and demanding (Andrade et al., 2016). The possibility of experiencing authentic and memorable experiences, even if virtual, provides greater consumer satisfaction and, consequently, a generation of greater value for the company (Martins, 2016). Thus, information and communication technologies (ICTs) are increasingly critical to the success of tourism (Morais & Cunha, 2018). Not being new this relevance (Sheldon et al., 2001), ICTs have allowed integration into global operations, reducing information costs and transaction time (Hassan, 2011). Technologies, particularly through social networks, have been constituted as powerful tools for promotion and competitiveness, strengthening strategies and operations (Buhalis, 2004). The market began to be seen on a global scale, became more relational (Lake, 2023),having forced a reorganization of many companies in the sector (Hassan, 2011; Aalbers et al., 2014), both on the supply and demand side (Buhalis, 2004).

The possibility of visualization of 3D virtual worlds, VR and augmented reality are some of the examples of how ICTs make it possible to explore and experience tourist products digitally in a pre-defined visit, and sometimes it is possible to perform virtual tours without having to travel to the destination (Rafael, 2022). In this sense, consumer behaviors have been changing to new formats in which tourism and ICTs merge (Rafael, 2022). With the use of VR, travel alternatives expand in the digital world (Correia & Brito, 2011). Currently, it is through digital technological resources that organizations try to captivate their customers, investing in the digital universe, where VR can be a useful tool in the dissemination of tourist offer (Milheiro, 2021).

Virtual tourism is expanding, and it may gain importance in the tourism sector. However, tourist companies must realize which virtual tools are best suited to attract and retain customers, and VR can be a good example of attraction (Milheiro, 2021). VR can become a powerful tool in the tourism sector, helping in the sustainable preservation of cultural and natural heritage, thus preserving sites that are already in degradation or even inaccessible to the public (Guttentag, 2010).

VR can be considered as a strategic form of greater persuasion (Milheiro, 2021) using sensory and psychological elements for greater involvement in the experience. The associated technology expands the two-dimensional vision to the panoramic view which brings a strong sense of presence and provides a new viewing experience and at the same time breaks the regional and seasonal limitations of conventional tourism (Rafael, 2022). For several years, airlines, travel and tourism agencies have used the technology associated with virtual reality to advertise holiday destinations to potential customers. Not a technological "contraption" (Chen, 2020), VR drives tourists to immersive virtual travel experiences (Lever, 2021). Some examples of VR applications in the world are the Grand Canyon VR Experience, which allows you to take a virtual powered kayak tour through the Grand Canyon, and this experience can be adapted to user preferences (experience illuminated by sun or moon, speed control of the ride (O'Donnell, 2021; Steampowered, 2022)); Google Earth VR, which presents in 3D several points around the planet, allowing the user to interact with the tool and choose the place you want to travel; Everest VR que permite escalar um Montanha Everest (Meireles, 2020); Qatar Airways where users are welcomed by a virtual flight attendant as well as interact with the crew (Lima, 2022); the Heritage Collection Travel Agency in the UK, which provides tours with crocodiles and zebras on a crossing of the Serengeti River (Bush, 2022).

3. Objectives and Methodologies

The main objective of this study was to understand the receptivity of the different stakeholders of the tourism market to the opportunity of digital transformation in the sector. The strong impacts and constraints on economic activity, both on the supply and demand sides, in the operationalization of commercial activities that occurred during the pandemic, showed a lack of alternatives, individual and collective, related to boosting the sector during the containment period. In this sense, the opportunity to carry out a study at the national level emerged, which would provide an overview of the opportunity to adopt virtual reality in this sector in Portugal.

The study was developed in two phases. In the first phase we sought to identify the interest of the potential of adopting virtual reality as an option to minimize the impacts of the pandemic and stimulate the resumption of economic activities by suppliers of tourism products and services, as, for example, travel agencies and tour operators, or those who may condition this offer, such as local or regional public government entities responsible for managing cultural heritage (e.g., monuments). And in the second phase, we tried to make the same analysis on the supply side, trying to understand to what extent the customers of tourist products and services consider relevant the access and availability of solutions in virtual reality format to increase the levels of knowledge and support to the decision making associated with the tourist offer.

It was chosen, as a methodology, to use a convenience sample, particularly regarding tour operators and customers in general. Through convenience sampling, as a non-probabilistic and non-random sampling technique, we sought to create samples according to the ease of access to respondents, considering the availability of stakeholders during the year 2022. Regarding the supply side, targeted mails were sent, and a reinforcement of this channel was made through LinkedIn. Regarding demand, the survey was disclosed by different channels (WhatsApp, Teams, LinkedIn, and email) and social networks (Facebook and Instagram). In this case, the Snowball technique was also adopted. On the supply side, it was also considered the possibility of a Focus group with some stakeholders to clarify the results obtained, if necessary.

4. Results Analysis

On the supply side, 780 surveys were sent, and 87 replies were received. Of the answers obtained, 90 % correspond to public stakeholders. Interestingly, for unidentified reasons, only 1 % of tour operators responded to the survey. This reduced participation, although it limits the study and the perception regarding the positioning of private stakeholders, as main agents in the tourist dynamics, constitutes an opportunity for the future development of the same.

Regarding the respondents' functions, it was found that 32 % occupy top management positions, 32 % intermediate management positions and 36 % operational management positions, which shows that the majority has decision-making responsibilities on the strategic and tacit development of their institutions (64 %). Regarding knowledge of VR, it was possible to verify that most individuals know virtual reality and its potential (98 %).

Regarding the potential and expected benefits of VR as a lever factor for tourism, all respondents (100 %) consider that it can enhance competitive advantages in the tourism sector, The main expected benefits correspond to the increase in the knowledge of destinations (20 %), the dynamization of the tourist offer (17 %) and the increase in the competitiveness of companies (2 %). However, 61 % of respondents mention all these benefits simultaneously.

Regarding the degree of familiarity, as users, with the associated technology, only 31 % of respondents say they have used this technology, it is evident that the vast majority (69 %) never used it. Among those who have had contact with this technology, the feeling generated by it is of greater accessibility to information (19 %), greater knowledge (14 %), greater curiosity (11 %) and greater sentimental relationship (2 %). The remaining (54 %) indicate benefits other than those previously indicated. However, 82 % of respondents consider that VR constitutes or may constitute an added value.

Interestingly, despite the expected benefits and feelings generated by those who have already experienced this technology, only 14 % of respondents have some type of current or planned project for the near future under VR. This finding shows that there has been no investment in these technologies by tour operators in Portugal. In addition, the remaining 86 % assume that they do not have projects in this area. Regarding the future strategy for the development of projects related to virtual reality, it was possible to determine that 22 % focus on historical heritage, 7 % on nature and 5 % on landscape.

Regarding the economic value generated through VR, or generation expectations, there is a positive response (14 %), in which it is assumed that VR generated or is expected to generate economic value to stakeholders who have invested or intend to invest in this type of technology. This is a reduced value, leaving some questions, such as, do stakeholders evaluate their investments? Do they know of any instruments for assessing them? This will be another opportunity to study in the future. Regarding respondents who do not have projects under the RV, 73 % answered that they consider this possibility, wanting more than half (52 %) to make investments from the improvement of existing technologies.

Regarding the promotion, dissemination, and promotion of tourism services, although there is a recognition of the relevance of digital, there is a significant part of respondents who still use traditional channels (43 %). However, it assumes some preponderance as a complement to traditional channels, namely through official websites (17 %) and social networks (22 %). It is clear that there is still no significant use of digital technologies, in particular virtual reality, but there is a desire for change, 59 % consider that the communication they make is not enough to reach the tourist/ client and 80 % admit that this should be improved.

Given the weak expressiveness of some results, it was understood that clarification of some dimensions expressed. In this sense, 10 operators were invited to clarify three important dimensions regarding the respective decision process. The first was limited to the identification of the factors that generate economic value with the investment in ICT. In this area, the most widely agreed justifying factors were: technological evolution and innovation; accessibility for people with motor difficulties; increased interactions and interactivity with customers; increased sales and quality of services provided; production and use of new content; improving competitiveness; improving dissemination and promotion; and increasing market share.

The second dimension focused on the potential for differentiation. In this case, it was possible to verify that there is no digital differentiation strategy, which seems to be a contradiction because, in general, they assume as very relevant technological innovation. Some inertia is evident, as they seek to monitor the market according to their financial availability. When encouraged to reflect on the potential of VR, they indicated the opportunity to develop more sentimental content; greater digital personalization of the offer; strengthening brand positioning; differentiation of marketing campaigns; and adopting a Storytelling perspective.

With regard to the last dimension analyzed, concerning the relevance of VR for tourism activity, the increased motivation to know more destinations was expressed; the possibility of developing new experiences, reducing the ecological footprint and protecting the planet; access to knowledge for people with motor disabilities; increase the sentimental relationship with the desired destination or tourist product; increase the quality requirements in tourist services; increase the potential for attracting tourists; increase the sensory relationship with the destination; the contribution to a greater enrichment of the visitor's experience; the provision and strengthening of scientific knowledge in the case of tourist destinations based on Cultural Heritage; the differentiating promotion of the destination, among others. As regards demand, around 1000 surveys were sent and 152 replies were received, mostly male (59 %). Regarding the training of respondents, 75 % have higher education, which shows a high level of knowledge and a better understanding of the challenges of technological innovation in the tourism sector. Regarding sensitivity and practices associated with tourism, the vast majority usually travel (88 %), being the most appreciated of leisure (53 %), cultural (31 %) and nature (11 %).

Regarding the openness to new technologies, 87 % consider themselves receptive to the use of new technologies in their activities and tourist needs. Most respondents (96 %) know what virtual reality is and, of these, 62 % already had a contact with this technology. However, only 23 % used it in the context of tourism. When confronted with VR in the decision-making on tourist destinations, it was observed that 66 % expressed their total agreement, considering that this would increase the information on destinations and products, increase the level of knowledge and facilitate better decision making.

Regarding the relevance of VR in the promotion of tourism, the vast majority (96 %) of individuals answered affirmatively that this can provide a differentiated promotion of tourist destinations through the Experienciation of the distinctive factors of the offer. In this sense, it can be deduced that, if there was a greater use of VR in tourism promotion, this could be a distinctive factor on the demand side. It should be noted that 80 % of respondents said that they would feel more confident in the proposed tourist attractions if there was the possibility of enjoying the VR, 85 % more motivated to look for information about tourist areas and 74 % available to develop emotional links with the destinations viewed.

Reinforcing the relevance of the potential of VR, the interest and willingness in its use is evident. Most respondents (95 %) consider that their use in tourism in Portugal should be a reality. Such expression and willingness to adhere to this paradigm should serve as a stimulus for stakeholders on the supply side to invest in VR in Portugal. The justification for this desire comes from 68 % of respondents highlight the advantage of being able to know better the destinations desired in the comfort of their homes or in the leisure time available. However, 86 % say they do not know virtual reality projects in Portugal. Given these elements, when questioning the main channels of access to tourist destinations, 30 % referred to the use of social networks, 26 % official websites, 19 % Youtube videos, 16 % maps and 9 % blogs.

5. Conclusion and Future Work

The comparison of the results shows that there is a knowledge of VR and its importance. On the supply side, more than half of the stakeholders surveyed consider that VR can bring increased competitiveness, enhance tourism supply, and increase knowledge of destinations. On the demand side, most are interested in the existence of technological solutions associated with VR that allow to increase knowledge about the destinations offered facilitating decision making.

On the supply side, this technology is more adopted in the promotion of heritage sites (22 %), nature (7 %) and landscape dimension (5 %). However, the use of VR is still little expressive, as the most used technological means in Portugal are social networks (26 %), YouTube (19 %) and maps (16 %). Only 26 % use VR software. However, on the supply side, the privileged form of communication goes towards the needs of the population, with a large bet on social networks.

In any case, we can consider that there is an opportunity for the adoption of this technology. On the supply side, this opportunity is reinforced by the fact that 59 % of respondents consider that the communication made is not enough to reach the diversity of customers. It should also be noted that, although most did not use VR, those who used it consider that there is greater accessibility to information (19 %), greater knowledge (14 %) and curiosity (11 %). Although they recognize the advantages of VR, it is possible to verify that most do not have short or medium-term projects associated with this technology, which can be justified by the difficulties of making investments associated with.

On the demand side, individuals consider that VR would help promote the destination, agreeing that it should be used in tourism in Portugal. Most respondents admit that with VR they would feel more motivated to seek information about a tourist area, as well as believe that it would allow the creation of an emotional bond. However, most do not know a VR project in Portugal.

Thus, being able to conclude that there is a window of opportunity on the supply side that is not being properly considered in the strategic plan given the desires and needs of the demand side. Although they consider that VR could be an asset to attract customers. It is expected that the tourism governing bodies in Portugal will soon consider the development of projects in this context, at various levels, because the time-to-market window, in the face of technological innovation, is increasingly narrow.

Regarding the limitations, the main limitation corresponded to this study still in the context of the COVID-19 Pandemic. The strong limitations to face-to-face interaction with stakeholders limited the number of responses and, consequently, the possibility of a more consolidated result. The results achieved result from the use of digital channels, such as mail and websites.

Regarding the future work, it may be interesting to carry out a new broader investigation on the subject, to validate some apparently contradictory results and a possible confirmation, or not, of the results obtained.

References

Aalbers, H. L., Dolfsma, W., & Blinde-Leerentveld, R. (2014). Firm reorganization: Social control or social contract?. *Journal of Economic Issues*, *48*(2), 451-460.

Andrade, A., Horodyski, G. S., & de Lima Medeiros, M. (2016). Augmented reality in tourism: Study of the game Pokemón Go. *Hospitality Journal*, 13, 1–21. *(In Portuguese).*

Buhalis, D. (2004). eTourism strategic and tactical impacts of information communication technologies for tourism. *Tourism & Development Journal*, (1), 57–66. from https://doi.org/10.34624/rtd.v0i1.14311.

Buhalis, D., & Law, R. (2008). Progress in information technology and tourism management: 20 years on and 10 years after the Internet – The state of eTourism research. *Tourism Management*, 29(4), 609–623.

Bush, E. (2022). *New luxury travel agency features virtual reality cinema room*. Available at: https://travelweekly.co.uk/news/travel-agents/new-luxury-travel-agency-features-virtual-reality-cinema-room.

Chandrasekaran, K. S., & Dhanalakshmi, N. (2020). The pandemic effect on the tourism industry. *Strad Research*, 7(9), 33–39.

Chang, C. L., McAleer, M., & Ramos, V. (2020). A charter for sustainable tourism after COVID-19. *Sustainability*, 12(9), 3671.

Chen, A. (2020). *Será que as Viagens Virtuais Vieram Para Ficar*. Available at: https://www.natgeo.pt/viagem-e-aventuras/2020/04/sera-que-viagens-virtuais-vieram-para-ficar.

Correia, R., & Brito, C. (2011). The importance of marketing for tourism development: The case of Montalegre. *Tourism & Development Journal*, (16), 127–143. Available at: https://doi.org/10.34624/rtd.v0i16.13395. *(In Portuguese)*

Guttentag, D. A. (2010). Virtual reality: Applications and implications for tourism. *Tourism Management*, 31, 637–651. Available at: https://doi.org/10.1016/j.tourman.2009.07.003.

Hassan, H. (2011). *Information technology and tourism management. Faculty of arts*. University of Coimbra. Available at: https://estudogeral.sib.uc.pt/handle/10316/19126. *(In Portuguese)*

Lake, D. A. (2003). Global governance: a relational contracting approach. In *Globalization and governance* (31-53). Routledge.

Lever, R. (2021). *Pandemic drives international travel (in virtual reality)*. Available at: https://exame.com/casual/pandemia-impulsiona-viagens-internacionais-em-realidade-virtual. *(In Portuguese)*

Lima, L. (2022). *Users can travel first class on the Qatar Airways metaverse*. Available at: https://exame.com/marketing/usuarios-podem-viajar-de-primeira-classe-no-metaverso-da-qatar-airways/. *(In Portuguese)*

Martins, L. (2016). *Augmented reality in hospitality: Potential application in the perspective of 4 and 5 star hotel guests in the Lisbon Region*. Institutional Repository of the Superior School of Hospitality and Tourism of Estoril. Available at: https://comum.rcaap.pt/handle/10400.26/19762. *(In Portuguese)*

Meireles, C. (2020). *Since we can't travel, we take you to the world through virtual reality*. Available at: https://www.metropoles.com/colunas/claudia-meireles/ja-que-nao-podemos-viajar-te-levamos-ao-mundo-atraves-da-realidade-virtual. *(In Portuguese)*

Milheiro, A. (2021). *Stakeholders' perceptions of virtual reality applications in tourism*. Institutional Repository of the Superior School of Hospitality and Tourism of Estoril. Available at: https://repositorio.ul.pt/handle/10451/50714. *(In Portuguese)*

Morais, E., & Cunha, C. (2018). *Information and communication technologies in tourism degrees – The evolution in Portugal*. Available at: https://bibliotecadigital.ipb.pt/bitstream/10198/17930/1/TIC%20Turismo.pdf. *(In Portuguese)*

Neuhofer, B., Buhalis, D., & Ladkin, A. (2014). A typology of technology-enhanced tourism experiences. *International Journal of Tourism Research*, 16(4), 340–350.

Neuhofer, B., Buhalis, D., & Ladkin, A. (2015). Technology as a catalyst of change: Enablers and barriers of the tourist experience and their consequences. In *Information and Communication Technologies in Tourism 2015: Proceedings of the International Conference in Lugano* (pp. 789–802). Switzerland, February 3–6, 2015. Springer International Publishing.

Nguyen, T. T. N. (2020). Business Plan-Travelholic Oy-An Online Travel Agency for Tour Operator in Vietnamese Market.

O'Donnell, A. (2021). *7 Great virtual reality travel experiences*. Available at: https://www.lifewire.com/virtual-reality-tourism-4129394

Rafael, C. (2022). *Virtual tourism and the pandemic: Bibliometric study*. RISTI. Available at: https://www.researchgate.net/profile/Irene-Hernandez-8/publication/359504702_La_experiencia_de_un_caso_de_ABP_en_un_curso_de_requerimientos_de_software/links/6240e2bd8068956f3c5393d2/La-experiencia-de-un-caso-de-ABP-en-un-curso-de-requerimientos-de-software.pdf. *(In Portuguese)*

Sheldon, M. et al. (2001). What is satisfying about satisfying events? Testing 10 candidate psychological needs. *Journal of Personality and Social Psychology*, 80(2), 325–339. Available at: https://doi.org/10.1037/0022-3514.80.2.325

Steampowered. (2022). *The grand canyon vr experience*. Available at: https://store.steampowered.com/app/407710/The_Grand_Canyon_VR_Experience/

Pedro Fernandes da Anunciação, Dorota Kuchta,
Cátia Cristina Ferro Guégués

Organizational Urbanism, Digital Transformation and Smart Cities. The Case of Civil Protection of a Portuguese City

1. Introdution

Smart cities are buzzword of the moment (Franke et al., 2015). Smart Cities represent a significant challenge in Information Systems (IS) applied to the urban context. Smart city expresses a new reality in which information and communication technologies (ICT) are incorporated in cities, contributing to a new digital ecosystem, of urban dimensions, which must be designed, architected, and managed from a systemic perspective (Camboim et al., 2019). Technology, embodied through the so-called smart cities, has been integrated into nearly all aspects of public and private urban life (Calzada et al., 2023). Everything that surrounds us has been becoming smart (Zait, 2017) and cities are now designated as «smart», because they now integrate a technological support and allow to innovate the services provided by public authorities. This infrastructure can be geared towards increasing the efficiency and effectiveness of urban infrastructures, such as water management, air quality control, or the management of municipal solid waste; but also, to innovation in services presented to citizens, improving the quality of life and the sustainability of a common space (Chamoso et al., 2020; Scuotto et al., 2016).

The concept of intelligence makes sense if it is linked not only to organizational efficiency and effectiveness, but especially to multidimensional sustainability (multifunctional and multifaceted context) of the urban system (Anunciação, 2015; Anunciação et al., 2014) (Mundula & Auci, 2013) for the benefit of citizens. Meeting citizens' requirements economically and efficiently is the most important objective of Smart Cities (Cimmino et al., 2014).

In this context, public local government entities have sought on the Internet-of-Things (IoT) a unique opportunity for the improvement of public services, as they now have data/ information on various dimensions of urban reality. However, the possibility of generating knowledge, through technologies, opens new requirements in the field of management of the diversity of factors that integrate urban activities, processes, and resources. In addition, it is emphasized that the introduction of new ICT brings out the complexity and difficulty related to the management and maintenance of a new large technological park.

A smart city should cover all urban dimensions and add in a technological structure the communicational dimension as well as that of services, making it more flexible, efficient, and sustainable using ICT to improve operations in the city for the benefit of its inhabitants (Mohanty, 2016). However, the simple introduction of ICT alone does not allow intelligence. Intelligence depends on the suitability of the actions developed in view of the nature of the problems found. The challenge is not in the adoption and introduction of technologies, but in the utility and availability of digital services and the reliability of technological infrastructure. The digital transformation process can be a trap if public organizations fail to create operational capacity associated with new digital requirements.

In this sense, the problem of smart cities will be a problem of architecture, first, and management, secondly, to the extent that it will require a capacity to intervene from public management in accordance with the opportunity associated with the availability of information on reality. IS/ ICT will provide data/ information in real time and require timely intervention of entities according to the urgency and nature of the problems identified. Reality requires the construction of a new management model that is based on a fast and coherent reading of the urban reality, minimizing problems or inconveniences for citizens. Cities will only be "smart" if those responsible transform data into information, information into knowledge and these support actions and these allow learning. The use of data should serve to improve the lives and safety of those living in cities and this is one of the main objectives of Smart Cities. Thus, advances in big data and IoT have given cities access to unprecedented information, providing an opportunity to define a data analysis strategy that allows the acquisition of insights that enable real-time monitoring of the various urban dimensions by identifying risk areas, forecasting, prevention and planning for the various interventions to be carried out in the context of population security (Warner & Mansker-Young, 2023). Big data and IoT offer unlimited possibilities to strengthen decision-making but systems and decision-makers need to be prepared.

Smart Cities require a new vision, principles, and requirements, according to the characteristics of a new environment that is expected to be intelligent (Hashem et al., 2016). This new environment should include the diversity of areas of intervention of the urban reality, processes, stakeholders, technologies, among others, and should be viewed in a vision and urban organization, to ensure greater capacity intervention and knowledge (Anunciação & Zorrinho, 2006). The scientific study of smart cities is a relevant opportunity in the field of IS management. Improving the intelligibility of the city should correspond to a strategic development plan that integrates technological potential into economic and social activities, identifying the benefits for citizens and for the sustainability of cities.

2. The Role of Civil Protection in Cities

The role of civil protection is aimed at protecting citizens from situations of risk, disasters and natural or environmental weather. It is expected that municipal civil protection services have a reactive and proportionate response capacity to disaster situations. The national civil protection system in Portugal is structured in three major levels: national, regional, and local. At the local level, the decision-making body consists of the mayor, the coordinator of the Municipal Civil Protection Commission, and, in accordance with that Law, the civil protection agents, who are part of the fire departments, the security forces, the armed forces, maritime and aeronautical authorities, national institute of medical emergency and other health services and forest sappers.

Local civil protection intervention areas may vary according to the specificity of the natural characteristics of the geographical area of incidence. In the case study, the risks associated with civil protection affect forest fires, given the location of settlements near forest areas; seismic activity, being located in a seismic zone; flooding, given the location at the mouth of a river; industrial accidents, being one of the largest industrial areas in the country; road accidents, being crossed by the main highways and national roads of Portugal; accidents with transport, for having an important port where several kinds of cargo are moved by the highway and railroad; landslides, having steep slopes and unstable soils; contamination of air and water, resulting from the presence of various industries; underwater landslide, being located in a coastal area where there are cliffs and undersea escarpments that can generate tsunamis; storms and strong winds, being located in an exposed coastal area at risk of storms; among other characteristics.

In this sense, given the diversity of potential areas of intervention should alert and warning systems to the population be prepared and trained for effective transmission of relevant information associated with emergencies. Crisis communication, which involves coordinating the dissemination of clear and accurate information to the population, should be associated with emergency plans and provide the general population with all the information necessary for safe protection against the size and characteristics of the expected or occurred situation.

Given the high number of stakeholders involved in civil protection interventions, there are some traditional problems, such as difficulties in controlling prevention and mitigation actions, poor organization, or disability, the lack or poor support of information systems and procedures for action and coordination between entities and their resources, among other aspects. In this case it can be said that in many situations, in terms of emergency, coordination is not the solution, it is the problem. Information is needed to generate knowledge, and this is obtained through learning.

3. Objectives and Methodology

The objective of this study was to analyze and evaluate some of the central elements to the digital transformation contextualized in the context of civil protection of a large Portuguese city. In this sense, the study was developed in two phases. The first corresponding to a survey and identification (As-Is) of the current coverage of IS in support of civil protection. And the second in identifying the necessary evolution (To-Be) for a better intervention in a smart city context, by identifying the main developments that should be considered in the near future.

A Focus working group was defined in which the following persons participated: elements of civil protection, city council, security forces and fire brigade, on behalf of the most requested stakeholders in situations involving civil protection. The brainstorming technique was adopted for reflection and greater interaction considering the various areas of responsibility and intervention of each of the stakeholders' representatives with the objective of the benefits of a sharing of specialized knowledge regarding resolution of potential situations in which they may be called to participate. Regarding the first stage, the assessment of As-Is focused on the contextualization of digital transformation from two macro-dimensions of digital transformation in civil protection, namely, identification, area of intervention and relationship between stakeholders and the characterization of existing IS and levels of integration. Subsequently, the challenges associated with digital transformation were identified, such as the identification of potential intervention areas, associated projects, availability of resources, among others.

The choice of these Focus group technique and brainstorming resulted from the fact of seeking to maximize with the individual participation of each specialist in a collective environment of sharing the generation of synergies at the level of knowledge generation and learning that facilitate and promote a multidisciplinary and transversal approach to the complexity of problems and to the search for the best solutions given the potential occurrences that may be registered and that can be developed in the context of regional civil protection.

Several meetings were always held in order to achieve, for the scenarios presented, a collective and consensual solution that, unanimously, is considered as the best from the perspective of all participants.

4. Analysis of the Results

Regarding the intervention of stakeholders and relationship with the local authority of civil protection, it was found that there is a knowledge of the field of intervention and responsibility of each stakeholder, which facilitates articulation regarding the organization of responsiveness to the specificity of each occurrence. Calls for interventions are made by the local civil protection authority. However, these are only issued after knowledge of the occurrences, showing a delay between the understanding of the occurrence and the respective evaluation and the summoning of the required stakeholders. Considering that the number of stakeholders that can potentially be involved in the responses to occurrences can be high, there is a difficulty in controlling prevention and mitigation actions, a poor organization or inability of the means and resources necessary to protect the population, a lack or weak IS support, weaknesses in the procedures of action and coordination between entities and their resources, significant gaps between the time of occurrence and response time, among other aspects.

In any case, it is also evident the existence of a weekly practice of briefings, carried out through online platforms with the aim of sharing information and looking for solutions for situations that need quick resolution or monitoring. There is thus a culture of reactivity in which all entities are involved.

Regarding the IS, it was found the absence of an IS supported by ICT dedicated to the treatment of occurrences, sufficiently timely and comprehensive for a connection between all the potentials involved in the civil protection of the population. The IS of the local civil protection authority consists essentially of the production of several reports, on paper, where all the characterizing elements of the various occurrences and respective actors and participations are described. This is an internal register of the local civil protection authority carried out after the event, which identifies and characterizes them, as regards, for example, the identification and description of the event, the actions taken, resources and means used and stakeholder participation. The lack of IS supported by ICT limits the ability to react to the seriousness of situations, the allocation and management of resources, the response to the urgency of relief, and, consequently, the sharing of information between stakeholders. In addition, as there is no place for automated data processing, there is a limitation to the development of knowledge and the appreciation of learning. Furthermore, these reports, stored in physical folders, are not available to other stakeholders. Access to reports by other stakeholders is subject to the authorization of the local civil protection authority.

Given the current logic of operation, it is common agreement the imperative need for a digital transformation that contemplates the development of an IS/ ICT that facilitates the identification of the complexity and nature of the occurrence, articulation of response capacities and timely warning to the population. This IS should integrate all stakeholders that make up the civil protection to facilitate the clarification of the severity of occurrences and ensure an adequate reaction to the necessary mitigation of the effects on the population, the economy and society.

The local civil protection authority is far from benefiting from the potential of new technologies, such as the Internet-of-Things, Artificial Intelligence or Analytics. The weaknesses or absence of IS/ ICT also contributes to the difficulties of articulation of the means and an integrated response among stakeholders. The timing of the interventions is a critical success factor for the response and performance of the participants.

With regard to the digital transformation advocated, focus group identified, in a future perspective, some areas of intervention, specifically in terms of urban security, water management, urban mobility, waste management, smart buildings, smart energy networks, Intelligent parking, integrated supply systems, intelligent mobility, among others. In this context, there are already some projects in perspective, namely:

- IoT solutions in the scope of environmental monitoring, through sensors installed in strategic locations for the collection of real-time data on air quality, temperature, and other weather conditions.
- environmental risk monitoring sensors, floods, landslides, in infrastructures such as bridges and buildings to analyze stability, among others.
- early warning systems, to notify the population about emergencies.
- geographical information systems (GIS), for mapping and analysis of spatial data, including risk and vulnerability data.
- fire-fighting drones, whose combination with a telecommunications tower infrastructure that allows real-time mobile connectivity, will enable the activation of UAV (Unmanned Aerial Vehicle) (Mohammed et al., 2014), capable of detecting a possible occurrence, for example, of fire within a radius of 15 kilometers.

Focus group also mentioned the desire to evolve to even more innovative solutions, which allow to increase the ability to anticipate and react to certain situations that require intervention. In this sense, three areas of digital transformation were highlighted:

- detection, using Artificial Intelligence (AI) and with network support of urban video surveillance cameras and sensors located in public transport, unusual movements of people, alerting to a potential emergency.
- monitoring of social networks to, using AI, interpret and detect expressions associated with hate speech, correlating these publications with the determination of an approximate geographical location.
- crisis management, support decision-making in emergency situations in public events.

However, when faced with the requirement of resources, tools, knowledge and capabilities to enable the recommended digital transformations, the following limitations were highlighted: lack of autonomy to make strategic investments; lack of autonomy in accessing investment decisions; lack of skills and technical skills associated with new technologies, such as AI, cybersecurity or software development; lack of IS/ ICT support for the current activity developed; lack of technical skills in the management of complex and integrated projects, to ensure synchrony in the intervention; and, limitations in management.

5. Conclusions

Prevention is always the best way to avoid disasters. Therefore, it is important that local authorities invest in measures and support systems aimed at prevention, communication and immediate information, in order to strengthen coordination between stakeholders. The alignment of a well-structured civil protection system within a frame of reference for a Smart Cities has significant protection advantages. Through an architectural and urban framework associated with IS/ ICT it will be possible to reduce disaster risks and improve the security of the population, allowing cities to respond quickly and effectively in emergencies, minimizing the damage caused, becoming more resilient. Investing in prevention and a civil protection system can reduce the costs of disaster damage and with the recovery of affected areas increases the confidence of the population in the ability of local authorities to protect it in emergency situations.

However, it should be noted that, conceptually, smart cities are not limited only to the introduction of ICT in the various urban areas. The creation of a new digital system to support urban management presupposes the development of a technically and economically well-structured project, as well as its support in a strategic development framework that covers the various areas of urban activity.

Although the approach can be flexible and agile, it is essential to ensure an overview for integration and interoperability between the various partners and information and operational systems. Digital transformation must be viewed and developed as a broad ecosystem, heterogenous and hybrid, however, cohesive and aligned. This requires technical and management knowledge sufficiently secure to bring «to completion» projects and investments for the development of a smart city.

The urban logic applied to the organizational domain must ensure responsible and transparent communication and involvement, with the aim of aligning expectations, maintaining support and ensuring the results that are intended to be achieved, in a strategic alignment between the parties and accompanied by a continuous effort of integration and governance.

To make a city "smart" it is necessary to formulate a long-term strategic plan. This challenge must presuppose a broad vision, policies and concrete objectives for the future of the city, where governance must take a central role in the development of systems to support its management.

5.1. Limitations and Future Work

The case study shows the complexity of the theme of smart Cities. Although it was developed based on the optics of civil protection, it would be interesting in the future to proceed to a deepening of the same. Some aspects that support this conviction relate to the relevance, for example, of being able to involve, in the Focus group, all stakeholders associated with the studied reality. Only with everyone's involvement will it be possible for each one to visualize the relevance of their performance in an urban intelligence context.

On the other hand, it would also be useful to frame the challenges of digital transformation in civil protection in a broader context of applicability of the concept of smart city to the city itself studied. It is important to identify the existence of possible strategies related to the digital transformation of the associated city and how they include the domain of civil protection in this transformation.

Another limitation is related to political power. This main stakeholder did not participate in the Focus group. Digital transformation decisions and technological investments in the public domain depend directly on public budgets and responsible political institutions.

It would also be important to involve citizens and analyze their receptiveness to the changes recommended, since resistance to change can be an obstacle to the modernization process.

Acknowledgments

The authors would like to thank the Setúbal Polytechnic University (Portugal) for the support given to the publication of this research work.

References

Anunciação, P. F. (2015). Organizational change through information systems: Metavision-project management model in internet banking. In *Handbook of research on effective project management through the integration of knowledge and innovation*, Chapter 23 (pp. 450–465).

Anunciação, P. F., & Zorrinho, C. (2006). *Organizational Urbanism – How to manage technological shock*. Lisboa: Sílabo Publishing *(In Portuguese)*

Anunciação, P. F., Esteves, F. J. M., & Santos, J. R. (2014). Some information systems requirements in view of organizational sustainability in an information society. *Information Resource Management Journal*, 27(1), 21–35.

Calzada, I., Pérez-Batlle, M., & Batlle-Montserrat, J. (2023). People-centered smart cities: An exploratory action research on the cities' coalition for digital rights. *Journal of Urban Affairs*, 45(9), 1537–1562.

Camboim, G. F., Zawislak, P. A., & Pufal, N. A. (2019). Driving elements to make cities smarter: Evidences from European projects. *Technological Forecasting & Social Change*, 142, 154–167.

Chamoso, P., González-Briones, A., De La Prieta, F., Venyagamoorthy, G. K., & Corchado, J. M. (2020). Smart city as a distributed platform: Toward a system for citizen-oriented management. *Computer Communications*, 152, 323–332. https://doi.org/10.1016/j.comcom.2020.01.059

Cimmino, A., Pecorella, T., Fantacci, R., Granelli, F., Rahman, T. F., Sacchi, C., & Harsh, P. (2014). The role of small cell technology in future smart city applications. *Transactions on Emerging Telecommunications Technologies*, 25(1), 11–20.

Franke, T., Lukowicz, P., & Blanke, U. (2015). Smart crowds in smart cities: Real life, city scale deployments of a smartphone based participatory crowd management platform. *Journal of Internet Services and Applications*, 6, 1–19.

Hashem, I. A. T., Chang, V., Anuar, N. B., Adewole, K., & Yaqoob, I. (2016). The role of big data in smart city. *International Journal of Information Management; Kidlington*, 36(5), October, 748.

Mohammed, F., Idries, A., Mohamed, N., Al-Jaroodi, J., & Jawhar, I. (2014, May). UAVs for smart cities: Opportunities and challenges. In *2014 International Conference On Unmanned Aircraft Systems* (ICUAS) (pp. 267–273). IEEE.

Mohanty, S. P. (2016). Everything you wanted to know about smart cities. *IEEE Consumer Electronics Magazine*, Piscataway, 5(3).

Mundula, L., & Auci, S. (2013). *Smart cities and a stochastic frontier analysis: A comparison among European Cities, IDEAS Working Paper Series from RePEc*. St. Louis, 2013.

Scuotto, V., Ferraris, A., & Bresciani, S. (2016). Internet of things: Applications and challenges in smart cities: A case study of IBM smart city projects. *Business Process Management Journal*, Bradford, 22(2), 357–362.

Warner, M., & Mansker-Young, S. (2023). *Thinking about becoming a smart city? 10 benefits of smart cities*. plante moran, July 14, Available at: https://www.plantemoran.com/explore-our-thinking/insight/2018/04/thinking-about-becoming-a-smart-city-10-benefits-of-smart-cities

Zait, A. (2017). Exploring the role of civilization competences for smart citie's development. *Transforming Government: People, Process and Policy*, Bradford, 11(3), 377–392.

Francisco Joaquim Madeira Esteves, Pedro Fernandes da Anunciação, Hélder Miguel da Graça Alexandre

Roadmap for Enterprise Architecture. The Cornerstone for the Evolution of Information Systems

1. Introduction

Any of the expressions that characterize the current society, «Information Society», «Knowledge Society», «Network Society», among others, refer the centrality and complexity of a new economic and social phenomenon. «Smart Cities», «Artificial Intelligence», Internet-of-Things, among others, are expressions of a new economic and business reality that challenges information systems (IS) architecture and management and marks a new paradigm for the consumers and companies' dynamics (Lin & Macvittie, 2022). All these expressions show architecture as the greater enabler of connectivity, relational interaction, functional integration, among others. Today`s business must be able to flexible and quickly adapt to market needs, but even minor changes to processes can involve rework in multiple Information Technology (IT) systems that were originally designed as application silos (Serrano et al., 2014).

Architecture can be defined as the conceptual structure and functional behavior, distinguishing the organization of data flows and controls, logical design, and physical implementation (Amdahl et al., 1964) or a field of studies focused on solving the basic problems of accessing, and using, the vast amounts of information available today (Resmini & Rosati, 2012). In today's increasingly volatile environments, evolvability is quickly becoming the most desirable characteristic of information systems. However, current IS still struggled to provide these high levels of evolvability (Mannaert et al., 2012).

If the current paradigm of society and economy lies in information and knowledge, as central assets to its operation, and in information systemas and information and communication technologies (IS/ ICT) as systems to support the development of economic and management activities, it is important that managers assume the relevance of the architecture of production systems to ensure the quality requirements of digital assets (Esteves & Anunciação, 2021). In this context, business architecture is a critical success factor for the competitiveness of economic organizations. The Enterprise Architecture (EA) refers to a comprehensive description of all the key elements and relationships that make up an organization (Kang et al., 2010). An EA relates organizational mission, goals, and objectives to work processes and to the technical or IT infrastructure required to execute them (Urbaczewski & Mrdalj, 2006) allowing a deep understanding of computer systems as an essential element of success of computer systems (Englander & Wong, 2021). EA can potentially align organization's business processes, information, information systems and technology towards a common goal, and supply the information required within this journey (Niemi & Pekkola, 2017).

EA management has become increasingly recognized as a crucial part of both business and IT management (Simon et al., 2013). Architecture should be seen as the «cornerstone» of IS/ICT, because allows companies to proactively assess and adjust policies and systems to achieve target business goals that monetize relevant business disruptions (Perez-Castillo et al., 2019). Considering that there are no economic organizations without management, management without information or information without SI, three important aspects in the architectural field should be highlighted as management paradigms:

- the conceptual domain, which comprises the coherence and harmony of concepts, instruments and the various existing dimensions (functional, informational and technological).
- the methodological field, which stresses the importance of framing architecture as an organizational project, the need to support top management and respect for existing specificities (rules and standards).
- the instrumental field, which emphasizes the importance of adopting and using a framework or a model for framing, developing, and managing IS/ICT.

Architecture should not be considered as an option in the field of IS/ICT. It is the architecture that depends on the efficiency and effectiveness of IS (adequacy to needs) and organizational performance (value and competitiveness). It is through architecture that the sustainability of IS, and business is expected, regarding its evolution, flexibility, continuity, security, and sustainability. The future will necessarily continue to pass through a relational logic, based on cooperation and integration of activities, information, and systems, among the various economic agents (logic of value creation in network).

It is important to adopt an architectural dimension for IS but not always the most recognized architecture references, frameworks or roadmaps are easily understood or adopted, requiring a few years of experience for proper use. Understanding methodologies' strengths and weaknesses play significant role in selecting appropriate methodology for each EA project (Rouhani et al., 2013).

2. Pragmatism of IS Architecture

Companies are open and interactive systems, in which process networks are constantly crossed articulated in horizontal (value chains and processes) and vertical (command/execution and control chains). The underlying dynamics presupposes interaction with various stakeholders and articulation at different levels of management, and the architecture of the various functional components, information and technology ensure a consistent functioning and reach of shared collective competitive advantages (Zieman, 2022).

This growing interconnection and integration of activities and their support systems (organizational, informational, technological, logistical, etc.) should be stronger the greater the value of the competitive advantages that are intended to achieve. In this sense, it is important that the depth of the relationships established and the degree of dependence of economic agents is based on a model or architectural matrix, which facilitates the framing of activities, the processing of information, generation of knowledge and communication between stakeholders, providing a similar (collective) reading of economic challenges.

It is in this sense that managers should develop a knowledge and a mastery of business, information, and technological systems, and these must be supported by an architectural vision that constitutes a structural and structuring element of the solutions adopted in the different areas mentioned. It is important that managers know how to architect the elements related to the recommended solutions and, above all, visualize the coherence of the articulation and integration between the different systems and integral elements. Explaining IS architecture (ISA) presupposes the ability to explain the interrelationships between business processes, application systems, technological infrastructures, as well as the identification of various stakeholders. This explanation must be supported by instruments (models, frameworks, policies, etc.) that facilitate the analysis and understanding of the IS, particularly regarding the following aspects:

- planning processes, which develop and harmonize strategic "roadmaps" across business domains and information systems and technologies.
- governance processes, which monitor adherence to an information systems and technologies strategy, which allow understanding.
- innovation processes, which provide a manageable environment for the introduction of new technologies that enable the identification of new business capabilities.

The objectives for the adoption of an architectural vision should aim, among other aspects, the development of a clear function for EA aligned with the strategic objectives of the business; the creation of a structure of government, supervision, control and accountability; compliance with principles and responsibilities relating to information governance and reference architectures; improving agility and flexibility in responding to market changes; and a common language between business and IT.

Generally, the relevance of ISA has been underestimated by managers and IS managers. In many cases, the urgency and pressure placed on the operability of technological technologies and systems, the preconceived technological proposals, the attractiveness of technological innovation or even the lack of sensitivity of top managers to these matters have caused this strand to be relegated to a secondary plan or even devalued. Not being an area of easy understanding, due to the multidisciplinary of domains it aggregates, the international reference architecture models are dense and require periods of time and significant experience for safe use by IS professionals. This is a subject that, at the level of education of students who are part of Information Systems Management courses, traditionally has a significant resistance, since it requires a systemic look from those who develop architecture activities and a significant knowledge of the various architectural levels that must integrate a roadmap for the development of associated projects.

Participating in architectural projects requires a rigorous and coherent line of thought in the field of management, to facilitate the reasoning and pragmatism of solutions within the IS/ICT. A company cannot be considered a patchwork of departments, directions, products, or workers. For the same reason, an IS should not constitute an archipelago of information, computer systems or even technologies. Their understanding necessarily involves the identification of the set of technological components, but also the principles, rules, procedures, techniques, activities, and processes that support the business and the organization. The specificity of the organizational system must dictate the singularity of the respective IS, and this singularity must be evident through the following aspects: architecture only makes sense if there is, at its base, a systemic perspective; the absence of an architectural perspective makes it difficult to read and understand the system; it should not be the system that conditions the architecture but the architecture that imposes itself on the system; there is no system without architecture and there is no architecture without system; and, it is in the system that one must find the reason for being and the purpose of it and it is in the architecture that one must find the respective justification.

In architecture, managers should find a conceptual framework to support the design and structuring of the IS, considering all stakeholders; an itinerary for the full use and exploitation of IS capabilities, stimulating their performance;

a reference for the aggregation of new elements, facilitating their management; and an instrument for the development, evaluation, and control of the IS. The better the architectural specification, the better the organizational flexibility, the easier it will be to understand its structure and the easier it will be to adapt to the evolving needs of the market and the constraints of competitiveness.

Architecture shows benefits at various levels. At the business level through the understanding of the value chain, the integration of processes and activities, the support to economic and organizational dynamics, as well as the perception of the role of each of the stakeholders; the identification of the best organizational structure to support economic activities, in the respective levels of responsibility and mode of operation; the profitability of organizational resources allocated to the activities developed; identifying the levels of efficiency, effectiveness and competitiveness required; identifying the relationships to be established between the various partners/stakeholders; identification of information dynamics between agents; among other aspects.

Organizations can use enterprise architecture frameworks to manage system complexity and align business and IT resources (Shah & El Kourdi, 2007). Although the importance of ISA in companies is understood, through the benefits generated, it is difficult to understand the complexity of its purpose and the reality of its operation. It is also rare to have the visibility of its "modus operandi" and/or its implementation in everyday life. However, we can have as drivers of benefits speed (in intervention on IS/ICT), reliability (of the operation of IS/ICT), strategy (of future development), interoperability (between systems), simplification (of their structure), cost reduction (in operation), among others.

The arguments presented for the relevance of architecture can also be reinforced when management is confronted with technological innovation. Since innovation is one of the main axes of evolution of society, it is responsible for forcing management to consider the need for architectural references, as a way to minimize the complexity of the administration of the new capabilities required by the systems. With the evolution of organizations and technology, IS has become increasingly complex and difficult to manage.

3. Objectives and Methodology

A detailed conceptual framework is still lacking (Stelzer, 2010). Given the reality of the lack of sensitivity and difficulty of IS professionals in economic organizations and students of IS management courses in universities, regarding the framework of the subjects associated with IS, emerged among some university professors of IS the opportunity to identify and propose a roadmap, simpler than international references, to explain the relevance and approach of architecture at the IS level.

Thus, the objectives of the study aimed to identify the set of central dimensions to the ISA to facilitate the assumption of the relevance of this theme, on the one hand, and the respective contextualization within the governance and management of IS, on the other. As mentioned earlier, architecture is a subject of difficult adherence in the training of future IS managers to the extent that the frameworks/ models internationally used usually generate some resistance to the ease in their adoption requires a considerable period for a total understanding and handling. This finding constituted the trigger for the identification of some central phases in the development of ISA, and it is expected in the future to be able to build a model or models to support their learning.

To this end, a set of seven ISA specialists, university professors and professionals, were invited with the aim of, through brainstorming sessions, identifying the central phases for an adequate understanding and use of this dimension at the IS level. This Focus group professionals with more than 10 years of experience in the field. The proposal presented below results from several interactions that were carried out both with students and with companies in which technical work of ISA was developed.

4. Roadmap Proposal for IS Architecture

Management must find in the architecture a reference framework and through a roadmap a roadmap that facilitates the identification of information (raw material), technologies (means of production) and users (consumers), as well as the dynamics associated with the treatment, storage and sharing of information and its adaptation to organizational needs. Figure 1 proposes a roadmap consisting of five stages.

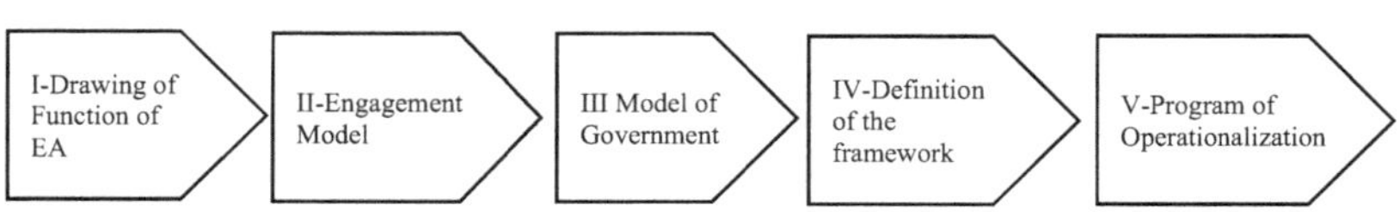

Figure 1. IS architecture roadmap

For the first stage, it should be considered:

I. Drawing of the EA function.
   a. Objectives
      Establish the framework and contribution of Business Architecture to the achievement of the strategic objectives of the Company, by defining its foundations and principles of action.
   b. Activities:
      i. Analysis, evaluation and validation of the current situation (As-Is) in terms of strategic objectives, current organic structure, existing documentation of processes and industry standards and regulation of the activity supported in sessions of identification and collection of information (face-to-face / remote / documentation).
      ii. Conducting interviews with different organizational units (Chief Information Officer, Business Engagement & Portfolio, Delivery & Solutions, Cybersecurity, and IT Services), to assess the current situation of the organization.
      iii. Consolidation of information and identification of guiding principles of the company including preparation of SWOT analysis, the design of the Stakeholder map and compliance requirements.
      iv. Definition of the Business Architecture Vision and Mission proposal with its framework in the organization structure.
      v. Establishment of the principles of Business Architecture in terms of alignment with business and technological drivers and regulatory and market principles.
      vi. Definition of Business Architecture operational indicators based on their applicability and contribution to IT and business performance.
      vii. vii. Presentation and approval of the document with the foundations for Enterprise Architecture – Enterprise Architecture Charter.
   c. Deliverables:
      i. Enterprise Architecture Charter comprising:
         1. Vision.
         2. Mission.
         3. Principles.
         4. Stakeholders.
         5. Objectives and indicators.

II. Engagement model
  a. Objectives
     Define an engagement model that integrates existing processes and is based on the principles of obtaining benefits for the business, creating dynamic models and clarity in assigning functions and responsibilities.
  b. Activities:
     i. Analysis of the IT operating model and interaction with the business.
     ii. Identification of control points for Enterprise Architecture in the existing operational model for existing processes, with the identification of their role and responsibility (RACI – Responsible, Accountable, Consulted, Informed) at the level of:
        a. Plan (Strategic Guidance, Planning, Design, Portfolio Management).
        b. Build (Requirements, Solution Design, Development, Quality).
        c. Deliver (Production, Compliance, Security); – Run (Management of Environments, Operation).
     iii. Presentation and approval of the document with the analysis of the impact of Business Architecture on existing processes and identification of gaps – Engagement Model.
  c. Deliverables:
     i. Engagement model
        1. Proposal for revision of existing procedures.
        2. Recommendations for new processes.
        3. Action plan.

III. Governance model
  a. Objectives
     Define the set of activities that the organization must perform to ensure that decisions are made and that responsibility is strengthened during the execution of activities that support the function of Enterprise Architecture.
  b. Activities
     i. Evaluation of the organizational model with typology definition: Distributed vs Federated vs Centralized.
     ii. Definition of proposed bodies to support the Enterprise Architecture, including the definition of functions and responsibilities and domains of architecture.
     iii. Design of the maintenance processes of Enterprise Architecture
        1. Design of controls for monitoring the government components of the Enterprise Architecture.

        2. Process design that ensures the introduction, implementation, evolution or discontinuation of reference architectures/solutions in the organization.
        3. Definition of a model for assessing compliance with architectural, regulatory and market principles.
    iv. Elaboration of the Business Architecture Policy – definition of scope, objective and audience, definition of custody of information and definition of decision criteria on new solutions/ projects.
    v. Reference architectures – definition of the template for architecture documentation and associated map identifier proposal.
    vi. Presentation and approval of the proposal of the document with the model of government and architecture policy.

c. Deliverables
    i. Government Model of Business Architecture
        1. Architectural domains.
        2. Committees.
        3. Roles and responsibilities.
        4. Processes.
    ii. Corporate Architecture Governance Model
        1. Policy of Enterprise Architecture.
        2. Document Template for Reference Architecture.
        3. Map of Reference Architectures (proposal).

IV. Definition of the Enterprise Architecture Framework

a. Objectives

Definition of the Enterprise Architecture implementation framework considering its organizational context. The goal will be the materialization of a comprehensive and consistent structure to develop, manage and maintain the Enterprise Architecture.

b. Activities
    i. Definition of the Architecture work products comprising the reference architecture model, the solution proposal evaluation model, and the reference architecture evolutionary roadmap model.
    ii. Identification of the basic and optional requirements for the selection of the support tool: definition of profiles and responsibilities and requirements for modeling, integration, and visualization.
    iii. Identification of artifacts (information assets) to be mapped in the metamodel.
        1. Definition of reference architecture entities by architectural domain.

2. Elaboration of the modeling guide.
3. Construction of a reference library.

iv. Identification of existing information sources for Enterprise Architecture and definition of the integration process (ETL) of entities.
v. Structuring indicators and views by architectural domain based on the defined metamodel.
vi. Presentation and approval of framework work products.

c. Deliverables
i. Templates of products of work.
ii. List of requirements for Enterprise Architecture support tool selection.
iii. Metamodel specification.
iv. Guide for modelling.
v. Map of integrations of existing information sources and data loading.
vi. List of views and indicators (baseline).

V. Operationalization Program
a. Objectives
Define the communication process of Business Architecture with the organization, identifying model and content. Structuring a framework implementation plan and resource capacity building.
b. Activities
i. Definition of the operationalization program
1. Roadmap for selection and implementation of the Enterprise Architecture support tool.
2. Government Implementation Plan of Enterprise Architecture.
3. Information modelling and integration plan.
4. Business Architecture instantiation plan in existing processes.
5. Implementation plan of views and indicators.

ii. Definition of the change management plan – model of communication with stakeholders, training and training, and communication and dissemination.

c. Deliverables
i. Operational program (supported on schedule).
ii. Change management plan.

5. Conclusions

The existence of a reference architecture for IS becomes increasingly important as well as the identification of a roadmap for its implementation. In this sense, it is important to assume that a good architectural choice is a necessary condition for organizational sustainability, which should be simple and understandable (easy to express and understand by the various actors, identifying the critical elements of the system, making simple what is complex); to provide an organizational vision (to map the modularity of the business and support systems, which must correspond not to a sum of elements but rather to a systemic set); and to be flexible (based on their design the possibility of evolution).

Given the complexity of the dimensions associated with EA, such as the level of business, processes, information, software and infrastructure, the adoption of a roadmap facilitates the definition of a path for the development and implementation of an architectural framework. The EA and ISA should identify and categorize the components of a company to better understand and manage the relationships between them to achieve specific results. The role of architecture corresponds to the viability of the configuration or reconfiguration of organizational assets according to the current economic and technological paradigms without "destroying".

Acknowledgments

The authors would like to thank the Setúbal Polytechnic University (Portugal) for the support given to the publication of this research work.

References

Amdahl, G. M., Blaauw, G. A., & Brooks, F. P. (1964). Architecture of the IBM system/360. *IBM Journal for Research and Development*, 8(2). (Reprinted in IBM Journal for Research and Development, 44(1/2), 2000).

Englander, I., & Wong, W. (2021). *The architecture of computer hardware, systems software, and networking: An information technology approach*. John Wiley & Sons.

Esteves, F. J. M. & Anunciação, P. F. (2021). Architecture – Essential dimension in information systems. *Information systems – Paradigms and solutions for management* (pp. 9–36). Plátano Publishing *(In Portuguese)*.

Kang, D., Lee, J., Choi, S., & Kim, K. (2010). An ontology-based enterprise architecture. *Expert Systems with Applications*, 37(2), 1456–1464.

Lin, G., & Macvittie, L. (2022). *Enterprise architecture for digital business – Transforming IT* (1st ed.). O'Reilly.

Mannaert, H., Verelst, J., & Ven, K. (2012). Towards evolvable software architectures based on systems theoretic stability. *Software: Practice and Experience*, 42(1), 89–116.

Niemi, E., & Pekkola, S. (2017). Using enterprise architecture artefacts in an organisation. *Enterprise Information Systems*, 11(3), 313–338.

Perez-Castillo, R., Ruiz, F., Piattini, M., & Ebert, C. (2019). Enterprise architecture. *IEEE Software*, 36(4), 12–19.

Resmini, A., & Rosati, L. (2012). A brief history of information architecture. *Journal of Information Architecture*, 3(2), 33–45.

Rouhani, B. D., Mahrin, M. N., Nikpay, F., & Nikfard, P. (2013). A comparison enterprise architecture implementation methodologies. In *2013 International Conference on Informatics And Creative Multimedia*, September (1–6). IEEE.

Serrano, N., Hernantes, J., & Gallardo, G. (2014). Service-oriented architecture and legacy systems. *IEEE Software*, 31(5), 15–19.

Shah, H., & El Kourdi, M. (2007). Frameworks for enterprise architecture. *It Professional*, 9(5), 36–41.

Simon, D., Fischbach, K., & Schoder, D. (2013). An exploration of enterprise architecture research. *Communications of the Association for Information Systems*, 32(1), 1.

Stelzer, D. (2010). *Enterprise architecture principles: Literature review and research directions.* In Service-Oriented Computing. ICSOC/ServiceWave 2009 Workshops: International Workshops, ICSOC/ServiceWave 2009, Stockholm, Sweden, November 23–27, 2009, Revised Selected Papers 2 (12–21). Springer Berlin Heidelberg.

Urbaczewski, L., & Mrdalj, S. (2006). A comparison of enterprise architecture frameworks. *Issues in Information Systems*, 7(2), 18–23.

Ziemann, J. (2022). *Fundamentals of enterprise architecture management.* Springer.

Lucia Zbihlejová

Self-Assessment of Bossing by Business Managers in Terms of Gender

1. Introduction

Managers are primarily business-minded and acting individuals with responsibility to the company as well as its employees. The decisive factor is therefore the quality of their personality as an active initiator and creator of progressive changes leading to a comprehensive quality of the organization. The aim of their work is employees, their incentive to work, influencing and guiding them in their performance, control, evaluation, remuneration and management of their professional career (Birknerová, 2009). A manager must provide subordinates with the necessary information, solve interpersonal relationships, work problems, communicate with people, know how to lead their subordinates and effectively motivate them. DiKamp (2000) presents the qualities of an effective manager who should be a leader, a role model for others, knowing oneself, learning permanently, enjoying change, having a vision, having a high value of ethics and values, communicating correctly, thinking positively, being excited, and so on. Slobodová and Šulík (2007) pay attention to the issue of selection of managers according to their abilities. They state that the main key to the success of any organization is to find and obtain the highest quality for highly specialized and key management positions. Properly filling these positions is an art that requires special procedures, skills and experience. It is effective to identify and detect, assess and evaluate them, as well as compare them with other personalities in terms of predictions for the future.

In this context, principles that the business manager cannot tolerate should be set. Examples include abuse of power or position, disrespect, wounds below the waist, bullying, blaming, or non-compliance with standards. These principles need to be adhered to not only by the subordinates or the working groups and teams but also by the managers themselves.

Rosener (1990) found out that men tend to use force that comes from formal authority and their status within the organization more often than women. Nielsen and Huse (2010) add that the leadership styles vary between the genders in accordance with the particular tasks and situations. Yukl (2002) states that there is no gender difference in the efficiency of managers, but there are gender differences in certain forms of their behavior. Combining the abovementioned, the proposed paper deals with an assumption that there are statistically significant gender differences in the self-assessment of bossing factors between business managers. Its main objective is, therefore, to contribute theoretically and methodologically to solving issues of self-assessment of bossing in the work of business managers (partial findings presented previously by Zbihlejova, & Birknerova, 2022).

2. Literature Review

Hirigoyen (2000) introduces workplace bullying as a phenomenon which dates back to the very beginnings of work as such but it was only in the late 20th century when it started becoming a major cause of tension increase, labor productivity reductions, and work absence caused by mental disorders naturally generated by it. Bullying can affect anyone anywhere but, in some industries, where it has the most suitable conditions to develop, its occurrence is more frequent.

In accordance with Yaman (2009), Senol et al. (2015) and others, *mobbing* is a *horizontal* form of workplace bullying which occurs between two or more people working on the same position within the hierarchy of an organization from the lowest working positions to the top management (i.e. just as a production worker can mob another production worker, a top manager can mob another top manager). When the initiator of aggression is a senior executive, this kind of bullying is called *bossing*. It is a type of *vertical* abuse directed from a higher-level position to a lower-level position within the organizational hierarchy (i.e. supervisor/manager can use bossing on the subordinates, or a top manager can use it to abuse a lower-level type of a manager). Arnejčič (2016) also reports that bossing is a form of "vertical wall" mobbing, occurring when a person tries to denigrate his or her subordinate.

In every field, besides mobbing, one can find a boss who resorts to bullying subordinates. Abusive supervision or bossing is a very specific mode of bullying in the workplace, i.e. mobbing and persecution by the boss, where the psychological coercion is initiated by the superior (Novák, 2004). Bossing is a specific form of mobbing where the aggressor is the manager or executive. Attacks are targeted at their subordinates in the form of pressure to enforce their obedience, respect and adaptation, possibly enforcing the "voluntary" resignation of a subordinate from the workplace (Topa & Moriano, 2013).

Russo and Popović (2016) also present bossing as a phenomenon occurring frequently in the workplace, where one or more supervisors apply ongoing aggression on a selected subordinate or group of subordinates. Dabu and

Drăghici (2013) present an overview of bullying practices in business organizations and its consequences on human health.

Bossing is an apparent cause of the decrease in the performance of employees and therefore performance of an organization, particularly in terms of its sustainability. However, Lu (2013) argues that bossing may quite contrarily inspire job passion among employees and thus improve the overall performance of an organization. In this context it is therefore crucial to distinguish between:

bossing = abusive supervision	bossing = requiring consistent performance of duties
performance decrease	*performance increase*

Here it should be pointed out that bossing is not aimed primarily at the performance increase or decrease; it is a form of satisfying one's psyche by means of bullying another person, i.e. creating the feeling of power, or it is a method used to get rid of an undesired employee.

Salin (2001) carried out a cross-sectional survey study among Finnish professionals with a university degree in business studies to analyze the prevalence and forms of workplace bullying among business professionals on managerial or expert positions. According to the results of her research, the respondents who had classified themselves as bullied also reported higher exposure rates to almost all the negative acts included.

Valentine and Fleischman (2017) conducted research on the sample of sales and business employees, where they studied workplace bullying and recorded positive links to Machiavellianism and negative links to job satisfaction. The authors state that the research on bullying in the US is in its infancy, and that their findings and theoretical implications suggest that "HR professionals and other business leaders need to address bullying in a manner that promotes decreased Machiavellianism and increased job satisfaction among employees, ultimately enhancing their ethical sensitivity" (Valentine & Fleischman, 2017, p. 302).

Ambrose and Ganegoda (2020) have recently examined how abusive behaviors of supervisors are perceived by their managers as well as their subordinates and found out that in the manager–supervisor–subordinate triads, there are differences between managers' and subordinates' view of abusive supervision, i.e. bossing.

The above research studies have inspired us to move the topic of bossing to the level of gender specifics, which is the essence of the next, research part of the chapter.

3. Materials and Methods

In order to find out whether there are statistically significant gender differences in the self-assessment of bossing factors between business managers, 631 business managers were addressed, of which 367 (58.2 %) were women and 264 (41.8 %) were men aged between 25 and 68 years (M = 33.91 years, SD = 9.355). 108 (17.1 %) of the approached business managers were from the top management, 161 (25.5 %) of business managers were from the middle management, and 362 (57.4 %) of business managers were first-level managers.

For the purposes of this study, we used the following research methodologies:

1. *BOSS methodology* (Birknerová et al., 2021)

The BOSS methodology is aimed at the issue of assessing downward workplace bullying, i.e. bossing on the basis of a psychometric approach. The BOSS methodology contains 17 items describing various forms of workplace bossing. The role of the respondents is to assess each item on a 5-point scale (1 = absolutely disagree, 2 = rather disagree, 3 = neither disagree nor agree, 4 = rather agree, 5 = absolutely agree). It specifies two bossing factors:

- *Communication-Aimed Bossing:* Respondents with high scores in a given factor feel that their superior does not allow them to comment on criticism, does not invite them to the operational or informal meetings of the working team, does not provide them with a turn to speak according to their interest during meetings, does not allow them access to undistorted information to fulfill their tasks, communicates with them minimally, abruptly terminates the conversation when they enter the room, carries out senseless and unjustified actions against their will, spreads gossip, defamation, unsubstantiated claims, half-truths, and intrigues about them, and ignores their opinions and casts doubt on their views.
- *Psyche-Aimed Bossing:* Respondents who score high in this factor feel that they are criticized by their superior for their political, religious, and other convictions, that the superior damages their belongings and the results of their work, threatens them with physical violence, sexually harasses them, questions their mental state, gives them defamatory nicknames, and denies them additional business education.

2. *BOSS(m) questionnaire* (Birknerová et al., 2022)

A modified version of the BOSS questionnaire – BOSS(m) enables the detection of bossing manifestations among managers in the business environment based on a psychometric approach. Manifestations of bossing are an important factor in predicting and interpreting undesirable behavior in various social contexts of business management work. The BOSS(m) methodology represents a dispositional approach for identifying the tendency towards undesirable forms of behavior of managers in various social contexts of work in the business environment. The Skewness and Kurtosis test of this modified version is presented in Table 1.

Table 1. Data distribution within individual BOSS(m) factors

	Communication-Aimed Bossing	**Psyche-Aimed Bossing**	**Bossing**
Skewness	.845	.890	.853
Kurtosis	−.105	.721	.872

Source: Own processing.

In terms of validation of the BOSS(m) methodology aimed at assessing the manifestations of bossing among managers in the business environment, correlation coefficients between the extracted factors of this methodology (Communication-Aimed Bossing and Psyche-Aimed Bossing) and overall score of the NAQ self-assessment methodology measuring mobbing in the workplace were analyzed (Table 2).

The NAQ questionnaire (Einarsen et al., 1994) contains 29 items that describe negative forms of behavior. Respondents answered how often they encountered the following forms of behavior in the workplace on a scale from 1 to 5 (1 – never; 2– occasionally; 3 – monthly; 4 – weekly; 5 – daily). The methodology is evaluated by one overall score, within which a higher value represents a higher rate of manifestations of negative behavior in the workplace.

Table 2. Correlation coefficients between BOSS(m) factors and total NAQ score

		Communication-Aimed Bossing	**Psyche-Aimed Bossing**
Total NAQ score	Pearson Correlation	.515**	.469**
	Sig. (2-tailed)	.000	.000
	N	631	631

Source: Own processing.

The obtained results of the validation study confirmed the existence of statistically significant correlation coefficients between the two factors of the BOSS(m) methodology and the overall score of the NAQ self-evaluation methodology aimed at measuring mobbing in the workplace. The higher the respondents scored in the NAQ methodology, the higher they scored in the mentioned factors of the BOSS(m) methodology. This finding suggests that the more the business managers assessed the manifestations of bullying (NAQ) as negative, the more negatively assessed was also the tendency to bossing in terms of communication and psyche.

Gender differences between the selected factors of bossing self-assessment by business managers were detected using BOSS(m) methodology. For identification of these differences, Student's t-test for two independent samples was used and calculated in the IBM SPSS Statistics 26 statistical software.

4. Results

The main aim of the research part of the chapter is to detect possible statistically significant differences in the self-assessment of bossing factors between business managers.

Table 3 illustrates the identified gender differences between the selected factors of bossing self-assessment by business managers using BOSS(m) methodology.

Table 3. Comparison of self-assessment of bossing factors between male and female business managers

BOSS(m)	**Gender**	**M**	**SD**	**t**	**p**
Communication-Aimed Bossing	female	1.901	.918	−3.023	**.003**
	male	**2.128**	.937		
Psyche-Aimed Bossing	female	1.390	.707	−2.078	**.038**
	male	**1.514**	.786		
Bossing	female	1.645	.741	−2.834	**.005**
	male	**1.821**	.798		

Source: Own processing.

The gender differences are graphically compared in Figure 1 for clearer demonstration.

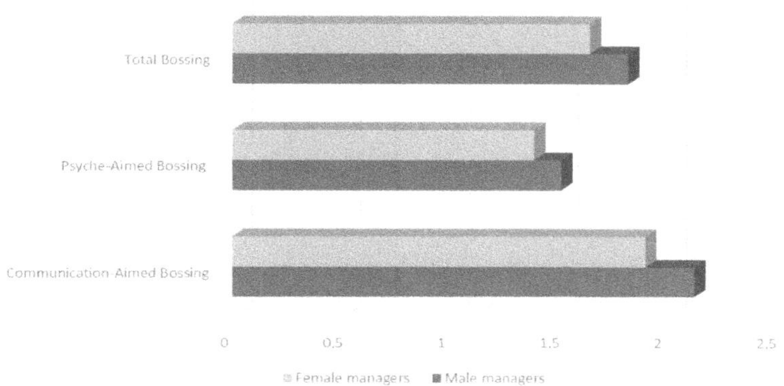

Figure 1. Comparison of self-assessment of bossing factors between male and female business managers (mean values)

Source: Own processing.

Table 3 and Figure 1 present the results of a statistical analysis aimed at comparing the self-assessment of bossing factors among business managers. In both factors of the BOSS(m) methodology, as well as in the overall Bossing score, the male business managers scored higher than the female business managers. However, it should be noted that both male and female business managers assessed bossing factors on the disagreement part of the scale (rather than the one expressing agreement). Statistically significant gender differences were, therefore, recorded only to the extent of their disagreement with the statements. Men did not completely rule out the tendency to criticisms and unsubstantiated claims against subordinates as compared to women, who judged the statements closer to the "complete disagreement" part of the scale.

5. Conclusions

In the presented chapter, the focus was on the differences in self-assessment of bossing in terms of the gender of the addressed business managers. In both bossing factors, as well as in the overall bossing score, the male business managers scored higher than the female business managers. As opposed to the original BOSS, which was designed primarily for employees and line managers to assess the possible bullying behavior directed from their superior towards them, BOSS(m) takes on a self-assessment quality by presenting the undesirable workplace behaviors by superiors in general, so that the managers can express their agreement/disagreement with these behaviors and thus indirectly indicate their own workplace behavior tendencies.

The problem of bossing and its negative consequences should be addressed at the level of the whole society, as well. Bossing, in its substance and effect, negatively affects the inner psycho-moral side of its victim (Celik & Peker, 2010). This personality component is the holder of significant social and legal characteristics, which the legal order recognizes and protects within the framework of the so-called personality law. Individual personal values can be divided into values of physical nature (life, health, physical integrity) and values of psycho-moral nature (freedom, honor, dignity, inner intimate sphere). Unauthorized interference with these personal values results in a violation of the basic personality right.

From the viewpoint of research on the given issue in business management, several steps could be taken. First of all, gender studies are currently much more complex, highlighting the variety of genders that need to be considered in such research studies. Furthermore, not only gender specifics but also the cultural context should be considered as a possible limitation or another study direction, as bossing can manifest itself differently within various cultures. In this sense, also the concept of staffing, i.e. upward bullying could be analyzed and further compared within various settings. As the results of presented analyzes suggest, the issue of bossing should be approached taking into account the hierarchy of an organization, as well. To what extent is bossing prominent on the different levels of management is yet another question provoking deeper discussion.

The BOSS(m) methodology can be also used by the hiring personnel, as it could serve as a tool for detection of the tendencies of the candidates to apply undesirable workplace behavior in the form of downward bullying – abusive supervision – bossing.

Acknowledgments

The compilation of this chapter was supported by the research grant project KEGA No. 018PU-4/2023.

References

Ambrose, M. L., & Ganegoda, D. B. (2020). Abusive according to whom? Manager and subordinate perceptions of abusive supervision and supervisors' performance. *Journal of Organizational Behavior, Special Issue: Contextualizing Workplace Mistreatment*, 41(8), 737–756.

Arnejčič, B. (2016). Mobbing in company: Levels and typology. *Organizacija,* 49(4), 240–250.

Birknerová, Z. (2009). Sociálna a emocionálna inteligencia, ich ponímanie, potreba a možnosti využitia pri príprave manažérov. *Manažment podnikania a vecí verejných – dialógy*, 4(10), 9–18.

Birknerová, Z., Zbihlejová, L., & Droppa, M. (2021). Assessment of abusive supervision – BOSS methodology. *Journal of Business Economics and Management,* 22(1), 197–216.

Birknerová, Z., Zbihlejová, L., & Gombár, M. (2022). *Posudzovanie prejavov bossingu. Metodika BOSSm18.* Prešov: Bookman.

Celik, S., & Peker, S. (2010). Mobbing perceptions of high school teachers. *Procedia: Social and Behavioral Sciences,* 9, 1617–1623.

Dabu, B., & Drăghici, A. (2013). Mobbing and bullying in business organizations and consequences on human health. *Scientific Bulletin–Economic Sciences,* 12(1), 63–71.

DiKamp. (2000). *Manažer 21. století.* Praha: Grada Publishing.

Einarsen, S., Raknes, B. I., Matthiesen, S. B., & Hellesøy, O. H. (1994). *Mobbing og harde personkonflikter. Helsefarlig samspill på arbeidsplassen* [Bullying and tough interpersonal conflicts: Health injurious interaction at the workplace]. Bergen, Norway: Sigma Forlag.

Hirigoyen, M. F. (2000). *Stalking the soul: Emotional abuse and the erosion of identity*. New York, NY: Helen Marx Books.

Lu, L. (2013). Abusive supervision and its organizational performance: A grounded study on the biography of Steve Jobs. *Journal of Manangement Case Studies,* 5, 20–31.

Nielsen, S., & Huse, M. (2010). The contribution of women on boards of directions: Going beyond the surface. *Corporate Governance: An International Review,* 18(2), 136–148.

Novák, T. (2004). *Jak bojovat se stresem* [How to fight stress]. Prague, Czech Republic: Grada Publishing.

Rosener, J. B. (1990). Ways women lead: The command-and-control leadership style associated with men is not the only way to succeed. *Harvard Business Review,* 11–12, 119–125.

Russo, A., & Popović, T. (2016). Workplace agression: Secondary analysis of Croatian research practice [Agresivnost na radnom mjestu: Sekundarna analiza istraživačke prakse u Hrvatskoj]. *Sigurnost: Časopis za Sigurnost u Radnoj i Životnoj Okolini,* 58(2), 121–135.

Salin, D. (2001). Prevalence and forms of bullying among business professionals: A comparison of two different strategies for measuring bullying. *European Journal of Work and Organizational Psychology,* 10(4), 425–441.

Senol, V., Avsar, E., Peksen Akca, R., Argun, M., Avsarogullari, L., & Kelestimur, F. (2015). Assessment of mobbing behaviors exposed by the academic personnel working in a university, in Turkey. *Journal of Psychiatry,* 18(1), 212.

Slobodová, E., & Šulík, I. (2007). Výber manažérov prostredníctvom kompetencií. *Jeneweingroup,* 05/2007, 26 p. [online]. Available at: http://www.jenewe ingroup.com/dokumenty/others/vyber_manazerov.pdf.

Topa, G., & Moriano, J. A. (2013). Stress and nurses' horizontal mobbing: Moderating effects of group identity and group support. *Nursing Outlook,* 61(3), 25–31.

Valentine, S., & Fleischman, G. (2017). From schoolyard to workplace: The impact of bullying on sales and business employees' Machiavellianism, job satisfaction, and perceived importance of an ethical issue. *Human Resource Management*, 57(1), 293–305.

Yaman, E. (2009). The validity and reliability of the mobbing scale (MS). *Educational Sciences: Theory & Practice,* 9(2), 981–988.

Yukl, G. (2002). *Leadership in Organizations*. Upper Saddle River: Prentice Hall.

Zbihlejova, L., & Birknerova, Z. (2022). Gender differences in self-assessment of the selected bossing and leadership factors by business managers. Paper presented at *19th Annual International Conference on SMEs, Entrepreneurship and Innovation: Management – Marketing – Economic – Social Aspects*; 25–28 July 2022, Athens, Greece.

Rossella Locatelli, Cristiana Schena, Alessandra Tanda

European Climate Change and ESG Regulation and Banks' Lending to SMEs

1. Introduction

Since the Brundtland Commission defined sustainable development in 1987, sustainability has been considered the ultimate objective of Corporate Social Responsibility (CSR). CSR has long been viewed as a discretionary aspect of a firm, secondary to the primary objective of shareholders' profitability. Historically, the literature focused on the drivers of sustainability disclosure, documented in non-financial statements relying on international standards (e.g., GRI) (Giannarakis et al., 2014; Bose et al., 2018), the purpose of profit versus non-profit companies, and the issue of shareholder versus stakeholder value creation (Freeman et al., 2004; Garriga & Melé, 2004; Parmar et al., 2010).

A change in policymakers and market attention towards climate change and sustainability brought to relevant regulatory initiatives – e.g., Non-Financial Reporting Directive (2014) and Corporate Sustainability Reporting Directive (2023) – that introduced new standards for social and environmental disclosure for listed companies, banks and insurance companies. These trends underscore the need to raise awareness on the topic for all companies, including SMEs. While not currently directly regulated, they may face indirect consequences of climate change regulations targeting banks, particularly regarding climate change risks.

To better understand the implications of the policy debate on sustainability for SMEs, this discussion paper focuses on the recent regulatory changes for banks, which serve as the primary financial providers for the short and long-term needs of SMEs. European banks are currently mandated to regard sustainability as a fundamental element in business and, among others, in their lending activity towards companies, including SMEs. SMEs face indeed added challenges in an intricate market landscape marked by the long-term effects of banking and sovereign debt crises, COVID-19 consequences, heightened geopolitical tensions, inflation, and climate change (Fenwick et al., 2022; Macchiavello & Siri, 2022).

2. Why Climate Risk Regulation Impacts SMEs?

As is well known, SMEs comprise the vast majority of corporates in Europe (97 % of firms), contributing to 53 % of the value added and 65 % of employment (European

Commission, 2021). SMEs still heavily rely on the banking sector to obtain funds for both their ongoing operations and long-term investments (Hoffmann et al., 2022).

In the past, shifts in regulatory provisions in the banking sector, including the revisions of Basel Accord, have affected SMEs through shifts in lending decisions and processes (Altman & Sabato, 2005). SMEs might however be unaware of the consequences of banking regulation on their loan accessibility (Carey & Flynn, 2005).

Sustainability may mirror this trend: integrating climate risk into banking regulations will directly impact SMEs through regulatory taxonomy (Westerberg & Gren, 2023) and indirectly affect banks' lending strategies (Mirza et al., 2023).

Currently, mandatory sustainability disclosure requirements[1] affect large and listed companies (Aureli et al., 2020). However, the Corporate Sustainability Due Diligence Directive, nowadays in discussion by EU authorities and consultations on sustainability reporting directive, lowers the threshold for disclosure, to include medium-sized companies. Moreover, it proposes that large companies disclose a comprehensive range of emissions, including those stemming from their value chain, which involve SMEs counterparties.

Company disclosure on ESG profile has been deemed necessary based on supporting evidence by the literature (e.g., Brooks & Oikonomou, 2018; Yu et al., 2021), but awareness of the consequences of disclosure for SMEs is still relatively unexplored (Gjergji et al., 2021). Gholami et al. (2022) find that listed SMEs evaluation might not benefit from better ESG performance in the long run and listed SMEs refrain from disclosing their ESG activities because of a shortage of essential resources. Similar results emerge for Polish (Martyniuk & Gostkowska-Drzewicka, 2022) and Hong Kong SMEs (Yip & Yu, 2023).

Systematic data collection and reporting are essential for both internal and external stakeholders and for developing a transition strategy. Non-compliance may restrict credit access for SMEs failing to provide information.

This topic is extremely relevant, because despite the development of Fintech credit providers[2], Fintech is nowadays considered complementary and not a substitute of the traditional lenders (Elsaid, 2021; Hodula, 2022). Hence, SMEs will

---

1 Including the Corporate Sustainability Report Directive, the Taxonomy Regulation, the Sustainability Reporting Standards by EFRA.

2 Fintech credit providers specifically provide prompt answer to SMEs financing needs via the employment of sophisticated tools, e.g., AI and machine learning (Tanda & Schena, 2019; Locatelli et al., 2021).

continue to have a strong connection with traditional banking systems and will be affected by changes in banking regulation.

Regulatory changes represent also an opportunity for SMEs to enhance and cultivate relationships with their lenders. The adoption of a more sustainable profile by a company is expected to produce a higher availability of credit or, at least, a lower cost of credit (Jung et al., 2018; Dunne & McBrayer, 2019). However, the incorporation of ESG evaluation in the lending process is still at its infancy and approaches by banks are very different (Calderon & Chong, 2014). To unlock a sustainable growth, it is crucial to enhancing the literacy of SMEs on financial and climate change aspects, so that SMEs can face these challenges successfully (Molina-Garcia et al., 2023).

3. Policy Measures for Sustainability

Sustainable development was defined in the World Commission on Environment and Development's 1987 Brundtland report as "development that meets the needs of the present without compromising the ability of future generations to meet their own needs" (Brundtland Commission, 1987). The definition seeks to reconcile economic development with the protection of social and environmental balance for future generations.

Since then, the European Union (EU) adopted a sustainable development strategy, introduced in 2001 and revised in 2006, articulating a vision where economic growth, social cohesion, and environmental protection were intertwined and mutually reinforcing. In 2009, the European Commission recognized the progress in integrating sustainable development principles across policies, including trade and development. It commended the EU's leadership in addressing climate change and promoting a low-carbon economy[3]. Sustainable development formally became one of the EU's long-term goals under Article 3(3) of the Treaty.

Following the 2015 Paris Agreement, there has been a notable shift in international policymaking, with a greater focus on climate change and finance as key drivers of sustainable development. Sustainable development became a prominent policy objective in Europe, formalized in 2019 by the European Green Deal (Figure 1).

Supranational financial regulatory bodies have also actively engaged in addressing climate-related concerns. In 2015 the Financial Stability Board (FSB)

3 https://gsfo.org/sustainable-finance-regulations-platform

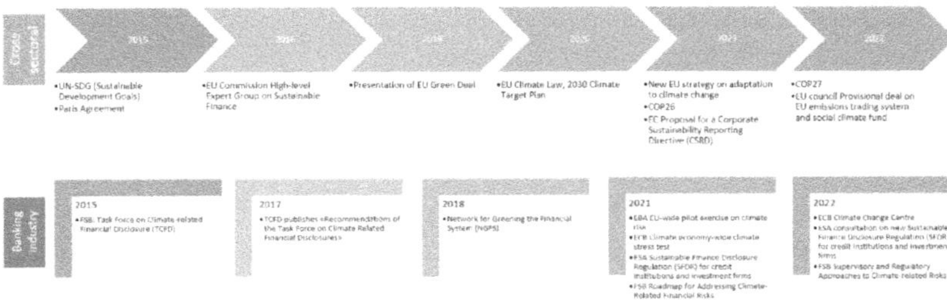

Figure 1. Main climate change policy initiatives since 2015
Source: Authors' elaboration.

formed a task force on climate-related financial disclosures, releasing recommendations in 2017. FSB oversees the Climate Risk Monitoring, provides recommendations for financial institutions to incorporate climate risk scenarios into their stress testing and risk assessment processes, to improve climate-related risk disclosures, not only in public reporting but also internally. FSB also provided guidance to policy makers, to incorporate climate risk considerations into supervisory frameworks and to ensure that financial institutions are adequately managing climate-related risks (FSB, 2021, 2022).

The Network for Greening the Financial System, the Task Force on Climate-related Financial Disclosures and the Principles for Responsible Banking cooperate to address climate-related financial risks for central banks and supervisory authorities, promote sustainable finance, and encourage financial institutions to adopt climate risk disclosure practices.

In June 2021 the EBA issued the Guidelines on Environmental, Social, and Governance Risk Management and the Report on Management of Environmental and Social Risks and Opportunities, that provide guidance and evidence on the integration of ESG risks into credit institutions and investment firms risk management processes and prudential requirements. The EBA shows that that over 50 % of bank exposures are linked to sectors subject to transition risk, and more than 33 % of counterparties can be labelled as "heavy emitters".

EBA also cooperates with the other European authorities: it supported the implementation of Sustainable Finance Disclosure Regulation (SFDR) by ESMA for credit institutions and investment firms (ESA, 2021), currently under consultation (ESA, 2023).

Also, the ECB has issued documents on climate change, such as the Guide on Climate-Related and Environmental Risks (ECB, 2020), instructing banks on these risks and their incorporation into their risk management processes. The 2022 Climate Risk Stress Test assesses the resilience of financial institutions to climate risks, identifying vulnerabilities and verifying their ability to withstand climate-related shocks (ECB, 2022, 2023).

The ECB performs supervisory assessment exercises and communicates its expectations regarding climate risk management, including the integration of climate considerations into banks' strategies and governance (e.g., ECB, 2023). Additionally, the ECB Climate Change Centre coordinates and enhances work on climate-related topics, promotes research, data analysis, and policies development.

The ECB also collaborates on these topics with international organizations, including the Task Force on Climate-related Financial Disclosures, the Network for Greening the Financial System and the Basel Committee on Banking Supervision.

4. Sustainability in the Banking Sector

Before discussing ESG sustainability for banks, we must underline that "sustainability" for banks has different interpretations.

First, it refers to the sustainability of banks' business models, in both the short-term (viability) and the long-term (sustainability). The sustainability of business models is mandated to banks by regulation, since the institution of the Single Supervisory Mechanism (ECB, 2023). This topic became especially relevant after the 2008 financial crisis, when traditional banks faced sustainability challenges to their business model. In those years, low interest rates negatively impacted profitability by thinning interest margins; additionally, labor and branch network costs, coupled with increased non-performing loans and heightened competition from new and existing players, added complexity to achieving satisfactory short and long-term profitability (Heilpern et al., 2009; Cosma et al., 2017).

Sustainability for banks is also interpreted in the light of the traditional and evolving role of banks in the real economy, i.e., for economic development and monetary policy transmission. This role also emerged during the COVID-19 crisis: the banking system was a primary channel for providing assistance to businesses and households in distress, e.g., through moratoria or loan guarantee extensions. Banks are therefore crucial to actively support a sustainable development (Yip & Bocken, 2018; Carè, 2018).

In relation to ESG sustainability, instead, banks need to consider their Environmental, Social and Governance performance when performing their business.

Like other companies, banks are increasingly expected to incorporate sustainability objectives into their strategies. The market is demanding more ESG information from both companies and banks (Gjergji et al., 2021; Yu et al., 2021), calling for transparent and genuine disclosure. Greenwashing practices are not only scrutinized by investors but also subject to legal sanctions (Ferrón-Vílchez et al., 2021). Some firms can even incorporate in their statutes the objective of a balance of interests between shareholders and other stakeholders.

But differently from other non-financial companies, banks face additional challenges. Banks are indeed mandated to incorporate ESG criteria into their financial activities, especially when evaluating lending options (e.g., EBA/LOM Guidelines). From SMEs' standpoint, this implies that banks can choose borrowers and provide incentives based on borrowers ESG performance. Consequently, SMEs will be involved in the process by the request of additional data on their ESG profile.

Moreover, banks must adapt their product and customer portfolios. Sustainable assets must be identified and classified on the balance sheets for both lending and investment portfolios. Simultaneously, on the liabilities side, banks encounter the challenge of refinancing with sustainable investments.

ESG risks also play a critical role in credit pricing, with lower ESG performance associated with a higher credit cost. This has implications for risk management processes and, ultimately, for the capital requirements associated with

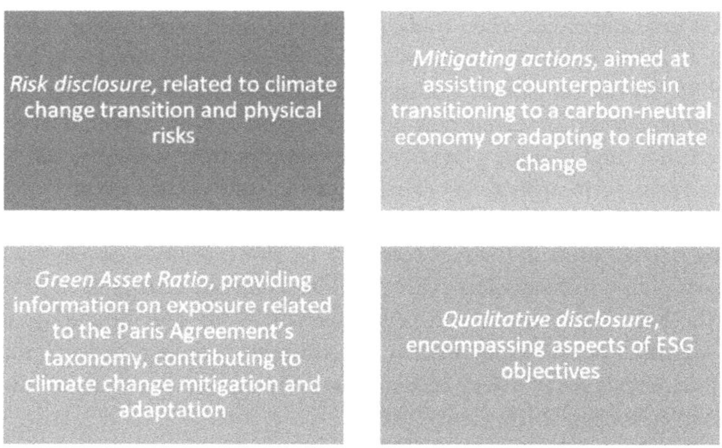

Figure 2. ESG disclosure areas for banks

Source: Authors' elaboration.

risk-weighted assets. This holistic ESG approach also necessitates the disclosure of ESG risks and sustainability actions, which should be reported to supervisory authorities and various stakeholders (Ferrón-Vílchez et al., 2021).

In this scenario, the European banking regulation (CRR2/CRD5) has undergone revision and the EBA received three mandates for evaluating the integration of ESG into prudential regulations. Nowadays, banks must follow disclosure guidelines on their ESG performance across various areas (Figure 2). These guidelines together with the Regulation on Disclosure of Investment Products and Financial Advice, the Taxonomy Disclosure, and the Non-Financial Statement Directive support the European Green Deal.

5. The Focus on Climate Change Risks

Over time climate change risks have gained importance as a component of ESG risk regulation. These can be physical or transition risk (Batten et al., 2016). Physical risk depends on geographical location of borrowers and is linked to climate change-induced losses resulting from catastrophes such as floods, storms, and rising sea levels. These events can damage assets and properties and affect companies, via the disruption of business, lack of revenue and high investment costs. It is a concern in the lending process, as banks will evaluate the value of firms' collateral and might decide on new loans also according to their current exposure[4] (Eceiza et al., 2020; ECB, 2021). It has reputational risk and credit risk implications.

Transition risk is linked to the shifts required for adopting a green economy and carries strategic implications. Its magnitude depends on the pace and nature of this transformation, whether it unfolds gradually and orderly or abruptly and chaotically (EBA, 2021; ECB, 2021).

A substantial body of literature discusses sustainability in non-financial companies (e.g., Pankratz et al., 2023), but the research on sustainability within the banking sector remains limited (e.g., Garbarino & Guin, 2021). Of these, many take a macroeconomic, financial stability, or prudential perspective (e.g., D'Orazio & Popoyan, 2019; Dafermos & Nikolaidi, 2021), whereas the managerial adaptation to climate change for banks remains underexplored (Furrer et al., 2012).

4 According to estimates, physical risk is highly concentrated: 70 % of exposures relate to 25 banks (ECB, 2022).

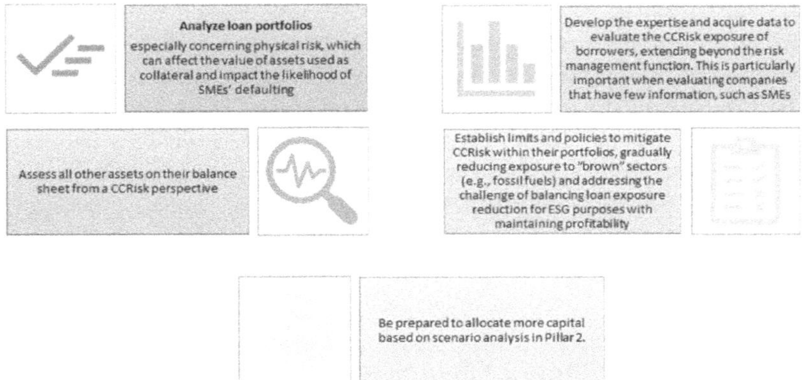

Figure 3. Actions to address CCRisk by banks
Source: Authors' elaboration.

To adequately address Climate Change Risk (CCRisk) banks must take several actions, depicted in Figure 3, that will affect SME lending policies and the related profitability, especially considering that banks will request higher interest rates to ESG-riskier SMEs.

European Authorities claim that climate risk poses a significant threat to banks' balance sheets and presents complex managerial and methodological challenges (ESBR, 2020; ECB, 2021, 2022)[5]. Unlike other risks, estimating CCRisk requires a high level of data granularity and a longer time horizon than ever before, combining the banks' own risks with those of their loan portfolio and banks still appear relatively unprepared to face this challenge.

Industry initiatives to encourage corporate borrowers to achieve net-zero emissions include the Glasgow Financial Alliance for Net Zero (GFANZ), born during the 2021 COP26 in Glasgow. The initiative is rooted in the UN's Race to Zero campaign and is dedicated to mobilizing the financial industry to achieve net-zero emissions by 2050, fostering climate resilience. As of January 2024, GFANZ encompasses over 675 financial institutions from 50 countries,

5 A rapid transition from high-emission borrowers to those operating in less carbon-intensive sectors could be destabilizing for non-financial companies and could hinder the green transition of heavy emitters.

collectively managing assets exceeding $130 trillion, of which 141 are banks, accounting for 41 % of global total assets.

6. The Consequences for SMEs

Sustainability has gained substantial importance in banking, driven by the demands of policymakers, regulatory authorities, and the market. These changes will affect SMEs severely, not only directly, but also indirectly, via the effects that new regulations will have on the lending channels. Especially SMEs will experience changes in the funds availability as banks are rethinking their lending policies to integrate ESG in the decision process.

Banks are indeed increasingly expected to play a crucial role in fostering sustainable development, financing eco-friendly initiatives, and facilitating the transition to a greener economy. Furthermore, banks are now required to incorporate ESG factors into their strategies and management, similar to other businesses responding to market pressures.

However, 'sustainability' in the banking industry presents unique complexities that affect lending to SMEs. ESG considerations permeate the core operations of banking and ESG risks impact banks' risks exposure. Understanding the effects of climate regulation on the banking sector is key for SMEs as they are not exempted from the transition to a more sustainable economic system. In the foreseeable future, the possibility to access external funds from banks and other channels for SMEs will also depend on their climate and ESG profile. Data will be a key issue in the design of the lending processes of banks. A lower availability of funds can be detrimental to the companies' investment strategy and can hinder the transition process to a more sustainable business model. SMEs are thus called to design strategies to improve their ESG profile and to collect and disclose relevant data.

References

Altman, E. I., & Sabato, G. (2005). Effects of the new Basel capital accord on bank capital requirements for SMEs. *Journal of Financial Services Research*, 28, 15–42.

Aureli, S., Del Baldo, M., Lombardi, R., & Nappo, F. (2020). Nonfinancial reporting regulation and challenges in sustainability disclosure and corporate governance practices. *Business Strategy and the Environment*, 29(6), 2392–2403.

Batten, S., Sowerbutts, R., & Tanaka, M. (2016). Let's talk about the weather: The impact of climate change on central banks. *Bank England Work. Pap.*, 603.

Bose, S., Khan, H. Z., Rashid, A., & Islam, S. (2018). What drives green banking disclosure? An institutional and corporate governance perspective. *Asia Pacific Journal of Management*, 35, 501–527.

Brooks, C., & Oikonomou, I. (2018). The effects of environmental, social and governance disclosures and performance on firm value: A review of the literature in accounting and finance. *The British Accounting Review*, 50(1), 1–15.

Brundtland Commission. (1987). *Brundtland report.*

Calderon, F., & Chong, L. C. (2014). Dilemma of sustainable lending. *Journal of Sustainable Finance & Investment*, 4(2), 192–209.

Carè, R. (2018). Exploring the role of banks in sustainable development. In R. Carè (Ed.), *Sustainable banking* (pp. 39–64). Palgrave Macmillan.

Carey, D., & Flynn, A. (2005). Is bank finance the Achilles' heel of Irish SMEs?. *Journal of European Industrial Training*, 29(9), 712–729.

Corporate Sustainability Reporting Directive (2023). Directive (EU) 2022/2464 of the European Parliament and of the Council of 14 December 2022 amending Regulation (EU) No 537/2014, Directive 2004/109/EC, Directive 2006/43/EC and Directive 2013/34/EU, as regards corporate sustainability reporting.

Cosma, S., Ferretti, R., Gualandri, E., Landi, A., & Venturelli, V. (2017). The business model of banks: A review of the theoretical and empirical literature. *The Business of Banking*, 131–167.

D'Orazio, P., & Popoyan, L. (2019). Fostering green investments and tackling climate-related financial risks: Which role for macroprudential policies?. *Ecological Economics*, 160, 25–37.

Dafermos, Y., & Nikolaidi, M. (2021). How can green differentiated capital requirements affect climate risks? A dynamic macrofinancial analysis. *Journal of Financial Stability*, 54, 100871.

Dunne, T. C., & McBrayer, G. A. (2019). In the interest of small business' cost of debt: A matter of CSR disclosure. *Journal of Small Business Strategy*, 29(2), 58–71.

EBA. (2021). *Consultation paper on draft ITS on Pillar 3 disclosures on ESG risks.*

ECB. (2020). *Report on institutions' climate-related and environmental risk disclosures.* November.

ECB. (2021). *Climate-related risk and financial stability,* July.

ECB. (2022). *Results of the 2022 climate risk stress test of the Eurosystem balance sheet.*

ECB. (2023). *The importance of being transparent. A review of climate-related and environmental risks disclosures practices and trends,* April.

Eceiza, J., Harreis, H., Härtl, D., & Viscardi, S. (2020). *Banking imperatives for managing climate risk*. McKinsey & Company.

Elsaid, H. M. (2021). A review of literature directions regarding the impact of fintech firms on the banking industry. *Qualitative Research in Financial Markets,* 15(5), 693–711.

ESA. (2021). *Joint ESAs final report on RTS on the content, methodologies and presentation of disclosures under SFDR*. JC-2021-03, February.

ESA. (2023). *Joint committee consultation paper on review of SFDR Delegated Regulation regarding PAI and financial product disclosures*. JC-2023-09, April.

ESBR. (2020). *Positively green: Measuring climate change risks to financial,* June.

European Commission. (2021). *Annual report on European SMEs 2020/2021,* July.

Fenwick, M., Tronel, J., van Wyk, S., & Vermeulen, E. P. M. (2022). ESG as a business model for SMEs. *ECGI – Law WP* (642).

Ferrón-Vílchez, V., Valero-Gil, J., & Suárez-Perales, I. (2021). How does greenwashing influence managers' decision-making? An experimental approach under stakeholder view. *Corporate Social Responsibility and Environmental Management,* 28(2), 860–880.

Freeman, R. E., Wicks, A. C., & Parmar, B. (2004). Stakeholder theory and "the corporate objective revisited". *Organization Science*, 15(3), 364–369.

FSB. (2021). *FSB roadmap for addressing climate-related financial risks,* July.

FSB. (2022). *Supervisory and regulatory approaches to climate-related risks*. Final report, October.

Furrer, B., Hamprecht, J., & Hoffmann, V. H. (2012). Much ado about nothing? How banks respond to climate change. *Business & Society,* 51(1), 62–88.

Garbarino, N., & Guin, B. (2021). High water, no marks? Biased lending after extreme weather. *Journal of Financial Stability*, 54, 100874.

Garriga, E., & Melé, D. (2004). Corporate social responsibility theories: Mapping the territory. *Journal of Business Ethics*, 53, 51–71.

Gholami, A., Sands, J., & Rahman, H. U. (2022). Environmental, social and governance disclosure and value generation: İs the financial industry different?. *Sustainability*, 14(5), 2647.

Giannarakis, G., Konteos, G., & Sariannidis, N. (2014). Financial, governance and environmental determinants of corporate social responsible disclosure. *Management Decision*, 52(10), 1928–1951.

Gjergji, R., Vena, L., Sciascia, S., & Cortesi, A. (2021). The effects of environmental, social and governance disclosure on the cost of capital in small and medium enterprises: The role of family business status. *Business Strategy and the Environment*, 30(1), 683–693.

Heilpern, E., Haslam, C., & Andersson, T. (2009, June). When it comes to the crunch: What are the drivers of the US banking crisis?. *Accounting Forum*, 33(2), 99–113.

Hodula, M. (2022). Does Fintech credit substitute for traditional credit? Evidence from 78 countries. *Finance Research Letters*, 46, 102469.

Hoffmann, M., Maslov, E., & Sørensen, B. E. (2022). Small firms and domestic bank dependence in Europe's great recession. *Journal of International Economics*, 137, 103623.

Jung, J., Herbohn, K., & Clarkson, P. (2018). Carbon risk, carbon risk awareness and the cost of debt financing. *Journal of Business Ethics*, 150, 1151–1171.

Locatelli R., Schena C., & Tanda A. (2021). A historical perspective on disruptive technologies. In T. King, F. S. Stentella Lopes, A. Srivastav, & J. Williams (Eds.), *Disruptive technology in banking and finance*. Palgrave Macmillan.

Macchiavello, E., & Siri, M. (2022). Sustainable finance and fintech: Can technology contribute to achieving environmental goals? A preliminary assessment of 'green fintech' and 'sustainable digital finance'. *European Company and Financial Law Review*, 19(1), 128–174.

Martyniuk, O., & Gostkowska-Drzewicka, M. (2022). Non-financial information reporting of Polish family and non-family companies. A comparative analysis. *Zeszyty Teoretyczne Rachunkowości*, 46(4), 69–91.

Mirza, N., Afzal, A., Umar, M., & Skare, M. (2023). The impact of green lending on banking performance: Evidence from SME credit portfolios in the BRIC. *Economic Analysis and Policy*, 77, 843–850.

Molina-Garcia, A., Dieguez-Soto, J., Galache-Laza, M. T., & Campos-Valenzuela, M. (2023). Financial literacy in SMEs: A bibliometric analysis and a systematic literature review of an emerging research field. *Review of Managerial Science*, 17(3), 787–826.

Non-Financial Reporting Directive (2014). Directive 2014/95/EU of the European Parliament and of the Council of 22 October 2014 amending Directive 2013/34/EU as regards disclosure of non-financial and diversity information by certain large undertakings and groups.

Pankratz, N., Bauer, R., & Derwall, J. (2023). *Climate change, firm performance, and investor surprises*. Management Science.

Parmar, B. L., Freeman, R. E., Harrison, J. S., Wicks, A. C., Purnell, L., & De Colle, S. (2010). Stakeholder theory: The state of the art. *Academy of Management Annals*, 4(1), 403–445.

Tanda, A., & Schena, C.-M. (2019). *FinTech, BigTech and Banks. Digitalisation and its impact on banking business models*. Palgrave.

Westerberg, J., & Gren, S. (2023). Exploring implications of the EU Taxonomy on funding and disclosure for Swedish SMEs. https://stud.epsilon.slu.se/19289/1/westerberg-j-gren-s-20230714.pdf

Yip, A. W., & Bocken, N. M. (2018). Sustainable business model archetypes for the banking industry. *Journal of Cleaner Production*, 174, 150–169.

Yip, A. W., & Yu, W. Y. (2023). The quality of environmental KPI disclosure in ESG reporting for SMEs in Hong Kong. *Sustainability*, 15(4), 3634.

Yu, E. P. Y., Tanda, A., Luu, B. V., & Chai, D. H. (2021). Environmental transparency and investors' risk perception: Cross-country evidence on multinational corporations' sustainability practices and cost of equity. *Business Strategy and the Environment*, 30(8), 3975–4000.

Fayaz Hussain Tunio, Agha Amad Nabi,
Khurram Ali Mubasher, Yi Ding

Measuring the Degree of Fiscal (De) Centralization of Pakistan: Theoretical Model Empirical Analysis

1. Introduction

Over the past few decades, Pakistan's government has attempted to decentralize its financial system, same as the USA, Canada, Switzerland, and Sweden. Fiscal decentralization was attempted three times in Pakistan: First in 1960 by General Ayub Khan, second in 1979, by General Zia ul Haq, and third in 2000 by General Pervez Musharaf, all in military regimes (Cheema et al., 2005; Jalal, 1995). The conventional theory of fiscal federalism arranges a universal framework for assigning functions to various governmental levels within appropriate financial tools for carrying out functions (Musgrave & Musgrave, 1959; Oates, 1972). Under a centralized system, the levels of public goods and services provision is determined by central government with uniform taxes to all citizens (Besley & Coate, 2003). Schiender (2003) explained that decentralization is the devolution of powers and authorities in provision of public goods and services from central government to last tier. Kincaid (2019) measured the fiscal (de) centralization of the USA and using five indicators. Kincaid also includes legislative and administrative measures. Further, Kaiser and Vogel (2019) and Lecours (2019) same model were used for assessing the degree of fiscal (de) centralization in Canada, and Germany and found mixed results. Cevik (2016a) analyzed that Pakistan's fiscal system is highly centralized from the revenue side. At the same time Pakistan has a decentralized political system it contains federal, provincial, and local governments.[1] Oates (1972) explained that federal states should be, decentralized or centralized fiscal & political institutions, so both go hand in hand. Weissert and Uttermark (2017) analyzed the health policy legislation and conclude with centralization. Tunio and Nabi (2021) Believed that Pakistan has decentralized political institutions and centralized fiscal institutions. However,

1 The federal government under Art-90 (1), the provincial governmentArt-129 (1), and the local government Art- 140-A (1) in the constitution of Pakistan

above literature depicted the fiscal centralization and political decentralization that generates the different questions. As a federalist country why Pakistan has institutional asymmetric? What are political and fiscal intuitions of Pakistan? How can we understand the institutional structure? Before analyzing these questions, we need to evaluate and measure the Pakistan's political and fiscal institutions. Therefore, it is important to measures the degree of fiscal institutions either it decentralized or centralized. This study used approach of (Kincaid et al., 2019) for measuring the degree of (de) centralization in Pakistan that is widely ignore in literature and did not attempted to quantify it through various dimensions and indicators.

Theoretical and empirical approaches are used to analyze the fiscal structure of Pakistan. On the theoretical side, we have employed the approach of Schneider (2003), Morozov (2016) and Kincaid et al. (2019) by used five indicators for measuring the degree of fiscal autonomy in Pakistan: Provincial own revenue, Provincial expenditure, Provincial tax autonomy, Federal transfers, and Provincial debt autonomy. Pakistan's fiscal system is highly centralized in the perspective of provincial own revenue, provincial tax autonomy, and provincial debt borrowing autonomy and provincial expenditure and federal transfers are confined in quite centralization scale.

Moreover, empirical estimations show that models are statistically fit, where the P-value is less than 5 %, and the data is significant at first different. Therefore, all variables have a significant impact on the dependent variable. All significant relationships indicate a direct relation to fiscal autonomy. Statistically strong links explain the variations in the dependent variable. A positive coefficient indicates that the increasing ratio of provincial own revenue, provincial expenditure, debt borrowing autonomy, and federal transfer variables have higher degrees at the national level. It means that the degree of fiscal centralization is also higher in the country.

The remaining parts of the paper are organized as: Section 2 literature review; Section 3 fiscal institutions. Section 4 is about the structure of financial institutions. Section 5 results and discussions and Section 6 about the conclusion.

2. Literature Review

Measuring the degree of fiscal institutions is still a complicated problem in under-developing countries like Pakistan. Nevertheless, the researcher has done sufficient work in the OECD, USA, and other developed countries. The extensive material is available to analyze and describe the fiscal federalism theory and measure the degree of fiscal structure in diverse ways and calculate various essential results. Therefore, we have an attempt to measure the degree of (de) centralization in Pakistan's context.

The theory of fiscal federalism was equally fixed in view of public finance dispersed in the 1950s and 1960s. Musgrave, Arrows, and Samuelson primarily addressed the traditional federalism approach that explained the distribution of regulatory powers between federal and states. Moreover, the conventional theory of fiscal federalism arranges a universal framework for assigning functions to various governments and appropriate fiscal tools for carrying out these functions (Musgrave & Musgrave, 1959; Oates, 1972). Under a centralized system, the levels of public goods and services are determined by a unitary government that denotes the central and state levels, where the expenditures are financed by uniform taxes to all citizens (Besley & Coate, 2003). The first generation FFT is primarily normative and assumes that public decision-makers are benevolent maximizes of the general public welfare (Musgrave & Musgrave, 1959; Oates, 1972). The second-generation FFT describes the decentralization of functions and budgetary responsibilities among government levels, which increases the institutional and regional competition among the regions (Oates, 2005). Furthermore, many factors could foster (de) centralization and remarked centralization increased at the start of the 20th century and decreased after World War II (Oates, 1972).

Kee (2003), defined, fiscal decentralization is a devolution of responsibilities from the central government to sub-tiers (State, Local & Municipal) specific to expenditures, revenue (Tax and No-tax), and administrative functions. Bahl and Cyan (2009) found that sub-tiers exercised over certain spending zones, especially on expenditure categories. Cyan (2011) wrote the sub states were highly dependent on transfer payments; it reconnects the revenue and expenditure responsibilities and increases accountability challenges for all lower tiers. Searle (2005) assumed that fiscal transfers are an essential job to guarantee the equal and efficient distribution of the public good's provisions and value. Köthenbürger (2002) concluded that the unclear design transfers could not do a good job, regardless of; they just financed 10 % of local expenditures. Shah (2005) defined the structure of financial organizations that pact with assigning tax revenue, expenses, and tax legislation procedures, along with income sharing arrangements between different government levels, which has pivotal implications for the most effective and equal provision of public goods. Iqbal et al. (2012) empirically analyzed the revenue, expenditure & composite variable and measured the positive trend on growth and spending devolution has a negative impact on GDP per capita growth. Another study by (Iqbal 2013) used time series data, examined the relationship between fiscal decentralization and inflation, and tracked the negative and insignificant relations. Ebel and Yilmaz (2002) took revenue, expenditure, and tax autonomy as indicators for measuring the degree of fiscal decentralization. Schneider (2003) used the four-dimensional model for financial degree measurement including revenue, expenditures, tax autonomy, and federal transfers. Perhaps, some theoretical literature on fiscal decentralization induces the federal and provincial political actors to decrease indebtedness. Baskaran (2010) explained, the limited number of studies expresses the impacts of government indebtedness on fiscal decentralization, and the researcher does not attempt to describe the determinants of public debt clearly. Kiewiet and Szakaty (1996) concluded for guaranteed debt in the perspective of the USA. de Mello (2000) described that the subnational tax powers typically lead to an upsurge in subnational deficits. Fornasari et al. (2000) worked on 32 developing countries and concluded that the decentralization of expenditures frequently contributes to the government sector. However, the revenue decentralization measure was used; the federal government deficit was negatively related to devolution. Rodden (2002) analyzed through different models and concluded that the degree of expenditure and revenue decentralization both tend to raise the total government deficits.

Chandio et al. (2024) and Ullah et al. (2022) analyzed the comparative federalism in context of India and Pakistan. Under the Rodden model of fiscal federalism, jurisdictions compete for capital based on low tax rates, and centralized systems will have higher spending and taxation than the decentralized structure (Rodden, 2004). Although Schneider (2003) and Morozov (2016) explained it suitably to analyze the fiscal degree of (de) centralization of an economy is in aspect of the subnational share of both expenditures and revenues. The main point is that the higher the percentage share of subnational government's expenses and taxes, the higher the (de) centralization. Kincaid (2019) statistically analyzes the US fiscal (de) centralization and uses five metrics. Kaiser and Vogel (2019), Kincaid (2019) and Lecours (2019) attempted to assess fiscal centralization in some developed federalist countries such as the USA, Canada, and Germany and found mixed results. Cevik (2016b) examined Pakistan's fiscal structure is strongly centralized on the revenue side. Simultaneously, Pakistan's constitution proves that the country has a decentralized democratic structure and comprises federal, provincial, and local governments. According to the theory of fiscal federalism (FFT), a federal country has an entirely decentralized or centralized fiscal and political system, both of which go hand in hand (Oates, 1972). Weissert and Uttermark (2017) studied various health policy regulations from 1977 to 2016 and identified centralization. These studies measure the flow of (de) centralization, not the degree of (de) centralization. Consequently

Dardanelli et al. (2019), explained the degree of centralization of federations has been widely debated in the literature since the federalist period, but no attempt has been made to measure it by means of various dimensions and indicators.

3. Research Methodology and Outcomes

This paper has used theoretical and empirical models for measuring the degree of (de) centralization in Pakistan. In theoretical models, theories are framed to enlighten, forecast, and understand phenomena. In many cases, to test and encompass the general awareness within the confines of critical leaping assumptions, that has measured the degree of fiscal autonomy by using the one dependent variable and five independent variables. In the empirical model, we have taken the same variables and analyzed the relationship coefficient & covariance between the dependent and independent variables. Moreover, we have put some more tests for measuring the significant level of data.

3.1. Theoretical Model

We have used different approaches in the theoretical model for indexing the dependent and independent variables. Therefore, table ten displays various researchers' methods for measuring the degree of fiscal (de) centralization. Therefore, we have put the same approaches for independent variables such as public expenditure, public revenue, tax autonomy, and federal transfers, and then we took the percentage share of each variable according to table ten's calculation. Furthermore, we have made public debt an independent variable; we analyze the provincial government's debt autonomy through this. Hence, we index as a percentage of public debt in provincial expenditures to measure capacity and contribution.

Furthermore, we have measured the dependent variable as a percentage of total government revenue, expenditure, tax autonomy, federal transfers, and public debt. The federal and provincial governments' share indicates the (de) centralization vis a vis higher the percentage specifies the centralization. Below, table two provides a unified understanding of the selection of the theoretical model.

3.1.1. Fiscal Autonomy

In the theoretical measures section, we have divided fiscal autonomy into five sub dimensions. The first degree of public revenue owns resources directly controlled by provincial governments, which can be defined as the proportion of own public revenues out of the total government revenue resources. The higher the proportion of provincial own revenue sources, greater the fiscal autonomy of the provincial government. Therefore, we measure it on basis of seven-point scale in percentage, 1 = 0–14 high centralized; 2 = 15–29 centralized; 3 = 30–44 quite centralized; 4 = 45–59 medium; 5 = 60–74 quite decentralized; 6 = 75–89 decentralized; 7 = 90–100 high decentralized. The scale is based on equivalent intervals at the top to capture the better distribution variation at the top end.

The second and third dimensions related to expenditure and tax autonomy, so we measured these dimensions alike first variables as the percentage higher at a provincial level greater than the fiscal autonomy. The fourth indicator, federal transfer, concerns the sphere based on federal transfers' percentage share in regional own revenue resources. Therefore, the limited sphere of federal transfers, the more autonomous provincial governments are allocating the federal government's funds. If a sphere of federal transfer is significant, it means higher centralization. We measure it as a percentage share of federal transfers in own provincial revenue. The fifth dimension is related to autonomy in borrowing; a provincial government can increase their spending via borrowing. However, greater autonomy in borrowing specified the higher fiscal decentralization. We measure this indicator using the same above scale.

3.1.2. Measuring Dimensions

The property of direction change is shifting over the measure from the highest to the lowest value, indicating a reduction in the provincial governments' fiscal autonomy and centralization. Variable change entailing the shift from a lowest to the highest value specifies an increase in the provincial government's fiscal autonomy and denotes decentralization. Morozov (2016) and Schneider (2003) measures the fiscal degree of (de) centralization of an economy as higher the percentage share of subnational government's expenditure and revenue, which shows the higher (de) centralization in the state. Below Table 1 shows the fiscal provision in constitution of Pakistan

Table 1. Fiscal provision in the constitution of Pakistan

Indicators	The Federal Government	The Provincial Government
Public Expenditure	Fourth schedule in the constitution of Pakistan under the Art-70(4) legislative list	Fourth schedule in the law of Pakistan under the Art-70(4) legislative list
Public Revenue	Fourth schedule in the constitution of Pakistan under the Art-70(4) legislative list	Fourth schedule in the law of Pakistan under the Art-70(4) legislative list

Table 1. Continued

Indicators	The Federal Government	The Provincial Government
Tax Autonomy	Fourth schedule in the constitution of Pakistan under the Art-70(4) federal legislative list	Agricultural income tax Art-162, Professional tax Art-163 and Fourth schedule in the law of Pakistan under the Art-70(4) legislative list
Federal Transfer	NFC award Art-160, Natural gas, and hydro-electric power Art-161	
Public Debt Autonomy	Public debts Borrowing Art-166	Public debt borrowing Art-167 and confined under Art-167(2)

Source: *Constitution of Pakistan organized by the author*

3.1.3. Operational Definitions

Fiscal autonomy: $$FD = \frac{Provincial\,Government\;Revenue}{Total\,Government\;Revenue + Federal\,Transfers + Provincial\,Debts}\text{'}100$$

Provincial expenditure: $$PE = \frac{Total\,Provincial\;Expenditures}{Total\,Government\;Expenditure}\text{'}\,\mathrm{g}$$

Provincial Own Revenue: $$POR = \frac{Provincial\,Own\,Revenue}{Total\,Government\;Revenue}\text{'}100$$

Provincial Tax Autonomy: $$PTA = \frac{Provincial\,own\,Tax\;Revenue}{Total\,Government\;Tax\;Revenue}\text{'}100$$

Federal Transfer: $$FT = \frac{Federal\,Transfer}{Provincial\,Own\,Revenue + Federal\,Transfers + Provincial\,Debts}\text{'}100$$

Debts Borrowing Autonomy: $$DBA = \frac{Provincial\,Debts}{Total\;provincial\;Exependitures}\text{'}100$$

3.2. Empirical Model

We estimate the model outlined in using annual time series data of Pakistan for the financial year 1979 2017 because of the data unavailability observations are limited. The official source of data collection is the Handbook of Pakistan

Statistics on Pakistan Economy 2015 by State Bank of Pakistan and Pakistan Economic Survey issued by Ministry of Finance. We have indexed the variables according to the bellow calculations for the analysis of the empirical model.

3.2.1. Descriptive Statistics

Table 2 statistics show that the provincial governments are highly dependent on federal transfers; simultaneously, provinces' tax autonomy is confined within 5.4 % by mean. Another Table then describes the minimum and maximum level of all variables, along with the standard deviation.

Table 2. Summary statistics on centralization measures

	Fiscal Autonomy	**Provincial Own Revenue**	**Provincial Expenditure**	**Provincial Tax Autonomy**	**Federal Transfer**	**Debt Borrowing Autonomy**
Mean	30.44722	11.02308	22.61538	5.425641	66.93077	10.66923
Median	30.16857	10.80000	21.30000	5.300000	69.40000	9.100000
Maximum	36.09762	20.10000	37.30000	8.100000	88.70000	21.60000
Minimum	22.92521	5.600000	16.90000	3.800000	33.40000	0.000000
Std. Dev.	2.852568	3.388561	5.353481	0.951928	14.36963	6.573037
Skewness	−0.146380	0.790140	1.446566	0.911809	−0.616374	0.280151
Kurtosis	3.258599	3.337335	3.964439	4.109463	2.683045	1.725221
Jarque-Bera	0.247946	4.243001	15.11307	7.404294	2.632709	3.150874
Probability	0.883404	0.119852	0.000523	0.024670	0.268111	0.206917
Sum	1187.441	429.9000	882.0000	211.6000	2610.300	416.1000
Sum Sq. Dev.	309.2116	436.3292	1089.071	34.43436	7846.483	1641.783
Observations	39	39	39	39	39	39

The summary statistic Table 2 suggests that expenditures are highly dependent on federal transfers, where the colossal dependency shows that provincial revenue is highly centralized. It seems to be correct for the entire period of our analysis. Furthermore, a small convergence between public expenditure public revenue, and transfers in the eighties because the variables' gaps have slightly lowered. Similarly, tax autonomy has a small variance and constant, while public debt autonomy has reduced in the last two decades. While the evolution of the averages suggests that there has been more variance within the variables; therefore, the country has significant changes in the degree of fiscal centralization.

Table 3. Fiscal correlation measures

	Fiscal Autonomy	Provincial Own Revenue	Provincial Expenditure	Provincial Tax Autonomy	Federal Transfer	Debt Borrowing Autonomy
Fiscal Autonomy	1					
Provincial Own Revenue	−0.168	1				
Provincial Expenditure	0.473	−0.522	1			
Provincial Tax Autonomy	−0.054	−0.069	0.529	1		
Federal Transfer	0.366	−0.928	0.662	0.086	1	
Debt Borrowing Autonomy	−0.327	0.480	−0.632	−0.1794	−0.701	1

3.2.2. Regression Analysis

The linear relationship occurs between the dependent and one independent variable. When there is only one independent variable in the linear regression model, the model has generally termed a simple linear regression model. When there is more than one independent variable in the model, the linear model is termed, multiple linear regression model.

$$(\mathrm{FA})_t = \beta_0 + \beta_1(POR)_t + \beta_2(PE)_t + \beta_3(PTA)_t + \beta_4(FT)_t + \beta_5(PDA)_t + \varepsilon_t \ldots\ldots\ldots(i)$$

Table 4. Regression analysis

Variable	Coefficient	Std. Error	t-Statistic	Prob.
FEDERAL TRANSFER	0.329767	0.117702	2.801711	0.0084***
DEBT BORROWING AUTONOMY	0.198357	0.098273	2.018427	0.0517**
PROVINCIAL EXPENDITURE	0.316594	0.122011	2.594796	0.0140***

(continued)

Table 5. Continued

Variable	Coefficient	Std. Error	t-Statistic	Prob.
PROVINCIAL OWN_ REVENUE	1.214434	0.379821	3.197384	0.0031***
PROVINCIAL TAX AUTONOMY	−0.995279	0.495027	−2.010555	0.0526**
CONSTANT	−8.896691	12.70382	−0.700316	0.4886
R-squared	0.513983	Mean dependent var		30.44821
Adjusted R-squared	0.440344	SD dependent var		2.852280
Prob(F-statistic)	0.000152	Akaike info criterion		4.494319

The model is statistically fit and explains the dependent and independent variables, where the P-value is less than 5 % of all variables. The variables public revenue, public expenditure, public debts, autonomy, and federal transfers significantly impact the dependent variable. All considerable relationships show a direct relation with the dependent variable.

In the regression, it has been observed that there are 39 observations, and R-squareis 51 %, which means that the model explains 51 % variation. The sign of the coefficient depicts whether there is a positive correlation between each independent variable. A positive coefficient indicates that the increasing ratio of variables such as public revenue, public expenditure, public debts, autonomy, and federal transfer, to some extent, reduces the degree of fiscal centralization. However, Arzaghi and Henderson (2005), Morozov (2016) and Cevik (2016a) explained that the degree of fiscal centralization can be measured by the percentage share of subnational government's expenditures and revenue in the total government expenditure and revenue: the lower the share is, the more centralized. Hence, our theoretical describes that the degree of Pakistan's fiscal system is highly centralized in all prospective.

Table 5. ARDL estimation

Variable	Coefficient	Std. Error	t-Statistic	Prob.*
Fiscal Autonomy (-1)	−0.656936	0.237849	−2.761988	0.0185***
Provincial Own Revenue (-1)	3.057728	0.945051	3.235517	0.0079***
Provincial Expenditure	0.446029	0.173519	2.570484	0.0260***
Provincial Tax Autonomy	−3.256625	1.309532	−2.486861	0.0302***
Federal Transfers (-1)	0.936709	0.306325	3.057892	0.0109***
Provincial debts Autonomy	0.415915	0.170479	2.439681	0.0328***

Table 5. Continued

Variable	Coefficient	Std. Error	t-Statistic	Prob.*
C	14.11657	23.09217	0.611314	0.5534
R-squared	0.883034	Mean dependent var		30.84356
Adjusted R-squared	0.638469	S.D. dependent var		2.699005
Prob(F-statistic)	0.015548	Akaike info criterion		4.020213

*Note: one, two and three stars showed the significant level at 10 %, 5 %, and 1 % respectively.

Above Table 5 shows that selection (using the Akaike Information Criterion) was used with a maximum of 4 lags for the regressors and one lag for the dependent variable. Out of the 3125 models evaluated, the procedure has selected an ARDL (1, 1, 0, 0, 1, 0) model – 1 lag for the dependent variable, and 4 for regressors. It is also noted that since the selected model has fewer lags than the maximum, the sample used in the final estimation will not match that used during selection. The rest of the output is the standard least-squares output for the selected model. Table 14 shows that fiscal autonomy, provisional own revenue, provincial tax autonomy, federal transfers, and provincial debt autonomy are significant.

4. Discussion

Our theoretical model explains that Pakistan's fiscal system is highly centralized in expenditure, revenue, tax autonomy, transfers, and debt autonomy. We measure the fiscal degree based on the above variables calculations and took the 39 years average of each variable. However, the mean of provincial expenditure is about 22.6, including transfer payments. It means that the federal government spends 77.4 % of the total government expenditures; based on our measured dimensions, the spending indicator is relatively high, which relies on scale 2, which expresses the centralization in the expenditure side. Our graph one explains that the federal government's highest level was spending about 82 % from 1979 to 1983, which induced the expenditure centralization. The 18th amendment, to some extent, gives relief to the provincial governments on the spending side in and after 2010. The provincial government's spending was recorded 36.9 % in FY 2018, which is still above our measured decentralization dimension and relies on a relatively centralized scale.

According to graph two, the era of 2014 to 2017 was represented by the period of centralization. At the same time, tax autonomy at the provincial level was declined sharply and trended toward high centralization. Therefore, it relies on our first measuring scale of highly centralized. According to the indicator's revenue resources and tax autonomy, most of the taxes depend on the federal government's domain, collecting the massive share of the revenue and transferring it through the NFC award among the provinces. Therefore, it increases the importance of transfer payments. The NFC award formula has been fixed, the percentage between the federal and provincial governments renewed as 42.5 % and 57.5 % in tax revenue.

The federal transfer indicator demonstrates that a large chunk of the provincial government's revenue comes through federal transfers. The provincial governments' dependency gradually increased since 1979, but the last four years from 2011 to 2017 denoted 88.7 % as its peak. However, it contributes 66.9 % based on an average in provincial revenue. The growing reliance of provincial governments on federal transfers raises the "degree of condition," which contends the country's fiscal centralization scale. Thus, federal transfers decline in scale five, relatively centralized.

The public debt autonomy variable is related to regional borrowing freedom; therefore, higher freedom denotes greater fiscal autonomy. If lower, the borrowing autonomy represents the fiscal centralization. The provincial borrowing scale is confined in scale one, high centralized. Because the federal government bound provinces under the FRDL Act-2005 amended in 2017 and Art-167(3) of the constitution, the provincial may not be borrowing loans without the federal government's consent. It is reduced debts borrowing autonomy of provincial governments and restricted provinces under the federal government permission. Impose of borrowing restrictions shape the fiscal system highly centralized. However, the fiscal system's overall provincial expenditures, own provincial revenue, provincial tax autonomy, federal transfers, and debt borrowing autonomy denoted high centralization.

5. Conclusion

This paper attempted to analyze and measure the degree of fiscal (de) centralization by using theoretical and empirical approaches. We concluded that Pakistan's fiscal system is highly centralized in revenue, expenditure, tax revenue autonomy, and debt autonomy.

The provincial government's revenue collection is about 11 % of the total government revenue, which denotes the scale of centralization. The perspective of provincial public expenditures is confined in scale 2 of centralization, which is recorded 22.6 % of total government expenditures, based on an average of the last 39 years. We have noted that provincial tax autonomy is confined within the first scale of centralization and recorded 5.4 % on average based on the 39 years' data set. Moreover, the provincial governments' dependency on transfer payments was increased in 2011–2017, recording 88.7 % highest, and denoted in the 6th scale of federal transfer measures. It is an average basis of 66.9 % of its provincial revenue. The provincial debt borrowing autonomy is restricted under the law of the constitution unless provinces take permission from the federal government. Compared with other federalist countries such as the USA and Canada, Pakistan has a high centralized fiscal system.

Our empirical model explains that the dependent variable is highly regressed on the independent variables in this study. In the regression, it has been observed that there are 39observations, whereas the data is significant at the 1st difference, and P-value recorded less than 5 %. The variables provincial own revenue, provincial expenditure, provincial debt autonomy, and federal transfers significantly impact the dependent variable. All significant relationships show a direct relation with the dependent variable. Statistically, significant relationships explain 51.3 % variation on the dependent variable. Furthermore, the Durbin-Watson state is displaying that there is no serial correlation among the variables.

References

Arzaghi, M., & Henderson, J. V. (2005). Why countries are fiscally decentralizing. *Journal of Public Economics*, 89(7), 1157–1189.

Bahl, R., & Cyan, M. (2009). Local government taxation in Pakistan. *International Studies Program Working Paper*, 09(09), 90.

Besley, T., & Coate, S. (2003). Centralized versus decentralized provision of local public goods: A political economy approach. *Journal of Public Economics*, 87(12), 2611–2637.

Cevik, S. (2016a). *Unlocking Pakistan's revenue potential* (p. 22).

Chandio, A. S., Tunio, F. H., & Korai, A. G. (2024). Federalism in South Asia: A constitutional analysis of India and Pakistan. *Cogent Arts & Humanities*, 11(1), 2299536. https://doi.org/10.1080/23311983.2023.2299536

Cheema, A., Khwaja, A. I., & Qadir, A. (2005). Decentralization in Pakistan: Context, content and causes. *SSRN Electronic Journal*. https://doi.org/10.2139/ssrn.739712

Dardanelli, P., Kincaid, J., Fenna, A., Kaiser, A., Lecours, A., & Singh, A. K. (2019). Conceptualizing, measuring, and theorizing dynamic de/centralization in federations. *Publius: The Journal of Federalism*, 49(1), 1–29. https://doi.org/10.1093/publius/pjy036

de Mello, L. R. (2000). Fiscal decentralization and intergovernmental fiscal relations: A cross-country analysis. *World Development*, 28(2), 365–380. https://doi.org/10.1016/S0305-750X(99)00123-0

Ebel, R. D., & Yilmaz, S. (2002). *On the measurement and impact of fiscal decentralization*. The World Bank. https://doi.org/10.1596/1813-9450-2809

Fornasari, F., Webb, S. B., & Zou, H.-F. (2000). The macroeconomic impact of decentralized spending and deficits: International evidence. *Annals of Economics and Finance*, 1(2), 403–433.

Iqbal, N. (2013). Fiscal Decentralization, Macroeconomic Stability and Economic Growth (Doctoral Dissertation). *Pakistan Institute of Development Economics*, Islamabad

Iqbal, N., Din, M. U., & Ghani, E. (2012). Fiscal decentralisation and economic growth: Role of democratic institutions. *The Pakistan Development Review* (51), 173–195

Jalal, A. (1995). *Democracy and authoritarianism in South Asia* (p. 50). Cambridge University Press.

Kaiser, A., & Vogel, S. (2019). Dynamic de/centralization in Germany, 1949–2010. *Publius: The Journal of Federalism*, 49(1), 84–111. https://doi.org/10.1093/publius/pjx054

Kee, J. E. (2003). Fiscal decentralization: Theory as reform. *VII Congreso Internatcional Del CLAD Sobre La Reforma Del Estado y de La Administracion Publica* (p. 34), Panama, 28–31 Oct. 2003.

Kiewiet, D. R., & Szakaty, K. (1996). Constitutional limitations on borrowing: An analysis of state bonded indebtedness. *The Journal of Law, Economics, and Organization*, 12(1), 62–97.

Kincaid, J. (2019). Dynamic de/centralization in the United States, 1790–2010. *Publius: The Journal of Federalism*, 49(1), 166–193. https://doi.org/10.1093/publius/pjy032

Köthenbürger, M. (2002). Tax competition and fiscal equalization. *International Tax and Public Finance*, 9(4), 391–408. https://doi.org/10.1023/A:101651 1918510

Lecours, A. (2019). Dynamic de/centralization in Canada, 1867–2010. *Publius: The Journal of Federalism*, 49(1), 57–83. https://doi.org/10.1093/publius/pjx046

Morozov, B. (2016). Decentralization: Operationalization and measurement model. *International Journal of Organization Theory & Behavior*, 19(3), 275–307. https://doi.org/10.1108/IJOTB-19-03-2016-B001

Musgrave, R. A., & Musgrave, R. A. (1959). The theory of public finance. In *The theory of public finance* (pp. XVII–628). McGraw-Hill Book Co.

Musharraf Cyan, R. B. (2011). Tax assignment: Does the practice match the theory? *Environment and Planning C: Government and Policy 2011*, 29(264), 280.

Oates, W. E. (1972). *Fiscal federalism*. New York: Harcourt Brace Jovanovich.

Oates, W. E. (2005). Toward a second-generation theory of fiscal federalism. *International Tax and Public Finance*, 12(4), 349–373. https://doi.org/10.1007/s10797-005-1619-9

Rodden, J. (2002). The dilemma of fiscal federalism: Grants and fiscal performance around the world. *American Journal of Political Science*, 670–687.

Rodden, J. (2004). Comparative federalism and decentralization: On meaning and measurement. *Comparative Politics*, 36(4), 481–500.

Schneider, A. (2003). Decentralization: Conceptualization and measurement. *Studies in Comparative International Development*, 38(3), 32–56. https://doi.org/10.1007/BF02686198

Searle, B., & Ahmad, E. (2005). On the implementation of transfers to subnational governments. *IMF Working Papers*, 05(130), 1. https://doi.org/10.5089/9781451861495.001; BSearle@imf.org; EAhmad@imf.org

Shah, A. (2005). *Fiscal decentralization and fiscal performance*. The World Bank. https://doi.org/10.1596/1813-9450-3786

Thushyanthan Baskaran (2010) On the link between fiscal decentralization and public debt in OECD countries; *Public Choice*; 145: 351–378; DOI 10.1007/s11127-009-9570-4

Tunio, F. H., & Nabi, A. A. (2021). Political decentralization, fiscal centralization, and its consequences in case of Pakistan. *Cogent Social Sciences*, 7(1), 1924949. https://doi.org/10.1080/23311886.2021.1924949

Ullah, I., Tunio, F. H., Ulllah, Z., & Nabi, A. A. (2022). The impact of capital account openness on income inequality: Empirical evidence from Asia. *Journal of Asian Finance, Economics and Business*, 9(2), 0049–0059.

Weissert, C. S., & Uttermark, M. J. (2017). Glass half full: Decentralization in health policy. *State and Local Government Review*, 49(3), 199–214. https://doi.org/10.1177/0160323X17741945

Marija Ham

Social Desirability Bias in Research in Sustainable Marketing

1. Introduction

Over the last few decades, a significant progress has been made in identifying the determinants of consumer behavior in the domain of sustainable marketing. Most of that research is based on self-reported attitudes, intentions and behavior, which introduced some major issues into the relevant discussions. Some of those issues refer to sample issues and non-response bias, namely a systematic error resulting from unwillingness to participate in the survey. (Ham et al., 2016)

Also, many of these studies have implicitly or explicitly assumed the influence of SDB that can affect the outcomes of the research and result in an inaccurate representation of actual attitudes and behavior. This phenomenon leads to over-reporting of what is socially desirable, under-reporting of what is not and confounds attempts to examine the nature of relationships between the variables under study (Nancarrow et al., 2001). Both survey and experimental research can be prone to such SDB. (Ried et al., 2022). Despite that assumption, most of the studies do not offer a solution for that problem, rather than merely recognizing it as a limitation of the study.

Cerri et al. (2019a) carried out a systematic literature review and revealed that the number of papers mentioning SDB steadily increased since the 1990s. However, the overall proportion of relevant papers discussing it is low, with most of those doing so giving no clear indication about its causes and/or consequences for data quality. Ried et al. (2022) also state that SDB has been addressed in only surprisingly few empirical studies in purchasing and supply management.

It should be stated that there are also some previous studies (Gatersleben et al., 2002; Chan & Lau, 2000; Kaiser et al., 1999), that have demonstrated that the influence of social desirability is not significant when it comes to environmental awareness. A study conducted by Chan and Lau (2000) showed that respondents were ready to express their apathy concerning environmental issues.

More recently, Dursun et al. (2019) identified nine groups of constructs that were empirically found to be vulnerable to SDB and pro-environmental consumption was one of them. Furthermore, Wheeler et al. (2019) used a structural equation model to assess the drivers of South Australian consumers' self-reported organic food purchasing frequency and provided empirical evidence that failure to account for self-deception bias generates considerable upward bias in estimated purchasing frequency, indicating the need for future organic purchasing surveys to control for SDB. Durmaz et al. (2023) conducted an experiment and revealed that the pro-environmental intention scale is vulnerable to SDB and that respondents tend to overreport about their pro-environmental intentions, particularly in non-anonymous survey conditions.

As stated in Cerri et al. (2019a), despite various methodological and statistical approaches have been suggested to counteract social desirability, their use in research about sustainable food has not been systematically reviewed before. The same can be stated for the sustainable marketing research in general. Therefore, this study aims to provide a systematic overview of the main ways to cope with social desirability in sustainable marketing research in order to enable academics as well as practitioners, that are increasingly doing research in this area, to gain a comprehensive insight in the state of the matter and main remedies available. Although different studies (Durmaz et al., 2023; Ried et al., 2022; Joyce, 2022; Cerri et al., 2019a) suggest different approaches to coping with social desirability, the present study focuses specifically on approaches that are relevant for research in sustainable marketing and it observes those issues and remedies through three main phases of research process: 1. Questionnaire design; 2. Data collection; and 3. Research results and interpretation. It applies qualitative methodology in order to focus more on the content of the studies and conclusions rather than on the number of studies (like Cerri et al. 2019a and Van de Mortel, 2008). The results can be considered as a check list for researchers in sustainable marketing in each of the phases of the research. By considering the complexity of the issue and providing a systematic overview of the remedies, it is possible to minimize the negative influence and to contribute to quality of the obtained results, developed models and consequently decisions made based on that research.

2. Social Desirability Bias

SDB has recently been defined by Durmaz et al. (2023) as the output of the tendency that makes respondents look favorable with regard to culturally derived norms and standards in test-taking situations. In the past, social desirability has been studied either as a characteristic of items or as an aspect of personality (Steenkamp et al., 2010).

SDB generally has two aspects, one being strategic and one more subconscious. The strategic one is often referred as image management where one tries to present themselves in a more favorable, morally or socially acceptable manner

(Joyce, 2022) and it can be regarded as a form of lying (Cerri et al., 2019b). A subconscious aspect refers to self-deception wherein respondents unconsciously answer in a way that reflects how they would like to think they behave or will behave (Wheeler et al., 2019) which means that a respondent has an unrealistic image of himself.

One of the definitions related specifically to measurement, states that SDB is the "tendency of some people to respond to items more as a result of their social acceptability than their true feelings" (Podsakoff et al., 2003, p. 882). Both "bad" behaviors and states may be under-reported and "good" behaviors and states may be over-reported (Ried et al., 2022). Participants engage in this self-protective behavior because they fear violating social norms (Jann et al., 2019). According to Cerri et al. (2019a), SDB has two different roots: (1) the need for social approval and impression management, and (2) item-specific conformity to existing social norms.

Social desirability is inarguably important in many different specific research domains, however in research on sustainable marketing it is particularly so. As stated by Ried et al. (2022), respondents in research related to sustainable supply chain management may want to appear more environmentally friendly, more socially empathetic or more committed to sustainable procurement initiatives, than they truly are.

SDB can cause systematic measurement errors and therefore poses a threat to the overall validity of study results (Ried et al., 2022) and therefore it is important to consider it and to apply the appropriate remedies as much as possible to minimize the negative effects. In this study we propose the process approach through three main phases of research and analyze the suggested remedies appropriate for sustainable marketing research.

3. Coping with Social Desirability in Different Phases of Research

3.1. Questionnaire Design

In the phase of questionnaire design, one of the frequently used techniques to mitigate SDB is indirect questioning, sometimes also referred to as other-based questioning, i.e., letting participants respond in terms of others' perspectives rather than their own. (Ried et al., 2022). This is a projective technique that makes responses seem more impersonal or general and especially makes self-reporting negative behavior or attitudes easier. When respondents are asked how people tend to behave or think, it is assumed that they will assess the general behavior based on their own and give a more truthful response. This is particularly important for sustainability research (Knemeyer & Naylor, 2011). In case of an in-person interview it reduces the embarrassment in front of the interviewer, especially regarding negative behavior.

There are also disadvantages of this technique. In case of any kind of outlier respondent, it is expected that a respondent will answer quite differently when asked about own opinion or behavior in contrast to opinion or behavior of others. His answer could in this case be honest but incorrect, if it is interpreted as his own characteristic. As stated in Ried et al. (2022, p. 4), "indirect questioning may have the potential to reduce social desirability issues; however, researchers should carefully consider whether it truly measures what it was intended to measure". This leads to the conclusion that indirect questioning should be limited to surveys within coherent groups or subsamples where high similarity of respondents can be assumed. Also, the fact that indirect questioning was used, should be carefully considered when interpreting the results. Also, the phrasing of the questions or statements could influence the social desirability influence. Avoiding too strong statements that may raise ethical issues and using softer phrasing can influence the SDB reduction. (Ried et al., 2022).

Furthermore, one of the social desirability remedies could be incorporating a scale for measuring social desirability in the preliminary or pilot survey. After testing the preliminary results, scales that are classified (based on factor analysis) together with the factor marking social desirability, could be excluded or changed. Also, as states in Carlson (2004), it is possible to include the social desirability scale in the final version of the questionnaire, and then to exclude from further analysis the responses in which the effect of social desirability is present at a level that exceeds the previously established maximum.

Van de Mortel (2008) carried out a review of health studies that applied social desirability statistical remedies. It identified 14,275 studies of which 0.2 % used a social desirability scale and of these, 43 % found that social desirability influenced their results. Cerri et al. (2019a) found, in their study on sustainable food (388 articles), that social desirability scales, were applied only in two studies.

By applying a scale of 32 questions that measures the influence of social desirability, Kaiser et al. (1999) measured the influence on each of the measured variables separately (pro-environmental knowledge, environmental values, intention of pro-environmental behavior, general pro-environmental behavior). However, they found that social desirability had only a marginal influence on all measured variables. Durmaz et al. (2023) found in their study that distinct SDB scales have different levels of relationship with respective scales of sustainable consumption intention.

Two of the most frequently used scales are a 33-item scale named Marlowe-Crowne Social Desirability Scale (Crowne & Marlowe, 1960.) and Balanced Inventory of Desirable Responding (BIDR) scale developed by Paulhus (1988). Steenkamp et al. (2010) revealed that Marlowe-Crowne scale was by far the most frequently employed social desirability response instrument in marketing literature. Marlowe-Crowne scale was mostly used to check for response bias in a construct of interest or to control for response bias when investigating the relationship between substantive constructs. The BIDR was used less frequently and mostly to control for response bias.

A shorter version of Marlowe and Crown's scale was proposed by Vésteinsdóttir et al. (2017). It consists of 10 items and was developed using item response theory. This scale was applied in a recent study of Joyce (2022) that examined the effects of social desirability on reported attitudes towards sustainably produced food and found that social desirability influences self-reported attitudes, however in a simulated shopping task, social desirability does not predict any behavior. This points to the conclusion that introducing a social desirability scale in a survey based on attitudes and intentions is beneficial and that alternative measures (such as the simulated shopping task) are less influenced by social desirability.

Ried et al. (2022) strongly recommend the use of SDB scales not only for the main data collection but also already in the pre- and pilot-testing stages of both surveys and behavioral experiments, in order to derive a better understanding of how strong SDB is, and consequently which and how many countermeasures might be needed to better mitigate this SDB.

3.2. Data Collection Procedure

One of the reasons why surveys in sustainable marketing suffer from socially desirable responding is the fact that anonymized data collection and analysis is not assured (Cerri et al., 2019b; Ried et al., 2022).The mode of survey administration, the degree of privacy protection, the interaction with the interviewer and the presence of acquaintances during survey completion determine the observability of survey completion which is according to Cerri et al. (2019b) one of the main conditions that lead to social desirability in surveys.

Holbrook et al. (2003) determined that telephone respondents were more suspicious about the interview process and more likely to present themselves in socially desirable ways than were face-to-face respondents. Furthermore, Tourangeau and Yan (2007) state that respondents are less likely to overreport socially desirable behaviors and to underreport socially undesirable ones when the questions are self-administered, when the randomized response technique or bogus pipeline is used, and when the data are collected in private. Similarly, Krumpal (2013) states that self-administration (compared to interviewer-administration) generally reduces SDB as well as randomized response technique (and it's alternative: The unmatched count technique) which guarantees the respondent to maintain privacy via the possibility of randomizing the answer (for more information on the technique and references to original literature, see: Krumpal, 2013)

In the context of sustainable consumption, Cerri et al. (2019b) investigated which factors are perceived by consumers as critical for socially desirable answering in self-reported organic fruit consumption and found that the presence of acquaintances during survey completion is a critical driver of survey misreporting.

Krumpal (2013) points out that data collection strategy called the 'Bogus pipeline procedure' decreases SDB. The term 'bogus pipeline' refers to any procedure that makes the respondent believe that an objective measurement instrument will be used, such as lie detector to reveal false responses. According to Roese and Jamieson (1993, p. 364), Bogus pipeline is based in the assumption that a respondent's desire to avoid appearing to be a liar or to be self-unaware would supersede the typically assumed tendency to exaggerate possession of favorable traits.

Also, one of the ways to reduce the potential bias of respondents in face to face surveys is to instruct the fieldworkers to simply and clearly explain to the respondents the importance of honestly expressing their true attitudes and to emphasize the fact that their answers would be analyzed and reported only on a collective basis (Chan & Lau, 2000, p. 345). Krumpal (2013) also point to the importance of data protection assurances but stresses the fact that confidentiality assurances that are too elaborate and sophisticated might have opposite effect.

As suggested by Tourangeau and Yan (2007), future survey procedures to encourage honest reporting are likely to involve new forms of computerized self-administration. There is some evidence that computerization increases the reporting of sensitive information in surveys relative to paper questionnaires, though the difference between the two may depend on other variables (such as whether the computer is a stand-alone machine or part of a network) because the latter could raise some online privacy issues.

3.3. Results and Interpretation

One of the main ways to check for social desirability influence in the results is comparing them to available secondary data or previous research. For example, self-reported behavior on buying sustainable products or recycling behavior can be compared to secondary data available for a specific market or area. Also, a comparison to previous studies results can flag cases of SDB. Significant deviations from previous results should, in the interpretation phase, be considered in the light of possible social desirability influence.

Also, a multiple-methods approach can be considered to verify and strengthen the results of a single survey or experiment since it allows for triangulation of the data which may enhance the external validity of a study with the potential to also lead to more robust interpretations in light of social desirability (Ried et al., 2022). Significant differences between results obtained from different methods should be fully disclosed and they can provide valuable methodological insights for future researchers.

As elaborated in the study by Krumpal (2013), two sorts of studies can be distinguished to assess the accuracy of survey reports and to compare two or more different methods: (1) validation studies and (2) comparative studies without validation data. Validation studies can be considered as the golden standard for testing the value of a method because they enable the researcher to compare individual survey responses with the true status of each individual as well as a comparison of survey estimates to the true means or proportions at the aggregate level (often from external data sources, such as administrative records). In contrast, comparative studies are experimental surveys comparing different survey conditions without the possibility of external validation with some objective criterion. In that case, when underreporting is expected, a higher survey estimate (mean or proportion) is assumed to be a more valid and vice versa.

4. Conclusion

Although it is present in many different research domains, investigating behavior and opinions within sustainable marketing is particularly susceptible to social desirability. This is mostly due to the very nature of issues involved and the fact that it is quite easy for respondents to understand which direction of answers is considered socially desirable.

It can be concluded that SDB needs to undoubtfully be considered when using self-report measures for assessing sustainable consumption behaviors or attitudes as also suggested by Durmaz et al. (2023). Thereby the issue of SDB needs to be considered when creating measurement instruments, collecting the data, analyzing data and interpreting the results. Every effort in that area could help to minimize the influence of SDB and contribute to the quality of results, robustness of theory and conclusions and optimize decisions made based on those data.

The present study aimed to provide researchers with a check list of issues and remedies through all of the three major phases of research whereby remedies applied in first two phases (questionnaire design and data collection process) are focused on preventing the influence of social desirability and the ones in the last phase (results and interpretation) are focused on detecting and interpreting that influence.

Researchers need to carefully choose between suggested approaches based on their specific research questions and aims of the research as well as specifics of the sample. Further, it would be advised not to rely on one approach alone, but to apply several in combination. (Ried et al., 2022). And finally, specific situational factors have to be considered such as current macroeconomic cycle phase or the existence of specific social impacts relevant for the sustainability topic such as the recent global pandemic or some major events related to ecology which can have a temporary influence on the results.

As Joyce (2022) concludes in a study on sustainably produced food, it is troubling that social desirability is in most studies mentioned superficially, stated briefly in the discussion section of papers with no real implications for the research. In the future of sustainable marketing research, it is necessary to invest efforts in dealing with social desirability in all three phases of research. In the phase of questionnaire design, the use of indirect questioning should be (carefully) considered as well as phrasing of the questions. Also, social desirability scales should be used more comprehensively. In this area, more research is needed to further refine those scales for specific research areas as well as to respond to the issue of the length of those scales (causing fatigue of respondents) without compromising on reliability and validity.

Furthermore, as also suggested by Cerri et al. (2019a), a better description of the data collection process is highly important, to better identify the limitations and strengths of a specific study. Although the assumption of anonymity and privacy of respondents seems as common sense, this is often neglected and violated during data collection in research in sustainable marketing where convenient samples in shopping situations are often used. Growing use of online surveys would seem to rectify this, however, in current conditions of comprehensive connectivity, development of online identity and growing online privacy issues, people could eventually become even more concerned about their privacy in online than in offline environment. This could lead to the situation where social desirability becomes more influential in online surroundings because the risk would be perceived as greater. Substantial work needs to be done in developing new specialized questioning techniques and data collection methods (bearing in mind also a dropping response rate due to saturation of consumers with online research). Also, the potentials as well as ethical considerations of some existing methods such as "Bogus pipeline" need more investigation within the domain of sustainable marketing.

And finally, although comparing research results to previous research is common practice in sustainable marketing literature, seldom is this used to detect and cope with social desirability. The same could apply to secondary data such as public records or aggregate data on any level. Efforts on multi methods approach and triangulation of data would contribute to robustness of conclusions and implications of academic research for practice.

References

Carlson, D. H. (2004). *Environmetal concern in South Africa: The development of a measurement scale*, Masters paper, University of South Africa.

Cerri, J., Testa, F., Rizzi, F., & Frey, M. (2019a). Factorial surveys reveal social desirability bias over self-reported organic fruit consumption. *British Food Journal*, 121(4), 897–909.

Cerri, J., Thøgersen, J., & Testa, F. (2019b). Social desirability and sustainable food research: A systematic literature review. *Food Quality and Preference*, 71, 136–140.

Chan, R. Y. K., & Lau, L. B. Y. (2000). Antecedents of green purchases – a survey in China, *Journal of Consumer Marketing*, 17(4), 338–357.

Crowne, D. P., & Marlowe, D. (1960). A new scale of social desirability independent of psychopathology. *Journal of Consulting Psychology*, 24(4), 349.

Durmaz, A., Dursun, I., & Kabadayı, E. T. (2023). Are they actually sustainable? The social desirability bias in sustainable consumption surveys. In *Dealing with socially responsible consumers: Studies in marketing* (pp. 533–560). Singapore: Springer Nature Singapore.

Dursun, İ., Kabadayı, E. T., & Durmaz, A. (2019). When to consider social desirability bias (SDB) in consumer behavior studies? A Review on SDB-vulnerable concepts. *Business & Management Practices*, 233.

Gatersleben, B., Steg, L., & Vlek, C. (2002). Measurement and determinants of environmentally significant consumer behavior. *Environment and Behavior*, 34(3), 335–362.

Ham, M., Mrčela, D., & Horvat, M. (2016). Insights for measuring environmental awareness. *Ekonomski vjesnik: Review of Contemporary Entrepreneurship, Business, and Economic Issues*, 29(1), 159–176.

Holbrook, A. L., Green, M. C., & Krosnick, J. A. (2003). Telephone versus face-to-face interviewing of national probability samples with long questionnaires: Comparisons of respondent satisficing and social desirability response bias. *Public Opinion Quarterly*, 67(1), 79–125.

Jann, B., Krumpal, I., & Wolter, F. (2019). Editorial: Social desirability bias in surveys – Collecting and analyzing sensitive data. *Journal for Quantitative Methods and Survey Methodology*, 13(1), 3–6.

Joyce, C. (2022). *The effects of social desirability on reported attitudes towards sustainably produced food.* Doctoral Dissertation, Dublin Business School.

Kaiser, F. G., Wölfing, S., & Fuhrer, U. (1999). Environmental attitude and ecological behaviour. *Journal of Environmental Psyhology*, 19(1), 1–19.

Knemeyer, A. M., & Naylor, R.W. (2011). Using behavioral experiments to expand our horizons and deepen our understanding of logistics and supply chain decision making. *Journal of Business Logistics,* 32(4), 296–302.

Krumpal, I. (2013). Determinants of social desirability bias in sensitive surveys: A literature review. *Quality & Quantity*, 47(4), 2025–2047.

Nancarrow, C., Brace, I., & Wright, L. T. (2001). Tell me lies, tell me sweet little lies: Dealing with socially desirable responses in market research. *The Marketing Review*, 2(1), 55–69.

Paulhus, D. L. (1988). Balanced Inventory of Desirable Responding (BIDR). *Acceptance and Commitment Therapy. Measures Package*, 41, 79586–79587.

Podsakoff, P. M., MacKenzie, S. B., Lee, J. Y., & Podsakoff, N. P. (2003). Common method biases in behavioral research: A critical review of the literature and recommended remedies. *Journal of Applyed Psychology*, 88(5), 879–903.

Ried, L., Eckerd, S., & Kaufmann, L. (2022). Social desirability bias in PSM surveys and behavioral experiments: Considerations for design development and data collection. *Journal of Purchasing and Supply Management*, 28(1), 100743.

Roese, N. J., & Jamieson, D. W. (1993). 20 years of bogus pipeline research – A critical review and metaanalysis. *Psychological Bulletin,* 114, 363–375.

Steenkamp, J. B. E., De Jong, M. G., & Baumgartner, H. (2010). Socially desirable response tendencies in survey research. *Journal of Marketing Research*, 47(2), 199–214.

Tourangeau, R., & Yan, T. (2007). Sensitive questions in surveys. *Psychological Bulletin*, 133(5), 859.

Van de Mortel, T. (2008). Faking it: Social desirability response bias in self-report research. *Australian Journal of Advanced Nursing,* 25(4), 40–48.

Vésteinsdóttir, V., Reips, U. D., Joinsonc, A., & Thorsdottir, F. (2017). An item level evaluation of the Marlowe-Crowne Social Desirability Scale using item response theory on Icelandic Internet panel data and cognitive interviews. *Personality and Individual Differences*, 107, 164–173.

Wheeler, S. A., Gregg, D., & Singh, M. (2019). Understanding the role of social desirability bias and environmental attitudes and behaviour on South Australians' stated purchase of organic foods. *Food Quality and Preference*, 74, 125–134.

Entela Abdul, Plarent Anamali

Enhancing Albania's Electronic Procurement System! Balancing Between Data Privacy and Transparency in Public Investment and Procurement

1. Introduction

Contracting Authorities during the development of procurement procedures, in compliance with public procurement rules, published in the Electronic Procurement System (EPS) and in the Bulletin of Public Announcements, the information considered necessary by the Law "On Public Procurement" for the competition of economic operators in this procedure. It is necessary to clarify that Electronic Procurement System (EPS) is a state database, created according to the legislation in force and used to carry out public procurement procedures. The purpose of this announcement is transparency and information, which enables economic operators to decide whether or not they meet the qualification criteria and whether or not they will participate in the procurement procedures. Referring to legal provisions in any case, announcements are made according to the format, part of the standard tender documents approved by law.

The purpose of the Contracting Authorities and of the Procurement Law itself is to increase the efficiency of procurement procedures and the good use of public funds by reducing expenses and increasing the quality of goods, works and services provided from the procurement procedures.

The lack of transparency and the narrowing of the competition by the Contracting Authorities directly affects the efficiency of the procurement procedures, as it aims to favor a certain economic operator and harm other competitors, undermining the equality in procurement procedures.

The involvement of technology has brought as a result that no procurement procedure can be announced or finalized until if all information is not made publicly endorsed and easily accessible by competing economic operators. This publication is monitored in all cases by the Public Procurement Agency (PPA), which verifies and controls case by case, the standard tender documents published by the contracting authorities. It is worth clarifying that in the public procurement sector in Albania (PPA) is a central institution under Prime Minister, which oversees the public procurement system, with the aim of ensuring efficiency and transparency in the public procurement process and administers the Electronic Procurement System (EPS).

Referring to legal provisions, in the event of winner notifications, cancellation notifications and contract notification turn out not to have been drawn up in accordance with the format and method defined by the law, the (PPA) does not make the publication but returns it recommending and guiding the Contracting Authority for the correct completion of the procedure. The decisions of the (PPA) are recommendatory/advisory and not binding regarding the information published by the Contracting Authorities in the (EPS). For this reason, the main responsibility and challenge between maintaining confidentiality and also not violating the right to information remains within the Contracting Authorities. The objectives of the procurements are to promote efficiency and effectiveness in the good management of public funds, but also to ensure equal and comprehensive treatment to the participants. Referring to the law, the way the technical qualification criteria are drawn up and published in the SPE can violate equality in the tender, violating integrity, competition, transparency and public trust.

On the other hand, the purpose of the law "On the protection of personal data" is the harmonization of legal changes with the Acquis Communautaire and the implementation of EU standards in the field of personal data protection.

The need to align the current legislation for the protection of personal data with the EU Acquis in this area is important in order to guarantee the highest European standards to Albanian citizens in the field of personal data protection at a time when the processing of personal data in the digital age has multiplied.[1] Also, the Procurement Law has been amended and aligned with European directives and standards. Referring to EU Directive 24/2014 "On public procurement", according to Bano and Ahmeti (2022, p. 211), it is foreseen that the awarding of public contracts must be in accordance with the principles of the Treaty on the Functioning of the European Union (TFEU), specifically with the free movement of goods, the freedom to provide services, as well as main principles such as equal treatment, non-discrimination, proportionality and transparency.

According the law, always in order to protect personal data, contractors as owners of their personal data, have the right to express their consent to the processing of this data by completing the confidentiality declaration, where they can request that a certain number of documents and information should not be made public to third parties who request it.

---

1 General Regulation for protection of personal data 2016/679 GRPR and Police Directive 2016/680.

However, the economic operator cannot classify as confidential, subject of data protection, the information related to the price of the offer, the list of prices, the catalog, information related to the selection criteria, public documents, and other information that must be made public in order to carry out and finalize the procurement procedure.

On the other hand, according to article 14 and 15, of the Law No. 119/ 2014 "On the Right to Information", regarding to the right to information, the parties participating in procurement procedures, also any interested entity too, has the right to request information about the documentation, facts and circumstances related to the procurement procedures, this obliging the Contracting Authority to respond within the legal deadlines.

However, the right to information in procurement procedures cannot be unlimited. According to article 17, of the Law No. 119/2014 "On the Right to Information" it is limited if it is necessary, proportionate and if the provision of information damages the right to a private life, trade secret, copyright, patents, etc. But referring to the legal provisions, the limitation of the right to information, due to subjective interests, does not apply when the holder of these rights have given their consent for the provision of information. Regardless of the legal provisions, the requested information is not restrained in case there is a higher public interest in providing it.

Referring to institutional practices, during the development of procurement procedures, an inconsistency is observed between the facts and circumstances of the legal provisions as well as the technical processes, where these legal provisions must be reflected in the (EPS). This brings technical and legal difficulties in the daily institutional practice, affecting the finalization of the procurement procedures and contract agreement.

Based on the qualitative analysis of the Procurement Law, on the institutional practices and the data obtained from it, in terms of the protection of personal data and confidentiality on the one hand, as well as the obligation of the Contracting Authority to make public the required information, the right to information, the analysis permeates into two main research objectives:

- Identification of the procedural actions of the Contracting Authorities for the protection of personal data and the confidentiality of procurement procedures, in the face of the right to information.
- Highlight the necessity of improvements and adjustments to the (EPS), implementing it in accordance with the legal framework and anticipating all circumstances and legal situations.

2. Literature Review and Development of Hypothesis

Comprehensive literature review, laws and legal changes forms the backbone of this study. Literature review is limited for public procurement procedures in the Albanian case as this topic has not been extensively elaborated by Albanian scholars.

According to Toçi (1974), the first concessions problems treatment, and developments in Albania started from a comparative and historical perspective. Bano and Ahmeti (2022), explore some country cases, including Albania, through historical and comparative lenses, emphasizing the need for a unified and harmonized legislation in line with international directives.

According to the article by Bosio et al. (2022), public procurements as observed and examined in 187 different countries stress that law and practices of different countries are connected and unified between them, bringing better practical results. This study also highlights that stricter laws improve the outcomes of procurement practices. While Mironov and Zhuravskaya (2016) treat unlawful procurements leading to corruption and favoritism with negative effects in public procurements toward politically connected bidders. Coviello and Mariniello (2014), emphasize the importance of transparency as well as the connection between the results of the auction and the public release of information.

This study is a contribution with innovative discussions and results in the field of treatment of the (EPS) problems while providing recommendations for the Albanian case, as lack extensive research exist regarding this sector.

Following the literature review and acknowledging the need for due attention to this subject in the case of Albania, the study posits the following hypothesis:

There is a significant discrepancy between the operational functionality of the new (EPS) and the legal provisions it was intended to embody, which suggests that the current legislative framework is not effectively guiding the practical application of the (EPS).

3. Research Methodology

This study employs qualitative descriptive and explanatory analyzes to critically examine the extent to which current and evolving legislation influences and regulates procurement practices and procedures. This rigorous examination aims to objectively assess the potential dichotomy creating between maintaining confidentiality and ensuring transparency within this domain.

To enrich the analysis, the study scrutinizes institutional practices and real-cases drawn from procurement activities. Empirical data are gathered through a series of six unstructured interviews with field-experts. These interviews, meticulously analyzed, identified and helped evaluate discrepancies between the (EPS) and legal provisions, specifically in the context of personal data protection.

The synthesis of insights from the literature review, statutory regulations, legal amendments, and expert interviews facilitates a nuanced exploration of the core issues and objectives outlined in this research. The outcome of this multifaceted investigation provides a foundation for formulating conclusions and actionable recommendations. These recommendations advocate for enhanced personal data safeguards that do not compromise the right to information, along with the technological refinement and legal-compliant implementation of the (EPS).

Furthermore, the findings advocate for the alignment of legislative reforms with the Acquis Communautaire, promoting the adoption of EU standards in the pursuit of harmonized legal and procedural frameworks.

4. The Historical Beginnings of Procurement Procedures in Albania

Our country lacks a longstanding tradition in the concessionary sector as well as in the development of public procurement and the attraction of foreign investments. According to Toçi (1974, p. 44), Albania encounters the first steps of concessionary developments around the 1920. At the end of the first world war, some main problems emerged, which were:

- reconstruction of the state;
- economic recovery and development;
- finding means and ways for development.

The first discussions about granting a concession were those of the kerosene concession, where there were many opinions and discussions from 1921 to 1925. The main elements analyzed were the way of granting the concession, the duration of the contractual conditions, the benefits and obligations of the Albanian state, and those of the concessionaire. Debates of the kerosene concession during this period were also included in the parliament of the time.

According to Toçi (1974, p. 52), in the parliament of 1923, after the presentation of the government's project for the kerosene concession agreement with the Anglo-Persian company, Luigj Gurakuqi presented a critical analysis regarding this agreement. In this discussion, he emphasized the fact that the language of the agreement should be precise and clear, where the contractual conditions should not be left evasive and not clearly defined, which could pave the way for damage to state interests. Of great importance in this discussion of Gurakuqi was the fact that he demanded the agreement to encourage free competition and to prohibit monopolization, this very progressive principle for the time in the function of protecting the national interest, and which has a well-regulated provision in the current law "On Public Procurement". Furthermore, in this discussion he requested to clearly define the term of the concession, as well as the share of the profit for the Albanian state, so that the profit was as large as possible.

According to Toçi (1974, p. 129), during the years 1921–1925 foreign investments in Albania were also developed in the field of transport and communication works. The goal and aim of our country at this time was the construction of communication roads and several bridges. For the construction of large automobile bridges, the Albanian government announced a public auction in 1923, which was won by a French company. The main condition was that the Albanian state would pay 1 million francs per year, as well as allow the use of forests and mines until repayment of construction costs.

Concessions had a rapid development even during the period of the monarchy, but after the second world war and the establishment of the communist regime, construction and economic development were no longer based on the concessions, and foreign investments were stopped.

5. Protection of Confidentiality in the Field of Public Procurement, Practical and Legal Limit with the Right to Information

Referring to the rules of public procurement and the principle of transparency based on the needs for public works, goods or services, the Contracting Authority at the beginning of each year draws up and publishes in the (EPS) the annual register of forecasts for public procurement procedure. The publication of the register of forecast aims a good planning, good use of public funds as well as the timely realization of public procurement procedures, since the Contracting Authorities cannot go outside the deadlines provided in the register and outside the limit fund provided. Also, the (PPA) publishes in the bulletin of public announcements, every Monday, the various notices related to the procurement procedures, which must be made available for the public according to the right to information. Referring to legal provisions and institutional practice, all information and documentation published in the (EPS) and in the bulletin of public announcements is easily accessible.

The Contracting Authorities also periodically publish electronically in the (EPS) the register of achievements, which contains public information about the procurement procedures carried out during the budget year, their finalization and the dates of the conclusion of the contracts. After the electronic publication in (EPS) the standard tender documents, as well as all the necessary information for the participation of economic operators in the tender, referring to article 28, of Decision of The Council of Ministers No. 285/2021 "On the Approval of Public Procureme Rules", the right arises that the economic operators who choose to compete in this procurement procedure, also complete the declaration of confidentiality.

Through this statement, the bidder (economic operator) defines the information or documents that he decides to keep confidential and for which the Contracting Authority is obliged to respect the protection of personal data. An economic operator may not make public and require the preservation of confidentiality for technical or commercial secrets. It is worth noting that various institutions and institutional practices occasionally encounter many difficulties in terms of defining the line between maintaining confidentiality and the right to information.[2] This is because the economic operators participating in the tender or any interested party have the right to address a request for information to the Contracting Authority and the latter is obliged to respond within 5 days of receiving the request.

According to article 81 of Law No. 162/2020 "On Public Procurement", it is worth noting that without avoiding the obligations arising from legal provisions, the contracting authorities may not make public some of the requested information, if such a thing contradicts the legislation on the protection of personal data or violates the public interest, legal interests and economic of the parties. Also, if some parts of the economic offer are declared confidential, then these documents will not be made available to anyone requesting that information.

During the administrative investigation procedure, According to article 129 of Law No. 162/2020 "On Public Procurement", the Public Procurement Agency (PPA) has the right to request information from any public administration body, as well as to receive any file or material of the procurement procedures, which are related to the administrative investigation. Also, during the investigation, the APP can perform various investigative actions, such as entering any office of public institutions and inspecting on-site acts or documents related to the case it is investigating.

2 Alisona Meçe, Procurement Specialist, DPÇK, Municipality of Tirana, (public institution of executive power), unstructured interview interviewed by Entela Abdul on November 27, 2023.

It is worth noting that these investigative actions carried out by the (PPA), even though they are provided for by legal provisions and justify investigative actions in the function of protecting a higher public interest, at the same time come in conflict with the protection of personal data and the declaration of confidentiality drawn up by the participating economic operators.

Subjects of personal data have the right to know how they have been processed and where their data may have been transferred. The Public Administration must provide these persons with the protection of personal data.[3]

The legislation itself has created an evasive and not clearly regulated situation in terms of the protection of the legal interests of economic operators during procurement procedures. Thus, on one hand there is the obligation not to violate personal data and simultaneously on the other hand the obligation to respect the right to information.

The fact that all systems are concentrated in a central system brings problems as it is completely hacked if the protocols are not followed. For data administration, although the law provides for the position of a personal data processor, in practice this position is not well regulated in terms of the contractual responsibility, that this person should have for monitoring, processing personal data, as well as liability in cases of their misuse, violation and hacking.[4]

6. Findings and Discussions

The Electronic Procurement System during the handling of complaints, causes serious problems since it does not follow the same path as the legal provisions.

In cases where the procurement procedures are suspended in the (EPS) due to legal deadlines and complaints handling procedures, various events and situations may occur. In such cases, the law requires undertaking various procedural actions, actions which cannot be technically reflected in the (EPS), causing serious problems in the finalization of procurement procedures. Referring to the institutional practice of public procurement and legal provisions, after confirming that the complaint has been submitted to the Public Procurement Commission (PPC), the Contracting Authority immediately suspends the procurement procedure in the (EPS) until the complaint is fully examined, and a decision has been provided by the (PPC). According the law, Public Procurement

3 Hatixhe Çollaku Bilabashi, ICT expert in private sector, unstructured interview, interviewed by Abdul, Entela dt. 19 tetor 2023.

4 Endri Plasari (IT expert, Lecturer at "Luarasi" University), unstructured interview, interviewed by Abdul, Entela dt. 13 tetor 2023.

Commission (PPC) is the highest administrative body in the public procurement sector, which examines and finally exhausts complaints about procurement procedures. PPC is considered by the latest legal changes in procurement sector, as a quasi-court.

During the handling of complaints regarding procurement procedures, either by the Contracting Authority or by the (PPC), the procurement procedure in the (EPS) continues to be suspended and it can be removed from the suspension only when the (PPC) issues a final decision on the review of the complaint.[5]

In view of these legal provisions and referring to the decision of (PPC) where it is quoted: "The (PPC) is foreseen by the law as a quasi-court of law"[6] as such, in its decision-making, the (PPC) applies the main principles of law.

It is worth noting that during the complaint review phase, when the procurement procedure is suspended in the (EPS), in institutional practice it happened that the lawyer/responsible employee for the procurement procedure, resigned from his position in this institution. In this case, the "Order of termination of employment relations", should also be reflected in his removal from the position of responsible person in (EPS), since they should no longer have the credentials to enter and change the tender documents in (EPS). To change the person responsible for the procurement in the (EPS), the Contracting Authority must technically unsuspend the procedure again and after changing the responsible person, resuspend the procurement procedure.[7]

The (EPS) did not technically foresee the resuspension and this procurement procedure was not resuspended, causing problems and impossibility of finalizing the procedure, lastly leading to the cancellation of this procedure. Subsequently, the (PPC) came to a decision that accepted the complaint of the economic operator and based on this decision, the reclassification and reevaluation of the offers in the (EPS) should have been done. This action was technically impossible as without suspension the deadlines for the announcement of the winner was

---

5 Article 24 of Law No. 162/2020 "On Public Procurement", specifies:"*…The Public Procurement Commission makes decisions on the complaints submitted to it, keeping in consideration, in addition to the general principles mentioned in Article 2 of this law, the following principles: impartiality in the examination of complaints, stability in decision-making, legality, speed and efficiency, access, public character, as well as the principle of contradiction*".

6 Decision of KPP no. 655/2018 dated 04.10.2018

7 Unstructured interview with former Procurement Specialist Lisandër Prekperaj, DPÇK, Municipality of Tirana, (public institution of executive power). Interviewed by Entela Abdul on November 25, 2023.

passed.[8] Finally, the Contracting Authority in this case sent a request addressed to the Public Procurement Agency for technical assistance regarding the handling of the case. The (PPA) replied that the Electronic Procurement System has no technical way to change the responsible person and the Procurement Unit.[9] This statement of the (PPA) confirms the fact that the legal framework and the (EPS) are not aligned with each other and do not change at the same pace. Since the legal framework prevails over the electronic system this inconsistency causes difficulties in the realization of public services and the finalization of procurement procedures.

7. Conclusions

- Dual Challenges in Procurement Processes:

The research evinces the dual challenges faced in procurement processes, emphasizing the delicate balance between safeguarding personal data and ensuring transparency. The controversy between the right to information and data confidentiality poses significant obstacles, necessitating careful consideration and legal alignment.

The practical and legal boundary between the protection of personal data and the right to information in the field of public procurement is not well regulated, as the legal framework and the best institutional practices need improvements and changes. The evolution of laws, such as the "On the protection of personal data" and amendments to the Procurement Law, has aimed to align with EU standards and enhance data protection. However, challenges arise in defining the limits of the right to information, especially when it comes to personal data, trade secrets, and other subjective interests.

The antagonism between data protection and transparency is evident in the dilemmas surrounding confidentiality. While economic operators have the right to withhold certain information through a confidentiality statement, it is essential to strike a balance to prevent misuse of this provision and ensure the integrity of the procurement process.

---

8 Unstructured interview with Procurement Specialist Ivona Lame, DPÇK, Municipality of Tirana, (public institution of executive power). Interviewed by Entela Abdul on November 27, 2023.

9 Unstructured interview with Procurement Specialist Sadika Veshi, DPÇK, Municipality of Tirana, (public institution of executive power). Interviewed by Entela Abdul on November 20, 2023.

- Historical innovations of procurement procedures:

Exploring the historical context of procurement procedures in Albania highlights the country's transition from limited concessionary traditions to a more structured approach. The early discussions and debates around concessions emphasized the importance of clear language, defined contractual conditions, and the encouragement of free competition – principles still relevant in the contemporary legal framework.

- Transparency and Efficiency in Procurement Procedures:

The primary objective of procurement procedures is to enhance efficiency and ensure the optimal use of public funds while maintaining the quality of goods, works, and services. Transparency is crucial in achieving these goals. The integration of technology, particularly the Electronic Procurement System, has played a vital role in making information easily accessible to economic operators, fostering competition, promoting accountability and preventing favoritism. However, challenges persist, especially in the proper implementation of the system and adherence to legal provisions.

- Legal Framework Misalignment and Technological Impact:

The research reveals inconsistencies between legal provisions and the technical processes within institutional practices, particularly in the Electronic Procurement System. The need for harmonization between legal frameworks and technological systems is evident to address these challenges adequately.

The new (EPS) does not follow the same path with the legal framework, not foreseeing all legal situations and circumstances, and violating the confidentiality of the procurement process, and the personal data of economic operators.

8. Recommendations

- Recommendations for further Improvement:

The research proposes recommendations for addressing the identified challenges. This includes enhancing the legal framework to better accommodate the intersection of personal data protection and transparency, refining the (EPS) to align with legal provisions, and promoting a more coherent and synchronized approach to legislation. The drafting of laws should aim to minimize conflicts, enhance public trust, and foster transparency while addressing emerging challenges in the digital age.

- Need for Legislative Harmonization:

It is recommended that Albania continues to improve and harmonize the legislation, particularly in personal data protection and the right to information, emerges as a critical need. Aligning national legislation with EU standards ensures that Albanian citizens benefit from the highest European standards, especially in the era of increased digital data processing. This should involve the continued emphasis on clear language, well-defined contractual conditions, and the promotion of free competition, as these principles have proven to be foundational in the current context. Such efforts will ensure that procurement processes are transparent, equitable, and benefiting to sustainable economic development.

- Recommendation for the compliance of legal framework with the development of technology

It is recommended to technically improve the electronic procurement system following the legal provisions.

Given that the law, in this case, prevails over the system, while the system must follow the legal provisions, recommended that the EPS should be improved by moving at the same path as the legal framework.

Since draft laws for both procurements and right to information are in the stages of public consultation yet to be approved, recommended that, all the problems observed during the practical implementation of these laws, but also this study, carried out in this field, should be taken into account to make the necessary legal improvements.

References

Administrative procedure code of the Republic of Albania. Tiranë: Alb Juris (2021).

Bano, E., & Ahmeti, E. (2022). *E Drejta e Konçensioneve dhe e Partneritetit Publik Privat.* Tiranë: Morava.

Bosio, E., Djankov, S., Glaeser, E., & Shleifer, A. (2022). Public procurement in law and practice. *American Economic Review 2022*, 112(4): 1091–1117. https://doi.org/10.1257/aer.20200738

Coviello, D., & Mariniello, M. (2014). Publicity requirements in public procurement: Evidence from a regression discontinuity design. *Journal of Public Economics*, 109, 76–100. https://EconPapers.repec.org/RePEc:eee:pubeco:v:109:y:2014:i:c:p:76-100

Civil Code of the Republic of Albania. Tiranë: Alb Juris (2018).

Civil Code of 1929. Tirane: Toena (1998).

Civil Code of the People's Socialist Republic of Albania. Tiranë (1982).

Civil Procedure Code of the Republic of Albania.Tirane: Alb Juris (2018).

DCM No. 285, dated 19.05.2021 "On the Approval of Public Procurement Rules".

Decision of the Public Procurement Commission No. 655/2018 dated 04.10.2018.

Directive (EU) 2016/680 of the European Parliament and European Council. 2016. Access: https://eur-lex.europa.eu/legal-content/EN/TXT/PDF/?uri=CELEX:32016L0680

Law No 9887 dated 10.03.2008 "For the protection of personal data".

Law/ 119/2014 "For the right of information"

Law No. 162 dated 23.12.2020 "On Public Procurement".

Law No. 49/2012 "On administrative courts and adjudication of administrative disputes".

Mironov, M., & Zhuravskaya, E. (2016). Corruption in procurement and the political cycle in tunneling: Evidence from financial transactions data. *American Economic Journal:Economic Policy*, 8(2), 287–321. https://EconPapers.repec.org/RePEc:aea:aejpol:v:8:y:2016:i:2:p:287-321

Regulation (BE) 2016/679 of the European Parliament and of the Council. (2016). https://www.idp.al/wp-content/uploads/2016/11/Rregullorja_AL_GDPR.pdf

Toçi, V. (1974). *Nderhyrja e kapitalit të huaj në Shqipëri dhe qëndrimi i qarqeve demokratike 1921–1925, Akademia e Shkencave e RPSh, Instituti i Histowrisë.* Tiranë: Mihal Duri.

Elira Luli, Mirela Metushaj

Socio-Political Transition and Vulnerabilities in the Western Balkans: A Comparative Study of Montenegro and Albania

1. Introduction

The Western Balkan societies have been in transition for the past three decades, facing challenges of state-building, socio-economic nature, and democratic consolidation after the conflicts of the 1990s. Albania and Montenegro have unique historical contexts that shape their current affairs and highlight their governance struggles towards the EU integration process. These countries are progressing in strengthening democratic institutions and aligning with EU standards. Montenegro and Serbia are involved in EU accession negotiations, while Albania and North Macedonia have received the green light to open the negotiations (although North Macedonia has some conditionality). Kosovo focuses on institution-building, international recognition, and economic development, but its relationship with Serbia poses significant obstacles. Bosnia and Herzegovina face challenges in implementing peace accords and suffers from political and ethnic tensions and divisions driving frequent deadlocks. Corruption, political polarization, weak institutions, and socio-economic gaps are priority issues in the region. Montenegro and Albania need to address corruption issues and strengthen the rule of law. Albania also faces challenges in judicial independence, political polarization, opposition, and captured institutions. These issues have been perpetually stressed for both countries to progress towards EU membership. "In both countries, institutions were pivotal to the reforms throughout their transition. This comprehensive process was lengthy and challenging due to each country's unique political, economic, social, and historical contexts." (Zotaj, 2023)[1]

Research Objective: This paper compares socio-political vulnerabilities and limitations in Montenegro and Albania during their transition period. The aim is to understand the challenges in establishing effective governance by examining three factors (Figure 1.):

1 Elda Zotaj, interview by authors, Google Form Questionnaire, November 14, 2023.

1. ***EU journey impact:*** Assessing how governance effectiveness has influenced the EU integration process.
2. ***Society-governance interplay:*** Analysing the relationship between citizens and governing institutions in promoting or hindering reforms.
3. ***Malign actor interference:*** Investigating Russia's role and potential negative influences on governance systems in Montenegro and Albania.

The three factors identified as units of analysis explored in this study are interrelated and crucial for understanding democratic deficiencies and other limitations in Albania and Montenegro. Socio-political structural weaknesses in state-building processes create vulnerabilities in democratic systems, while the path to EU integration presents opportunities and challenges for democratic progress. The influence of malign actors domestically plays a significant role in shaping the political landscape by impeding the development of democratic institutions, slowing the EU integration path, and highlighting the threats and vulnerabilities faced by these countries in their pursuit of democratic consolidation. With a particular emphasis on fortifying the levers of democracy and preventing rapid backsliding, this study critically examines the prospects and potential avenues for advancing the development of resilient structures and institutions that effectively address public needs and aspirations within the complexities and adversities of the prevailing circumstances. The study objective is accomplished by deconstructing inherent vulnerabilities in both countries and their effects on establishing efficient governance based on the abovementioned factors. Exploring these explicit weaknesses is crucial for understanding and addressing the democratic decline in Albania and Montenegro. After a qualitative comparative case analysis, the study discusses the similarities at the macro level and the differences at the micro level based on the data derived from the literature utilization and in-depth interviews. Subsequently, drawing upon these findings, the study concludes with recommendations for each study case.

2. Literature Review and Development of Hypothesis

The state's role in transition societies has been extensively researched, discussed, and debated (Mitchell, 2002; Fukuyama, 2012; Mann, 2012). The literature review aims to synthesize existing scholarship to deeply understand how specific states in the Southeast European region navigate and impact transitioning societies. Fukuyama's book on the origin of political order explores the historical development of the state and its role in societal transitions. He emphasizes the importance of state institutions by highlighting that "… political institutions are necessary and cannot be taken for granted" (Fukuyama, 2012), adding that societal progress and stability "... rest on a hidden institutional foundation of property rights, rule of law, and basic political order" (p. 13), and how differences arise between societies struggling to build efficient and democratic institutions and those enjoying the benefits of modern institutions, with norms and culture playing a vital role because "... institutions reflect the cultural values of the societies in which they are established." (Fukuyama, 2012, p. 14). Furthermore, Fukuyama (2012, p. 16) emphasizes the importance of governance and legitimacy, highlighting the aim of the rule of law and accountable governance to restrict the state's power through transparent rules and subordination to the people's will. He argues that institutional flexibility and adaptability are imperative in successful transitions, particularly in accommodating evolving social, economic, and political dynamics. However, the study cases reveal challenges in achieving flexibility and adaptability, particularly due to pressing issues such as corruption, captured institutions, weak rule of law, and the influence of regressive foreign forces, especially in Montenegro. These circumstances have led to the interaction of "shadowy elite networks" and a "strong oligarchy" with political elites, undermining the moral relationship of responsibility and accountability between the government and society (Fukuyama, 2012, p. 400; p. 385).

Mitchell's book "Rule of Experts: Egypt, Techno-Politics, Modernity" (2022) delves into the state's role in transitions and economic development, with a focus on policies and strategies in Egypt. Mitchell argues that the state can perpetuate inequality (Mitchell, 2002, p. 226) and emphasizes the need for comprehensive planning that considers potential political forces affecting the execution process (Mitchell, 2002, p. 233). Mann's work explores the reciprocal relationship between the state and society, with societal forces shaping state development and vice versa (2012). According to Mann, the state, or the political network, is considered the fourth and final network capable of providing regulations and a judicial system for sustained periods (Mann, 2012, p. I, 49). Recognizing the diversity within societies and how different groups may influence power dynamics and governance is essential. However, an aspect of extensive interest by scholars in the SSE region is how societies, despite their complexity and diversity, may be exploited by external or internal political forces for specific agendas or become disinterested and indifferent to contestation possibilities to challenge state authority when necessary. Scholars highlight the significance of active participation and inclusion of diverse social groups in successful state-building, as it contributes to legitimacy and effective governance (Sen, 1999). Ethnic divisions can hinder nation-building efforts and shape power dynamics during transitions

(Robinson, 2006); hence, how these groups are exploited is imperative for successful and efficient interactivity at top-down-bottom-up levels.

As this research scrutinizes specific study cases in the SSE region, a scholarly concern has also been the causes of the lengthy transition and failures to democratize in some countries of SEE, exploring the 6-Western Balkan countries or specific cases. Scholars who have explored Albania (Tafili, 2015; Jusufi, 2017; Margariti, 2021) and Montenegro (Vukovic, 2011, 2015; Pavleviq, 2019) focus on the impacts of transition and deficiencies in implementing democratic systems. In the recent literature, authors (Kalemi, 2019; Margariti, 2022; Kolasi & Kolasi, 2023) deal with other factors such as political culture, political elite, and neoliberal strategies posing challenges to the democratization process. In the case of Montenegro, scholars such as (Bajrović et al., 2018) focus on Russian influence. (Stankov, 2023) deals with democratic vulnerabilities of Small Systems but focuses on External Actors' influence in Montenegro and how they might explore identified vulnerabilities. Laštro, Bieber, and Marović (2023) explore the long-standing dominance of Montenegro's Democratic Party of Socialists (DPS) through programmatic flexibility, co-optation, repression, control, clientelism, and the ongoing transition towards a more competitive multiparty system. In this case, the analysis scrutinizes explicitly the trinomen (as explained above) to understand under-covered deficiencies at the micro-level across cases.

In the current literature, Western Balkan countries are often treated or perceived as a collective entity when addressing their macro-level challenges despite variations in specific circumstances. These challenges include combatting corruption and organized crime and fortifying the rule of law, institutions, Civil Society, and electoral systems. Nevertheless, at the micro-level, the obstacles related to democratic implementation arise from distinct contextual factors and persistent deficiencies. It is imperative to comprehend these unique characteristics to effectively address these issues' root causes.

While previous scholarship has extensively explored the concepts of democratic backsliding, deficiencies, and transitional challenges, this study offers a distinct contribution to the field by correlating specific factors that bear specific impeding hints, their interplay, and how they impact the structural shortcomings in the state-building processes, in both cases.

In the cases of Albania and Montenegro, the criteria posed by the EU for membership, closely tied to democratic consolidation, have primarily been technical and achievement-focused rather than aimed at rectification. Consequently, the transition process has been protracted and arduous for both countries. Identifying the idiosyncratic specifics at the micro-level and formulating policies accordingly is instrumental in resolving macro-level challenges that bear similarities between the two countries, albeit progressing at different paces in their EU integration processes. Considering the abovementioned, this study sheds light on overlooked issues in Southeast European studies, revealing their adverse impact on governance, independent institutions, disillusioned citizens, and the limited opportunities for new political leaders and elites to emerge, particularly in Albania.

2.1. Development of Hypothesis

The research hypothesis posits that specific socio-political structural weaknesses encountered by Montenegro and Albania at the ***micro level*** during their transitional period significantly impede good governance and hinder democratic progress. The research question tries to deconstruct inherent vulnerabilities in both countries and their effects on the interplay between society and governance, the influence of malign actors, and the challenges encountered in the EU integration process. (Figure 1)

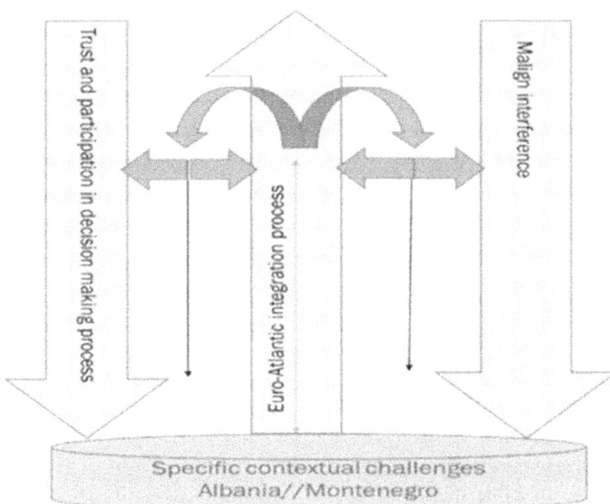

Figure 1. Deconstruction of interrelated factors impacting a lengthy transition and effective governance in both countries

Source: Own elaboration.

2.2. Why These Three Factors Identified as Units of Analysis?

These interconnected factors exert complex influences on one another. The reciprocal interaction between society and government can shape society's values, beliefs, and demands, thereby molding governance structures and policies. In turn, governance structures, conduct, and policies can influence societal behavior and expectations. However, malign actors, driven by malevolent intentions, may exploit vulnerable areas within the relationship between society and government, weaknesses within governance systems, and possible social divisions. The consequences of their actions could manifest in disruptions to governance processes, manipulation of public opinion, social unrest, and challenges to EU integration efforts. These repercussions directly disrupt EU integration through the incitement of identity conflicts, the weakening of top-down and bottom-up relationships, and the engendering of political disagreements within these states aspiring to join the block as soon as possible. As a result, societal perspectives, preferences, and reactions may be negatively impacted, potentially leading to decreased governance responsiveness toward public interest. This creates exploitable voids that allow certain malign actors to amplify their presence further and exploit certain divisions and weaknesses within society and state.

3. Research Methodology

The research methodology involves a comparative case analysis, delving into the macro and micro levels to qualitatively distinguish differences and specific details for each country. This approach aims to comprehensively understand the structural weaknesses and their impact on governance and democratic progress in Albania and Montenegro, focusing on three ***units of analysis***. These factors are studied to gain insights into their interrelatedness and influence on the broader context of good governance and democratic consolidation in both countries.

At the same time, these factors can also be considered ***variables*** due to their potential to change or have different values in the cases context. For instance, the level of EU integration, the dynamics of society-governance interplay, and the extent of malign actor interference can vary in each study case, diversely impacting governance effectiveness and democratic progress at the macro level. At the same time, in each country, specific ***interfering variables*** impact the value of correlation, such as deteriorating political factors in Albania and the schism among the populace and politicians, polarized between pro-Russian and pro-Serbian orientations in Montenegro. These specific variables contribute to the nuanced understanding of the challenges and complexities faced by each country during transition periods.

In addition to the existing data collection process, in November 2023, in-depth interviews were conducted with four experts specializing in EU Integration/EU Law, Government-society relationships, and Malign Interferences. The interviews were facilitated through Google form questionnaires, allowing for efficient data collection and convenient insights from the experts. Their academic backgrounds and research focus in the relevant thematic areas made them well-suited to provide valuable perspectives on the study cases, which were elaborated and synthesized in the last section of the findings and discussions. The data collection process relies on current literature sources within the scholarly context of transitional studies, mainly focusing on Southeast European literature. Academic journals, scholarly articles, and reports provide a rich foundation of existing knowledge and insights on the topic. Qualitative content analysis is used to systematically examine textual data from these sources, identifying key themes, patterns, and hints related to enduring structural weaknesses during lengthy transitions. Additionally, secondary sources such as analyzes, press clippings, and surveys supplement primary sources, ensuring an up-to-date comprehensive understanding of the research subject. These insights from experts have informed the development of well-informed recommendations for addressing the identified structural weaknesses.

4. Study Case – Montenegro

Montenegro took the path towards independence as a sovereign state after a referendum in 2006. Before this, Montenegro and Serbia formed a federation comprising the Republic of Serbia and the Republic of Montenegro, which lasted until 2003. It was then transformed into a political union until Montenegro's final secession in 2006. During this period, the Albanian and Bosniak minority[2] played a significant role in supporting Montenegro's separation from Serbia, evidenced by the referendum result showing 55.5 % in favor of secession. Additionally, the international community, including the EU and US, strongly supported Montenegro's peaceful journey towards becoming an independent and sovereign state.

Montenegro sought independence due to unfair responsibility for problems linked to Serbia, jeopardizing its EU rapprochement. This was tied to the EU

2 Demographic profile of the country: Montenegrin 45 %, Serbian 28.7 %, Bosniak 8.7 %, Albanian 4.9 %, Muslim 3.3 %, Romani 1 %, Croat 1 %, other 2.6 %, unspecified 4.9 % (2011 est.)

ultimatum for Serbia to surrender Serb General Ratko Mladic (The Robert Schuman Foundation, 2006, par. 9).

Although having experienced dictatorship before the 90s, "unlike Albania, Montenegro was open to emigration, free movement within Europe, loans and aid, and concessional foreign investments. It was also considerably more open in terms of creativity and freedoms compared to Albania." (Bytyçi, 2023)[3]

Post-independence, Montenegro focused on establishing itself as an independent state and gaining international recognition. Despite challenges, it made impressive progress, showing a strong commitment to Euro-Atlantic integration.

4.1. EU Integration Journey of Montenegro

Its path toward EU integration began immediately after 2006. At first glance, it appeared disadvantaged due to the long coexistence with Serbia and due to past legacies and conflicts after the 90s. Nevertheless, Euro-Atlantic integration turned forthwith into a foreign policy priority. EU "took a positive approach" regarding its progress, and "… Montenegro benefited from the EU's need to tell a positive story with regard to the Western Balkans, more difficult in the context of, say, Serbia, FYROM, Albania or Bosnia & Herzegovina." (Morrison, 2011, p. 3) The international assistance for Montenegro to progress and transform during this path has been paramount and well exploited, with headway in sectors such as the economy, infrastructure, and tourism sector, increasing employment opportunities until the global crisis in 2008 erupted. "The post-referendum boom was essentially reversed by the onset of the global economic downturn, and the economy contracted sharply in 2009" *(ibid, 35)*. However, even after the economic crisis, the economic situation in the country began to rebound, and the country adopted a forward-looking approach to absorb funds from the EU through existing initiatives in the region for the development of different sectors.

In 2010, determined to implement reforms and democratize the country, Montenegro obtained the status of candidate country, and in 2012, officially opened negotiations with the EU, thus becoming a frontrunner in the integration process in the Western Balkans region. "Montenegro has better performed in its road toward accession in the European Union, having opened all the negotiating chapters and successfully closed three of them to date." (Kalemaj, 2023)[4] Nonetheless, the country's integration has faced challenges, leading to limited

3 Enver Bytyçi, interview by authors, Google Form Questionnaire, November 15, 2023.
4 Kalemaj Ilir, interview by authors, Google Form Questionnaire, November 17, 2023.

progress and a stalled momentum towards EU membership. According to the "Key findings of the 2022 Report on Montenegro", political tensions, government instability, and gridlock in decision-making processes have hindered Montenegro's institutional functioning, including an incomplete Constitutional Court, amplifying political uncertainty. "Still, the inability of political parties to reach agreement on top appointments to the judiciary holds the country hostage in both the EU integration process and much-needed results in the fight against corruption and organized crime." (FH, 2022, par.6) Montenegro's Parliament has faced boycotts, government changes, and disruptions in legislation-making, hindering political dialogue and accountability. To enhance Parliament's role in EU accession, improved regulation and cooperation between the government and Parliament are necessary. Strengthening the legal framework is crucial for promoting collaboration between state institutions and civil society. Nevertheless, moderate progress in public administration reform and its judicial system has been shown. One significant issue is the prevalence of corruption, despite the "positive trend in the work of the Anti-Corruption Agency" (European Commission, 2022), which undermines transparency, accountability, and the effective functioning of institutions. Organized crime remains partially addressed at contentious levels, considering "systemic deficiencies that exist across the board in its criminal justice system, including the way organized crime cases are handled in courts." *(ibid 2022)* Despite internal opposition to joining NATO, the country was continuously praised for its achievements regarding EU integration, NATO membership, and its success story in the international community.

The success story was one side of the coin. Another side of the coin is the influence of political elites and vested interests, which can hinder progress in implementing necessary reforms and consolidating democratic institutions. Since 2006, the country showed problems with the alternation of political elites and "decades of state capture" (Saric, 2020, par.5) until the departure of its long-time ruler, Milo Djukanovic, in the parliamentary elections of 2022, when DPS experienced an electoral defeat although very narrowly. The United States and its European allies overlooked Milo Djukanovic's transgressions due to his leadership in Montenegro's NATO and EU accession, despite consolidating party patronage and corruption (ibid, par. 9). The lack of change in the national government, dominated by a party connected to the League of Communists, complicates Montenegro's success story due to historical patrimonial power, limited political alternation, and dependence on state resources. Komar (2020, p. 67) asserts that Montenegro's ruling party (DPD) is viewed as the best defender of Montenegrin statehood against territorial ambitions, particularly from Serbia, despite its flaws and questionable practices. On the other side, the county has long experienced "the consequences of a dysfunctional system of checks and balances" and a "lack of true competitiveness" (Komar, 2020, p. 77) at least until 2022. The case shows how " 'newborn' institutions, which lack bottom-up legitimacy, can be substantively eroded without losing their appearance." (ibid, 77)

Montenegro's political elite is undergoing rejuvenation, but the country faces deep political crises, competing national identities, corruption, abuse of power, and instability. Despite a rise in the National Democratic Governance rating, the conduct of the new parliamentary majority and Prime Minister Zdravko Krivokapić's government has been flawed, leading to political polarization and slow decision-making.

4.2. Trust and Participation of the Society in the Decision-Making Process in Montenegro

From what was presented above, the relationship between the government and society in Montenegro can be characterized as complex. While Montenegro has a democratic system with mechanisms for citizens to hold the government accountable, there are challenges in effectively exercising this accountability. Bytyçi (2023)[5] argues that, although having had "a stable governance until a few years ago, and not descending into anarchy or paralyzing internal political conflict," yet, the single-party dominance for decades, coupled with corruption, clientelism, and lack of transparency, has limited competition, consolidated power, and eroded citizen trust in the government. The citizens of Montenegro are formally engaged in political and civic activities, and their support and belief in the potential for change and the influence of their votes are essential. They have high expectations and are unwilling to accept an outcome that could be described as "awakened hope – betrayed expectations" (Stoiljković et. Al, 2020, p. 17). The Westminster Foundation for Democracy's (2022, p. 16) survey in Montenegro revealed a lack of trust in politicians among the youth, with 57.1 % expressing no trust in any politicians. Additionally, 48.6 % feel their concerns are not being addressed, and 55.3 % believe that individual rights and liberties are not respected. The survey also found that younger individuals are less politically engaged than older citizens, with only 28.6 % following political affairs and 41.6 % understanding critical political issues. Another Friedrich-Ebert-Stiftung (FES) survey found that one-fifth of respondents, mainly young and educated individuals, expressed a desire to leave Montenegro. Similarly, the Westminster Foundation for Democracy survey indicated that 70.3 % of Montenegrin youth

5 Enver Bytyçi, interview by authors, Google Form Questionnaire, November 15, 2023.

have contemplated leaving the country, with 36.2 % occasionally considering it and 14.0 % already making serious preparations. In Montenegro, voting carries an additional psychological burden, as "parental political views have a significant influence, with 66.0 % of respondents sharing their mother's political stance and 63.9 % sharing their father's" (Westminster Foundation for Democracy, 2022, pp. 48–49).

4.3. Partners and Influences in Montenegro

One of Montenegro's major alliances is with NATO (North Atlantic Treaty Organization), as Montenegro became a member in 2017. "The EU is perceived as Montenegro's most important foreign policy partner, followed by Russia and the USA." It has collaborated with the United States on various initiatives, but "positioning of the USA behind Russia is obviously a consequence of the lower level of US engagement in Montenegro since Montenegro became a member of NATO alliance" (FES, 2020, p. 16). According to (Stanko, 2023, p. 8), in Montenegro, Russia has a significant "economic and cultural influence" due to its limited strategic capabilities compared to NATO in the Mediterranean. Additionally, Montenegro has close ties with neighboring countries. "Russia is the largest foreign direct investor in Montenegro," while "Serbia is the largest contributor to the tourism industry." Montenegro aligns fully with EU's foreign and security policy, including responding to Russia's aggression against Ukraine. The society is "deeply divided over ethnic and religious matters, amid the nation's ambition to join the European Union by 2025" (Mikovic, 2023, par.1), and promoting inclusivity and addressing the concerns of minority communities remain challenging for fostering social cohesion and a sense of belonging among all citizens. Bytyçi[6] stresses that Montenegro continues to grapple with a schism among its populace and politicians, polarized between pro-Russian and pro-Serbian orientations, in contrast to those advocating for a pro-Western alignment. Notably, Montenegro harbors influential political factions, demonstrating Eastern inclinations. To the same stance is Zotaj[7], noting that although "the EU, is a key donor and advocates for regional democratization and development," wielding substantial influence in its integration initiative, still, "Russia's greatest influence is on local political actors, due to the close proximity of the Montenegrin political class to Russia."

6 Enver Bytyçi, interview by authors, Google Form Questionnaire, November 15, 2023.
7 Elda Zotaj, interview by authors, Google Form Questionnaire, November 14, 2023.

The relationship between Montenegro and the Serbian Orthodox Church is intricate, reflecting the divisions within Montenegro's political landscape between those who identify as Montenegrins with a pro-Western orientation and those aligned with Serbs who lean towards Moscow and oppose Montenegro's independence and integration in Euro-Atlantic structures. Despite Montenegro formally separating from Serbia in 2006, the Serbian Orthodox Church still retains control over the Montenegrin church. "Russia builds on this societal division, supporting pro-Russian organizations through various channels, whose political actions ultimately shape the face of Montenegrin democracy." (Stanko, 2023, p. 8)

The signing of the agreement between the government and the Serbian Orthodox Church recently exacerbated the situation.[8] Although criticism was faced from pro-European political forces, including President Djukanovic's party, and experts/advisers for giving the Church disproportionate power and inflaming internal divisions, he continued and "committed" a "political self-sabotage." (Leka, 2022, par.7) The attempt to advance reconciliation between the conservative (pro-Russian and pro-Serbian) Democratic Front and pro-European factions in Montenegro, aimed at resolving "property disputes with the church" (ibid, par.8), ended up exacerbating divisions and escalating political tensions. "Critics say the agreement undermines Montenegro's national interests, describing it as a tool for Serbia and Russia to increase their influence in the country."(ibid, par. 10) As "Russia's intervention remains a sharp issue, for historical and social reasons" (Ruçi, 2023)[9], Montenegro's decision to pursue NATO membership in 2017 strained the relationship between the two. Diplomatic strains between the two countries stem from a 2016 coup attempt in Montenegro linked to Russian nationals and Serbian nationalist denial of Montenegrin identity, using church and media influence to promote Russian agendas. Stanko (2022, p. 7) suggests that autocracies like Russia and China may impede democratic reforms and cause democratic backsliding, mainly when dysfunctional institutions are in place. Montenegro is a state with established legal and political frameworks, but its concept of nationhood faces differing perspectives. The population is divided, with many supporting Euro-Atlantic integration, while a notable Serbian minority favors connections with Russia and Serbia, which complicates efforts to build a cohesive "civic society" (Bieber, 2010, p. 964). The

8 Mr. Abazović faced backlash for silently signing the Basic Agreement with the SOC on August 3, 2022, without media presence or prior announcement.

9 Hektor Ruçi, interview by authors, Google Form Questionnaire, November 20, 2023.

Serbian community, significant in number (28.73 %)[10], has been less supportive of further integration, notably after Montenegro joined NATO and in light of the situation in Ukraine. In contrast, Albanian and Bosnian minorities have actively contributed to Montenegro's independence and generally support integration with NATO and the EU. Montenegro's challenge lies in reconciling these varied stands on nationhood and ensuring an inclusive approach to national identity, essential for the country's ongoing democratic development and stability.

5. Study Case – Albania

Since its 1912 independence, Albania has been ethnically homogenous (98.1 % Albanian) and politically varied, having been a monarchy and then a communist state under Enver Hoxha (1944–1990), who imposed stringent societal controls and isolationist policies, distancing Albania from the Soviet Union and China (Gjeta, 2021). Post-Hoxha, Albania struggled with the legacy of communism during its transition, especially after the Berlin Wall fell in 1989, a period highlighting its economic weaknesses and international isolation (*ibid*). In the early 1990s, Albania experienced significant protests calling for the end of authoritarianism, democratization, and better living standards, which catalyzed its shift to democracy and a market economy, reflecting "an aspiration for European integration and values and an end to isolation," according to (Gjeta, 2021). The transition was complicated by the lack of established dissidents, as intellectuals and clergy had been suppressed, making it difficult to dislodge entrenched communist leaders. The "presence of the communist regime's legacy in public administration, judiciary, and political parties has hindered progress in Albania" (ibid, 2021).

5.1. EU Integration Journey of Albania

After the regime change, Albania promptly established diplomatic ties with the European Economic Community (EEC) in 1991 and advanced on a clear path toward European integration, unaffected by the conflicts in former Yugoslavia. By 1992, it was the first in the region to sign both a Trade and Economic Cooperation Agreement and a Joint Political Declaration with the European Community.

10 **Please refer to**: https://eurydice.eacea.ec.europa.eu/national-education-systems/montenegro/population-demographic-situation-languages-and-religions#:~:text=Life%20expectancy%20at%20birth%20in%202021%20is%2073.8%20years.&text=According%20to%20the%202011%20Census,3.31%25%2C%20Croats%200.97%25.

Albania faced a "state failing"(Jusufi, 2017, p. 82) momentum in the decade following the regime change, undermining early democratic and state-building efforts, with the 1997 crisis significantly impeding EU integration progress. "The catalyst and trigger of the collapse were the country's war-like economic structures, such as the pyramid schemes that emerged during this period, which benefited from the uncontrolled and ungoverned order." *(ibid)* The widespread civil unrest and loss of public trust in government institutions resulted in instability and damaged Albania's credibility on the international stage. After this period, "Albania's integration process has faced challenges, including corruption, political polarization, and an unchanged political establishment" (European Commission, 2022). The country was granted visa liberalization in 2010 and received candidate status for EU membership in 2014. However, the journey towards integration has been lengthy and challenging, with difficulties in meeting EU criteria and requirements (Braka, 2022). The domestic political landscape has hindered Albania's development, with accusations of reforms being overly politicized (European Commission, 2022). On the other hand, "the impasse between Sofia and Skopje has obstructed Albania's negotiation start" (Braka, 2022). Although "Albania received candidate country status almost ten years ago, has yet to officially open negotiations"(Bytyçi, 2023), becoming now even more vulnerable to "Beleri case"[11], and the intention of Greece to "not be able to agree on the upcoming phases of the membership process, including the approval of the evaluation report on unresolved standards."(Media Ditari, 2023, par.3)

Albania's EU integration is hindered by limited reform progress, requiring enhanced collaboration and societal involvement in administration and governance. While there are improvements in public administration, the judiciary, and anti-corruption measures, persistent challenges include corruption, organized crime, and media freedom (European Commission, 2022). Effective reform and adherence to EU standards remain essential for Albania's EU accession process.

5.2. Trust and Participation of the Society in the Decision-Making Process in Albania

Albanian citizens' limited involvement in decision-making is influenced by a rigid cultural legacy inherited from the totalitarian regime, shaping a perception of subservience to government dictates. The dominance of two main political parties perpetuates loyalty and obedience, resulting in a deep division along

11 For more information on the case, please see: https://www.ekathimerini.com/news/1225971/albanias-eu-hopes-hinge-on-beleri-case-athens-says/

political lines, hindering social cohesion and compromising democratic governance. Such conditions severely limit incentives and opportunities for citizen participation and the expression of opposing viewpoints as "a result of political culture" (Bytyçi, 2023).[12] Luli (2021, p. 31) stresses that representative governance, while aiming for inclusivity and consensus, often fails to represent citizens' interests genuinely. Trust and sympathy are often expressed as submission to autocratic leaders rather than aiming at fostering active involvement in decision-making. The prevailing sentiment toward political parties in power, policy, and law formulation happens through general silent approval. Albania's Civil society is perceived as weak, "constrained, less proactive, and primarily operates for the sake of maintaining a façade" (Bytyçi, 2023)[13], encountering frequent financial shortcomings. In cases of commitments from its side, it seriously requires consideration of its recommendations by governmental structures. Conversely, or as a consequence, "… it has not functioned as a robust agent that effectively mediates between the government and citizens." Instead, it operates in a self-serving manner, primarily serving its interests and those of different governing bodies/actors, often becoming an inconsequential lever in policy/decision-making and failing to prompt meaningful reactions (Luli, 2021, p. 31).

The Westminster Democratic Foundation's study (2021) highlights a lack of proactive engagement by Civil Society Organizations (CSOs) in developing sustained relationships with state institutions and actively participating in policy and legislative processes. Collaborative efforts between CSOs and state institutions primarily revolve around project-based initiatives, leading institutions to view CSO contributions as less genuine, fostering mutual mistrust in their cooperation (Luli, 2021, p. 7). The Institute for Democracy and Mediation's survey (IDM, 2023, pp. 4–5) reveals the institutions with the lowest public trust in Albania, including political parties (29.5 %), Parliament (33.8 %), the prosecution (35.2 %), and the courts (36.2 %). Conversely, international organizations are the most trusted, with over 70 % of respondents expressing trust, although this has declined since 2019. The central government (59.4 %) and municipalities (60.2 %) are seen as lacking transparency by over half of the surveyed citizens. Albania's National Report (2020, p. 7) indicates that approximately one-third (23.2 %) of its population comprises 661,365 young individuals aged 15–29. Despite their significant numbers, a decline in youth engagement in political processes and governance decision-making has been observed, linked to a loss

---

12 Enver Bytyçi, interview by authors, Google Form Questionnaire, November 15, 2023.

13 (ibid)

of trust in the existing political establishment and limited alternative options beyond established political figures.

This trend has led to a significant wave of youth emigration, known as the "brain drain," primarily due to limited short-term opportunities and the absence of long-term prospects. Hoxhaj (2023, par. 1) notes that in 2022, approximately 46,460 Albanians left the country, marking a 10.5 % increase from 2021, with the majority (about 36,000) being young people, highlighting too the severe repercussions of youth migration and brain drain in Albania, particularly evident in the healthcare system. Over the past decade, around 3,500 healthcare professionals have migrated from Albania to Germany. The brain drain also affects critical sectors like tourism and agriculture, intensifying the detachment of young individuals from societal functions, including political party involvement. Albanian political parties, existing for over thirty years, have become closed systems dominated by party politics, hindering the participation of young individuals and stifling innovative ideas. In such a way, the rejuvenation of political elites exhibits limited opportunities for meaningful change.

On the other hand, the Albanian opposition is experiencing notable internal polarization and fragmentation, representing a challenging phase during the country's 33-year transition. Internally, there is a lack of consensus on fundamental values and principles guiding the opposition's mission, failing to translate these ideals into tangible joint actions and outcomes. The stalemate between opposing political factions within the democratic party after the elections of 2021 is compounded by declining democratic participation indicators, citizen skepticism, dissatisfaction with political figures and governance practices, diminished trust in institutions, and slow integration, contributing to an increase in authoritarian tendencies in the political landscape. According to Berdufi and Krasniqi (2022, p. 42), the reliance on strong leaders, increased government control, and problematic elections without accountability have eroded the social foundation of functioning democracy in Albania and the region. This erosion is further compounded by the weakening of watchdog institutions, civil society, citizens' voices, and critical media.

5.3. Partners and Influences in Albania

Albania is fully aligned to the Euro-Atlantic path, values, and standards. It has been a NATO member since 2010 and aspires to the highest citizens support[14]

14 For 95.7 % of Albanians, EU membership is very important, while for only 0.4 % it is not important. (source: euronews.al) https://euronews.al/en/do-albanians-still-want-to-join-the-eu/

(almost at a similar level with Kosovo) in the region to become an EU member. As regards the EU's Common Foreign and Security Policy, Albania maintained full alignment with all relevant EU decisions and declarations, including with the EU restrictive measures following Russia's unprovoked aggression against Ukraine. As a non-permanent member since January 2022, Albania has been actively engaged in the UN Security Council in promoting and defending the rules-based international order. (EU Commission, 2022, par. 19). The US plays a significant role in Albania's development and political sphere, maintaining a consistently cohesive relationship. The US supports Albania's EU membership aspirations and assists in security, economic development, and democratic governance while promoting stability and regional cooperation in the Western Balkans. Both the EU and the US encourage Albania to implement reforms and address challenges like corruption, the rule of law, and organized crime, fostering Albania's path towards Euro-Atlantic integration, democratic consolidation, and regional stability. Hence, "Albanian citizens exhibit the highest levels of trust in Western, Euro-American partnership" (Bytyçi, 2023)[15]

Albania's strong alignment with the West is profoundly ingrained and resolute within its unified society, allowing it to progress without hesitation. External actors attempting to obstruct Albania's integration processes face challenges and must seek alternative approaches to hinder progress. The main obstacles to Albania's integration stem from internal political dynamics and the political establishment rather than external actors, such as Russia, aiming to pursue geopolitical goals. Aside from the US and EU, Turkey maintains robust economic and cultural ties with Albania, actively supporting its Euro-Atlantic integration and progress without any intentions to counter the presence of the EU and NATO in the region. Footage of Russia's interference in Albania includes alleged meddling in elections, spreading disinformation, and financially supporting political actors aligned with Russian interests. However, no crises or impasses have been created due to Russia's lack of support in Albanian society, absence of Orthodox religious connections, and possible overt political affiliations that the public would condemn, if they were to exist and be recognized. Given the Russian aggression in Ukraine, thorough investigations and joint efforts are needed to counter interference in critical sectors like banks, telecommunications, media, real estate, and political linkages.

15 Enver Bytyçi, interview by authors, Google Form Questionnaire, November 15, 2023.

6. Interview Findings[16] and Discussions

Data analysis from literature and in-depth interviews indicates that Albania and Montenegro share similarities and distinct challenges in their democratic consolidation efforts and improving governance models and practices. At the macro level, they encounter similar issues with specific foundational or enduring roots in their development and persistence modus. What "they have in common is yet a dysfunctional justice system, political instability, corruption, and organized crime features" (Kalemaj, 2023; Bytyçi, 2023; Zotaj, 2023), issues featured too in EU and international reports.

The findings indicate specific areas (Euro-Atlantic integration path, citizens' participation and trust, and malign interference) where these countries' vulnerabilities to structural weakness lie and how they interrelate. (Figure 2).

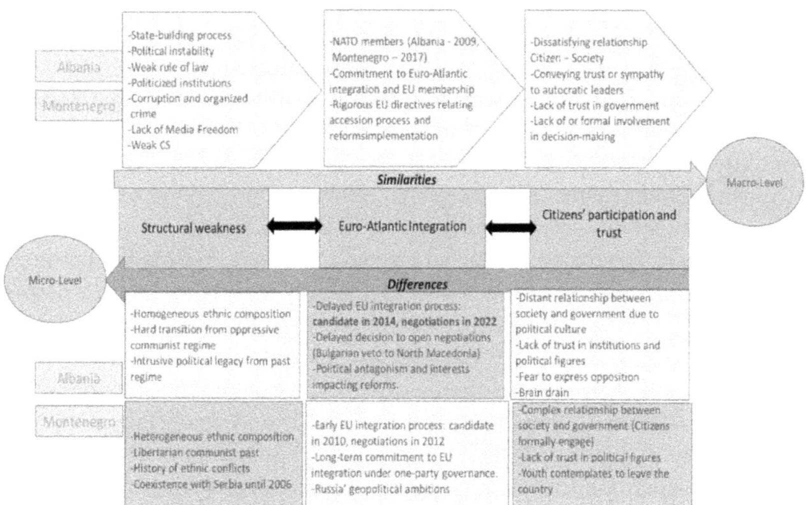

Figure 2. Areas of similarities (macro – level) and convergences (micro -level) between Albania and Montenegro

Source: Own elaboration.

---

16 All the authors cited in this section have contributed their expertise through comprehensive interviews for this article. The process involved online questionnaires via Google Forms conducted in November 2023. (Annex 1).

The distinct challenges of each study case are grounded and developed in historical, socio-political, contextual, and structural differences. Although crucially significant, these challenges are overshadowed by the urgent need to address pressing issues such as corruption, organized crime, media freedom, and the rule of law, similar to some extent in both countries.

While both countries "have moved from communism to democracy" (Bytyçi, 2023), Albania took the transformation path, transitioning from one of the most oppressive totalitarian regimes in the region. In contrast, Montenegro experienced a more libertarian form of communism but coexisted with Serbia until 2006 and lived a decade marked by ethnic conflicts in the post-90s.

Montenegro has a diverse ethnic makeup with significant minority populations, which poses challenges in addressing inter-ethnic relations and safeguarding minority rights. In contrast, Albania is more ethnically homogeneous. Both countries are NATO members and committed to Euro-Atlantic integration, with Montenegro emerging as a frontrunner in the region for EU membership. However, Albania faced delays in opening negotiations due to Bulgaria's veto on North Macedonia, and the "Beleri Case" recently seems to have put another obstacle in Albania's EU accession process. As Bytyçi (2023) notes, Montenegro maintained governance stability throughout the transition, avoiding the anarchy and political turmoil Albania experienced in the late 90s. However, unlike Albania, Montenegro's integration process is hindered by conflicts between pro-Russian/Serbian and pro-Western factions. While powerful pro-Eastern political groups exist in Montenegro, they are absent in Albania. Currently, "fears exist that a pro-Russian and pro-Serbian party, part of the new coalition government in Montenegro, may endanger the pace of reforms in Montenegro." (Kalemaj, 2023).

Nevertheless, both countries have political instability due to internal or external factors, and "the instrumentalization of state institutions for electoral effects and political gains has been a disturbing and hindering phenomenon for the success of reforms" (Zotaj, 2023). Still, internal political factors have hindered Albania more than Montenegro, resulting in periods of severe political deadlocks that have impacted a protracted and tiring EU journey. Regarding the rule of law, Albania has made some progress in establishing a new justice system through rigorous reforms, albeit slower, but still needing to show results.

The relationship between citizens and society is complex and unsatisfactory in both countries. Zotaj (2023) notes that advancements have been made in legislative aspects and civic engagement to bolster citizen participation in the policy-making process. However, these efforts still need improvements to meet requisite standards. Notwithstanding both states' generally weak civic engagement, as the exploited literature indicates, Bytyçi (2023) still distinguishes Montenegro's relatively active, more structured, and citizen-oriented civil society. Moreover, the media is deemed more independent and critical. Compared to Albania, Montenegro also faces fewer criticisms in international reports concerning civil society and freedom of speech.

Nevertheless, in both countries, "a vibrant civil society with powerful social movements that seek to create a more fair and equal partnership between society and governments and empower citizens is absent" (Kalemaj, 2023). Until now, internal issues have shunned citizen engagement and trust in the government, and though mechanisms for citizen accountability exist, challenges remain in effectively exercising this accountability. Interestingly, citizens in both countries tend to show trust or sympathy towards autocratic leaders rather than actively participating in decision-making processes.

The younger population is dissatisfied with their leaders and political landscape. Most youth in Montenegro contemplate leaving the country, while Albania has been experiencing a profound brain drain in the last five years. The critical issue of brain drain is an immediate priority to tackle, which poses multifaceted ramifications on Albania's social, economic, and political fabric. This phenomenon demands immediate attention and accurate political address to mitigate its adverse effects.

Consequently, there is a palpable disinterest amongst the youth in actively participating in politics and governance, alongside contemplation of emigration due to a lack of confidence in a better future within the country. Addressing these concerns should be done promptly and attentively.

Montenegro has experienced prolonged dominance by a single political party, limiting political competition and consolidating power. Meanwhile, Albania has seen the dominance of two main political parties, with citizens feeling divided along political lines. Albania's distant relationship between society and government can be partially attributed to the enduring influence of a rigid political and cultural legacy inherited from the totalitarian regime, which viewed citizens as subservient to government dictates. The inter-party polarization within the right wing is particularly worrisome, resulting in a state of paralysis with limited participation in decision-making processes and increased animosity, leading to an imbalance of power, a decrease in accountability, and an unchecked leftwing majority that may undermine the system of checks and balances. The opposition is recently navigating its most arduous period in over three decades.

While Montenegro has taken steps towards changing its old political establishment, Albania has established an impeding political environment for the emergence of new leaders. Albania's political establishment has displayed a tenacious resistance to change, dismissing any prospects for political transformation and rejuvenation. Rather than embracing genuine rejuvenation, political figures often view it as a temporary hiatus following an electoral defeat, falsely promising altered political agendas upon their return.

There is a lack of trust among Albanian citizens towards political parties, the Parliament, prosecution, and the courts. The fear of expressing opposition is also evident among Albanian citizens.

In Montenegro, citizens lack trust in political figures, yet the voting process still carries a psychological burden. Even about the EU, "the understanding of the EU's concept, in terms of rights and obligations, is hardly perceived by ordinary citizens. Predominantly, they perceive national governments as the primary bearers of these rights and obligations" (Ruci, 2023) in both countries. Malign influences challenge Montenegro's integration and state-building efforts, primarily due to divisions related to national identity issues, which create vulnerabilities for potential interference. The interference propensity is more significant "due to Montenegro's strategic value to Russia for access to the Adriatic Sea, and also because almost 33% of the Montenegrin population is of Serbian nationality, which harbors strong affinities with Moscow." (Bytyçi, 2023) In contrast, Albania's strong Western orientation and solid national identity leave no room for exploitation of identity and other vulnerable gaps. However, "a commonality in both countries is that several media outlets in Montenegro and Albania are sponsored by and disseminate Russian propaganda." (Bytyçi, 2023) Russian interference has had a more pronounced political impact on Montenegro, particularly during NATO membership pursuit, which strained relations with Russia and escalated tensions over alleged Russian involvement in a failed coup attempt.

Bytyçi (2023) identifies other differences: Albania still needs to construct a rule-of-law state, while Montenegro needs to construct a state fully oriented towards Euro-Atlantic structures. Albania needs to sever the ties of politics with organized crime and combat corruption, whereas Montenegro has more pronounced issues with corruption, albeit at slightly lower levels than Albania. Albania needs to elevate its citizens' living standards, while Montenegro ranks higher in this regard.

These differences might be at a lesser level noticed during the integration process, but they indicate where greater engagement and improved policies are needed. Despite the increased commitment from the EU, especially in the Russia-Ukraine conflict context, to boost the integration of the Western Balkans, there still needs to be more cohesion and decision-making power within the EU. "EU decision-making is often influenced by individual member states' interests, sympathies, or antipathies towards Montenegro or Albania." (Bytyçi,

2023). In fact, under the pretext of adhering to standards and fulfilling reforms, certain states instrumentalize bilateral disagreements to obstruct the process. On the other side, these countries need to understand that "more institutional mechanisms in place and faster implementation of reforms to speed up the EU integration can serve as bulwarks to protect themselves against malign influences." (Kalemaj, 2023) Moreover, Zozaj (2023) stresses that "the fulfillment of obligations by the states to the Stabilization and Association Agreement, and the acceleration of the negotiation processes for Chapters 23 and 24 related to the "Judiciary and Fundamental Rights" and "Justice, Freedom, and Security," would be effective for improving democratic standards and guiding the countries towards EU accession advancement. Currently Montenegro's progress in the above-mentioned chapters is crucial for its EU accession negotiations. As a leading candidate in the region, its advancements could result in membership by 2030, serving as a positive stimulus and example for other Western Balkan countries aiming for EU integration.

7. Recommendations

Albania:

- Albania should strengthen democratic processes by reinforcing its democratic institutions, including electoral systems, to ensure transparency, integrity, and resilience against obscure funding. It is necessary to encourage open dialogue to address the high political polarization within the right wing and among political parties while emphasizing the importance of national interests over partisan interests and creating spaces for shared decision-making to help promote and foster a more unified and collaborative political environment. At the same time, establishing inclusive platforms or forums where representatives from different political parties can engage in constructive discussions and work towards common goals is crucial.
- Implementing comprehensive education programs is crucial to promoting civic education and educating the younger generation about democratic values, tolerance, ethics, integrity, and human rights to counter politically divisive narratives, especially in the long run.
- Create favorable conditions for professional growth and opportunities: Develop policies and initiatives that promote entrepreneurship, innovation, and career advancement within the country, including – providing access to funding, mentorship programs, research grants, and networking opportunities to

nurture and support local talents, encouraging them to stay and contribute to the nation's development.

- Responsible structures and actors should work to enhance the quality of education and research institutions. Investing in education and research institutions to improve the quality and relevance of academic programs and research opportunities is imperative. By providing competitive academic resources, scholarships, and partnerships with international institutions, talented individuals will have fewer incentives to seek educational and research opportunities elsewhere.
- Create a conducive business environment that stimulates job creation, economic growth, and career opportunities; a goal to be achieved through favorable investment policies, tax incentives for businesses, and targeted economic development initiatives that attract both local and foreign investments, providing employment opportunities for skilled professionals.
- Encourage networks and collaborations between local professionals and those who have migrated abroad. Establish platforms for knowledge sharing, professional networking, and mentorship programs that facilitate connections and exchange of expertise, fostering a sense of belonging and support among skilled individuals.
- Improve the work-life balance and quality of life by enhancing social and cultural amenities, healthcare services, infrastructure, and overall quality of life within the country. Time is due to create an attractive living environment with sufficient recreational opportunities, affordable housing options, and a robust social support system contributing to the retention of the younger generation.

Montenegro:

- Montenegro should prioritize efforts to strengthen democratic institutions, improve governance operability, and practically align its laws and practices with EU standards for effective state-building, accountability, and progress in the EU integration process. This situation highlights the need for the new government coalition to address its internal divisions and develop a cohesive and unified approach that aligns with its overarching goals and objectives related to the Euro-Atlantic agenda.
- Promote media literacy programs and critical thinking skills among the population to enable citizens to discern and counter disinformation and fake news. Educating the public about the risks of foreign interference and promoting responsible media consumption can help build resilience against manipulation attempts.

- Foster international collaborations: Strengthen cooperation with international partners, particularly those in the European Union and the United States, to share best practices and expertise in countering foreign interference- including exchanging information, coordinating efforts, and jointly addressing common challenges related to disinformation campaigns and cybersecurity.
- Collaborating with international partners on information sharing, capacity building, and joint exercises can enhance Montenegro's readiness to mitigate foreign interference risks.
- Monitor and address ethnic tensions: Carefully monitor areas with potential ethnic tensions and proactively address grievances through dialogue, inclusivity, and democratic processes.
- Fostering inclusive dialogue is imperative to encourage open and constructive discussions and debates, bridge identity gaps, and promote understanding, especially among younger generations. Strengthening social cohesion requires investments in community projects, cultural exchanges, and joint social activities to build trust and foster a shared sense of identity.
- It is necessary to implement measures to enhance transparency and integrity in political financing and lobbying activities, reducing the vulnerability of the political system to outside influence. Strengthening anti-corruption measures can also mitigate the risk of external actors exploiting corrupt networks for their agenda.

8. Annex 1 – (In-depth interviews)

Interview dates: November 2023 (Online, through Google Form Questionnaire)

The experts interviewed for this study are esteemed lecturers and scholars in International Relations/Political Sciences and EU Studies. Their expertise and knowledge in Southeast European studies make them well-versed in the subject matter and highly qualified to provide insights and analysis on the region's dynamics and challenges.

Table 1. Experts list

1) Prof. Assoc. Dr. Enver Bytyçi	Professor of Political History and International Relations
2) Prof. Assoc Dr. Ilir Kalemaj	Professor of International Relations
3) Dr. Elda Zotaj	Lecturer of EU studies
4) LLM Hektor Ruçi	Lecturer of EU Law

References

Bajrović, R., Garčević, V., & Kraemer, R. (2018). Changing by a thread: Russia's Strategy of Destabilization in Montenegro. Russia Foreign Policy Papers. Retrieved from: https://www.fpri.org/wp-content/uploads/2018/07/kraemer-rfp5.pdf

Bërdufi, D., & Krasniqi, A. (2022). Democracy state and autocratization features in the Republic of Albania. *Journal of Liberty and International Affairs*, 8(3), 34–46. https://e-jlia.com/index.php/jlia/article/view/741

Bieber, F. (2010). Das politische system montenegros. In W. Ismayr (Ed.), *Die politischen Systeme Osteuropas* (pp. 941–966). Wiesbaden: VS Verlag.

Bieber, F., Laštro, C., & Marović, J. (2023). Mechanisms of Dominance: Understanding 30 Years in Power of Montenegro's Democratic Party of Socialists. Comparative Southeast European Studies, 71(2), 210-236. Retrieved from: https://econpapers.repec.org/article/bpjsoeuro/v_3a71_3ay_3a2023_3ai_3a2_3ap_3a210-236_3an_3a5.htm

Braka, M. (2022). *Negociatat u hapën, sa duhet të presim për t'u anëtarësuar në Bashkimin Europian?* [Negotiations have been opened, how long should we wait for membership in the European Union?]. Faktoje.al. Retrieved from: https://faktoje.al/negociatat-u-hapen-sa-duhet-te-presim-per-tu-anetaresuar-ne-bashkimin-europian/

Deloy, C., & Levy, H. (2006, May 22). *The European elections monitor: Montenegro – Independence referendum*. By, Fondation Robert Schuman, Retrieved from: https://www.robert-schuman.eu/en/monitor/518-after-twenty-four-years-of-union-with-serbia-montenegro-is-independent-again

European Commission. (2022a). *Key findings of the 2022 report on Albania*. Retrieved from: https://ec.europa.eu/commission/presscorner/detail/en/COUNTRY_22_6103

European Commission. (2022b). *Key findings of the 2022 report on Montenegro*. Retrieved from: https://ec.europa.eu/commission/presscorner/detail/en/COUNTRY_22_6103

FES (Friedrich Ebert Stiftung). (2020). Stoiljković, Z., Vukanović, M., & Uljarević, D. (Eds.). (2020). When the political elite underestimates citizens: Parliamentary elections in Montenegro. Democracy and human rights analysis. https://library.fes.de/pdffiles/bueros/belgrad/16629.pdf

Freedom House. (2022). *Nation in transit 2022: Country report – Montenegro*. https://freedomhouse.org/country/montenegro/nations-transit/2022

Fukuyama, F. (2011/2012). The Origins of Political Order: From Prehuman Times to the French Revolution. Farrar, Straus and Giroux.

Gjeta, A. (2021, May 21). *Albania remains hostage to its communist past*. Balkan Insight. Retrieved from https://balkaninsight.com/2021/05/21/albania-remains-hostage-to-its-communist-past/

Hoxhaj, A. (2023). *Albania's brain drain: why so many young people are leaving and how to get them to stay*. The Conversation. Retrieved from: https://theconversation.com/albanias-brain-drain-why-so-many-young-people-are-leaving-and-how-to-get-them-to-stay-207455

Institute for Democracy and Mediation (IDM). (2023). *Public opinion survey 2022: Trust in governance* (10th ed.). Tirana: Author. Irma Semini, Besjana Kuçi, Marsela Dauti, & Sheila Hafizi. Retrieved from: https://www.undp.org/sites/g/files/zskgke326/files/2023-07/tig2022_report-alb.pdf

Jusufi, I. (2017). Albania's transformation since 1997: Successes and failures. *CIRR,* XXIII (77), 81–115. https://hrcak.srce.hr/file/262691

Komar, O. (2020). The elephant in the room: Illiberal politics in Montenegro. *Southeast European and Black Sea Studies*, 20(1), 61–80. https://doi.org/10.1080/14683857.2020.1703495

Leka, P. (2022). Montenegro's problematic relationship with the Serbian Orthodox Church. *Emerging Europe*. https://emerging-europe.com/news/montenegros-problematic-relationship-with-the-serb-orthodox-church/

Lukšić, I., & Katnić, M. (2016). The Making of a State: Transition in Montenegro. Cato Journal, 36(3), 659-709. https://www.cato.org/sites/cato.org/files/serials/files/cato-journal/2016/9/cj-v36n3-12.pdf

Luli, E. (2021). Roli i shoqërisë civile në garantimin e transparencës dhe llogaridhënies në qeverisje [The role of civil society in ensuring transparency and accountability in governance]. *Kuvendi (Journal)*, 15, 30–42. Retrieved from: https://staging.parlament.al/Files/Informacione/revista15.pdf

Mann, M. (2012). A theory of the modern state. In M. Mann (Ed.), *The sources of social power* (pp. 44–91). Cambridge: Cambridge University Press. https://doi.org/10.1017/CBO9781139381314.005

Margariti, G. (2021). End of transition, but failure to democratize: Democratic consolidation in Albania analyzed in the frame of political elite normative preference for democracy. In Proceedings of the International Conference on Social Science, Humanities and Arts (iCSHA), Vienna, Austria. https://www.dpublication.com/wp-content/uploads/2021/06/400_4021.pdf

Media Ditari. (2023). *ZBARDHET DEKLARATA/Fredi Beleri nuk është më vetëm çështje e drejtësisë, Greqia ia vendos si kusht Shqipërisë për të mos bllokuar integrimin* [The declaration is revealed/ Fredi Beleri is no longer just a matter of justice, Greece sets it as a condition for Albania not to block integration]. Ditar.al. https://ditar.al/qeveria-shqiptare-perbuz-parimet-themelore-te-shtetit-te-se-drejtes-ja-deklarata-e-greqise-derguar-27-anetareve-te-

Mikovic, N. (2023). *Montenegro is entering a new political era*. Europe, Politics, Diplomatic Courier. https://www.diplomaticourier.com/posts/montenegro-is-entering-a-new-political-era

Mitchell, T. (2002). *Rule of experts: Egypt, techno-politics, modernity*. University of California Press.

Morrison, K. (2011). *Change, continuity, and consolidation: Assessing five years of Montenegro's independence*. LSEE Papers on South Eastern Europe. http://eprints.lse.ac.uk/48039/1/__Libfile_repository_Content_LSEE_Change%2C%20continuity(author).pdf

Raporti Kombetar/National Report. (2020). *Rinia ne Shqiperi 2020* [Youth in Albania 2020]. K. Pulaha, A. Mustafaraj, E. Osmanaj, & A. Hazizaj (Eds.). https://www.crca.al/wp-content/uploads/2022/10/RAPORTI-TE-RINJTE-NE-SHQIPERI-2019-2020_0-1.pdf

Robinson, M. (2006). *Promoting polyarchy: Globalization, US intervention, and hegemony*. Cambridge University Press.

Rrapaj Kolasi, J., & Kolasi, K. (2023). The Political Economy of Passive Revolution in Albania: The Neoliberal Paradox and Transformation-Democratization Nexus. Journal of Balkan and Near Eastern Studies, 25(6), 963-981. DOI: 10.1080/19448953.2023.2167342 https://ideas.repec.org/a/taf/cjsbxx/v25y2023i6p963-981.html

Saric, D. (2020). The Winds of Political Change in Montenegro. Center for Strategic and International Studies. Retrieved from: https://www.csis.org/blogs/european-election-watch/winds-political-change-montenegro

Sen, A. (1999). *Development as freedom*. Oxford University Press.

Stankov, N. (2023, May). Democratic vulnerabilities of small systems: External actors' influence in Montenegro. In *Western Balkans at the crossroads: Democratic backsliding and external actors' influence*. Prague Security Center. https://www.pssi.cz/download//docs/10412_democratic-vulnerabilities-of-small-systems-external-actors-influence-in-montenegro.pdf

Stoiljković, Z., Vukanović, M., & Uljarević, D. (Eds.). (2020). *When the political elite underestimate citizens: Parliamentary elections in Montenegro. Democracy and human rights analysis*. Friedrich Ebert Stiftung. https://library.fes.de/pdf-files/bueros/belgrad/16629.pdf

The Robert Schuman Foundation. (2006, May 22). *The European elections monitor: Montenegro – Referendum on independence*.

Vukovic, I. (2011). The post-communist political transition of Montenegro: Democratization prior to Europeanization. Journal of Contemporary

European Studies, 1(2), 2010. https://www.researchgate.net/publication/263351273_The_post-communist_political_transition_of_Montenegro_Democratization_prior_to_Europeanization

Westminster Foundation for Democracy. (2021). *Pjesëmarrja e Shoqërisë Civile në Vendimmarrje në Shqipëri* [Civil society participation in decision-making in Albania]. B. Bino, R. Qirjazi, A. Dafa, & G. Vurmo (Eds.). Retrieved from https://idmalbania.org/wp-content/uploads/2021/11/Pjesemarrja-e-OSHC-ne-Vendimarrje-ne-Shqiperi-1.pdf

Westminster Foundation for Democracy. (2022). *Survey on Youth perceptions and attitudes towards politics in Montenegro*. Retrieved from: https://www.wfd.org/sites/default/files/2022-04/Youth%20perceptions%20and%20attitudes%20towards%20politics%20in%20MNE.pdf

Makhmudov Samariddin, Khamdamov Shoh-Jakhon,
Turaev Abdurakhim Nortojiyevich, Qamariddin
Qo`ldoshev Mansurovich

The Impact of Digital Technologies in the Service Sector of the National Economy: The Case of Uzbekistan

1. Introduction

The advent of digital technologies has been a transformative force across global economies, markedly shaping the service sector's landscape. As the world increasingly embraces digitalization, its impact on economic structures and productivity has become a focal point for research and policy formulation. This article aims to dissect and understand the influence of digital technologies on the service sector of Uzbekistan's national economy, a thriving and rapidly evolving market.

The development of information and communication technologies has a huge impact on various spheres of society, including the services market. In recent years, Uzbekistan has actively sought to modernize its economy and develop ICT, which opens up new opportunities and causes significant changes in the services market.

ICTs play an important role in Uzbekistan's services market, having a significant impact on its development. ICT development opens new opportunities for entrepreneurs and consumers of services, improves the quality of services provided and contributes to economic growth.

Roztocki, Soja and Weistroffer (2017) present a comprehensive framework linking Information and Communication Technologies (ICTs) to socioeconomic development. Their framework highlights the role of various ICTs such as computing resources, the Internet, mobile telephony, GPS, and Wi-Fi in enabling activities like e-commerce, e-government, and online learning. The authors emphasize how these activities contribute to the socioeconomic development of individuals, organizations, and countries. The study underscores the significant impact of ICTs on education, health, income, and overall quality of life, as well as on the global competitiveness and resources of organizations, and the national economy and labor market.

One of the main areas where ICTs have a significant impact is in the field of e-commerce. Uzbekistan is experiencing an increase in the number of Internet users, which opens up new opportunities for entrepreneurs to offer their services online. E-commerce is becoming increasingly popular and convenient for consumers, which contributes to the growth of transaction volume and development of the service market.

The development of ICT also affects the quality of services provided. The introduction of new technologies makes it possible to automate processes and improve the efficiency and accuracy of service delivery. For example, in the banking sector, ICT enables customers to make transactions quickly and conveniently, as well as to access their accounts and information about financial services.

However, the development of information and communication technologies also causes certain challenges and problems in the service market. One such challenge is the security of customer data and information. With the growth of online transactions and the use of electronic payment systems, there is a risk of hacker attacks and identity theft. Therefore, enterprises and government agencies need to pay great attention to information protection and ICT security.

Uzbekistan, with its strategic position and burgeoning market, offers a unique case to examine the effects of digital infrastructures on economic services. The service sector, a critical component of the nation's economy, is poised for significant transformation influenced by digitalization. Our study leverages comprehensive panel data, encompassing 104 observations from 13 regions over an eight-year period, to assess how the integration of digital technologies correlates with service sector performance.

We explore the relationship between the proliferation of personal computers, internet connectivity, and the skilled ICT workforce on the volume of services provided in the national economy. By employing a POLSE, FEE, and REE, our research navigates through the intricate dynamics of digital technology implementation and its economic ramifications.

In delving into the statistical data provided by the Statistical Agency under the President of the Republic of Uzbekistan, we shed light on the nuanced impacts of digitalization. This introduction sets the stage for a deeper exploration of our methodology, analysis, and the resultant recommendations that could guide policymakers and business leaders in strategically harnessing digital technologies to amplify the service sector's contribution to the national economy. The overarching goal is to provide a clear and empirical understanding of the digital landscape's potential to drive service sector growth, which is crucial for Uzbekistan's economic future.

2. Literature Review and Development Hypothesis

Guo and Wang (2023) investigate the impact of the digital economy on high-quality urban economic development, focusing on Chinese cities. Their study provides evidence of the transformative effects of digitalization on urban economies, highlighting how digital technologies influence various aspects of economic activities in urban settings. By analyzing data from Chinese cities, the authors offer insights into the role of the digital economy in shaping urban development strategies and fostering economic growth in urban areas.

The International Monetary Fund (IMF, 2018) offers a policy paper on measuring the digital economy, providing a valuable resource for understanding the complexities of digitalization and its impact on economic indicators. The paper discusses methodologies and frameworks for measuring the digital economy, shedding light on the challenges and opportunities associated with quantifying digital activities. By offering insights into measurement techniques, the IMF contributes to policymakers' ability to assess and respond to the growing influence of the digital economy on national and global economic landscapes.

Presented a case study on the implementation of ICTs in education, focusing on teacher education institutions in Pakistan (Majoka et al., 2013). Their study explores the challenges and opportunities associated with integrating ICTs into educational practices, particularly in developing countries. By examining the implementation process in teacher education institutions, the authors offer valuable insights into the factors influencing the effective use of ICTs in educational settings, highlighting the importance of infrastructure, training, and pedagogical strategies.

(Mills et al., 2018) delve into the integration of digital skills within journalism and mass communication curriculums, with a specific emphasis on the Middle East. Their research underscores the escalating significance of digital proficiencies in journalism, especially considering the evolving technological milieu and shifting media environments. Through an extensive survey of programs across the Middle Eastern region, the authors pinpoint potential areas necessitating curriculum revisions to ensure students are adequately equipped with the digital competencies essential for thriving in the profession.

Wang and Zhou (2022) analyze the impact of green finance on enterprise innovation using data from Shanghai and Shenzhen A-share listed companies. Their study provides empirical evidence of the positive influence of green finance on innovation within enterprises. By identifying the mechanisms through which green finance promotes innovation, the authors offer valuable insights for policymakers and businesses seeking to foster sustainable development through financial initiatives.

(Chen & Chen, 2018) develop a spillover model to describe the relationship between financial resource agglomeration and green innovation. Their study examines the impact of financial agglomeration on local industrial R&D efficiency, highlighting the significant role of financial factors in shaping innovation dynamics. By elucidating the complex interactions between financial resource allocation and innovation outcomes, the authors contribute to our understanding of the mechanisms driving sustainable development.

A series of studies (Khamdamov et al., 2022; Turayeva et al., 2022; Yusupov et al., 2022; Muftaydinova et al., 2022; Khamdamov, 2021; Burkhanov et al., 2022) explore various aspects of the relationship between digital technologies and economic development in Uzbekistan. These studies investigate topics ranging from the impact of Central Bank policies on economic stability to the use of modern digital technologies in financial services and healthcare. Collectively, they provide valuable insights into the role of digitalization in shaping economic trajectories in Uzbekistan and offer recommendations for policymakers and industry stakeholders.

(Tran et al., 2023) examine the nexus between natural resource depletion, rent, and commitments made at the COP26 summit, focusing on empirical evidence from Vietnam. Their study sheds light on the complex relationships between environmental sustainability, economic development, and international agreements. By analyzing the implications of natural resource management strategies on rent distribution and climate commitments, the authors offer insights into the challenges and opportunities associated with sustainable development agendas.

The reviewed literature provides a multifaceted understanding of the intersections between digitalization, economic development, and sustainability. From frameworks linking ICTs to socioeconomic development to empirical analyzes of green finance and innovation, these studies offer valuable insights for policymakers, businesses, and researchers seeking to navigate the complexities of the digital economy and foster sustainable development pathways. Moreover, the studies examining the specific context of Uzbekistan and Vietnam highlight the diverse challenges and opportunities associated with digital transformation in different regional contexts, emphasizing the need for context-specific policy interventions and strategies.

3. Research Methodology

The methodology section of a research article delineates the systematic process undertaken to answer the research questions or test the hypotheses. It includes the overall research design, data collection, and analytical techniques, ensuring replicability and reliability of the study.

3.1. Research Design

This study is rooted in an empirical research design that utilizes quantitative methods to evaluate the impact of digital technologies on the service sector of Uzbekistan's national economy. The design is structured to capture the multifaceted relationship between digital infrastructures – namely personal computing equipment, internet connectivity, and ICT workforce – and the service sector performance.

3.2. Data Collection

Data for this study were obtained from the Statistical Agency under the President of the Republic of Uzbekistan, accessed through their official website (www.stat.uz). The dataset comprises panel data consisting of 104 observations across 13 regions of Uzbekistan over an 8-year span. Variables included in the dataset encompass the number of personal computers, the number of internet-connected computers, the size of the ICT workforce in enterprises and organizations, and the corresponding volume of services in the national economy.

3.3. Methods

The analysis of the research included assessing the Gauss-Markov conditions and conducting Shapiro-Wilk and Durbin Watson tests within the framework of the Pooled OLS estimator model. Correlation matrices and graphical matrices were developed to assess the relationships between dependent and independent variables. During the model selection process, Fixed effects estimator and Random effects estimator models were also considered, and the Hausman test was used to determine the most appropriate model.

The regression analysis of panel data is a statistical approach used to examine data that includes spatial and temporal series elements. A brief summary of the panel data models is presented below. Panel data encompass observations across a constant time period T for N entities. These panel data points are jointly applied in the equations as it.

The Pooled OLS estimator model approach is distinguished by its simplicity and combines time series and spatial data. This model does not account for individual and temporary changes and represents the relationships of corporate data over different periods. Additionally, the regression is established using data relevant to the i factor and t time.

Accordingly, the model form of the Pooled OLS estimator is reflected as follows:

$$y_{it}=\alpha_0 + \alpha_1 x_{1it} + \varepsilon_{it} \quad (1)$$

Here,

i=1…n, t=1…t, it- number of observations

y_{it} – represents the dependent variable for the **i** observation at time **t**,

x_{it} – represents the independent variable for the **i** observation at time **t**,

α_0– is the intercept term,

α_1 – represents the slope coefficient for x_{it},

ε_{it} – is the error term, which expresses the deviation of the actual yit from the value predicted by the model.

The fixed effects estimator model is one of the econometric models used to assess the relationship between the dependent variable and independent variables. The fixed effects estimation technique is particularly relevant and widely used in applied econometrics, especially in the analysis of panel data where there is a continuous observation of the same regions, companies, or countries at different time points.

The fixed effects estimator model is expressed in the following form:

$$Y_{it} = \beta_o + \beta_i x_{1it} + \beta_z x_{zi} t + y_1 d_1 + y_z d_z + y_{n-1} y_{n-1} + u_{it} \quad (2)$$

The random effects estimator is an econometric model used to assess the relationship between the dependent variable and one or more independent variables. This model allows the inclusion of time-varying variables that Fixed Effects models cannot accommodate and implies a more efficient estimation when there is a correlation between random effects and independent variables.

The model is expressed as follows:

$$y_{it} - \theta\overline{y}_I = \beta_0 + \beta_1\left(x_{1it} - \theta\overline{x}_{1i}\right) + \beta_2\left(x_{2it} - \theta\overline{x}_{2i}\right) + \left(a_i - \theta\overline{a}_I\right) + \left(u_{it} + \theta\overline{u}_I\right) \quad (3)$$

According to the research, the factors affecting digital technologies in the service sector of the national economy were expressed as independent variables.

y- the volume of the service sector in the national economy (dependent variable),
x_1- the number of personal computers in enterprises and organizations in the country (independent variable),
x_2- the number of computers connected to the internet network in enterprises and organizations in the country (independent variable), and
x_3- the number of employees working in the field of information and communication technologies in enterprises and organizations in the country (independent variable).

The following hypotheses were reflected in the construction of the econometric model according to the research.

3.3.1. *Null Hypothesis (H0)*

There is no statistically significant relationship between the volume of the service sector in the national economy and the number of personal computers in enterprises and organizations in the country, the number of computers connected to the internet in enterprises and organizations, and the number of employees working in the field of information and communication technologies in enterprises and organizations.

3.3.2. *Alternative Hypothesis (Ha)*

There is a statistically significant relationship between the volume of the service sector in the national economy and the number of personal computers in enterprises and organizations in the country, the number of computers connected to the internet in enterprises and organizations, and the number of employees working in the field of information and communication technologies in enterprises and organizations.

3.3.3. *Validity and Reliability*

To ensure the validity and reliability of the econometric models, diagnostic tests including multicollinearity, autocorrelation, and heteroskedasticity assessments were conducted. The Hausman test's p-value of 0.62 confirmed the REE model's suitability for this analysis.

3.3.4. Ethical Considerations

The study adheres to ethical considerations by ensuring the data is used solely for research purposes, maintaining the confidentiality of any sensitive information, and crediting the data source.

The methodology section concludes by emphasizing that this approach provides a robust framework to analyze and interpret the impact of digital technology on the service sector, offering a foundation for evidence-based recommendations in the subsequent sections of the research article.

4. Analysis and Results

4.1. Matrix of Relationships Between Dependent and Independent Variables

These hypotheses would be tested using econometric modeling, where the null hypothesis typically represents the skepticism toward the existence of an effect

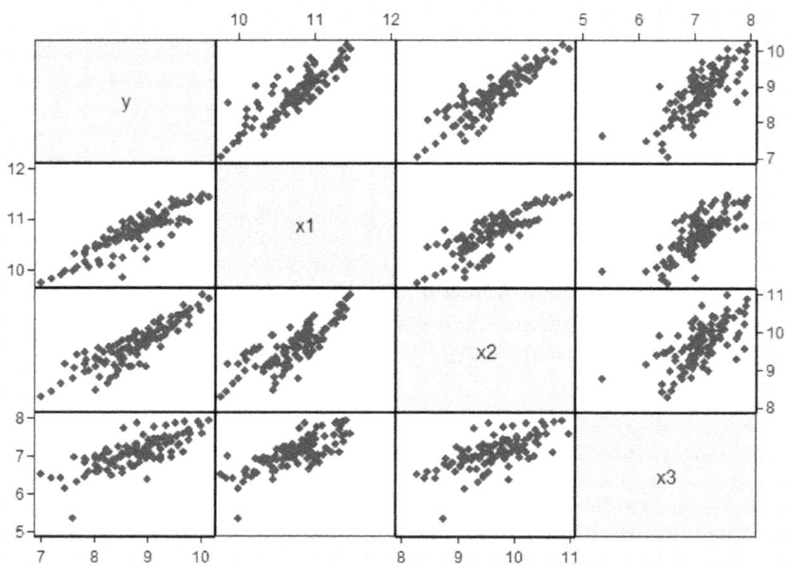

Figure 1. A graphical matrix of the relationship between the dependent variable and the independent variable

Source: It was developed by the authors based on Stata software.

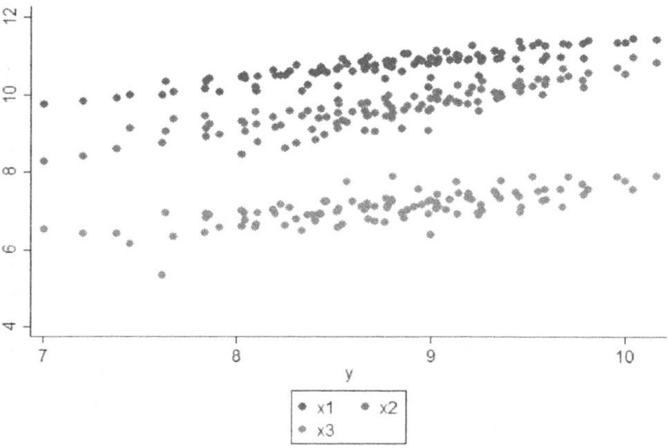

Figure 2. A graphical matrix of the relationship between the dependent variable and the independent variable

Source: It was developed by the authors based on Stata software.

or relationship, while the alternative hypothesis represents the assumption that there is some statistically significant relationship to be observed. The results of the econometric analysis would either provide evidence to reject the null hypothesis in favor of the alternative or not, depending on the statistical significance of the relationships among the variables.

Based on the information provided in the above images 1 and 2, there is a strong correlation between the dependent and independent variables, accompanied by a clear density phenomenon. Additionally, a noticeable correlation is observed at the points of data density, which show solid clustering and a concentrated distribution along the axes. The data density phenomenon indicates the presence of concentration and clustering of data points on the graph.

A graphical histogram of the dependent variables in the study is shown in the figures below. (See Figure 3).

In Figure 3, we have the graphical histogram of the dependent and independent variables. In this case, one can observe the central tendency, dispersion, and shape of the histogram data for the dependent and independent variables. It also indicates another important aspect of identifying boundary and extreme values for these variables.

In the next phase of the research, we examined the relationships between each of the dependent and independent variables using the correlation matrix in the Stata software program. (Refer to Table 1)

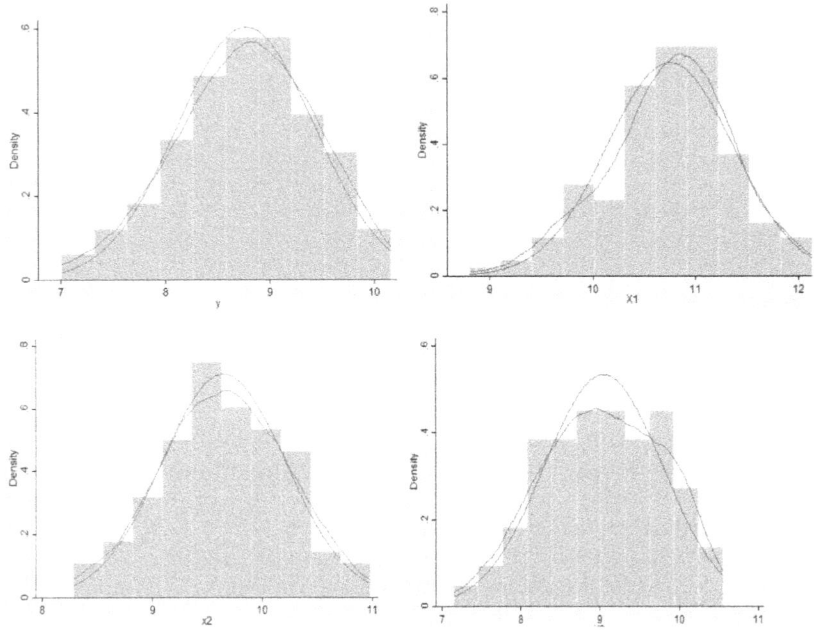

Figure 3. A graphical histogram of the dependent and independent variables
Source: It was developed by the authors based on Stata software.

Table 1. Correlation matrix of relationships between dependent and independent variables

Variables	(1)	(2)	(3)	(4)	(5)
(1) y	1.000				
(2) x1	0.699	1.000			
	(0.000)				
(3) x2	0.626	0.706	1.000		
	(0.000)	(0.000)			
(4) x3	0.686	0.362	0.731	1.000	
	(0.000)	**(0.000)**	**(0.000)**		

Source: It was developed by the authors based on Stata software.

Based on the data in Table 1, there is a high and strong correlation between the dependent and independent variables. Additionally, the correlation matrix indicates the absence of multicollinearity among the influencing factors.

In the next stage, econometric models such as the Pooled OLS estimator (POLSE), Fixed effects estimator (FEE), and Random effects estimator (REE) were evaluated. Furthermore, Shapiro-Wilk and Durbin Watson tests were conducted for the Pooled OLS estimator (POLSE) model.

Additionally, the Hausman test was utilized to determine the appropriateness of the Fixed effects estimator (FEE) and Random effects estimator (REE) model indicators, and the VIF indicator, which expresses the condition of multicollinearity, was assessed (see Table 2 for details).

Table 2. Indicators of econometric models based on panel data for the study

№	Indicators of the model	1st model	2nd model	3rd model
		POLSE model	FEE model	REE model
1	y	*	*	*
2	x_1	0.57 (0.12)	0.22 (0.13)	0.34 (0.14)
3	x_2	0.60 (0.07)	0.89 (0.08)	0.83 (0.06)
4	x_3	0.21 (0.09)	0.20 (0.08)	0.21 (0.08)
5	F test	206.42 (0.0000)	340.74 (0.0000)	
6	R^2	0.86	0.84	0.85
7	Chi-square			996.95 (0.0000)
8	Adj R^2	0.85		
9	Durbin Watson	0.59		
10	Shapiro-Wilk	0.23		
11	Vif	3.15		
12	Hausman			0.62

Source: It was developed by the authors based on Stata software.

According to Table 2, econometric models based on panel data were analyzed for each indicator and tests.

4.2. Pooled OLS Estimator (POLSE) Model Analysis

An analysis of the econometric equation indicators under the pooled OLS estimator model is presented below (See Table 3).

Table 3. Pooled OLS Estimator (POLSE) model indicators

y	Coef.	St.Err.	t-value	p-value	[95 % Conf	Interval]	Sig
x1	.577	.125	4.61	0	.329	.826	***
x2	.61	.075	8.17	0	.462	.758	***
x3	.215	.093	2.32	.023	.031	.398	**
Constant	−4.837	.71	−6.81	0	−6.246	−3.427	***
Mean dependent var	8.775		SD dependent var		0.662		
R-squared	0.861		Number of obs		104		
F-test	206.416		Prob > F		0.000		
Akaike crit. (AIC)	11.062		Bayesian crit. (BIC)		21.639		
*** *p*<.01, ** *p*<.05, * *p*<.1							

Source: It was developed by the authors based on Stata software.

The research utilized the Pooled OLS estimator (POLSE) model to conduct hypothesis testing. The null hypothesis (H_0) posited that the dependent variable (y) is equal to zero, while the alternative hypothesis (H_1) proposed that (y) is not equal to zero. The test results show that, with the F-statistic and the t-statistic being below the significance level of 0.05, the null hypothesis is rejected in favor of the alternative hypothesis. The outcomes obtained from the hypothesis test using the Pooled OLS model demonstrate its statistical significance and practical importance in enhancing our understanding of the relationships between the dependent variable and independent variables within the model.Тадқиқот бйўича ишлаб чиқилган Pooled OLS estimator (POLSE) модел қуйидаги кўринишга бўлди.

$$y=0.57x_1+0.61x_2+0.21x_3-4.43 \quad (4)$$

Source: It was developed by the authors based on Stata software.

According to the Pooled OLS estimator (POLSE) model, a 1 % increase in the number of personal computers in enterprises and organizations within the country leads to a 0.57 % increase in the volume of the service sector in the national economy. Furthermore, a 1 % increase in the number of computers connected to the internet in enterprises and organizations leads to a 0.61 % increase in the volume of the service sector in the national economy. Additionally, a 1 % increase in the number of employees working in the information and communication technologies sector in enterprises and organizations results in a 0.21 % increase in the volume of the service sector in the national economy.

In this study, we tested the important conditions of the Gauss-Markov theorem for the first model using the Pooled OLS estimator econometric equation.

The study presents the results of numerous statistical evaluations conducted to test the Gauss-Markov assumptions in the Pooled OLS econometric equation. *Durbin Watson* and *Shapiro Willke* tests were carried out, and the results showed that the null hypothesis (H_0) H_0:$y=0$ *ва* H_1:$y\neq 0$ is significant when the significance level exceeds the value of 0.05. Thus, in this research, the alternative hypothesis was not supported.

The VIF (Variance Inflation Factor) indicator was also calculated by model of Roztocki, Soja, and Weistroffer (2017) and Majoka, Fazal, and Khan (2013) to check for multicollinearity in the Pooled OLS estimator econometric equation, and its value was found to be 3.15. This value indicates the presence of significant multicollinearity within the model, and it is expressed with a confidence interval between.

4.3. Analysis of the Random Effects Estimator Model

The econometric equation parameters for the Random Effects Estimator model are presented in Table 4 of the research.

Table 4. Indicators of the random effects estimator model

y	Coef.	St.Err.	t-value	p-value	[95 % Conf	Interval]	Sig
x1	.348	.147	2.37	.018	.06	.635	**
x2	.832	.067	12.45	0	.701	.963	***
x3	.218	.083	2.63	.008	.056	.38	***
Constant	−4.537	1.062	−4.27	0	−6.618	−2.455	***
Mean dependent var	8.775		SD dependent var		0.662		
Overall r-squared	0.822		Number of obs		104		
Chi-square	996.954		Prob > chi2		0.000		
R-squared within	0.850		R-squared between		0.793		
*** *p*<.01, ** *p*<.05, * *p*<.1							

Source: It was developed by the authors based on Stata software.

According to the Random Effects Estimator model, the Chi-square statistic formed a value of 996.95. This expresses a positive condition between the observed and expected values. This indicates that the model fits the data and that the independent variables represent a positive forecast of the dependent variable.

The R-squared value constituted 0.85, explaining 85 % of the dependency in the dependent variable. This signifies the model's fit to the data and emphasizes the strength of the independent variables in making a positive prediction for the dependent variable.

The developed Random Effects Estimator model for the research took the following form.

$$y=0.34x_1+0.83x_2+0.21x_3-4.53 \tag{6}$$

Source: It was developed by the authors based on Stata software.

According to the Random Effects Estimator (REE) model results, a 1 % increase in the number of personal computers in enterprises and organizations in the country leads to a 0.34 % increase in the volume of the service sector in the national economy. Furthermore, a 1 % increase in the number of computers connected to the internet network in enterprises and organizations in the country results in a 0.83 % increase in the volume of the service sector in the national economy, and a 1 % increase in the number of employees working in the field of information and communication technologies in enterprises and organizations leads to a 0.21 % increase in the volume of the service sector in the national economy.

n the econometric model using the Random Effects Estimator (REE), the Hausman test resulted in a value of 0.62. According to the test results, the null hypothesis (H_0) $H_0{:}y=0$ nd the alternative hypothesis $H_1{:}y\neq0$ are significant when the level of significance p>0.05. In this research, the alternative hypothesis was rejected, which indicates that the Random Effects Estimator model is a more optimal model compared to the Fixed Effects Estimator model.

Additionally, the test recorded a p-value greater than 0.05, which indicates that the condition for the Hausman test has been met. This demonstrates that the Hausman test was appropriately applied to the data and that the results are reliable.

4.4. Analysis of the Fixed Effects Estimator (FEE) Model

The econometric equation indicators for the Fixed Effects Estimator (FEE) model in the research are presented in the following Table 5.

Table 5. Analysis of the Fixed Effects Estimator (FEE) model

y	Coef.	St.Err.	t-value	p-value	[95 % Conf	Interval]	Sig
x1	.225	.196	1.15	.253	–.164	.614	
x2	.895	.084	10.64	0	.728	1.062	***
x3	.205	.09	2.29	.025	.027	.383	**
Constant	–3.734	1.544	–2.42	.018	–6.804	–.665	**
Mean dependent var	8.775		SD dependent var		0.662		
R-squared	0.841		Number of obs		104		
F-test	340.738		Prob > F		0.000		
Akaike crit. (AIC)	–119.193		Bayesian crit. (BIC)		–108.615		
*** *p<.01*, ** *p<.05*, * *p<.1*							

Source: It was developed by the authors based on Stata software.

The Fixed Effects Estimator (FEE) model developed in the research is characterized by these statistics, indicating that the model can explain 84 % of the variability in the dependent variable within the entities being analyzed, which is a relatively high explanatory power. This implies that most of the variation in the dependent variable can be explained by the changes within the entities across time rather than by differences between the entities. The actual value of 340.73 may refer to a test statistic, coefficient, or another model parameter that is notably high, suggesting a significant effect or relationship within the data under consideration. The specifics of the model's appearance would depend on the variables included and the structure of the econometric equation used.

$$y=0.22x_1+0.89x_2+0.20x_3-3.73 \qquad (7)$$

Source: It was developed by the authors based on Stata software.

The results of the Fixed Effects Estimator (FEE) model suggest that in the country, a 1 % increase in the number of personal computers in enterprises and organizations leads to a 0.22 % increase in the volume of the service sector in the national economy. Moreover, a 1 % increase in the number of computers connected to the internet in enterprises and organizations results in a 0.89 % increase in the volume of the service sector in the national economy. Additionally, a 1 % increase in the number of employees working in the field of information and communication technologies in enterprises and organizations leads to a 0.20 % increase in the volume of the service sector in the national economy.

This FEE model analysis underscores the positive impact of technological advancement and digital connectivity on the service sector's growth. The results indicate that investments in digital infrastructure and the ICT workforce can have a meaningful and positive effect on the economic sector that is increasingly becoming central to modern economies.

5. Findings and Discussion

5.1. Interpretation of Findings

Our study's findings illustrate a clear and positive impact of digital technology on the service sector of Uzbekistan's national economy. The econometric analysis, particularly the Random Effects Estimator (REE), has revealed a nuanced relationship between digital infrastructure investments and service sector performance.

5.1.1. Personal Computers in Enterprises

The positive coefficient for personal computers suggests that technology plays a fundamental role in increasing the efficiency and capacity of service delivery. The finding that a 1 % increase in personal computers corresponds to a 0.34 % increase in service volume aligns with the global understanding that ICT infrastructure is a cornerstone of modern economic development.

5.1.2. Internet-Connected Computers

Perhaps most striking is the substantial impact of internet connectivity. The 0.83 % increase in service volume for every 1 % increase in internet-connected computers underscores the transformative effect of the internet on business operations and service delivery.

5.1.3. ICT Workforce

The positive coefficient associated with the ICT workforce suggests that human capital within this sector is crucial for leveraging technology to drive service sector growth. The 0.21 % increase in service volume for every 1 % increase in ICT employees highlights the importance of skilled professionals in maximizing the potential of digital infrastructures.

5.2. Implications for Policy and Practice

The implications of these findings are significant for policymakers and business leaders. The strong positive relationship between digital infrastructure and service sector performance indicates that investments in ICT can lead to tangible economic benefits. For Uzbekistan, a strategic focus on enhancing digital skills and infrastructure, particularly internet connectivity, could stimulate growth in the service sector, which is a vital component of the national economy.

Moreover, the preference for the REE model over the FEE model, as indicated by the Hausman test, suggests that while individual regional characteristics are important, the overarching national policy and economic environment play a more critical role in shaping the impact of digital technologies on the service sector.

5.3. Comparison with Existing Literature

Our findings resonate with existing literature that affirms the critical role of digital infrastructure in economic growth. Studies from various global contexts support the notion that ICT investment not only boosts service sector performance but also serves as a catalyst for broader economic development. The substantial impact of internet connectivity found in this study is particularly aligned with literature emphasizing the role of digital connectivity in modern economies.

5.4. Limitations of the Study

While the study provides valuable insights, it is not without limitations. The analysis is confined to available data, which may not capture all aspects of digital technology's impact. Moreover, the study focuses on the aggregate level impact, which might mask regional disparities or sector-specific nuances. Future research could explore these dimensions in greater depth.

5.5. Future Research Directions

Subsequent research could extend this study's findings by examining the long-term effects of digital infrastructure investments on the service sector. Moreover, comparative studies involving other Central Asian countries could provide a broader regional perspective on the digital transformation's economic implications.

6. Conclusion

The findings indicate a clear positive correlation between investment in digital technologies and the growth of the service sector. The preferred Random Effects Estimator (REE) model, substantiated by a Hausman test p-value of 0.62, suggests that enhancing digital infrastructure – notably, increasing the number of personal computers, internet-connected computers, and skilled ICT workers – can lead to measurable improvements in the service sector's volume and efficiency.

These results highlight the significant impact of ICT-related variables on the service sector of the national economy. While personal computers play a crucial role, the presence of internet-connected computers and a skilled ICT workforce has an even more direct and positive effect on the growth and development of services in the economy.

7. Recommendations

7.1. Strategic Investment in PCs and Internet Connectivity

The evidence suggests that a systematic increase in the number of personal computers and internet connections within enterprises can significantly boost the service sector's volume. Investments should, therefore, be directed towards upgrading digital infrastructure to ensure widespread access to these technologies.

7.2. Enhancing ICT Workforce Skills

The service sector's growth is noticeably influenced by the availability of skilled ICT professionals. It is recommended to focus on education and training programs that can increase the quality and quantity of the ICT workforce, thus driving innovation and efficiency in services.

7.3. Policy Frameworks to Support Digital Transformation

Policymakers should consider developing supportive frameworks that encourage the adoption of digital technologies in the service sector. This could include incentives for digital infrastructure investment, subsidies for training, and the creation of technology hubs.

7.4. Monitoring and Evaluation

Establish a continuous monitoring mechanism to assess the impact of digital technology investments on service sector performance. This will help in making informed decisions and adjustments to strategies as necessary.

7.5. Public-Private Partnerships

Encourage collaboration between the government and private sector entities to leverage resources for the development of digital infrastructure and to foster an environment conducive to technological innovation.

By acting on these recommendations, Uzbekistan can harness the full potential of digital technologies to catalyze growth and enhance the competitiveness of its service sector in the national and global economy.

References

Burkhanov, A. U., Tursunov, B., Uktamov, K., & Usmonov, B. (2022, December). Econometric analysis of factors affecting economic stability of chemical industry enterprises in the digital era: In case of Uzbekistan. In *Proceedings of the 6th International Conference on Future Networks & Distributed Systems* (pp. 484–490).

Chen, S. Y., & Chen, D. K. (2018). Smog pollution, government governance and high-quality economic development. *Economic Research*, 53(02), 20–34.

International Monetary Fund (IMF). (2018). Measuring the digital economy. *Policy paper*, February, 7. Retrieved from https://www.imf.org/en/Publications/Policy-Papers/Issues/2018/04/03/022818-measuring-the-digital-economy. Accessed 20 August 2018.

Khamdamov, S. J. (2021, December). Calculating share of factors of intensive economic growth in Uzbekistan. In *The 5th International Conference on Future Networks & Distributed Systems* (pp. 393–397).

Khamdamov, S. J., Usmanov, A. S., Abdulazizova, O., Isaev, F., Kholbaev, N., Makhmudov, S., … & Kholbaeva, S. (2022, December). Econometric modeling of Central Bank refinancing rate in Uzbekistan. In *Proceedings of the 6th International Conference on Future Networks & Distributed Systems* (pp. 253–257).

Majoka, M. I., Fazal, S., & Khan, M. S. (2013). Implementation of information and communication technologies (ICTs) in education course: A case from teacher education institutions in Pakistan. *Bulletin of Educational Research*, 35(2), 37–53. ISSN: 0555–7747.

Mills, A., Sanders, A. K., & Hussain, S. (2018). Digital skills implementation in journalism and mass communication curriculums: A census of programs in the Middle East. *Paper presented at the Qatar Foundation Annual Research Conference*, Qatar, 19-20 March.

Muftaydinova, S. K., Chuprynin, V. D., Fayzullin, L. Z., Buralkina, N. A., Muminova, Z. A., Asaturova, A. V., … & Abdullayev, S. I. (2022, December). Expression of the tyrosine Kinase Receptor (EPHA1) in the Eutopic and Ectopic Endometrium of patients with deep infiltrative endometriosis: Use of modern digital technologies. In *Proceedings of the 6th International Conference on Future Networks & Distributed Systems* (pp. 416–421).

Roztocki, N., Soja, P., & Weistroffer, H. R. (2017). *Enterprise systems in transition economies: Research landscape and framework for socioeconomic development.* Information Technology for Development. https://doi.org/10.1080/02681102.2017.1377148

Tran, T. K., Lin, C. Y., Tu, Y. T., Duong, N. T., Thi, T. D. P., & Shoh-Jakhon, K. (2023). Nexus between natural resource depletion and rent and COP26 commitments: Empirical evidence from Vietnam. *Resources Policy*, 85, 104024.

Turayeva, G., Berdiyev, G., Eshpulatov, D., Alimova, D., Odilbekov, A., Davletova, D., … & Burxanov, A. (2022, December). Opportunities to use financial services–"1 C program". In *Proceedings of the 6th International Conference on Future Networks & Distributed Systems* (pp. 556–561).

Wang, Y. L., & Zhou, Y. L. (2022). Green financial development and enterprise innovation. *Financial Research*, 1–15. https://doi.org/10.16538/J.CNKI.jfe.20615.101.100010000005

Wang, W., Jiang, H., Shoukat, A., & Usmanovich, B. A. (2023). Quantifying the impact of green growth and digital transformation on health: New insights from Asian economies. *Environmental Science and Pollution Research*, 1–10.

Yusupov, S., Boymuradov, S., Bobamuratova, D., Shukhratova, M., Marupov, I., Akramova, D. T., … & Muradova, D. A. (2022, December). Diagnostic aspects of zygomatico-orbital complex fractures with the use of modern digital technologies. In *Proceedings of the 6th International Conference on Future Networks & Distributed Systems* (pp. 399–403).

Jasurbek Ataniyazov, Elshod Alimardonov,
Anvar Saidmakhmudovich Usmanov, Shoh-Jakhon
Khamdamov, Samariddin Makhmudov

The Impact of Financial and Industrial Capital Integration on Economic Stability

1. Introduction

World experience shows that the driving force of the modern economy is large corporate business structures. They occupy an intermediate position between the state and the market. It is precisely large-scale production that forms supply and demand, determines the most important prerequisites for winning a competitive struggle. The victory is determined by the dynamics of costs due to the growth rate of labor productivity. Achieving these goals requires high-tech production, capital turnover rates, mobility in staff development, etc. All this is possible in large-scale production, where favorable conditions are created for the formation, use and reproduction as a whole.

Ensuring the monopoly position of large corporations in the world market is facilitated by a high degree of concentration of scientific and technical potential in one's hands. By expanding the range of functions and services, corporations are naturally transformed into financial-industrial groups (FIGs).

FIG has established itself as a more advanced organization of industrial and financial capital, which is able to preserve and ensure further development of competitive industries, give new impetus to development, allow using its state support to find and win its place in the internal and external economic environment.

A characteristic feature of the development of financial-industrial groups is their multidisciplinary orientation, which allows them to respond quickly to changes in market conditions. The main purpose of creating financial-industrial groups is to create favorable conditions for investment activity through the use of effective investment mechanisms, distribution of responsibility, conducting operations in the domestic and foreign securities market.

Modern FIGs are diversified multifunctional structures, resulting from the combination of financial and industrial capital. The main purpose of creating financial-industrial groups is to increase the efficiency of production and financial operations; enhancing competitiveness in the domestic and foreign markets;

the growth of the economic potential of its participants, attracting investment, expanding markets.

2. Literature Review and Development Hypothesis

Industrial-financial group is a new type of enterprise group establish upon the mutual penetration and alliance in capital and management between industrial organizations and financial organizations, as well as a consequence of self-organization coevolution on industrial-financial integration from claims model to equity model (Wei & Lei, 2009). Through self-organization and other-organization strategies, industrial-financial group merges multi-industries with finance industry and forms an industrial-financial system that fuses various subsystems.

The study by Qing et al. (2023) investigates the impact of financial inclusion and human development on ecological sustainability in G-20 countries. The study highlights the importance of government effectiveness in decreasing ecological footprints and suggests community awareness and regulatory measures as ways to improve outcomes.

Khamdamov et al. (2022) explore the application of econometric models to predict the Central Bank's refinancing rate in Uzbekistan, contributing to financial policy planning and economic forecasting in the region. Turayeva et al. (2022) discuss the "1 C Program" and its potential to enhance access to financial services, offering insights into digital finance's role in economic development. Tran et al. (2023) examine the relationship between natural resource depletion, rent, and COP26 commitments in Vietnam, offering empirical evidence that informs resource management and environmental policy. Gong et al. (2023) investigate sustainable economic development in resource-rich regions through an interdisciplinary lens, emphasizing resource productivity, technological innovation, and ecosystem resilience. Shoh-Jakhon (2023) delves into the theoretical and methodological aspects of intensive economic growth, contributing to the broader discourse on sustainable economic development.

According to self-organization theory (Haken, 1988) to achieve industrial-financial group system synergic effect and improve synergic value is mainly depend upon the order parameter of industrial-financial group system, i.e. the self-organization transition of synergic development ability.

However, due to the research of synergic development ability is still in the beginning phase, there are rarely existing documents concerning synergic development ability.

Teece et al., Shuen (1997) had recognized the importance of synergic development ability and researched the status of enterprises' resource integration capability in enterprises innovation capability. Kaplan & Norton (2006) used Blanced Scorecad (BSC) theory to research how enterprises create enterprise synergic development ability through organize synergic ability. Zheng Shenghua et al., (2007) researched the basic framework of enterprise alliance capability and the mechanism to raise alliance performance by utilizing self-organization theory. Tang & Wang (2008) researched the enterprise strategic transformation capability by applying self-introduction theory. In general, the current researches either place emphasis on the single factor analysis on synergic development ability and ignore the system factor synergic ability, or restricted to general description and lack of normative analysis.

3. Data & Methodology

The methodology section outlines a comprehensive approach to evaluating the economic benefits of financial-industrial groups (FIGs) in the national economy. Utilizing the multiplier model, the study aims to quantify the economic impact of increased investments in the industrial sector resulting from financial-industrial integration. The method involves calculating the multiplier effect of investments on GDP growth, incorporating second-generation panel techniques like the method of momentum quantile regression (MMQR) and augmented mean group (AMG) to analyze the cross-sectional interdependence, panel co-integration, and stationary characteristics among variables. This robust analytical framework provides a detailed examination of how FIGs can contribute to sustainable economic growth and stability by fostering domestic and foreign investments in the industrial sector.

On the basis of the revealed size of the investment potential, the optimal way of calculation of economic benefit of formation FIG for national economy is the model of the multiplier (Xue et al., 2023).

Speaking about the multiplier of investments (m), we consider the phenomenon of the increased influence of a gain of investments (ΔI) on a gain of level of the income (ΔY) that is expressed by the following record:

$$m^{*}\Delta I = \Delta Y \quad (1)$$

The increase in volume of investments (ΔI) leads to growth of incomes in the branches making the capital blessings, and this circumstance causes increase in consumer expenses (ΔC). Hence, the increase in investments causes consumption growth. Both these increments together taken, are equaled to an income increment, ΔI + Δ with = Δ U. But the cumulative effect of increase in investments can be stretched much further. The increase in the income caused by investments can cause the further growth of investments in turn. This last effect is known under the name of a principle of derivative demand or a principle of an acceleration (Chen et al., 2023). In order to apply the multiplier model, to calculate the long-term economic effect from the inflow of domestic investment from the financial and credit sphere into the production sector, it is necessary to determine the predicted value of the multiplication coefficient.

Let's accept, that ΔYn is a required indicator of macroeconomic effect in the form of the future gain of gross national product. Then, according to the formula of the multiplier it is possible to express size of a gain of gross national product as follows (Cuaresma & Glocker, 2023):

$$\Delta Yn = mn * \Delta\ In \qquad (2)$$

Where mn - multiplication coefficient, which is a discrete value;

ΔIn - a potential gain of investments;

ΔYn - required size of a gain of gross national product, characterizing itself economic benefit in a consequence of formation FIG in national economy.

As financial and industrial groups promote growth of domestic and foreign investments into national economy, and in particular in the industry in our analysis the size of a gain of investments ΔIn, will be directly defined by financial and industrial integration. Such approach is dictated to that financially - industrial integration means the certain sizes of not used financial reserves of domestic credit system as potential investments into the industry. The decision of the given equation (2), and, hence, and calculation of possible effect from financial and industrial integration, thus, is reduced to initial definition of discrete factor mn.

The multiplication factor is a multiplier that shows the excess of GDP growth in comparison with the initial increase in investment due to the level of business activity in the economy and the value of marginal propensity to consume (MPC) (Huang et al., 2023). Thus, the multiplier is expressed in a following kind:

$$m = l / (1 - MPC)$$

However, as MPC represents size defined by especially tactical market factors and psychological features of behaviour of consumers of demand in the market it becomes obvious, that calculation of the multiplier on the basis of MPC - is impossible. The acceleration factor also is the discrete size depending on level of solvent demand and investment activity in economy. Proceeding from it, in a kind of step-type behaviour of indicators m and i it is the most expedient to apply to their calculation the dispersive analysis.

Let's admit, it is necessary to calculate prognostic size of a discrete indicator X, if its values - x_i on a time interval - I, where i = (1,2,3 ….n), and (n) the-required future period of time are known. We will designate through: p_i=P (X=x_i), where i = (1,2,3…. n) probabilities of these values, that is probability of the event, consisting that the size X will accept value x_i and events X=x_i, at i = (1,2,3…. n) form full group of events, hence, to their probability we will present in a kind:

$$p_1+p_2+p_3+ \dots \dots \dots . p_n=1$$

Such conformity of possible values to their probabilities represents the law of distribution of a random variable X that is a basis for carrying out of the dispersive analysis. According to the probability theory, results of the dispersive analysis that will be more exact, than high a variation number of discrete sizes will be subjected to the analysis (Hajipour et al., 2023). The first stage is calculation of average prognostic values in the form of a population mean of a discrete random variable under the formula (Liu et al., 2023):

$$M(X)=\sum_{i=1}^{n} x_i p_i$$

Where $\sum_{i=1}^{n} p_i =1$.

Average, most probable value of required size X, it is necessary to add with a possible deviation that is to develop the theory of errors consisting in calculation of admissible error prognostic values. If it is known, that the random variable population mean makes M (X), and actual value - X, a random variable equal to a difference: X - M (X), it is considered to be a deviation of a random variable X during the concrete moment of time.

On the basis of it, it is necessary to define a dispersion that is degree of disorder of a random variable counted in the form of a population mean of a square of a deviation of this size from its population mean that assumes the following air Bakhshalizadeh et al., 2023:

$$D(X)=\sum_{i=1}^{n}\left(x_i-\sum_{i=1}^{n}x_ip_i\right)^2*p_i \tag{3}$$

Calculation of average size of an error of a population mean is reduced to calculation of an average square-law deviation of this size defined under the formula (Khamdamov, 2021):

$$\partial(X)=\sqrt{D(X)} \tag{4}$$

Let's transform the formula (4) substitution as D (X) - expressions (3) therefore the formula of an error of a random variable looks like:

$$\partial(X)=\sqrt{\sum_{i=1}^{n}\left(x_i-\sum_{i=1}^{n}x_ip_i\right)^2} \tag{5}$$

Thus, knowing a population mean and possible size of an error in the form of an average square-law deviation on the basis of the dispersive analysis, it is obviously possible to express prognostic value of casual discrete size in a following kind:

$$X=\sum_{i=1}^{n}x_ip_i\pm\sqrt{\sum_{i=1}^{n}\left(x_i-\sum_{i=1}^{n}x_ip_i\right)^2*p_i} \tag{6}$$

Where x_i - possible values of a discrete random variable;

p_i - probabilities of occurrence of these values;

i = (1,2,3...n) - represents a time interval;

X is required prognostic value of a discrete random variable.

If to take into consideration that fact, that the casual discrete size X on each time interval i accepts unique value then we will receive, that probabilities of reception of any values are identical at any variation number and can be expressed in the form of (Stecher & Baumgärtner, 2024):

$$P_i = 1/n = \text{const, where } i = (1,2,3\ldots.n)$$

Hence, it is necessary to transform the formula (6) taking into account equal to probability of occurrence of a random variable X that will be expressed in a kind:

$$X = \sum_{i=1}^{n} \frac{x_i}{n} \pm \sqrt{\sum_{i=1}^{n} \left(x_i - \sum_{i=1}^{n} \frac{x_i}{n} \right)^2 * \frac{1}{n}} \qquad (7)$$

The carried out discrete analysis allows, having applied the formula (7) to define prognostic value of factor m_n.

When calculating the multiplication factor, the values of the random variable x_i will be the coefficient values for a certain time period i, that is: $x_i = m_i$, however, the analyzed time period should be set as i = (1,2,3 ... n-1), since n is the unknown future time period for which the predicted values are calculated, and therefore, the value of n in the formula (7) will correspond to the value (n-1). Multiplier coefficients according to the formula (1), are calculated as a ratio of GDP growth to growth investments for each time period:

$$m_i = \Delta Y_{i/} \Delta I_i$$

Where i = (1,2,3 … n-1).

By substitution of expression (7) in the formula (6), forecast the size of the multiplier (m_n) pays off as follows:

$$m_n = \sum_{i=1}^{n-1} \frac{\Delta Y_i}{\Delta I_i * (n-1)} \pm \sqrt{\sum_{i=1}^{n-1} \left(\frac{\Delta Y_i}{\Delta I_i} - \sum_{i=1}^{n-1} \frac{\Delta Y_i}{\Delta I_i * (n-1)} \right)^2 * \frac{1}{n-1}} \qquad (8)$$

Thus having defined values of factor m_n under the formula (8) accordingly, and then having substituted them in the formula (1), possibility to calculate possible economic benefit of financially - industrial integration in the form of gross national product and public welfare gain in national economy is represented. The total expression modeling economic benefit of financial and industrial integration assumes the following air:

$$\Delta Y_n = \Delta I_n * \left[\sum_{i=1}^{n-1} \frac{\Delta Y_i}{\Delta I_i * (n-1)} \pm \sqrt{\sum_{i=1}^{n-1} \left(\frac{\Delta Y_i}{\Delta I_i} - \sum_{i=1}^{n-1} \frac{\Delta Y_i}{\Delta I_i * (n-1)} \right)^2 * \frac{1}{n-1}} \right] \qquad (9)$$

Where ΔY_n - required size of a gain of gross national product,

ΔI_n - Potential volume of investments initiated by financially - industrial integration,

ΔY_i - A gain of gross national product,

ΔI_i - A gain of investments for each i th analyzed period on a time interval i = (1,2,3.... n), and n - the future period of time.

4. Analysis and Results

With reference to the Republic of Uzbekistan economy macroeconomic indicators of gross national product and total volume of investments are presented in the following table.

Table 1. Volume of Gross National Product and Investments in The Republic of Uzbekistan for 2015-2021

Indicator (billion UZS)	2015	2016	2017	2018	2019	2020	2021
Gross National Product	171369	199325,1	302536,8	406648,5	529391,4	602193,1	734587,7
Investments into a fixed capital	44810,4	51232	72155,2	124231,3	195927,3	210195,1	239552,6

Source: State Committee on Statistics of Uzbekistan

Since for calculating the multiplication factor according to formula (15), GDP and investment increment values are used as arguments, it is necessary to calculate them based on the data in Table 1 as the difference of indicators for the current and previous periods. The growth rates of GDP and investment are presented in the following table.

Table 2. Size of A Gain of The Macroeconomic Indicators of The Republic of Uzbekistan for 2016-2021

Indicator (billion UZS)	2016	2017	2018	2019	2020	2021
Gross National Product	27956,1	103211,7	104111,7	122742,9	72801,7	132394,6
Investments into a fixed capital	8739,5	22678,4	52076,1	71696,0	14267,8	29357,5

Source: State Committee on Statistics of Uzbekistan

Having made the substitution of the data of Table 2 into formula (8), we obtain, on the basis of dispersive analysis, the magnitude of the multiplication coefficient, expressed as an average forecast value taking into account possible deviations. As the analysis of macroeconomic indicators is spent for an interval with 2016 on 2021 that is for last 5 years, and the potential gain of gross national product pays off for 2022 to value change (n) in the equation (8) and (9) there will correspond number 6. Data of corresponding calculations are presented in Table 3.

Table 3. Estimated Indices of Variance Analysis of The Distribution of The Random Value of The Multiplication Coefficient

Indicators	**2017**	**2018**	**2019**	**2020**	**2021**
Multiplication coefficient	4,55	2,00	1,71	5,10	4,51
Mathematical expectation (average)	3,31	3,31	3,31	3,31	3,31
Deviation	1,24	-1,31	-1,60	1,79	1,20
Deviation square	0,31	0,35	0,51	0,64	0,29
Dispersion (disorder)	0,86	0,86	0,86	0,86	0,86
Average square deviation	0,92	0,92	0,92	0,92	0,92

Source: Developed by authors.

So, on the basis of the corresponding calculations, the average predicted value of the multiplication coefficient (m_n) is determined taking into account possible errors: m_n=3,31±0,92. Thus, having determined the value of the coefficient m_n by the formula (8), it is necessary then to substitute it in the formula (1) and obtain the function of GDP growth from the argument in the form of potential investment inflows in the framework of financial and industrial integration, where the multiplication factor is constant m_n=3,31±0,92= const. Being expressed differently, we receive function of economic benefit of financial and industrial integration which has the following appearance:

$$\Delta Y_n = \Delta I_n * (= 3{,}31 \pm 0{,}92)$$

Where

ΔY_n - Required size of a gain of gross national product,

ΔI_n - The potential volume of investments initiated by financially - industrial integration, n - corresponds predictive to the period.

Thus, to calculate economic benefit of financial and industrial integration, it is necessary to reveal potential volume of investments initiated by creation FIG.

Thus, at an existing state of affairs the potential volume of investments of bank system of the country within the limits of financial and industrial integration can make about 3658 billion UZS that corresponds to size of the unallotted income.

If the value of the potential investment volume ΔI_n =3500, as well as the value of the multiplication coefficient m_n =3,31±0,92, is known, then substituting them into an expression it is possible to determine the economic effect of financial and industrial integration. The value of the macroeconomic effect should be calculated taking into account a possible deviation of ±0,92, therefore, if the average value of the multiplication coefficient is taken as $m_{\circ}$ = 3,31, then the minimum value of the coefficient is expressed as m_1=3,31-0,92=2,39; and the maximum value of the multiplier will be expressed as m_2=3,31+0,92=4,23. Thus, we will calculate the magnitude of the economic effect from the formation of financial-industrial groups with two possible variants of the multiplication factor, which characterizes the potential fluctuation of the macroeconomic market conditions. Results of calculations are presented in the following table.

Table 4. Potential Economic Benefit From Financial-Industrial Integration into National Economy

Economic benefit (billion UZS)	**The values of multiplier coefficients (m)**	
	m_1 =2,39	**m_2 = 4,23**
Potentially possible gain of GNP	8365	14805

Source: Developed by authors.

According to calculations, integration of real sector of economy and financially-credit system is capable to render positive effect in the form of a gain of volume of production of industrial production that will be expressed in a gain of an indicator of GNP. In other words, financial and industrial integration is capable to stimulate economic growth of national economy, to raise public welfare.

Along with it, FIG provides effective synthesis of manufacture with scientific and technical progress and attraction of considerable additional volumes of investments from the internal and international financial markets, and also achievement of high competitiveness of made production. It gives to a problem of creation and the state support of these perspectives for economy of Uzbekistan of institutes paramount value.

The variation of the macroeconomic effect in this process from 8365 to 14805 billion UZS will naturally depend on the fundamental economic factors of the multiplication factor lying in nature, such as propensity to consume, inflation rate, changes in the legal field, political stability, the situation on world market etc.

5. Conclusion

The conclusion of the research highlights the positive macroeconomic impact of financial and industrial integration, emphasizing its role in financial stabilization and investment stimulation within the national economy. It asserts the integration's capability to boost national income and public welfare over several years, highlighting the effectiveness of combining industrial and banking capital in financial-industrial groups. This integration not only facilitates economic growth and improves the macroeconomic situation in Uzbekistan but also enhances the country's business activity index and international reputation. The research suggests that the variability of macroeconomic effects depends on fundamental economic factors, advocating for the formation of financial-industrial groups as a pivotal strategy for Uzbekistan's economic development and competitiveness on the global stage.

Summarizing the consideration of the integration of financial and industrial capital, the following should be noted:

Combining industrial and banking capital into financial-industrial groups is essentially the main form of organization of the production system, making the technological complex of efficient economies of most of the economically developed countries of the world, the entire world economy, being an expression of the progress of modern social production and at the same time a condition for its further development. development.

The process of creating and developing FIGs is not only a successful experience of growing coherence and interdependence of the functioning of all organizational units in the structure of financial and industrial capital in accordance with the achieved level of socialization of production, breaking into international markets, but also shows the successful experience of managing the state industrial sector a number of European countries.

References

Bakhshalizadeh, S., Nasibulina, B., Kurochkina, T., Ali, A., Mora-Medina, R., & Ayala-Soldado, N. (2023). Multivariate analysis of trace elements in starry sturgeon (Acipenser stellatus) spine in different areas of the Caspian Sea. *Marine Pollution Bulletin*, 194, 115–289.

Chen, H., Xu, H., Liu, Y., & Ren, X. (2023). Seismic demand estimation of isolated buildings with nonlinear bearings subjected to linear response spectra. *Journal of Building Engineering*, 67, 105–995.

Cuaresma, J. C., & Glocker, C. (2023). Production structure, tradability and fiscal spending multipliers. *Journal of International Money and Finance*, 138, 102–921.

Gong, X., Wong, W-K., Peng, Y., Khamdamov, S., Albasher, G., Hoa, V. T., & Nhan, N. T. T. (2023). Exploring an Interdisciplinary Approach to Sustainable Economic Development in Resource-Rich Regions: An Investigation of Resource Productivity, Technological Innovation, and Ecosystem Resilience. *Resources Policy*, 87(Part A), 104–294. https://doi.org/10.1016/j.resourpol.2023.104294

Hajipour, V., Hekmat, S., & Amini, M. (2023). A value-oriented Artificial Intelligence-as-a-Service business plan using integrated tools and services. *Decision Analytics Journal*, 8, 100–302.

Haken H. (1988). Information and self-organization: A macroscopic approach to complex system. *Journal of Management*. Springer-Verlag, 18(4), 657–680.

Huang, J., Wang, Y., Luan, B., Zou, H., & Wang, J. (2023). The energy intensity reduction effect of developing digital economy: Theory and empirical evidence from China. *Energy Economics*, 128, 107–193.

Jianxiong, T., & Guoshun, W. (2008). Self-organization "Research on the Enterprises Strategic Transformation Ability". *Science of Science and Management of S. &T.*, 41(09), 171–175.

Kaplan, R. S., & Norton, D. P. (2006). Alignment: "Using the Balanced Scorecard to Create Corporate Synergies". *Journal of Accounting and Organizational Change*, 41(4), 320 p.

Khamdamov, S. J. (2021). Calculating Share of Factors of Intensive Economic Growth in Uzbekistan. In *The 5th International Conference on Future Networks & Distributed Systems* (pp. 393–397).

Khamdamov, S. J., Usmanov, A. S., Abdulazizova, O., Isaev, F., Kholbaev, N., Makhmudov, S., & Kholbaeva, S. (2022). Econometric Modeling of Central Bank Refinancing Rate in Uzbekistan. In *Proceedings of the 6th International Conference on Future Networks & Distributed Systems* (pp. 253–257).

Liu, Q., Liu, W., Dong, M., Li, Z., & Zheng, Y. (2023). Residual useful life prognosis of equipment based on modified hidden semi-Markov model with a co-evolutional optimization method. *Computers & Industrial Engineering*, 182, 109–433.

Qing, L., Li, P., & Mehmood, U. (2024). Uncovering the potential impacts of financial inclusion and human development on ecological sustainability in the presence of natural resources and government stability: Evidence from G-20 nations. *Resources Policy*, 88, 104–446.

Shenghua, Z., Mingjie, R., & Renyong, C. (2007). Research on the basic framework of alliance ability and the mechanism of improve alliance performance. *Science of Science and Management of S. & T.*, 7(4), 122–128.

Shoh-Jakhon, K. (2023). Theoretical and Methodological Aspects of Intensive Economic Growth in Ensuring Sustainable Economic Development. Social and Economic Studies within the Framework of Emerging Global Developments Volume 3, 283.

Stecher, M., & Baumgärtner, S. (2024). Quantifying agents' causal responsibility in dynamical systems. *Ecological Economics*, 217, 108086.

Teece, D. J., Pisano, G., & Shuen, A. (1997). Dynamic capabilities and strategic management. *Strategic Management Journal,* 18(7), 509–533.

Tran, T. K., Lin, C. Y., Tu, Y. T., Duong, N. T., Thi, T. D. P., & Shoh-Jakhon, K. (2023). Nexus between Natural Resource Depletion and Rent and COP26 Commitments: Empirical Evidence from Vietnam. *Resources Policy*, 85, 104024.

Turayeva, G., Berdiyev, G., Eshpulatov, D., Alimova, D., Odilbekov, A., Davletova, D., & Burxanov, A. (2022). Opportunities to Use Financial Services–"1 C Program". In *Proceedings of the 6th International Conference on Future Networks & Distributed Systems* (pp. 556–561).

Xue, Z., Yang, C., Dong, L., Bao, W., Wang, J., & Fan, P. (2023). Recent advances and conceptualizations in process intensification of coal gasification fine slag flotation. *Separation and Purification Technology*, 304, 122–394.

Yao, W., & Lianghai, L. (2009). Evolutionary Game Analysis of Industrial-financial Group System. *Chinese Journal of Management*, 8(4), 657–680.

Shoh-Jakhon Khamdamov, Zokir Mamadiyarov, Muxlisa Mahmudova, Jurabek Yusufovich Boltayev, Nasiba Sattorova

Digitalization and Taxation: Analyzing the Impact on Household Finances in Uzbekistan

1. Introduction

The onset of digitalization has ushered in a new era in the global economic landscape, fundamentally altering how financial systems operate, including the realms of taxation and household finance. In Uzbekistan, this transformation is particularly poignant, given the country's ongoing socio-economic reforms aimed at enhancing the well-being of its population. This study delves into the intricate relationship between digitalization, taxation policies, and their combined effect on household incomes and expenditures.

Digital technologies have revolutionized many aspects of everyday life, including how governments implement and manage taxation. This paper begins by examining the current state of Uzbekistan's economy, highlighting the significant strides made in digital infrastructure and its integration into financial systems. The role of digitalization in streamlining tax collection processes, broadening the tax base, and ensuring compliance is a focal point of discussion.

Furthermore, the introduction explores the concept of digital financial inclusion and its implications for household income and expenditure. With an increasing shift towards online transactions, e-commerce, and digital banking, there is a need to understand how these changes influence household financial behaviors and, in turn, how they are taxed.

The paper aims to bridge the gap in existing literature by providing a comprehensive analysis of how digitalization has impacted tax policies and, consequently, household finances in Uzbekistan. The introduction sets the stage for a detailed examination of the transformation brought about by digitalization in the realm of taxation and its far-reaching effects on the economic status of households.

In doing so, this study seeks to offer insights into the benefits and challenges of digital tax systems, the shifting landscape of household income and expenditure in a digitalized economy, and the implications for policy-making in Uzbekistan.

The overarching goal is to contribute to a deeper understanding of the interplay between digitalization and taxation, providing a foundation for informed decision-making and strategic planning in the country's fiscal and economic policies.

2. Literature Review and Development Hypothesis

Digital finance has a significant impact on household finances. It promotes household financial substitution for consumption, increases household leverage ratio, expands household consumption, and enhances household insurance purchases (Maksym et al., 2022). Digital finance improves information dissemination efficiency, enhances financial participation, and increases household income, leading to these effects (Apeti & Edoh, 2023). The impact of digital finance on household finances is more pronounced in households with low to moderate savings rates, low to average income households, urban areas, and households with low educational levels. The government should guide residents to consume rationally, promote digital financial literacy, and expand the coverage of digital finance in rural areas. Digital finance has a stronger impact on household consumption in East China compared to middle and West China, particularly in the areas of digital financial payment, insurance, and monetary fund businesses (Zhang et al., 2023).

Nancen, Liu (2023) as mentioned in this paper investigated the influence of digital finance on consumption of urban and rural inhabitants using the instrumental variable approach and propensity score matching method based on survey data of Chinese household finance in 2017.

The findings of Guo et al. (2023) demonstrate that the incorporation of digital inclusive finance holds the capacity to effectively stimulate enterprise digital transformation. Moreover, the extent of inclusion and utilization will further bolster the process of digitization within enterprises. Finally, we make a valuable contribution to the expanding body of scholarly work that investigates the effects of digital technologies on the administration of taxes (Bellon et al., 2022). The level of fiscal decentralization exerts a positive and notable influence on the technical efficiency of tax collection. Additionally, it is observed that tax structure decisions and the proportion of indirect to direct taxes play a significant role in determining tax collection efficiency. Lastly, we derive certain policy implications from our analysis (Martínez et al., 2022). But, There is a need to focus on the broader digital ecosystem of tax administration and not just technology acceptance models (Bassey et al., 2022). The increasing peril to the efficient management of governmental authority in the monetary domain has been significantly less apparent yet equally significant (Kudrle, 2021).

In Uzbekistan, modern studies have been conducted on the scientific-theoretical and practical foundations of the financial mechanism of consistently increasing the incomes of the population and regulating income inequality between its social strata (Khamdamov et al., 2022).

According the hypothesis of income inequality and health dependence, income distribution has a strong influence on population mortality and health (Yusupov et al., 2022; Muftaydinova et al., 2022). Evidence for the hypothesis supports redistributive policies aimed at reducing income inequality. With some exceptions, including Turayeva et al. (2022), Khamdamov (2021), Tran et al. (2023), Gong et al. (2023), support this hypothesis. Also, according to Shoh-Jakhon (2023), income inequality promotes research and development, and technological development, which leads to economic growth.

3. Analysis and Results

Various types of income and statistical indicators are used to analyze, measure and evaluate the level of income of the population. We will consider their most common types.

Table 1. Population income groups and their elements

No	Income group	Source of income
1	Salary	Income from the main job; Income from non-main work; Funds of military personnel; Seasonal income; Others
2	Income from the sale of labor results	Farm income; Income from personal property; Household income; Right; Others
3	Income from business activities	Income from business activities; Others
4	Return on capital	Dividends from shares; Rent; Capital gain; Interest on deposits; Others
5	Risk return	Payment of insurance risk; Bond advances; Lottery winnings; Achievements in sports competitions; Achievements in games; Achievements in various competitions; Others
6	Deferred income	A gift; Sponsorship assistance; alimony; Income left to the heirs of the author; Others
7	Social income	Payment for temporary disability; Pregnancy and postpartum payment; Birth allowance; disability benefits; Others

(continued)

Table 1. Continued

No	Income group	Source of income
8	Loan income	Bank loans; Enterprise loans; Debt amounts received from individuals; Others
9	Other income	Others

Source: Developed by authors.

In the table above, we can see that part of the population's income is spent on ensuring material well-being, and the rest is spent on using services. The composition of needs is affected not only by the increase in monetary income, but also by the change in the composition of the population, the growth of its scientific and cultural level. In economic literature, people's incomes are divided into nominal, discretionary and real incomes depending on the level of use. Nominal income describes the amount of monetary income excluding taxes and prices. Discretionary income is nominal income after deduction of taxes and other mandatory payments. Personal household plays an important role in the formation of personal and family income. In the complex socio-economic period of society's development, the private economy remains the main source of income for some groups of the population.

By improving the system of taxation of individuals, the conceptual basis for increasing their real income and stabilizing income inequality should be the system of taxation of the population's income should be directed to ensure the principles of vertical and horizontal equality, regardless of the social importance of their activities.

It is known that the optimal tax system in the modern economic space is the formation of a tax regime based on the principles of social justice for taxpayers with the same income or based on income from different activities. This tax system, first of all, forms the economic basis of taxpayers' willingness to pay taxes to the state budget. If we look at it from this point of view, one of the other problems in the system of taxation of individuals is the existence of horizontal inequality, which means that the tax regime of the same approach does not apply to taxpaying individuals with the same income.

In particular, the tax system should ensure a balanced tax burden for the category of taxpayers with the same income level. In addition, the differentiation of tax rates depending on specific types of activity creates problems of vertical inequality.

The current income taxation system is based on flat-scale tax rates, and this taxation system does not meet the criteria of marginal utility of income. In this regard, it is worth noting that the usefulness of 1.0 million UZS of income depends on the level of profitability of individuals who dispose of this income. For example, the benefit of 1.0 million UZS of income for the rich population is lower than that of poor individuals. An increase in income increases its total utility (TU) and ensures a decrease in marginal utility (MU).

As can be seen from Figure 1, the more balanced the distribution of incomes in the society is, first of all, by reducing the difference in the level of income degradation, it will have opportunities to balance the distribution of the marginal and total utility level among the social class of the population. The level of fair distribution of benefits in society affects the formation of social well-being.

At a certain stationary point (In-1) of the population income level, the total utility of income (TU(I)) is less than the marginal utility (MU(I)). In this case, the economic or social value of the income is very high, and the income in this interval is typical for the low-income population. The interval (In+1) in which the total utility of income (TU(I)) is greater than the marginal utility (MU(I)) is provided at the stationary point, and the incomes in this interval belong to the rich society stratum of the population. In exaggeration, the value of 1 million

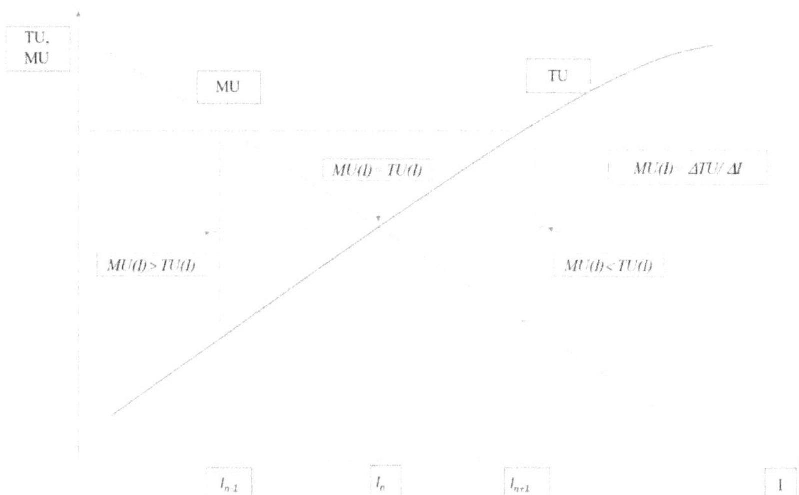

Figure 1. Income of the population and the effect of its change on the change in the total and marginal utility of income

Source: Developed by authors.

UZS is very high for an individual who earns 5 million UZS a month compared to an individual who earns 50 million UZS a month.

While the system of taxation of population incomes on a flat scale has a positive effect on the composition of consumption and the rate of accumulation from the point of view of ensuring macroeconomic stability, it creates the risk of increasing income inequality between social strata of the population.

There are 3 main established models of the system of taxation of individual incomes, and in the practice of Uzbekistan, a system of flat taxation or a system of proportional taxation is used from the system of progressive taxation. The purpose of the transition to this practice of taxation is, first of all, to improve the tax administration, to increase the personal income of the population by reducing the tax burden, and to increase the income to the budget due to the increase of the tax base by legalizing their informal income.

However, the system of income taxation based on a flat scale is ineffective compared to the progressive taxation system in terms of regulating and balancing incomes in the presence of differences in the level of income of the population in terms of wages and other sources of income.

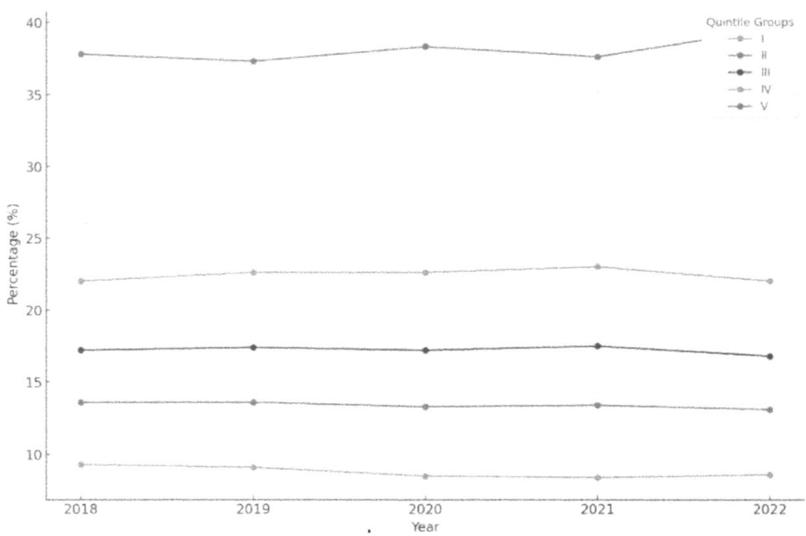

Figure 2. Income distribution by quintile groups(2018–2022)
Source: Developed by authors.

In the segment of progressive tax rates, a higher weight of the number of taxpayers in the lower ranges of income is assumed, and in the conditions of transition to a flat scale (the current taxation system), the 12% tax rate is set, and conclusions are drawn on the increase in the tax burden for the population with low income. In reality, IMF experts confirmed that taxpayers in the income range of the minimum wage make up the majority of total taxpayers. It can be seen from Figure 3 below that in 2018, the incomes in the 1–3 minimum wage range made up about 18% of the total population income, and when added with the 3–4 minimum wage incomes, they made up about 25% of the total income.

Under the conditions of the flat-scale taxation system, the comparative analysis of the tax burden in the income range confirms that there is a relatively equal distribution of the tax burden for the low-income population and the high-income population. Analyzes show that there is a relative equalization of the tax burden on a progressive and flat scale in the range of 8–9 minimum wages.

In other words, as a result of the introduction of the flat taxation system, setting the central rate at 12% ensures an increase in the tax burden on the low-income population and a decrease in the tax burden on the high-income population.

So, in the above case, due to the relatively equal distribution of the tax burden at different levels of incomes, the effect of the tax system is to increase the difference between incomes.

We can see this in the following statistical data on the incomes of the population and their distribution by different groups in the following years.

Table 2. Uneven distribution of incomes of the population of the Republic of Uzbekistan by 20% groups of the population

Quintile groups	2018	2019	2020	2021	2022
I	9.3	9.1	8.5	8.4	8.6
II	13.6	13.6	13.3	13.4	13.1
III	17.2	17.4	17.2	17.5	16.8
IV	22.0	22.6	22.6	23.0	22.0
V	37, 8	37, 3	3 8, 3	37.6	39.5
The coefficient of differentiation of population incomes by quintile groups	4.0 6 5	4.0 99	4,506	4, 4 7 6	4,604

Source: Developed by authors.

From the data of Table 2, we can see that in parallel with the introduction of the system of personal income taxation based on a flat scale from 2019, the coefficient of population income differentiation by quintile groups is 4,506 in 2020, 4,476 in 2021, and 4,604 in 2022, making it a higher indicator compared to 2018–2022. Therefore, the level of differentiation between the incomes of the population is high. We can see this from the comparative analysis of the income index of the population by categorizing the income of the population according to the 10% group.

Table 3. Uneven distribution of incomes of the population of the Republic of Uzbekistan by 10% groups of the population

Decile groups	2018	2019	2020	2021	2022
I decile	3.9	3, 7	3, 4	3, 3	3.5 _
II decile	5.4	5, 3	5, 1	5, 1	5.1
III decile	6.4	6.4	6.2	6, 2	6.1
IV decile	7, 3	7, 3	7, 1	7.2	7.0
V decile	8.1	8.2	8.1	8.2	7.9
VI decile	9.1	9.2	9.1	9, 3	8.9
VII decile	10.3	10.5	10.5	10.6	10.2
VIII decile	11.7	12.1	12.1	12.5	11.9
IX decile	14.1	14.7	14.8	15.2	14.7
X decile	23.7	22.6	23.5	22.5	24.8
Coefficient of stratification by groups of 10 % of population income	6.1	6.0	6.9	6.8	7.0

Source: Developed by authors.

From the data of Table 3, we can see that the coefficient of differentiation of population income by decile groups was 6.1 in 2018, and this indicator will be 7.0 by 2022.

Although the level of income of the population affects their desire to consume and save, the increase in the level of income also affects the increase in the marginal propensity for investment activity through savings. So, naturally, taxes not only affect the nominal value of the income of the population, but also affect the consumption and savings rate of households by affecting the purchasing power parity expressed through its real value.

This, in turn, creates opportunities to regulate the current and future development of the country's economy by influencing household consumption and savings standards through the tax system.

Table 4. Comparative analysis of the impact of flat scale and progressive taxation system on population consumption and savings funds

Alternatives to Personal Income Tax								
Types of scales	**Progressive (statistics based on 2018 data)**				**Flat scale (2021 statistics)**			
Income range	1 M W	up to 5 M W	up to 10 M W	Above 10 M W	1 M W	up to 5 M W	up to 10 M W	Above 10 M W
Rates, %	0	7.5	16.5	22.5	12			
Share of the income range in the total paid tax, in %	–	38.7	41.9	18.4	17.6	42.8	23.1	16.3
Average marginal rate, in %	9.6				12			
The composition of the population's expenses on the consumption of personal income after tax payment, in percent								
Consumption, (C)	100	100	68.91	64.81	100	100	61,32	43,64
Savings (S)	–	–	21.86	19.37	–	–	12.37	14.51
Investments (I)	–	–	9.23	15.82	–	–	26,31	41.85
The impact of the introduction of a flat scale of income tax on the ratio of population consumption and savings funds								
Consumption, (C)					–	–	−7.59 _	−21.17
Savings (S)					–	–	−9.49	−4.86
Investments (I)					–	–	+17.08	+26.03

Source: Formed by the author based on the information of the State Statistics Committee of the Republic of Uzbekistan

It can be seen from Table 4 above that in the system of taxation until 2018, the marginal tax rate calculated on the basis of the tax rates in the section of the (progressive) income range was 9.6%.

4. Findings and Discussion

In the system of taxation based on a flat scale, the system of taxation at the rate of 12% applies, the incomes in the first (1 MW) and second (up to 5 MW) intervals are mainly spent on the formation of the consumer budget to spend on consumer needs, and the system does not change in both taxation systems. While a change is observed in the ratios of consumption and accumulation of personal income formed in the third and fourth intervals, we can see the increase of investment passion (+17.08; +26.03), which embodies the target direction of savings.

The research underscores the critical role of digital financial inclusion in providing equitable access to financial services and highlights potential risks such as cyber security and digital fraud. Additionally, the need for evolving tax policies to accommodate the shift towards digital transactions and e-commerce is emphasized. Policy recommendations are made to strengthen digital tax systems, address the digital divide, and develop comprehensive tax policies for digital transactions, aiming to ensure a fair and equitable tax system and enhance public awareness and capacity building in digital taxation.

5. Conclusions and Suggestions

The above cases can systematize the following conclusions on income tax:

First, personal income tax is a tax that plays the role of the main fiscal factor in the formation of budget revenues, and it is a tax that has a high impact on the income of the population.

Secondly, although the transition from a progressive taxation system to a taxation system based on a flat scale is necessary to reduce the tax burden in the general context, this provides a relatively high tax burden for low-income residents in the income range. A reduction in the tax burden is observed for the income-earning population in the upper income range.

These circumstances have led to an increase in the influence of the tax system on the consumer spending of the population on the macro scale of the income tax from individuals.

Thirdly, the current system of personal income taxation, which is one of the main tools of the macroeconomic regulatory system, has the feature of accumulating the income of the population created in the country as savings and stimulating investment activity.

Fourthly, it is desirable to introduce a non-taxable minimum in order to improve the consumption expenses of the population receiving income from personal income tax, to reduce the tax burden on them and, ultimately, to comply with the principle of social justice in the taxation of income.

Impact of Digitalization on Taxation: The study concludes that digitalization has significantly transformed the taxation landscape in Uzbekistan. Digital tax platforms have enhanced the efficiency of tax collection, reduced evasion, and improved compliance. However, there is a need to continuously adapt these systems to address emerging challenges such as cyber security and digital fraud.

Influence on Household Income and Expenditure: Digitalization has also reshaped household financial behaviors, particularly in terms of income management and expenditure. The shift towards digital transactions and e-commerce has implications for tax policies, which must evolve to capture these new forms of income and spending.

Digital Financial Inclusion and Equity: The research highlights the critical role of digital financial inclusion in ensuring equitable access to financial services. While digitalization offers opportunities for enhanced financial participation, it also poses the risk of widening the digital divide, potentially exacerbating income inequalities.

Policy Implications: The findings underscore the importance of formulating policies that not only harness the benefits of digitalization in taxation but also address its socio-economic implications. Policies should aim to bridge the digital divide, ensuring that digital tax systems are accessible and equitable for all segments of the population.

5.1. Suggestions

Strengthening Digital Tax Systems: There is a need for continuous investment in and enhancement of digital tax systems to ensure they remain robust, secure, and adaptable to changing technologies and economic conditions.

Addressing the Digital Divide: Policies should focus on reducing the digital divide, particularly in rural and underserved areas, to ensure equitable access to digital financial services and tax systems.

Comprehensive Tax Policies for Digital Transactions: The government should develop comprehensive tax policies that effectively capture income and expenditures from digital transactions and e-commerce, ensuring a fair and equitable tax system.

Capacity Building and Public Awareness: Initiatives to enhance the capacity of tax officials and the general public in understanding and utilizing digital tax systems are crucial. Public awareness campaigns can help in increasing compliance and trust in the digital taxation process.

Research and Continuous Monitoring: Ongoing research and monitoring are essential to assess the impact of digitalization on taxation and household finances. This will help in identifying trends, challenges, and opportunities, enabling timely policy interventions.

So, as a general conclusion, it is worth noting that the policy of regulating the incomes of the population by means of taxes should perform the task of preventing and balancing the stratification of incomes in the conditions of optimal social usefulness of the incomes at their personal disposal (MU(I)=TU(I)).

References

Apeti, A. E., & Edoh, E. D. (2023). Tax revenue and mobile money in developing countries. *Journal of Development Economics*, 161, 103014.

Bassey, E., Mulligan, E., & Ojo, A. (2022). A conceptual framework for digital tax administration-A systematic review. *Government Information Quarterly*, 39(4), 101754.

Bellon, M., Dabla-Norris, E., Khalid, S., & Lima, F. (2022). Digitalization to improve tax compliance: Evidence from VAT e-Invoicing in Peru. *Journal of Public Economics*, 210, 104661.

Gong, X., Wong, W.-K., Peng, Y., Khamdamov, S., Albasher, G., Hoa, V. T., & Nhan, N. T. T. (2023). Exploring an interdisciplinary approach to sustainable economic development in resource-rich regions: An investigation of resource productivity, technological innovation, and ecosystem resilience. *Resources Policy*, 87(Part A), 104294. https://doi.org/10.1016/j.resourpol.2023.104294

Guo, B., Feng, Y., & Lin, J. (2023). Digital inclusive finance and digital transformation of enterprises. *Finance Research Letters*, 57, 104270.

Khamdamov, S. J. (2021). Calculating share of factors of intensive economic growth in Uzbekistan. *The 5th International Conference on Future Networks & Distributed Systems* (pp. 393–397).

Khamdamov, S. J., Usmanov, A. S., Abdulazizova, O., Isaev, F., Kholbaev, N., Makhmudov, S., & Kholbaeva, S. (2022). Econometric modeling of central bank refinancing rate in Uzbekistan. In *Proceedings of the 6th International Conference on Future Networks & Distributed Systems* (pp. 253–257).

Kudrle, R. T. (2021). Moves and countermoves in the digitization challenges to international taxation. *Technology in Society*, 64, 101453.

Maksym, D., Nataliia, K., & Olha, P. (2022). Digitalization of the financial services market: Advantages and risks for households. *Naukovij vìsnik Polìssâ*, 160–177. https://doi.org/10.25140/2410-9576-2022-2(25)-160-177

Martínez, Y. U., Arzoz, P. P., & Arregui, I. Z. (2022). Tax collection efficiency in OECD countries improves via decentralization, simplification, digitalization and education. *Journal of Policy Modeling*, 44(2), 298–318.

Muftaydinova, S. K., Chuprynin, V. D., Fayzullin, L. Z., Buralkina, N. A., Muminova, Z. A., Asaturova, A. V., … Abdullayev, S. I. (2022). Expression of the Tyrosine Kinase Receptor (EPHA1) in the Eutopic and Ectopic Endometrium of patients with deep infiltrative endometriosis use of modern digital technologies. In *Proceedings of the 6th International Conference on Future Networks & Distributed Systems* (pp. 416–421).

Nancen, L. (2023). Comparative analysis between digital finance and consumption capacity of urban and rural residents. *Highlights in Business, Economics and Management*, 11, 346–354. https://doi.org/10.54097/hbem.v11i.8154

Shoh-Jakhon, K. (2023). Theoretical and methodological aspects of intensive economic growth in ensuring sustainable economic development. *Social and Economic Studies within the Framework of Emerging Global Developments*, 3, 283.

Tran, T. K., Lin, C. Y., Tu, Y. T., Duong, N. T., Thi, T. D. P., & Shoh-Jakhon, K. (2023). Nexus between natural resource depletion and rent and COP26 commitments: Empirical evidence from Vietnam. *Resources Policy*, 85, 104024.

Turayeva, G., Berdiyev, G., Eshpulatov, D., Alimova, D., Odilbekov, A., Davletova, D., … & Burxanov, A. (2022). Opportunities to use financial services–"1 C Program". In *Proceedings of the 6th International Conference on Future Networks & Distributed Systems* (pp. 556–561).

Yusupov, S., Boymuradov, S., Bobamuratova, D., Shukhratova, M., Marupov, I., Akramova, D. T., … & Muradova, D. A. (2022). Diagnostic aspects of zygomatico-orbital complex fractures with the use of modern digital technologies. In *Proceedings of the 6th International Conference on Future Networks & Distributed Systems* (pp. 399–403).

Zhang, X., Li, J., Xiang, D., & Worthington, A. C. (2023). Digitalization, financial inclusion, and small and medium-sized enterprise financing: Evidence from China. *Economic Modelling*, 126, 106410.

Shoh-Jakhon Khamdamov, Nigora Ravshanovna Bazarova, Samariddin Makhmudov, Elshod Alimardonov, Anvar Saidmakhmudovich Usmanov, Jurabek Yusufovich Boltayev

Analyzing the Economic and Financial Implications of Consumer Credit Practices in Commercial Banks

1. Introduction

The role of consumer credit in economic development and financial stability has garnered significant attention in the field of financial economics. As a pivotal component of banking services, consumer credit extends beyond mere financial transactions, influencing economic growth, consumer behavior, and overall financial well-being. This study delves into the complex dynamics of consumer credit issued by commercial banks, which serve as both facilitators of and gatekeepers to financial resources for individuals and businesses.

Today, the granting of loans by commercial banks is considered one of the fundamental elements of financial intermediation (Pradhan et al., 2015). The process of lending to individuals by commercial banks is one of the key drivers of economic and financial systems, supporting economic growth, bolstering personal investments, and contributing to overall financial stability (Mamadiyarov et al., 2024).

Maintaining a balance between acquiring loans and managing risks is crucial to ensure the positive impact of lending on individuals and broader economy (Filis, 2010). As banking operations continue to evolve, stakeholders, including regulators, banks, and consumers, increasingly recognize the need for collaborative efforts to shape responsible lending practices and foster sustainable economic development (Khamdamov, 2021; Khamdamov et al., 2022). In this regard, the provision of loans to individuals by commercial banks significantly influences their financial well-being and quality of life.

Lending, whether short-term, medium-term, or long-term, is one of the services provided by financial institutions to their clients. Put differently, banks extend credits and advances as a means to initiate investment and development activities, supporting individuals, businesses, and even governments in their growth endeavors or overall economic development of the country (Boyd et. al., 2001).

Commercial banks play a leading role as institutions for accumulating, preserving, and allocating financial resources, thereby contributing to the strength in economic growth and development areas (Mamadiyarov, 2021). To effectively carry out this crucial function, banks must identify opportunities, assess risks, and anticipate future trends in financial markets and economic sectors.

Moreover, it is imperative for banks to understand their capabilities, impact scope, and future prospects in accumulating financial assets and directing them towards prudent investments (Marques et al., 2013). Additionally, in line with the country's revenue sources or economic policy, commercial banks conduct their activities based on the fundamental principles of profitability, liquidity, and payment ability, enabling them to extend loans and advances to their diverse clientele (Bhuiyan & Chowdhury, 2020). Furthermore, the legal framework governing the credit activities of commercial banks is shaped by numerous factors, including prevailing interest rates, volume of deposits, local and foreign investment volumes, liquidity indicators, and institutional foundations (Shoh-Jakhon, 2023; Tran et al., 2023) .

The significance of consumer credit in the financial sector and its impact on broader economic parameters has been extensively studied, indicating diverse findings across different contexts. Scholars like Kalam (2020) and Omar et al. (2022) highlighted the correlation between household debt levels and economic stability, suggesting that excessive consumer credit can precipitate financial crises. In contrast, studies by Hu, Zhai, and Zhao (2023) argued that responsible consumer lending has the potential to stimulate economic growth by enhancing consumer spending and investment.

2. Literature Review

Key economic and financial indicators used to analyze the impact of consumer credit practices on commercial banks include factors like the Consumer Price Index, Government Expenditure, Interest Rates, Money Supply (Dery & Serletis, 2021). Additionally, the effectiveness of credit and deposit practices in commercial banks is evaluated through econometric analysis based on banking data (Luo et al., 2021). Furthermore, the distribution of credit at commercial banks is influenced by variables such as Third Party Funds, bank performance metrics (CAR and LDR), credit interest rates, Non-Performing Loans (NPL), as well as external factors like BI Certificate, BI Rate, and exchange rates (Tao et al., 2021). These indicators play a crucial role in understanding and assessing the impact of consumer credit practices on the overall performance and stability of commercial banks.

The evolution of the stock market has been influenced by various factors over time. Initially perceived as a physical place for trading, the market has transformed into a mechanism balancing supply and demand, emphasizing competition and free pricing (Tolmasquim et al., 2021). Recent developments include the rise of algorithm-based trading, leading to high-frequency trading and the replacement of human traders with algorithms (Wang et al., 2021). Macro and microeconomic factors like inflation, interest rates, foreign direct investments, exchange rates, and money supply significantly impact the stock market, with money supply playing a more substantial role (Kulu & Bondzie, 2024). Analyzing stock market dynamics at a micro level through stock networks has provided insights into market evolution, such as the recovery of the 2008 financial crisis from an evolutionary perspective (Wang et.al., 2024).

Recent research has further explored the role of macroeconomic variables in shaping consumer credit practices. According to the findings by Bhattacharyya, and Nain (2011), interest rates and inflation significantly affect the lending behaviors of banks, which in turn influence consumer credit availability. Furthermore, empirical work by He et al. (2024) demonstrated that banks' profitability, often measured through metrics such as Return on Equity (ROE), directly impacts their lending capacity and risk tolerance levels.

Null Hypothesis (H0) is the absence of a substantial correlation is present among the lending rates extended to individuals by the banking sector, the mean short-term deposit interest rate for individuals, inflation rate, and the capital ROE of commercial banks.

Alternative Hypothesis (Ha) is a notable correlation existings among the lending rates to individuals by the banking sector, the average short-term deposit interest rate for individuals, inflation rate, and the capital return on equity (ROE) of commercial banks. The lack of such a correlation highlights the potential significant impact of unexplored variables on the determination of lending activities to individuals by commercial banks.

Despite extensive studies on the macroeconomic implications of consumer credit, fewer investigations have been focused on the integrative effects of short-term deposit rates, inflation, and bank profitability on consumer credit rates within commercial banks (Turayeva et al., 2022). This gap suggests a need for a detailed econometric analysis to understand how these variables interplay at a granular level in the banking sector.

3. Data and Methodology

3.1. Data Description

This study utilizes a comprehensive dataset from January 2018 to October 2023, provided by the Central Bank of Uzbekistan and the National Statistics Agency of Uzbekistan. The dataset comprises monthly observations of key economic indicators relevant to the consumer credit market within the commercial banking sector. The variables included are:

3.2. Methodological Approach

To examine the relationships between consumer credit rates and the selected economic indicators, this study employs the Autoregressive Distributed Lag (ARDL) model. The ARDL approach is particularly suitable for small sample sizes and integrates variables irrespective of their integration orders.

3.3. ARDL Model Specification

Below is the Autoregressive Distributed Lag (ARDL) model

Here:

$$Y_t = \beta_0 + \beta_1 y_{-1} + \beta_2 y_{-2} + .. + \beta_p y_{t-p} + \mu_1 x_{-1} + \mu_2 x_{t-2} + .. + \mu_q x_{-q} + \vartheta_1 z_{-1} + \vartheta_2 z_{-2} + \ldots + \vartheta_r z_{t-r} + \varepsilon_t \quad (1)$$

Y_t represents the dependent variable at time;

$y_{t-1}, y_{t-2}, \ldots, y_{t-p}$ – represent the lagged values of the dependent variable;

$x_{t-k}, x_{t-k-1}, \ldots, x_{t-k-q}$ – represent the lagged values of the independent variables;

$z_{t-1}, z_{t-2}, z_{t-r}$ – represent the lagged values of other variables influencing the dependent variable;

$\beta_0, \beta_1, \ldots \beta_p, \mu_1, \mu_2 .. \mu_q, \vartheta_1, \vartheta_2 \ldots \vartheta_r$ denote the coefficients to be estimated, ε_t t represents the error term.

In the context of the study, the banking sector's lending rates to individuals (dependent variable) are influenced by several factors, including the average short-term deposit interest rate for individuals, inflation rate, and capital return on equity (ROE) of commercial banks (independent variables).

The following hypotheses were formulated in developing the econometric model:

Variables:
y (dependent variable)- lending rates to individuals by the banks;
x_1 (independent variable)- average short-term deposit interest rate for individuals;
x_2 (independent variable)- inflation rate;
x_3 (independent variable)- capital return on equity (ROE) of commercial banks.

Based on the reviewed literature, this study posits the following hypotheses to be tested through econometric modeling:

Null Hypothesis (H0): There is no significant relationship among the lending rates to individuals by the banking sector, the average short-term deposit interest rate for individuals, inflation rate, and the capital ROE of commercial banks.
Alternative Hypothesis (Ha): There is a significant relationship among the lending rates to individuals by the banking sector, the average short-term deposit interest rate for individuals, inflation rate, and the capital return on equity (ROE) of commercial banks. The absence of such a relationship indicates the potential significant role of other factors not considered in this study in determining lending activities to individuals by commercial banks.
Null Hypothesis (H0), H_0:$\beta_1 = \beta_2 = \beta_3 = 0$
Alternative Hypothesis (Ha): at least one $\beta_i \neq 0$

The coefficients associated with the independent variables in the multiple regression model forecasting lending rates to individuals in the national banking system.

Null Hypothesis (H_0) indicates that all coefficients are equal to zero, demonstrating the absence of any relationship. The alternative hypothesis (H_a), on the other hand, confirms that at least one of the coefficients is not equal to zero, signifying the presence of a significant relationship.

4. Analysis

In the research, the time-series analysis of dependent and independent variables yielded the following analytical graph representation (see Figures 1 and 2).

The data presented in Figure 2 above demonstrates a notable association between the variables, suggesting a strong interconnection within particular circumstances. The concentration of data points in the graphical depiction highlights a substantial correlation, underscoring their inclination to form clusters around a focused distribution pattern. In the following phase of the study, an

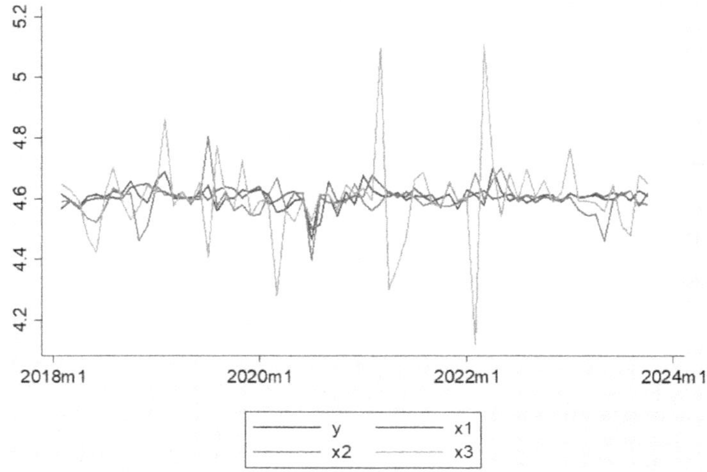

Figure 1. Graphical matrix of dependent and independent variables
Source: Developed by authors.

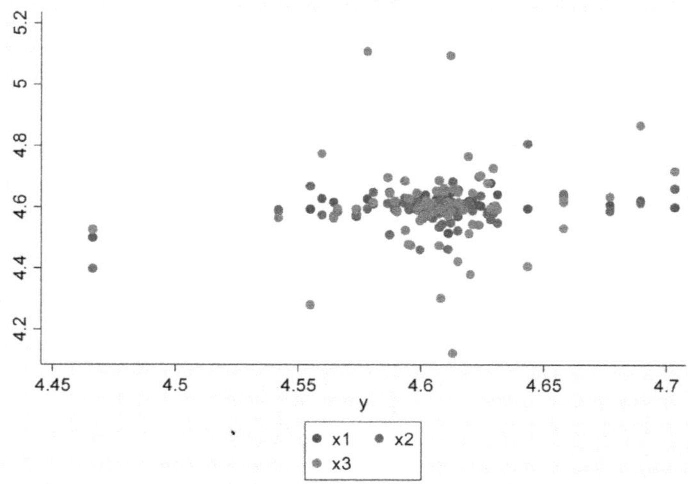

Figure 2. Scatterplot between dependent and independent variables
Source: Developed by authors.

analysis of correlation matrices for every combination of dependent and independent variables was conducted using Stata software (refer to Table 1).

Table 1. Correlation matrix of dependent and independent variables

Variables	(1)	(2)	(3)	(4)
(1) y	1.000			
(2) x_1	0. 4602	1.000		
	(0.0042)			***
(3) x_2	0.3921	−0.1725	1.000	
	(0.0013)	(0.3413)		***
(4) x_3	0.3783	0.2529	−0.1423	1.000
	(0.0057)	**(0.1800)**	**(0.2202)**	**

Source: Calculated by authors.

The correlation between dependent and independent variables indicates a high, strong, and moderate level of correlation, suggesting significant relationships between them. Additionally, the correlation matrix presented in Table 1 demonstrates the absence of multicollinearity between the dependent variable and the independent variables.

In the subsequent stage, a Unit-root test was conducted to determine the stationarity status of dependent and independent variables (see Table 2).

Table 2. Unit-root test statistics for dependent and independent variables

O'zgaruvchilar	Test Statistic	1 % Critical Value	5 % Critical Value	10 % Critical Value	p-value for Z(t)
Bog'liq o'zgaruvchi (y)	-8.031	−3.750	−3.000	−2.630	0.0000
Mustaqil o'zgaruvchi (x1)	-6.599	−3.750	−3.000	−2.630	0.0000
Mustaqil o'zgaruvchi (x2)	−7.130	−3.750	−3.000	−2.630	0.0000
Mustaqil o'zgaruvchi (x3)	−9.993	−3.750	−3.000	−2.630	0.0000

Source: Calculated by authors.

Based on the information provided in Table 2, the Unit-Root test yielded a statistic of (-8.031) for the dependent variable and statistics of (-6.599, -7.130, and -9.993) for the independent variables. The results of the Unit-Root test indicate that both dependent and independent variables have achieved stationarity. This is further supported by the minimal values of McKinnon's critical values (Zhou, 2024), Z(t) = 0.00.

The purpose of conducting time series analysis is to achieve stationarity, as it simplifies the modeling process and enhances the reliability of statistical inference. Therefore, the positive outcome of the Unit-Root test signifies the attainment of stationarity in the data, eliminating the need for further differentiation or adjustments.

Likewise, after the initial integration of both dependent and independent variables, the Unit-Root test values indicated stationarity. An econometric model was then developed based on the ARDL model used in the research. Below is the econometric model formulated based on the ARDL model:

$$\Delta y_{it} = \alpha_0 + \alpha_1 \sum_{p=1}^{n} \Delta y_{i,t-p} + \alpha_2 \sum_{p=1}^{n} \Delta x_{1i,t-p} + \alpha_3 \sum_{p=1}^{n} \Delta x_{2i,t-p} + \alpha_4 \sum_{p=1}^{n} \Delta x_{3i,t-p} + \quad + \mu_1 y_{i,t-p} + \mu_2 x_{1i,t-1} + \mu_3 x_{2i,t-1} + \mu_4 x_{3i,t-1} + \varepsilon_{i,t} \tag{2}$$

Here: $\Delta \mathbf{y}_t$ - denotes the change in the lending rates to individuals by the banking sector;

y_{t-1} - represents the lagged lending rates to individuals by the banking sector;
x_1- signifies the average short-term deposit interest rate;
x_{2} - denotes the inflation rate;
x_3- stands for the capital return on equity (ROE) of the banking system;
Δ denotes the first difference coefficient;
α_0 represents the constant, while α_1, α_2, α_3, and α_4 represent the short-term elasticity coefficients,
μ_1, μ_2, μ_3, and μ_4 indicate the long-term dynamic multipliers, **n** represents the remaining number of observations, and **p** denotes the lag length.

Equation (2) outlines the linear ARDL model, which provides short and long-term forecasts. Additionally, in the subsequent step, the ARDL model's econometric equation was formulated using Stata software, as shown in the following table (refer to Table 3).

Table 3. Coefficients of the ARDL(1,0,0,1) model regression equation

ARDL			(1,0,0,1) regression			
Sample:			2018m2 – 2023m10			
Number of obs			= 68			
R-squared			= 0.6936			
Adj R-squared			= 0.6473			
Log likelihood			= 152.			
Root MSE			= 0.0269			
D.y	**Coef.**	**Std.Err.**	**t**	**P>t**	**[95 %Conf.**	**Interval]**
ADJ						
y						
L1.	−1.186	0.113	−10.520	0.000	−1.412	−0.961
LR						
x1	0.383	0.104	3.700	0.000	0.176	0.590
x2	0.161	0.055	2.910	0.005	0.050	0.272
x3	0.085	0.032	2.680	0.009	0.022	0.148
SR						
x3						
D1.	−0.065	0.024	−2.690	0.009	−0.114	−0.017
_cons	2.026	0.666	3.040	0.003	0.695	3.358

Source: Calculated by authors.

According to the results of the ARDL (1,0,0,1) model, the R-squared value indicates the proportion of variability in the dependent variable explained by the model. In this case, an R-squared value of 0.69 suggests that approximately 69 % of the variability in the dependent variable is accounted for by the explanatory variables in the ARDL model. A higher R-squared value indicates a better fit of the model to the observed data.

As per the regression model analysis, the positive econometric results demonstrated by the estimated coefficients imply a successful detection of variations in the explanatory factors of the ARDL model. The substantial R-squared value, together with favorable log-likelihood probabilities and minimal RMSE, collectively suggest a strong alignment of the model with the data, indicating the capture of a notable portion of the key economic associations.

5. Results and Discussion

As a result of the 1 % increase in the average short-term deposit interest rate in the national banking sector, the interest rates on loans to individuals by the banking sector increase by 0.38 %. Similarly, with a 1 % increase in the inflation rate in the national banking sector, the interest rates on loans to individuals by the banking sector increase by 0.16 %. Additionally, when the capital profitability (ROE) indicator of the banking system increases by 1 %, the interest rates on loans to individuals by the banking sector increase by 0.08 %.

In the next step of the research, the ARDL(1,0,0,1) model underwent a CUSUM diagnostic test. (Refer to Figures 3 and 4).

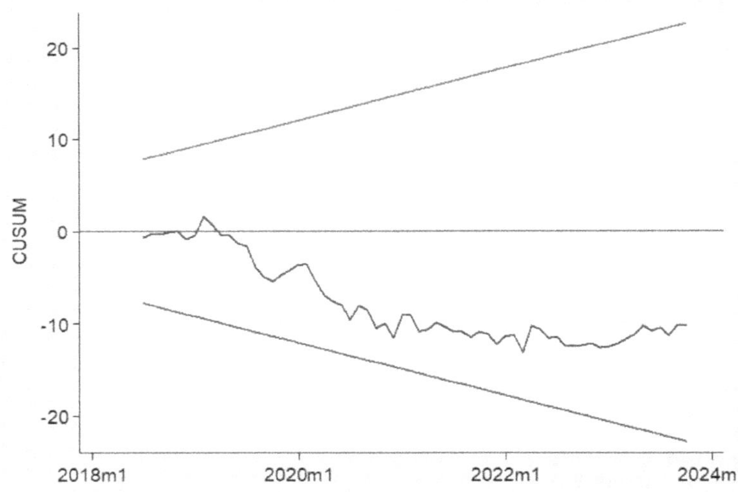

Figure 3. CUSUM diagnostic test graph 1

Source: Developed by authors.

The analysis of the data presented in Figures 3 and 4 indicates that the CUSUM diagnostic test statistic remained within critical bounds consistently, and no significant deviations were detected. Additionally, the null hypothesis H0, affirming the stability of systematic conditions, remained unaltered.

The Durbin-Watson test yielded a result of 2.13 for the ARDL (1,0,0,1) model. Furthermore, the Shapiro-Wilk W test produced a value of 0.08, the Breusch-Godfrey LM test resulted in 0.47, and the Breusch-Pagan test yielded a value of

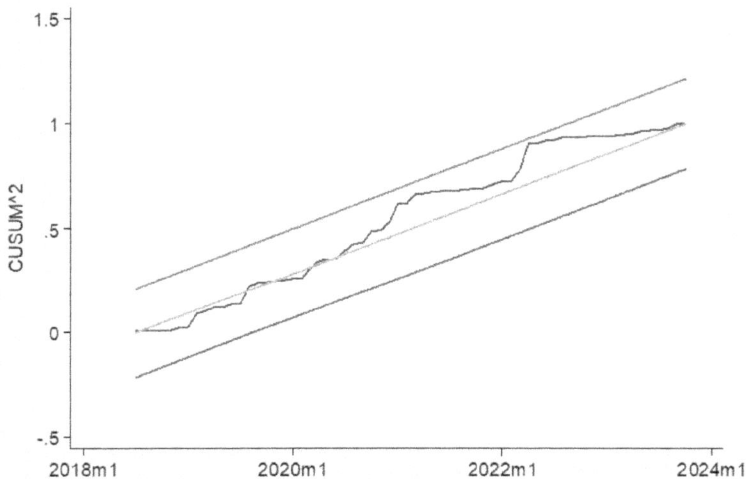

Figure 4. CUSUM diagnostic test graph 2
Source: Developed by authors.

0.58.Tadqiqot davomida birlamchi gipoteza H0: $y = 0$ va uning muqobil H1: $y \neq 0$ r>0,05 bo'lgan muhimlik darajasida statistik sinovdan o'tkazildi.

After conducting the Durbin-Watson, Shapiro-Wilk W, Breusch-Godfrey LM, and Breusch-Pagan tests, the decision to reject the null hypothesis was based on the criterion of $p > 0.05$. Thus, it can be concluded that there is no evidence of autocorrelation among the error terms in our study, affirming the appropriateness of the Gauss-Markov assumptions regarding the independence of errors in the econometric model.

6. Conclusion

Based on the analysis and conclusions drawn from the study on the mutual influence of personal loan interest rates, average deposit interest rates, inflation rates, and the banking system's capital profitability (ROE) in the national banking sector, the following recommendations and suggestions have been formulated:

The results indicate that a 1 % increase in the average interest rates on short-term deposits in the national banking sector is associated with a 0.38 % increase in personal loan interest rates. This positive relationship suggests that banks may be passing on some of the costs of raising funds (reflected in short-term deposit rates) to consumers in the form of higher loan interest rates.

The findings suggest that a 1 % increase in the inflation rate in the national banking sector leads to a 0.16 % increase in personal loan interest rates. This relationship implies that commercial banks may adjust loan interest rates in response to changes in inflation to maintain purchasing power and preserve profitability in real terms.

The results indicate that a 1 % increase in the profitability of the banking system's own funds (ROE) leads to a 0.08 % increase in personal loan interest rates. This suggests that for banks influenced by ROE, higher profitability may result in an increase in personal loan interest rates. The response of banks to changes in profitability levels by adjusting interest rates reflects their optimization of income through interest rate adjustments.

Furthermore, the econometric results allow us to observe the influence of changes in key financial indicators on personal loan interest rates in the banking sector.

References

Bhattacharyya, S., & Nain, A. (2011). Horizontal acquisitions and buying power: A product market analysis. *Journal of Financial Economics*, 99(1), 97–115.

Bhuiyan, E. M., & Chowdhury, M. (2020). Macroeconomic variables and stock market indices: Asymmetric dynamics in the US and Canada. *The Quarterly Review of Economics and Finance*, 77, 62–74.

Boyd, J. H., Levine, R., & Smith, B. D. (2001). The impact of inflation on financial sector performance. *Journal of Monetary Economics*, 47(2), 221–248.

Dery, C., & Serletis, A. (2021). Interest rates, money, and economic activity. *Macroeconomic Dynamics*, 25(7), 1842–1891.

Filis, G. (2010). Macro economy, stock market and oil prices: do meaningful relationships exist among their cyclical fluctuations?. *Energy Economics*, 32(4), 877–886.

He, B., Jie, W., He, H., Alsubih, M., Arnone, G., & Makhmudov, S. (2024). From resources to resilience: How green innovation, fintech and natural resources shape sustainability in OECD countries. *Resources Policy*, 91, 104856.

Hu, D., Zhai, C., & Zhao, S. (2023). Does digital finance promote household consumption upgrading? An analysis based on data from the China family panel studies. *Economic Modelling*, 125, 106377.

Kalam, K. (2020). The effects of macroeconomic variables on stock market returns: Evidence from Malaysia's stock market return performance. *Journal of World Business*, 55(8), 1–13.

Khamdamov, S. J. (2021). Calculating share of factors of intensive economic growth in Uzbekistan. In *The 5th International Conference on Future Networks & Distributed Systems* (pp. 393–397).

Khamdamov, S. J., Usmanov, A. S., Abdulazizova, O., Isaev, F., Kholbaev, N., Makhmudov, S., & Kholbaeva, S. (2022). Econometric modeling of Central Bank refinancing rate in Uzbekistan. In *Proceedings of the 6th International Conference on Future Networks & Distributed Systems* (pp. 253–257).

Kulu, E., & Bondzie, E. A. (2024). Mobile money, credit to deposit ratio and monetary policy: Empirics from Ghana. *Transnational Corporations Review*, 16(3), 200060.

Luo, S., Yu, S., & Zhou, G. (2021). Does green credit improve the core competence of commercial banks? Based on quasi-natural experiments in China. *Energy Economics*, 100, 105335.

Mamadiyarov, Z. (2021). Analysis of factors affecting remote banking services in the process of bank transformation in Uzbekistan. *Financial and Credit Activity Problems of Theory and Practice*, 1(36), 14–26.

Mamadiyarov, Z., Hakimov, H., & Askarov, S. (2024). Development of retail banking services in the context of digital transformation. *Financial & Credit Activity: Problems of Theory & Practice*, 1(54).

Marques, L. M., Fuinhas, J. A., & Marques, A. C. (2013). Does the stock market cause economic growth? Portuguese evidence of economic regime change. *Economic Modelling*, 32, 316–324.

Omar, A. B., Ali, A., Mouneer, S., Kouser, R., & Al-Faryan, M. A. S. (2022). Is stock market development sensitive to macroeconomic indicators? A fresh evidence using ARDL bounds testing approach. *Plos One*, 17(10), e0275708.

Pradhan, R. P., Arvin, M. B., & Ghoshray, A. (2015). The dynamics of economic growth, oil prices, stock market depth, and other macroeconomic variables: Evidence from the G-20 countries. *International Review of Financial Analysis*, 39, 84–95.

Shoh-Jakhon, K. (2023). *Theoretical and methodological aspects of intensive economic growth in ensuring sustainable economic development. Social and economic studies within the framework of emerging global developments* (Vol. 3, p. 283).

Tao, Y., Qiu, J., Lai, S., & Zhao, J. (2021). Renewable energy certificates and electricity trading models: Bi-level game approach. *International Journal of Electrical Power & Energy Systems*, 130, 106940.

Tolmasquim, M. T., de Barros Correia, T., Porto, N. A., & Kruger, W. (2021). Electricity market design and renewable energy auctions: The case of Brazil. *Energy Policy*, 158, 112558.

Tran, T. K., Lin, C. Y., Tu, Y. T., Duong, N. T., Thi, T. D. P., & Shoh-Jakhon, K. (2023). Nexus between natural resource depletion and rent and COP26 commitments: Empirical evidence from Vietnam. *Resources Policy*, 85, 104024.

Turayeva, G., Berdiyev, G., Eshpulatov, D., Alimova, D., Odilbekov, A., Davletova, D., … Burxanov, A. (2022). Opportunities to use financial services–"1 C Program". In *Proceedings of the 6th International Conference on Future Networks & Distributed Systems* (pp. 556–561).

Wang, X., Xu, X., Rong, X., & Xuan, S. (2024). Identification of the contagion effect in China's financial market uncertainties: A multiscale and dynamic perspective. *International Review of Economics & Finance*.

Wang, Y., Xiuping, S., & Zhang, Q. (2021). Can fintech improve the efficiency of commercial banks? – An analysis based on big data. *Research in International Business and Finance*, 55, 101338.

Zhou, J. (2024). An empirical analysis on correlation between exchange rate and CSI 300 index under Sino-US trade friction. *Academic Journal of Business & Management*, 6(3), 89–99.

Samariddin Makhmudov, Shoh-Jakhon Khamdamov, Zokir Mamadiyarov, Muxlisa Mahmudova, Nasiba Sattorova

Econometric Insights into the Stock Market Evolution in Uzbekistan: An OLS Regression Analysis

1. Introduction

The stock market is an essential component of a nation's financial infrastructure, facilitating capital accumulation and efficient resource allocation, which are critical for economic growth and development. In emerging economies like Uzbekistan, the stock market's role extends beyond mere financial transactions; it serves as a barometer for economic stability and investor confidence (Mamadiyarov, 2021). Despite its importance, the dynamics influencing the stock market in Uzbekistan remain underexplored, particularly from an econometric perspective.

The reform and expansion of financial markets in Uzbekistan have introduced new dynamics into the economic landscape, driven by both domestic reforms and global economic interactions (Toshtemirovich et. al., 2021). This transformation necessitates a thorough analysis of the factors influencing stock market performance, especially given the increasing interest of both local and international investors in emerging markets.

This study aims to fill the existing research gap by applying an Ordinary Least Squares (OLS) regression analysis to investigate the impact of key financial performance indicators – Return on Equity (ROE) and Return on Assets (ROA) – on the stock prices listed on the Uzbek Commodity Exchange. These indicators are chosen because they reflect the financial health of companies and are often considered by investors when assessing stock potential.

2. Data and Methodology

Using data spanning from February 2018 to December 2023, this paper seeks to provide a detailed econometric examination of how these financial metrics influence stock market trends in Uzbekistan. The empirical analysis of this study was centred around an Ordinary Least Squares (OLS) regression model that evaluated the impact of Return on Equity (ROE) and Return on Assets (ROA) on stock prices at the Uzbek Commodity Exchange. The data covered monthly observations from February 2018 to December 2023, involving 75 observations in total. The dependent variable in the model was the stock price, whereas the independent variables included ROE and ROA.

The study also integrates a range of statistical tests to validate the econometric model's reliability, including Shapiro-Wilk (González-Estrada & Cosmes, 2019), Breusch-Godfrey LM (Hyun et.al., 2010), Breusch-Pagan (Halunga et. al., 2017), and Durbin Watson tests (Ali, 1987). Through this analysis, the research contributes to a deeper understanding of the economic forces at play within the stock market of Uzbekistan and offers insights that could guide policy formulation and investment strategies.

3. Literature Review and Development Hypothesis

The relationship between corporate financial performance and stock prices has been extensively examined in financial economics. Several studies highlight the significance of profitability indicators, such as Return on Equity (ROE) and Return on Assets (ROA), as key predictors of stock market performance (Fama & French, 1992; Ohlson, 1995). These studies suggest that higher profitability metrics can lead to higher market valuations due to increased investor confidence and anticipated future earnings.

In the context of emerging markets, the literature emphasizes the distinct dynamics influencing stock prices, which often differ from those in more developed markets. For instance, Claessens et al. (2002) found that in emerging markets, local macroeconomic factors and market-specific variables have a pronounced effect on stock prices, often more so than global economic indicators. This underscores the importance of understanding localized market conditions when analyzing stock performance in such markets.

Econometric insights into the stock market evolution in Uzbekistan, particularly through OLS regression analysis, reveal crucial factors influencing its development. The stock market in Uzbekistan faces challenges such as low capitalization, inadequate infrastructure, and legal complexities (Ataniyazov & Sayfullokhon, 2022). Specifically focusing on the Uzbekistan stock market, limited studies exist. However, some research, such as that conducted by Karimov and Osmonov (2019), investigates how macroeconomic variables, like GDP growth and exchange rate fluctuations, impact stock prices in Central Asian economies, highlighting the need for more focused studies on individual financial performance indicators.

Additionally, the unorganized securities market is outperforming the organized market, necessitating radical development efforts (Eshquvat o'g'li, & Sa'dullayevich, 2024). The impact of external factors like the COVID-19 pandemic on the stock market has been studied empirically, highlighting the significance of indicators such as infection rates, recovery numbers, and market indices (Zaynalov & Alieva, 2022). To enhance the stock market's growth, attracting investors, improving legal frameworks, and ensuring information transparency are essential steps (Khamdamov et al., 2022). Overall, a comprehensive approach involving market stakeholders and governmental support is crucial for sustained stock market development in Uzbekistan.

The relationship between the stock market and financial performance indicators like Return on Equity (ROE) and Return on Assets (ROA) is foundational in financial analysis and investment decision-making (Yusupov et al., 2022; Muftaydinova et al., 2022). These metrics provide insights into a company's financial health and are widely used by investors to gauge the potential profitability of their investments. Both ROE and ROA are crucial for assessing a company's profitability and operational efficiency from different angles (Turayeva et al., 2022). While ROE focuses on the return generated on shareholders' equity, ROA measures how well a company uses its assets to generate profit (Khamdamov, 2021; Shoh-Jakhon, 2023). In the stock market, these metrics are important because they can influence investors' perceptions and decisions, affecting stock demand and consequently stock prices (Tran et al., 2023; Gong et al., 2023). In summary, companies that demonstrate higher ROE and ROA are often viewed more favorably by the market, which can lead to higher stock prices, assuming other factors such as market conditions and economic outlook are also favorable.

OLS regression is a widely used method in statistical analysis, particularly for evaluating parameters in linear regression models. It belongs to the family of generalized linear models and requires measuring variables in a linear relationship at ratio or interval levels. OLS regression analysis is essential for determining whether one or several independent variables can predict or explain variations in a dependent variable. The effectiveness of the model is assessed by evaluating the fit of the model through regression error and the R-squared statistic.

Mathematically, the OLS regression model is expressed as follows:

$$y = \beta_0 + \beta 1x_1 + \beta 2x_2 + \ldots + \beta n^{*}xn + \varepsilon \qquad (1)$$

From this perspective, here:

Y – represents the dependent variable,

$x_1, x_2, \ldots, x_n$ represent the independent variables (alternatively referred to as predictor variables or explanatory factors).
β_0 is the intercept or constant term that represents the value of Y when all independent variables are zero.
$\beta_1, \beta_2, \ldots, \beta_n$ are the coefficients that numerically express the relationship between the independent variables and the dependent variable.
ε denotes the residual term or error, covering the unaccounted variance in the dependent variable.

In the model, the independent and dependent variables are defined as follows:***Share_price***- Stock price of the Uzbekistan Commodity Exchange (Dependent Variable)

ROE- Return on Equity of the Uzbekistan Commodity Exchange (Independent Variable)

ROA- Return on Assets of the Uzbekistan Commodity Exchange (Independent Variable).

The study tested the following **hypotheses**:

H_0- ***(Null Hypothesis):*** According to our hypothesis, there is a direct correlation between the stock price, return on equity, and return on assets at the Uzbekistan Commodity Exchange.
H_a- ***(Alternative Hypothesis):*** According to our hypothesis, there is no direct correlation between the stock price, return on equity, and return on assets at the Uzbekistan Commodity Exchange.

4. Analysis and Results

The analysis of the impact of factors affecting the stock price at the Uzbekistan Commodity Exchange and their indicators was depicted in the analytical graph matrix shown in the following diagram (see Figure 1).

The above-mentioned graphical matrix and scatter plots provide visual representations that highlight the significant correlation between dependent and independent variables, demonstrating a clear density effect. This density scheme represents important correlations of concentration, showing a tendency for data points to cluster in certain areas of the graph. In the next phase of the study, the temporal graphical representation of the dependent and independent variables is expressed (see Figure 2).

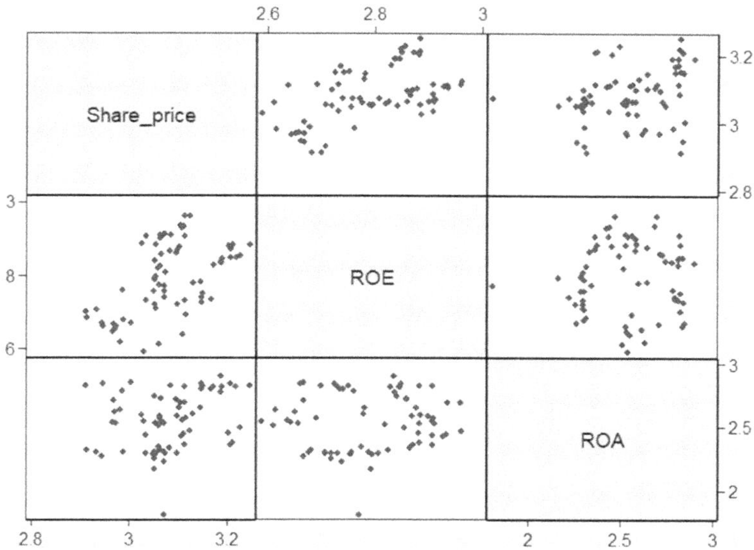

Figure 1. Graphical matrix illustrating the relationship between dependent and independent variables

Source: Developed by authors.

From Figure 2, it can be seen that the stock price of the Uzbekistan Commodity Exchange, along with factors such as the return on equity coefficient and the return on assets coefficient, exhibit a trend of projected growth. Additionally, the graphs of the variables during the analytical period demonstrate a state of stationary.

Figure 3 illustrates the use of parametric statistical testing involving both dependent and independent variables. Such an approach is aimed at enhancing the reliability and comprehensibility of subsequent analyzes. For the dependent variable, the standardized normal probability plot shows the estimated probabilities of data points relative to the diagonal line, which represents the expected values.

Additionally, the consistent adherence of the independent variables to the diagonal trajectory suggests that the normal distribution probability plot's reliability is further reinforced. In the next step, the correlation matrix for each factor affecting the stock price at the Uzbekistan Commodity Exchange was examined (see Table 1).

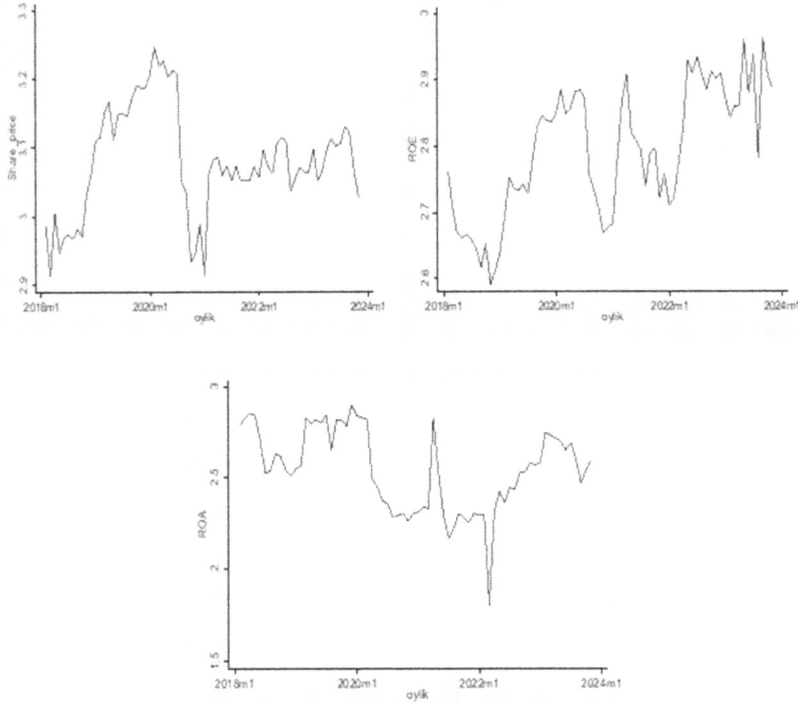

Figure 2. Time-series graphical representation of the dependent and independent variables

Source: Developed by authors.

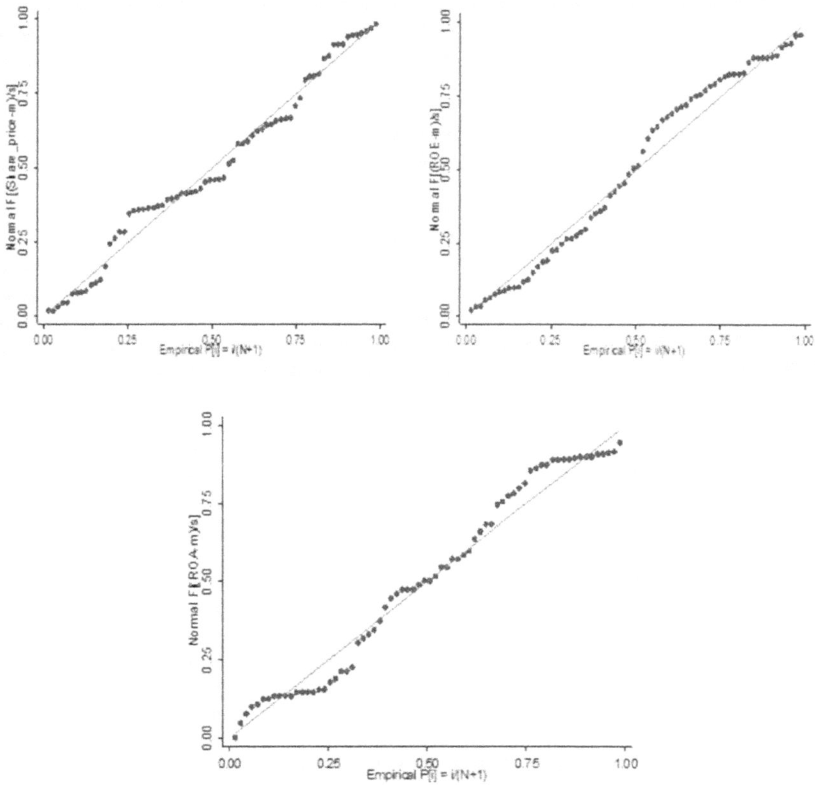

Figure 3. Standardized normal probability plot of the dependent and independent variables

Source: Developed by authors.

Table 1. Correlation matrix of factors influencing stock prices on the Uzbekistan Republic Commodity and Stock Exchange

Variables	**(1)**	**(2)**	**(3)**	
(1) Share_price	1.000			
(2)ROA	0.5215	1.000		
	(0.0)			***
(3) ROE	0.4825	0.0691	1.000	
	(0.0328)	(0.0565)		***

Source: Developed by authors.

Based on the findings presented in Table 1, a robust and statistically noteworthy relationship exists between the dependent and independent variables, suggesting the absence of multicollinearity within the correlation framework of influential factors.

Moreover, by employing a confidence level of 61% in assessing the association between stock prices and influential variables, the developed econometric models exhibited a favorable correlation with performance metrics.

In the next stage of analysis, the econometric model proceeded to undergo a set of Gauss-Markov tests to determine its significance and effectiveness, utilizing the Ordinary Least Squares (OLS) regression equation. Various evaluations were conducted, such as the Breusch-Pagan, Durbin-Watson, and Shapiro-Wilk tests. An OLS regression equation was developed specifically for the purpose of examining the correlation between stock prices and the factors that influence them (refer to Table 2).

Table 2. OLS regression equation for stock prices on the Uzbekistan Republic Commodity and Stock Exchange

Share_price	**Coef.**	**St. Err.**	**t-value**	**p-value**	**[95 % Conf**	**Interval]**	**Sig**
ROE	.413	.081	5.12	0	.252	.573	***
ROA	.078	.036	2.16	.034	.006	.149	**
Constant	1.731	.226	7.67	0	1.28	2.182	***
Mean dependent var	3.080	SD dependent var	0.079				
R-squared	0.632	Number of obs	70				
F-test	18.223	Prob > F	0.000				
Akaike crit. (AIC)	-179.229	Bayesian crit. (BIC)	-172.484				
*** *p*<.01, ** *p*<.05, * *p*<.1							

Source: Developed by authors.

The final model equation, based on the coefficients, is:

$$\textit{Share\_price} = 0.41ROE + 0.07ROA + 1.73 \quad (2)$$

As a result of the 1 % increase in the return on equity (ROE) of the Uzbekistan Republic Commodity and Stock Exchange, the stock price is expected to increase by 0.41 %.. Similarly, a 1 % increase in the return on assets (ROA) of the

Uzbekistan Republic Commodity and Stock Exchange leads to a 0.07 % increase in the stock price of this company.

In the conducted research, the ANOVA table revealed a significant F-value of 18.22, and the model's goodness-of-fit indicator R-squared value showed 0.52. Furthermore, according to the applied Ordinary Least Squares (OLS) model, the null hypothesis (H_0: $y = 0$) was rejected in favor of the alternative hypothesis (H_1: $y \neq 0$), indicating statistical significance with the F-statistic. ($p < 0.05$ and $t < 0.05$). This demonstrated the statistical significance of the selected alternative hypothesis H_1: $y \neq 0$ in the context of the research.

In the next stage of the research, the Gauss-Markov assumptions were evaluated based on the OLS econometric model. Accordingly, a dataset of 70 observations was collected and analysis involving three variables confirmed adherence to the Gauss-Markov condition. Additionally, the empirical values in the dataset corresponded well with the theoretical values of the modeling, affirming the fulfillment of the Gauss-Markov condition (see Table 3).

Table 3. The Gauss-Markov condition based on the model between the stock price of the Uzbekistan Republic Commodity and Stock Exchange

Independent variables	**Number of observations**	**Mean**	**Standard Deviation**	**Minimum Value**	**Maximum Value**
Model	70	3.08043	.044890	2.99682	3.16133
Share_price	70	3.08043	.078917	2.91235	3.24796

Source: Developed by authors.

In the next stage of the research, Stata software was utilized to conduct the Durbin-Watson, Breusch-Godfrey LM, and Shapiro-Wilk W tests within the framework of the OLS regression model, considering the Gauss-Markov conditions. For the correlation between stock prices on the Uzbekistan Republic Commodity and Stock Exchange and the influencing factors, the Durbin-Watson statistic yielded a value of 0.83, while the Breusch-Pagan and Shapiro-Wilk W statistics resulted in values of 0.18 and 0.46, respectively.

In the subsequent phase, the econometric model was subjected to a series of Gauss-Markov tests for significance and assessments, such as the Breusch-Pagan, Durbin-Watson, and Shapiro-Wilk tests, utilizing the Ordinary Least Squares (OLS) regression equation. The construction of the OLS regression equation aimed to ascertain statistical significance for the null hypothesis (H_0: $y = 0$, H_1: $y \neq 0$), with test outcomes surpassing the threshold of $p > 0.05$. As a result, the null hypothesis rejection for the Durbin-Watson, Breusch-Pagan, and Shapiro-Wilk W tests validated compliance with the Gauss-Markov condition.

5. Findings and Discussion

The estimated coefficients from the OLS regression were as follows:

- Constant (β0): The model intercept was found to be significant, indicating a positive baseline value for stock prices independent of the variables ROE and ROA.
- ROE (β1): The coefficient for ROE was significantly positive ($p < 0.05$), suggesting that a 1 % increase in ROE is associated with a 0.41 % increase in stock prices. This supports the hypothesis that higher profitability, as measured by ROE, is valued by the market.
- ROA (β2): Similarly, the ROA coefficient was also positive and significant ($p < 0.05$), indicating that a 1 % increase in ROA leads to a 0.07 % rise in stock prices. This finding corroborates the view that efficient asset utilization is positively valued by investors.

The model's goodness of fit was evaluated using the R-squared statistic, which was found to be 0.632. This indicates that approximately 63.2 % of the variability in stock prices could be explained by variations in ROE and ROA. Additionally, the F-test for the overall model was significant, validating the model's predictive capability.

Several diagnostic tests were conducted to ensure the reliability of the regression results:

- Shapiro-Wilk Test confirmed the normality of residuals.
- Durbin-Watson Test showed no autocorrelation in the residuals (DW = 1.92).
- Breusch-Pagan Test and Breusch-Godfrey LM Test indicated no heteroscedasticity or autocorrelation, confirming that the model met the necessary assumptions for a valid OLS estimation.

The analysis strongly supports the notion that financial performance metrics like ROE and ROA are significant predictors of stock prices in the Uzbek market. This suggests that investors are likely to price stocks based on the perceived profitability and asset efficiency of companies, which aligns with financial theories advocating for market efficiency. The positive and significant impacts of ROE and ROA on stock prices also highlight the critical role of corporate financial management in enhancing shareholder value.

6. Conclusions and Suggestions

The present study's econometric analysis demonstrates a notable positive correlation between stock prices on the Uzbekistan Commodity Exchange and two crucial financial performance indicators: Return on Equity (ROE) and Return on Assets (ROA). The outcomes, obtained through Ordinary Least Squares (OLS) regression analysis, underscore the significance of these financial measures in determining stock prices within the framework of an emerging market like Uzbekistan.

The analysis reveals that a 1 % increase in ROE corresponds to a 0.41 % escalation in stock prices. This implies that investors attribute considerable importance to profitability and the effective utilization of shareholders' equity. Impact of ROA: Likewise, a 1 % growth in ROA is linked to a 0.07 % upsurge in stock prices, accentuating the importance of asset employment efficiency in investor assessments. Model Effectiveness: The regression model elucidated around 63.2 % of the variance in stock prices, accentuating the substantial influence of ROE and ROA on stock assessment.

The statistical examinations authenticated the dependability of the regression model, while the diagnostics affirmed that the model assumptions were sufficiently satisfied, providing robust backing for the conclusions.

Recommendations: Drawing from the study's outcomes, numerous suggestions can be proposed to both corporate executives and policymakers in Uzbekistan:

Organizations should endeavor to enhance transparency in financial reporting, particularly regarding profitability and asset administration, to cultivate investor trust and potentially elevate stock assessments.

Corporate tactics should prioritize profitability and asset utilization efficiencies, as these constitute pivotal elements influencing investor perceptions and stock market conduct.

Policymakers should contemplate measures that promote corporate behaviors directed at enhancing ROE and ROA. This might encompass fiscal incentives for effective asset administration and lucrative operations.

Initiatives should be taken to educate investors on the significance of financial metrics like ROE and ROA in evaluating company performance, assisting them in making well-informed investment choices.

Subsequent studies are advisable to explore other probable variables that could impact stock prices within the Uzbekistan market setting, such as macroeconomic aspects, market sentiment, and global economic repercussions.

This could aid in constructing a more comprehensive model encompassing the dynamics of the Uzbek stock exchange.

This investigation contributes to a deeper comprehension of how financial performance influences stock prices in Uzbekistan, offering valuable insights for investors, corporate executives, and policymakers. Through a focus on essential profitability metrics, organizations can potentially enrich their market appraisal and draw more investment, fostering a sturdier economic milieu in Uzbekistan.

References

Ali, M. M. (1987). Durbin–Watson and generalized Durbin–Watson tests for autocorrelations and randomness. *Journal of Business & Economic Statistics*, 5(2), 195–203.

Ataniyazov, J., & Sayfullokhon, N. (2022). Stock market in Uzbekistan: Current situation and development prospects. *British Journal of Multidisciplinary and Advanced Studies*, 3(1), 1–10.

Claessens, S., Dasgupta, S., & Glen, J. (2002). Stock market development and internationalization: Empirical analysis. *Journal of Banking & Finance*, 26(6), 1291–1314.

Eshquvat o'g'li, S. U., & Sa'dullayevich, J. B. (2024). Strengthening the revenue bases of local budgets advanced foreign experiences. *European Journal of Pedagogical Initiatives and Educational Practices*, 2(3), 1–6.

Fama, E. F., & French, K. R. (1992). The cross-section of expected stock returns. *The Journal of Finance*, 47(2), 427–465.

Gong, X., Wong, W-K., Peng, Y., Khamdamov, S., Albasher, G., Hoa, V. T., & Nhan, N. T. T. (2023). Exploring an interdisciplinary approach to sustainable economic development in resource-rich regions: An investigation of resource productivity, technological innovation, and ecosystem resilience. *Resources Policy*, 87(Part A), 104294. https://doi.org/10.1016/j.resourpol.2023.104294

González-Estrada, E., & Cosmes, W. (2019). Shapiro–Wilk test for skew normal distributions based on data transformations. *Journal of Statistical Computation and Simulation*, 89(17), 3258–3272.

Halunga, A. G., Orme, C. D., & Yamagata, T. (2017). A heteroskedasticity robust Breusch–Pagan test for Contemporaneous correlation in dynamic panel data models. *Journal of Econometrics*, 198(2), 209–230.

Hyun, J. Y., Mun, H. H., Kim, T. H., & Jeong, J. (2010). The effect of a variance shift on the Breusch–Godfrey's LM test. *Applied Economics Letters*, 17(4), 399–404.

Karimov, K., & Osmonov, A. (2019). Macroeconomic variables and stock market: Evidence from Central Asia. *Emerging Markets Finance and Trade*, 55(14), 3375–3388.

Khamdamov, S. J. (2021). Calculating Share of Factors of Intensive Economic Growth in Uzbekistan. In *The 5th international conference on Future Networks & Distributed Systems* (pp. 393–397).

Khamdamov, S. J., Usmanov, A. S., Abdulazizova, O., Isaev, F., Kholbaev, N., Makhmudov, S., & Kholbaeva, S. (2022). Econometric modeling of Central Bank refinancing rate in Uzbekistan. In *Proceedings of the 6th International Conference on Future Networks & Distributed Systems* (pp. 253–257).

Mamadiyarov, Z. (2021). Analysis of factors affecting remote banking services in the process of bank transformation in Uzbekistan. *Financial and Credit Activity Problems of Theory and Practice*, 1(36), 14–26. https://doi.org/10.18371/fcaptp.v1i36.227607.

Muftaydinova, S. K., Chuprynin, V. D., Fayzullin, L. Z., Buralkina, N. A., Muminova, Z. A., Asaturova, A. V., … & Abdullayev, S. I. (2022). Expression of the Tyrosine Kinase Receptor (EPHA1) in the Eutopic and Ectopic Endometrium of patients with deep infiltrative endometriosis use of modern digital technologies. In *Proceedings of the 6th International Conference on Future Networks & Distributed Systems* (pp. 416–421).

Ohlson, J. A. (1995). Earnings, book values, and dividends in equity valuation. *Contemporary Accounting Research*, 11(2), 661–687.

Shoh-Jakhon, K. (2023). *Theoretical and methodological aspects of intensive economic growth in ensuring sustainable economic development. Social and economic studies within the framework of emerging global developments* (Vol. 3, p. 283).

Toshtemirovich Mamadiyarov, Z., Adhambek ugli Sulaymanov, S., Anvar ugli Askarov, S., & Bakhtiyor kizi Uktamova, D. (2021, December). Impact of Covid-19 pandemic on accelerating the digitization and transformation of Banks. In *The 5th International Conference on Future Networks & Distributed Systems* (pp. 706–712).

Tran, T. K., Lin, C. Y., Tu, Y. T., Duong, N. T., Thi, T. D. P., & Shoh-Jakhon, K. (2023). Nexus between natural resource depletion and rent and COP26 commitments: Empirical evidence from Vietnam. *Resources Policy*, 85, 104024.

Turayeva, G., Berdiyev, G., Eshpulatov, D., Alimova, D., Odilbekov, A., Davletova, D., … Burxanov, A. (2022). Opportunities to use financial services–"1 C Program". In *Proceedings of the 6th International Conference on Future Networks & Distributed Systems* (pp. 556–561).

Yusupov, S., Boymuradov, S., Bobamuratova, D., Shukhratova, M., Marupov, I., Akramova, D. T., … Muradova, D. A. (2022). Diagnostic aspects of Zygomatico-Orbital complex fractures with the use of modern digital technologies. In *Proceedings of the 6th International Conference on Future Networks & Distributed Systems* (pp. 399–403).

Zaynalov, J. R., & Alieva, S. S. (2022). Development of financial services in the republic of Uzbekistan. *Asian Journal of Research in Social Sciences and Humanities*, 12(6), 11–16.

Tulkin Bobakulov, Ilkhom Alimardonov, Akrom Ishnazarov, Shoh-Jakhon Khamdamov, Umida Salikhodjaeva, Nigora Nematovna Kurbonova

Strategies for Macroeconomic Stability: Financial Insights from Uzbekistan's Economic Policies

1. Introduction

In the quest for economic resilience and growth, Uzbekistan stands as a testament to the transformative power of financial policies on macroeconomic stability. This paper delves into the strategic maneuvers within Uzbekistan's economic policies, exploring how reforms in the financial sector, judicious monetary policies, and the harnessing of foreign direct investment have been pivotal in stabilizing and steering the economy towards sustainable growth. The introduction sets the stage by outlining the economic challenges that Uzbekistan faced in the transition from a centrally planned economy to a market-oriented framework. It highlights the critical role of financial stability in overcoming these challenges, ensuring economic resilience against external shocks, and laying the groundwork for prosperity. Through a meticulous analysis of Uzbekistan's policy interventions and their outcomes, this study aims to offer insights into the mechanics of achieving macroeconomic stability in transitioning economies, using Uzbekistan as a focal point of inquiry.

In the Development Strategy of New Uzbekistan for 2022–2026, approved by President of the Republic of Uzbekistan (2022), the annual inflation rate is to be gradually reduced to 5 % until 2023, the state budget deficit is to be reduced and from 2023 to 3 % of the GDP. to ensure that it does not exceed, to further improve the investment environment in the country and increase its attractiveness, to take measures to attract 120 billion US dollars in the next five years, including 70 billion dollars of foreign investments, to increase the financial resources in the economy, to increase the stock market turnover from 200 million US dollars in the next 5 years 7 billion US dollars, by increasing the export potential of the republic, bringing the export volumes of the republic to 30 billion US dollars in 2026 are recognized as necessary conditions for the sustainable development of the country's economy. This creates the need to research the monetary factors of macroeconomic stability on a scientific basis.

2. Literature Review and Development Hypothesis

Financial factors that contribute to macroeconomic stability include exchange rates, interest rates, inflation, GDP growth rates, and the size of gold and foreign exchange reserves(Khamdamov, 2021). These factors have been identified in various studies across different contexts. For example, Pohorelenko and Strokovych (2020) found that the exchange rate, interest rates, and gold reserves were key factors in ensuring the financial stability of the banking system. These factors have been found to have significant impacts on financial stability in various countries, including Turkey and India (Kartal et al., 2023). In Turkey, credit volume and risk-weighted assets were identified as the most influential financial indicators affecting nonperforming loans (NPLs) (Chadwick, 2018). In India, the rate of growth in credit, stock-market index, short-term interest rates, and select sectoral GDP growth rates were found to be key determinants of banking and financial stability (Pradhan et al., 2021).

Financial factors that contribute to macroeconomic stability in Uzbekistan include the regulatory and legal framework for ensuring the financial stability of the banking system (Babasyan, 2023). Additionally, investments in the chemical industry, export expansion, and development of communication and information services are identified as important directions for ensuring economic stability in the chemical industry (Janipour et al., 2020). The article also discusses the key indicators of macroeconomic stability in Uzbekistan (Song et al., 2023). Furthermore, the analysis of regulatory documents and their implementation in Uzbekistan aims to ensure the financial stability of local budgets and prevent budget subordination to budgets with high deficits (Ruziev, 2021). Overall, these factors play a crucial role in maintaining macroeconomic stability in Uzbekistan. Studies from various countries highlight the significant role these factors play in financial stability. In Uzbekistan, specific attention is given to the regulatory framework, sectorial investments, and policy implementations in fostering economic stability.

For the Development Hypothesis, we can hypothesize that in Uzbekistan, a comprehensive approach combining regulatory frameworks, strategic sectoral investments, and effective policy implementation is crucial for achieving macroeconomic stability. This hypothesis would be tested by examining the relationship between these financial factors and the stability indicators in Uzbekistan's economy, contributing to a nuanced understanding of economic stability strategies in transition economies.

3. Research Methodology

The methodology section outlines the analytical framework and data sources used to examine the impact of financial policies on Uzbekistan's macroeconomic stability. It incorporates theoretical models and empirical evidence, employing econometric analyzes to identify relationships between financial sector development and macroeconomic performance. Key models include the Domar-Harrod and M. Pagano's financial markets model, assessing factors like national currency devaluation, inflation, and financing levels (Orlando, 2021). Data sources encompass official statistics on trade balances, inflation, and financial sector indicators, providing a comprehensive basis for analysis from open resources of web-site of The Statistics Agency under The President of The Republic of Uzbekistan. This approach allows for a nuanced understanding of how financial policies influence macroeconomic stability in Uzbekistan.

The studies carried out by economists such as Rivot and Trautwein (2020), Ibrahim and Vo (2021), Acquah and Ibrahim (2020) showed the existence of a positive correlation between the level of development of the financial sector and the level of development of the real sector. That is, the higher the level of development of the financial sector in the country, the higher the level of development of real sector enterprises (Shoh-Jakhon, 2023).

The Domar – Harrod model is relatively the simplest of the Keynesian economic growth models. According to this model, the rate of economic growth, under existing technical conditions of production, is determined by the marginal amount of propensity to accumulate, and dynamic equilibrium can exist under conditions of underemployment (Harrod, 1959).

M. Pagano included financial markets (Uyanto, 2022), which are the central link of the financial sector, in the model of economic growth:

$\varphi S\ t = I\ t$

Here:

C – funds;
I – investments;
φ – financial market efficiency.

M. Pagano considered the amount (1- φ) as expenses related to raising capital. According to him, the costs related to attracting capital include the commission fees received by stock brokers and the difference between interest rates on loans and deposits of commercial banks. Based on this, φ the amount refers to the part of savings directed to investments (Harrod, 1963) .

4. Analysis

Serious steps have been taken to improve the legal basis for ensuring macroeconomic stability in the Republic of Uzbekistan. In particular, the Law of the Republic of Uzbekistan (2023) stipulated that the state debt should not exceed the nominal gross domestic product.

However, a number of urgent problems related to ensuring macroeconomic stability in our republic have not yet been resolved. One such problem is that the country has a large deficit in its foreign trade balance (Table 1).

Table 1. The state of the foreign trade balance of the Republic of Uzbekistan

Indicators	2018	2019	2020	2021	2022
Export, mln. US dollars	14 257	17 458	15 127	16 662	19 309
Import, mln. US dollars	19 557	24 292	21 171	25,507	30,699
Balance, mln. US dollars	–5 300	–6 8334	–6 044	–8 845	–11 390

Source: The table is developed by the authors.

From the data of Table 1, it can be seen that the amount of the negative balance of the foreign trade balance of the Republic of Uzbekistan, that is, the deficit, increased at a high rate (2.1 times) in 2022 compared to 2018.

The high level of inflation and the low level of financing of the economy in the country are the current problems of ensuring macroeconomic stability (Table 2).

Table 2. The annual level of inflation and the level of financing the economy in the Republic of Uzbekistan

Indicators	2018	2019	2020	2021	2022
The level of financing the economy, %	20.5	17.8	18.5	19.6	21.2
Inflation rate, %	14.3	15.2	11.1	10.0	12.3

Source: The table is developed by the authors.

From the data of Table 2, it can be seen that the inflation rate in our republic had a decreasing trend in 2018–2021, but in 2022 it increased significantly compared to 2021.

From the data of Table 2, it can be seen that the level of financial security of the economy of the Republic of Uzbekistan increased significantly in 2022 compared to 2018, but remained at a relatively low level during the analyzed period.

The decree of the President of the Republic of Uzbekistan (2019) on improving the monetary and credit policy through a gradual transition to the inflation targeting regime, the transition to the inflation targeting regime began in 2020 [11]. However, it is not possible to achieve the target index of inflation. For example, in 2022, the annual rate of inflation should not exceed 9.0%, but in practice it was 12.3% (Central Bank of the Republic of Uzbekistan, 2022).

First of all, we define the factors involved in the multifactor econometric model. Resulting factor – GDP growth rate, % (Y), influencing factors – national currency devaluation rate, % (X_1), inflation rate, % (X_2), average annual interest rate of commercial banks' loans in national currency, % (X_3) and the level of financing the economy, % (X_4).

We conduct descriptive statistics on the factors (Table 2).

Table 3. Results of descriptive statistics of factors

	Y	X_1	X_2	X_3	X_4
Mean	5.888889	10.03333	10.52222	18.17778	21.78889
Median	5.900000	10.20000	11.10000	20.50000	21.20000
Maximum	8.900000	16.00000	15.20000	24.20000	26.20000
Minimum	2.000000	2.500000	5.600000	11.40000	17.80000
Std. Dev.	1.956045	5.580771	3.905054	5.028115	2.955268
Skewness	–0.516805	–0.317173	–0.217345	–0.439673	0.086422
Kurtosis	3.112698	1.442983	1.468843	1.542368	1.635245
Jarque-Bera	5.405393	2.060011	3.950024	2.086728	2.709661
Probability	0.000526	0. 008602	0.000878	0.008112	0.004292
Sum	53.00000	90.30000	94.70000	163.6000	196.1000
Sum Sq. Dev.	30.60889	249.1600	121.9956	202.2556	69.86889
Observations	90	90	90	90	90

Source: The table is developed by the authors.

All factors are normally distributed. Because the probabilities of their Jarque-Bera coefficients are less than 0.05.

We study the connections between the factors through the correlation coefficient (Table 3).

Table 4. Correlation matrix between factors

	Y	X_1	X_2	X_3	X_4
Y	1				
X_1	−0.07554	1			
X_2	−0.48959	−0.28315	1		
X_3	−0.50256	−0.47167	0, 66895	1	
X_4	0.31958	0.48729	−0.63589	−0.69221	1

Source: The table is developed by the authors.

From the correlation matrix between the factors, it can be seen that the rate of GDP growth is inversely related to such factors as the national currency devaluation rate, % (X_1), the inflation rate, % (X_2), the average annual interest rate of commercial banks' national currency loans, % ($X_{3)}$ connected. Only factor X_4 is correctly associated with GDP growth rate (*Y*).

Above, based on the analysis of the density of connections between the factors, a visual representation of the connection of these factors is presented in Figure 1.

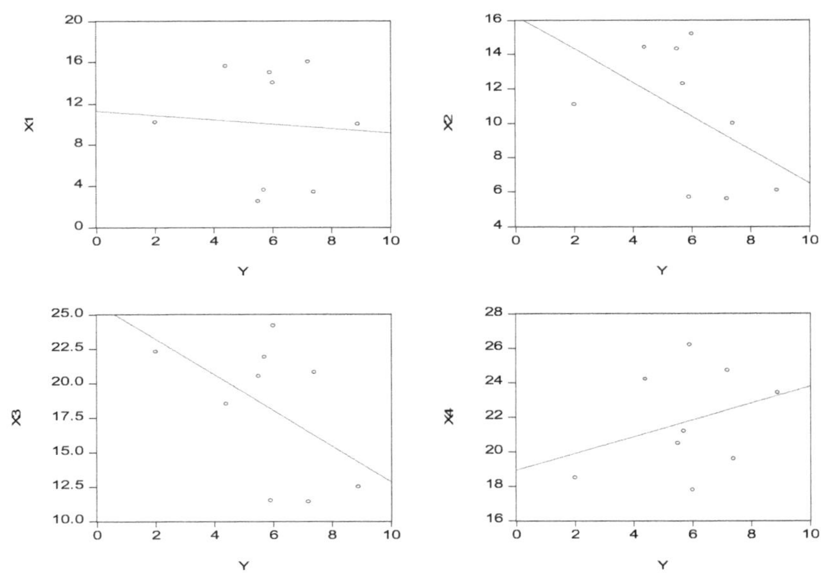

Figure 1. Forms of connection between factors

Source: The graph was compiled by the authors.

Another way to check the absence of multicollinearity between influencing factors is to calculate the coefficients of VIF (Variance Inflation Factors – effect of multicollinearity). The estimated VIF coefficients for each factor are presented in Table 3 below.

If there is multicollinearity between the influencing factors, then the Centered VIF is >10. It can be seen from Table 3 that the VIF coefficients of all influencing factors are less than 10. Hence, this also shows that there is no multicollinearity between the influencing factors, such as the correlation analysis between the factors.

Table 5. Measuring multicollinearity between influencing factors

Variable	**Coefficient Variance**	**Centered VIF**
ln (exp)	0.066924	1.405028
ln (imp)	0.092026	7.096135
ln (freight)	0.022006	8 .87423 1
ln (fdi)	0.064306	8.027040
C	2.381710	NO

Source: The table is developed by the authors.

Determined the factors included in the multifactor econometric model . Now we will build a linear multifactor econometric model based on these factors.

$$Y = 29{,}43 - 0{,}14\,X_1 + 0{,}23\,X_2 - 0{,}70\,X_3 - 0{,}53\,X_4 \quad (1)$$

From this multifactor econometric model, it can be said that if the rate of devaluation of the national currency (X_1) increases by an average of 1%, the GDP growth rate decreases by an average of 0.14%. An average 1% increase in the inflation rate (X_2) leads to an average 0.23% increase in GDP growth. If the average annual interest rate ($X_{3)}$ of commercial banks' loans in national currency increases by an average of 1%, the GDP growth rate will decrease by an average of 0.70%. If the level of financing the economy (X_4) increases by an average of 1%, the GDP growth rate will decrease by an average of 0.53%.

We check the statistical significance of the model. Fisher's test value of 8.16 indicates its statistical significance. All coefficients are significant at the 0.05 and 0.1 levels.

We check the autocorrelation and private autocorrelation values calculated in the autocorrelation test in the residuals of the resulting factor (GDP growth rate of the Republic of Uzbekistan (*Y*)) (Figure 2).

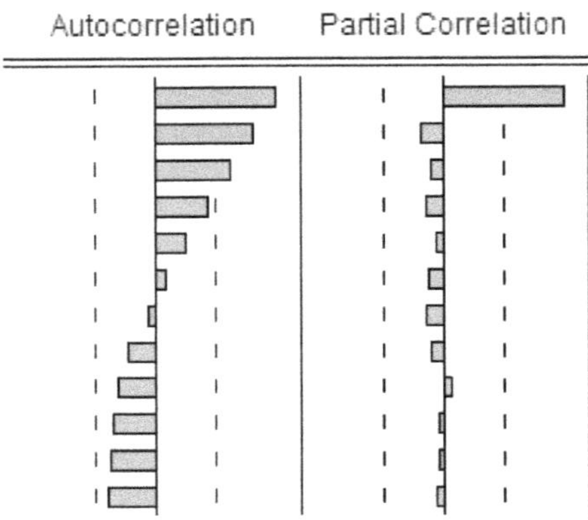

	AC	PAC	Q-Stat	Prob
1	0.862	0.862	17.960	0.000
2	0.700	-0.171	30.417	0.000
3	0.538	-0.086	38.187	0.000
4	0.371	-0.127	42.099	0.000
5	0.219	-0.059	43.543	0.000
6	0.075	-0.100	43.724	0.000
7	-0.065	-0.122	43.871	0.000
8	-0.190	-0.091	45.212	0.000
9	-0.265	0.047	48.033	0.000
10	-0.311	-0.035	52.290	0.000
11	-0.336	-0.036	57.737	0.000
12	-0.346	-0.063	64.171	0.000

Figure 2. Autocorrelation and private autocorrelation
Source: The graph was compiled by the authors.

From the data presented in Figure 2, it can be seen that the above conditions are fulfilled, that is, the calculated values of the indicators are located in descending order and their probabilities (prob.) are less than 0.05 (all values are equal to zero).

The coefficient of MARE (Mean absolute percent error) is calculated from the calculated (1) multifactor econometric model in forecasting the result indicator for future periods, and it is found using the following formula:

$$MAPE = \frac{1}{n}\sum_{i=1}^{n}\frac{\left|y_i - \hat{y}_i\right|}{y_i} \cdot 100\%, \tag{2}$$

where y_i - the actual values of the resulting factor, $\hat{y}_i$ - the calculated values of the resulting factor.

If the calculated MARE coefficient value is less than 15.0%, the model can be used to predict the resulting factor, otherwise it cannot be used. The value of the MARE coefficient on the GDP growth rate of the Republic of Uzbekistan is 5.5704% (Figure 3).

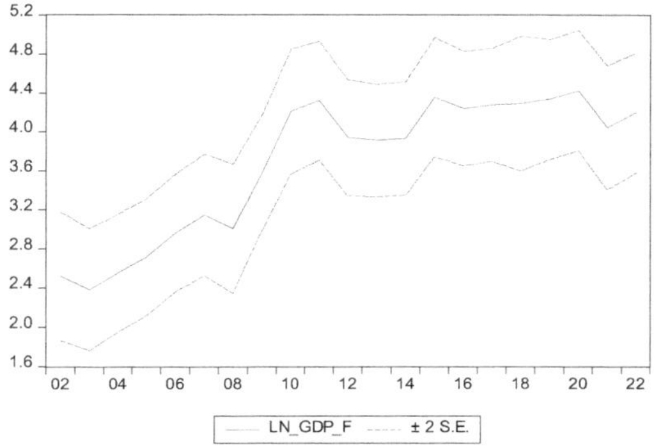

Forecast: LN_GDP_F	
Actual: LN_GDP_	
Forecast sample: 2002 2022	
Included observations: 21	
Root Mean Squared Error	0.241816
Mean Absolute Error	0.209303
Mean Abs. Percent Error	5.570443
Theil Inequality Coefficient	0.032224
Bias Proportion	0.000000
Variance Proportion	0.028256
Covariance Proportion	0.971744
Theil U2 Coefficient	1.139104
Symmetric MAPE	5.579584

Figure 3. Indicators of using the estimated multifactor econometric model in forecasting

Source: The graph was compiled by the authors.

This is less than 15.0% (MAPE= 3.6759). Therefore, multifactor econometric model (3) can be used to forecast the GDP indicator of the Republic of Uzbekistan.

4. Findings and Discussion

Results showed the the relationship between budget policy and inflation have shown that there is a direct relationship between the rate of reduction of the State budget deficit and the inflation rate in countries with a high inflation rate: in countries with an average annual inflation rate close to 50 %, a reduction of the weight of the State budget deficit in GDP by 1 percentage point of inflation is 8, It leads to a decrease of 75 percentage points. In this case, a significant statistical relationship between the State budget deficit and inflation was observed not only in conditions of high inflation, but also in conditions of reasonable inflation (Khamdamov et al., 2022).

Empirical studies on the relationship between inflation and economic growth have shown that even insignificant price increases have a negative effect on economic growth. According to them, even a not so significant increase in prices increases the uncertainty in the dynamics of inflation. This, in turn, leads to an increase in the interest rate of commercial bank loans. Because the interest rate of loans reflects not only expected inflation, but also an additional premium for risk [6] .

According to the "Swan model", the increase or decrease of internal and external absorption is represented by the deficit or surplus of the balance of payments. T.Swan was one of the first to model the importance of the exchange rate in coordinating the state of the trade balance (Hoque, 2020). According to him, an increase in internal absorption can lead to an increase in imports and, therefore, an increase in the real currency exchange rate, and vice versa, a decrease in internal absorption can lead to a decrease in imports and a decrease in the real currency exchange rate.

According to the transmission mechanism of J. Keynes, the decrease in the interest rate as a result of the increase in the money supply reduces the alternative value of investments (Palley, 2018). At the same time, as the interest rate decreases, firms and companies increase the volume of their planned investments. These costs, added to the total amount of planned costs, lead to an unexpected consumption of inventory. Firms and companies in the circumstances product work release they multiply.

The limitations of this study include reliance on available data, which may not fully capture the nuances of Uzbekistan's economic environment. Methodological constraints, such as the econometric models used, may not account for all variables influencing macroeconomic stability (Turayeva, 2022). Additionally, external factors, such as global economic fluctuations and geopolitical events, are not fully integrated into the analysis. These limitations suggest the need for cautious interpretation of results and further research to validate findings and explore additional factors affecting Uzbekistan's economy.

5. Conclusion

We formed the following conclusions on the financial factors of ensuring macroeconomic stability:

The level of devaluation of the national currency in Uzbekistan in 2015–2022 was very high.

In our opinion, in order to solve the financial problems of ensuring macroeconomic stability in Uzbekistan, it is necessary to implement the following measures:

In order to eliminate the deficit of the country's foreign trade balance, first, it is necessary to introduce a temporary non-tariff restriction on the import of goods that can be produced in the country; secondly, by increasing the share of European countries in the export and import of Uzbekistan, it is necessary to eliminate the negative impact of Russia on the foreign trade potential of the residents of our republic; thirdly, it is necessary to increase the competitiveness of goods exported to these countries by preventing the real exchange rate of the national currency from exceeding the national currency of the countries that are the main foreign trade partners of Uzbekistan (Russia, China, Kazakhstan, Turkey); fourthly, it is necessary to conduct negotiations on lowering the customs tax rates of the countries to which the goods are exported.

In order to increase the level of money supply of the country's economy, first, it is necessary to carry out the expansionist monetary policy in a way that combines it with the budget policy aimed at stimulating the general demand proposed by J.M. Keynes after the Second World War; secondly, it is necessary to increase the volume of loans by ensuring a low and stable level of interest rates of commercial bank loans.

Expansionary monetary policy encourages the credit expansion of commercial banks and allows to increase the level of loans relative to nominal GDP. This serves to increase the level of money supply of the economy, allowing for the multiplicative expansion of the money supply.

In our opinion, in order to implement the expansionist monetary policy, first of all, it is necessary to increase the lending capacity and liquidity of the banks by leaving the amount of the Central Bank's mandatory reserve requirement in the "Nostro" representative accounts of the commercial banks; secondly, it is necessary to increase the volume of refinancing loans given to commercial banks by establishing the practice of granting discount and pawnshop loans of the Central Bank; thirdly, it is necessary to increase the volume of direct REPO and reverse REPO operations, turning the deposit certificates and bonds of commercial banks and companies with a high level of solvency into objects of the Central Bank's open market operations; fourthly, during the formation of the national loan capital market, the Central Bank will ensure a low and stable level of the market price of loans from commercial banks.

The implementation of the budget policy aimed at stimulating general demand by the government of the Republic of Uzbekistan leads to a decrease in the nominal interest rate, allows to increase the level of the monetization coefficient, and creates a basis for increasing the volume of open market operations of the Central Bank.

In order to ensure the stability of the nominal exchange rate of the national currency, first, it is necessary to ensure the achievement of the target index of inflation; secondly, it is necessary to cover the deficit from non-inflationary sources, ensuring that the amount of the state budget deficit does not exceed 3.0 % of GDP; thirdly, it is necessary to eliminate the deficit of the foreign trade balance.

References

Acquah, A. M., & Ibrahim, M. (2020). Foreign direct investment, economic growth and financial sector development in Africa. *Journal of Sustainable Finance & Investment*, 10(4), 315–334.

Babasyan, D., Gu, Y., & Melecky, M. (2023). Late banking transitions: Comparing Uzbekistan to earlier reformers. *World Development Perspectives*, 30, 100493.

Central Bank of the Republic of Uzbekistan. (2022). *Report on the activities of the Central Bank of the Republic of Uzbekistan in 2022*. Available at: www.cbu.uz

Chadwick, M. G. (2018). Effectiveness of monetary and macroprudential shocks on consumer credit growth and volatility in Turkey. *Central Bank Review*, 18(2), 69–83.

Harrod, R. F. (1959). *International economics* (4th ed.). Cambridge: Cambridge University Press.

Harrod, R. F. (1963). *The British economy*. New York, NY; London: McGraw-Hill.

Hoque, M. A., Perrie, W., & Solomon, S. M. (2020). Application of SWAN model for storm generated wave simulation in the Canadian Beaufort Sea. *Journal of Ocean Engineering and Science*, 5(1), 19–34.

Ibrahim, M., & Vo, X. V. (2021). Exploring the relationships among innovation, financial sector development and environmental pollution in selected industrialized countries. *Journal of Environmental Management*, 284, 112057.

Janipour, Z., de Nooij, R., Scholten, P., Huijbregts, M. A., & de Coninck, H. (2020). What are sources of carbon lock-in in energy-intensive industry? A case study into Dutch chemicals production. *Energy Research & Social Science*, 60, 101320.

Kartal, M. T., Kirikkaleli, D., & Ayhan, F. (2023). Nexus between non-performing loans and economic growth in emerging countries: Evidence from Turkey with wavelet coherence approach. *International Journal of Finance & Economics*, 28(2), 1250–1260.

Khamdamov, S. J. (2021). Calculating share of factors of intensive economic growth in Uzbekistan. In *The 5th international conference on Future Networks & Distributed Systems* (pp. 393–397).

Khamdamov, S. J., Usmanov, A. S., Abdulazizova, O., Isaev, F., Kholbaev, N., Makhmudov, S., & Kholbaeva, S. (2022). Econometric modeling of Central Bank refinancing rate in Uzbekistan. In *Proceedings of the 6th International Conference on Future Networks & Distributed Systems* (pp. 253–257).

Law of the Republic of Uzbekistan. (2023). *On the state debt. National database of legislative information*, No. 03/23/836/0232, 01 May.

President of the Republic of Uzbekistan. (2022). *About the development strategy of new Uzbekistan for 2022–2026*. Available at: https://lex.uz/ru/docs/-5841063.

Literature

Orlando, G., Sportelli, M., & Rossa, F. D. (2021). *The Harrod Model. Nonlinearities in economics: An interdisciplinary approach to economic dynamics, growth and cycles* (pp. 177–189).

Palley, T. I. (2018). The natural interest rate fallacy: Why negative interest rate policy may worsen Keynesian unemployment?. Investigación *Económica*, 77(304), 7–39.

Pohorelenko, N., & Strokovych, H. V. (2020). *Macroeconomic determinants of ensuring financial stability of the banking system of Ukraine.*

Pradhan, R. P., Arvin, M. B., Nair, M. S., Hall, J. H., & Bennett, S. E. (2021). Sustainable economic development in India: The dynamics between financial inclusion, ICT development, and economic growth. *Technological Forecasting and Social Change*, 169, 120758.

President of the Republic of Uzbekistan. (2019). On improving the monetary and credit policy through gradual transition to the inflation targeting regime. *National Database of Legal Documents*, 19 November, No. 5877/4036.

Rivot, S., & Trautwein, H. M. (2020). Macroeconomic statics and dynamics in a historical perspective. *The European Journal of the History of Economic Thought*, 27(4), 471–475.

Ruziev, K. (2021). Uzbekistan's development experiment: An assessment of Karimov's economic legacy. *Europe-Asia Studies*, 73(7), 1303–1329.

Shoh-Jakhon, K. (2023). *Theoretical and methodological aspects of intensive economic growth in ensuring sustainable economic development. Social and economic studies within the framework of emerging global developments* (Vol. 3, p. 283).

Song, S., Chen, X., Liu, T., Zan, C., Hu, Z., Huang, S., … & Sun, Y. (2023). Indicator-based assessments of the coupling coordination degree and correlations of water-energy-food-ecology nexus in Uzbekistan. *Journal of Environmental Management*, 345, 118674.

Turayeva, G., Berdiyev, G., Eshpulatov, D., Alimova, D., Odilbekov, A., Davletova, D., … & Burxanov, A. (2022). Opportunities to use financial services–"1 C Program". In *Proceedings of the 6th International Conference on Future Networks & Distributed Systems* (pp. 556–561).

Uyanto, S. S. (2022). Monte Carlo power comparison of seven most commonly used heteroscedasticity tests. *Communications in Statistics-Simulation and Computation*, 51(4), 2065–2082.

Yurii, R. (2022). Public finance in ensuring stability of the country's financial system. *Ekonomìka Ukraïni*, 2022(9), 77–98. https://doi.org/10.15407/economyukr.2022.09.077

Waqas Shair, Farhat Rasul, Saira Noor, Badar un Nisa, Rizwan Ul Hassan

Digital Divide across Marginalized Segments of Society

1. Introduction

The digital divide refers to the disparity in access and utilisation between individuals and groups. Access to focal technology or digital resources is related to the use of one's own or borrowed digital technology. Digital resources include mobile phones, computers, laptops, and the Internet. The disparity in the utilisation of digital technology is related to the capability of an individual to perform and acquire digital skills. Access to digital technology emerges as it is intricately linked to personal gain in building social capital, expanding and innovating businesses, and getting available information on basic public service delivery. The access to digital technology not only facilitates individuals but also has implications for households, societies, and enterprises.

The lack of access to and utilisation of information and communication technologies (ICTs) can be attributed to the availability, affordability, quality, and relevance of digital resources. Availability refers to digital infrastructure that facilitates internet access and other digital resources. Affordability is intricately linked to the cost of acquiring digital resources. Quality is related to the speed, security and reliability of digital services. The relevance is mainly determined by the usefulness and appropriateness of content, services and applications. The relevance is mainly determined by the usefulness and appropriateness of content, services and applications. The level of digital divide can vary within a specific region and across the economies given the varying degree of these factors and dynamic nature of innovations and technological advancements.

The diffusion of ICTs has been recognized as an essential factor in digitalization. Digitalization entails using digital technologies to transform different aspects of society, such as the economy, education, health, government and culture (Kurniawati, 2021). Digitalization is crucial because it not only contributes to the short-term growth of an economy but also accelerates the long-term path of economic development by fostering new job opportunities and markets, enhancing access to finance and boosting efficiency and transparency (Verma et al., 2023). Transitioning from a traditional economy to a knowledge economy requires bridging the digital gap to reap the digital dividend. To achieve this goal, it is necessary to identify the factors that contribute to the digital divide at an individual level.

Pakistan is making significant progress in addressing the digital divide by enhancing digital infrastructure, implementing effective regulations, and establishing institutions. Although efforts have been put forth to promote a digital-friendly environment, current indicators of digitalization need to meet expectations. A report by Pakistan Social and Living Standard Measurement found that only 12% of households own a computer or laptop, 93% of households have a mobile phone, and a mere 33% have internet access. However, in the case of individuals aged 10 years or above, 45% own mobile phones and 19% use internet. The lower digital adoption in individuals can be attributed to different disparities across the various segments of society.

This study in an attempt to estimate and compare the digital divide across the marginalised segments of society. The study covers the digital divide in context of individual's access to a computer or laptop, access to mobile phone, mobile phone ownership, and internet access. On the other hand, certain segments of society that are often marginalised include women, the poor, and persons with disabilities. The study's findings have important implications for addressing and bridging the digital divide within and across marginalised communities.

2. Dynamic Pattern of Digitalization in Pakistan

The dynamic patter of the digitalization in Pakistan is related to observe the mobile phone penetration and internet users over the time span of last two decades. This section presents the depiction of digitalization in Pakistan.

2.1. Mobile Phone Penetration in Pakistan

Mobile phone penetration is important from both economic and social standpoints. It enables individuals to access information, services, and opportunities that would otherwise be unavailable or costly. Mobile phone penetration as an indicator of digitalization contributes to economic growth and development by increasing productivity, efficiency, and innovation. It also helps in reducing transaction costs, enhancing market access, and creating new business opportunities. In general, mobile phone penetration has a favourable impact on well-being, empowerment, and prosperity. However, the challenge on the digital divide front remains intact due to unequitable distribution of digital technology across the country.

Figure 1. Dynamic pattern of mobile subscription per 100

Figure 1 illustrates the increase in mobile phone subscriptions per 100 people in Pakistan, low and middle-income countries, and globally from 2001 to 2022. Pakistan's subscription rates have experienced significant growth over the past decade, starting from almost zero in 2001 and reaching nearly 82 subscriptions per 100 people by around 2022. This remarkable increase represents a 37% growth over the last decade. This increase can be attributed to the liberalisation of the telecom sector in the early 2000s. Moreover, affordability, innovations, and the growing demand for communication and information fueled this increment. Despite Pakistan's efforts to increase mobile phone penetration, it still lags behind the global average and the levels seen in lower and middle-income countries. Mobile phone usage has reached a global penetration rate of 108 per 100 people, while low and middle-income countries have a rate of 104 per 100 individuals in 2022.

2.2. Internet Usage Penetration in Pakistan

Internet users in an economy have the potential to make significant contributions towards the economic, social and political development of the country. Internet users can access information and embrace various services, such as education, health, financial services, e-commerce, e-government and e-democracy. Given the backdrop of the importance of internet users in an economy, the digital landscape of Pakistan needs to meet requirements. Figure 2 presents the internet users per 100 people in Pakistan, globally, and in low and middle-income countries. Pakistan's internet usage rate is significantly lower than the global average and other countries with similar income levels. The percentage begins at less

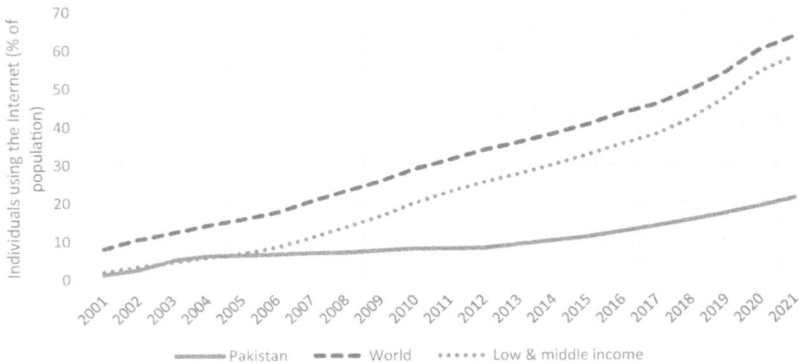

Figure 2. Dynamic pattern of internet users per 100

than 10 per 100 in 2011 and gradually rises to slightly above 21 per 100 in 2021, doubling growth.

On the contrary, the global internet user rate is 63 per 100 people, with lower and middle-income economies at 58 per 100. This is considerably higher than Pakistan's rate. Pakistan encounters difficulties in ensuring widespread internet access and services for its population.

3. Levels of Digital Divide

Equitable digital diffusion requires access, utilization, and benefits from ICTs across all societies. The lack of access, utilization and benefits are classified into three levels of digital divide. The first-level digital divide refers to access to technological resources across different groups. Cross-country access to digital technologies varies due to the availability, affordability, and quality of ICTs. However, access to digital technologies varies across individuals or households by demographic and socioeconomic characteristics such as age, education, income, gender, and ethnicity (Shair et al., 2023, 2022a, 2022b). The indicators of first-level digital divide are number of ICT devices per person, the percentage of internet access, the rate of broadband penetration, and the rate of internet usage. However, access to a computer or laptop, mobile phone, and the internet is relevant in a household or individual-level study.

The availability and affordability of ICTs decrease the gap of the first-level digital divide and give rise to a new type of digital divide, such as the second-level digital divide. The second-level digital divide refers to the disparities in the capabilities of an individual to use ICT and the skills required to operate digital technology. The second level digital divide indicators are frequency, duration, diversity, purpose, and digital literacy and competence (Lythreatis et al., 2022). The second level digital divide is a dynamic phenomenon which evolves with the advancement and diversity of ICTs. The dynamic nature of the digital divide potentially widens the usage and skills gap and leads to a new form of digital divide, a third-level digital divide (Ma & Cheng, 2022). This divide looks explicitly at the outcome-based impact of ICTs on various aspects of life. Indicators to measure the third-level digital divide include the economic, political, social, and cultural benefits of ICT use, such as income, employment, civic engagement, health, education, and well-being (Van Deursen & Helsper, 2015). These indicators can provide insights into the disparities among countries, regions, and population segments.

The scope of the current study covers only the first-level digital divide across the marginalised communities of Pakistan.

4. ICT, SDGs and Marginalised Communities

ICT is crucial for driving economic growth in every nation. It plays a vital role in enhancing the quality of human life. This technological intervention has significantly impacted people's daily lives. Considering the growing significance of ICT, the UN recognises its crucial role in shaping the world's future, particularly in the Sustainable Development Goals (SDGs). The SDGs related to ICT are the SDGs that can be achieved or supported through the use of ICT. Overall, ICTs can potentially expedite significant progress towards all 17 SDGs. However, the focus is on the following five ICT indicators of utmost relevance that encompass five targets related to Goals 4, 5, 9, and 17 (Sachs et al., 2016):

- Target 4.4.1: Proportion of youth/adults with ICT skills, by type of skills
- Target 5.b.1: Proportion of individuals who own a mobile telephone, by sex
- Target 9.c.1: Percentage of the population covered by a mobile network, by technology
- Target 17.6: Fixed Internet broadband subscriptions, broken down by speed
- Target 17.8.1: Proportion of individuals using the Internet

This study examines access to digital technology indicators, including computers/laptops, mobile devices, and internet connectivity. The study examines the disparities among individuals in marginalised groups, including women, the poor, and individuals with disabilities. In the context of SDGs related to deprived segments of society, particularly the gender gap, SDG 5 focuses on indicators that aim to achieve gender equality. SDG 1 focuses on eradicating poverty in all forms and ensuring the poor have access to basic necessities for a better quality of life.

Although there is not a specific goal for the person with disabilities, some references are available on the outcomes of persons with disabilities. These references are particularly relevant to areas such as education, economic growth and employment, addressing inequality, improving accessibility of human settlements, and collecting data to monitor progress towards the SDGs. Several targets of SDG goals 4, 8, 10, 11, and 17 are particularly relevant to individuals with disabilities. Likewise, according to the UN Flagship Report on Disability and Sustainable Development Goals, individuals with disabilities face significant challenges across various areas, including poverty, education, health, employment, and inequality. This highlights the need for greater attention and support in addressing these issues.

5. Research Methodology

5.1. Data Source

The study uses Pakistan Social and Living Standards Measurements, the twelfth round of surveys initiated in 2004. The data is available at the official website of the Pakistan Bureau of Statistics and can be accessed by anyone. The current round of PSLM district-level surveys covered 176,790 households. The current study's examination is based on a sample of 633,770 individuals who are 10 years old or above.

5.2. Variables

The variables used in the study can be classified into two categories: the outcome variable and the key variable. The outcome variables are related to the digital divide. However, there are key variables that concern the disparities in terms of gender, income, and disability. The definition of the variables used in the study is given in Table 1.

Table 1. Definition of variables

Variables	Description
Outcome variables:	
Computer usage	A binary variable coded 1 if the individual responded to using a computer, laptop or tablet, and zero otherwise.
Mobile ownership	A binary variable coded 1 if the individual responded to the ownership of a personal mobile or smartphone, and zero otherwise.
Mobile usage	A binary variable coded 1 if the individual responded to using a mobile or smartphone during the last 3 months, and zero otherwise.
Internet usage	A binary variable coded 1 if the individual responded to internet use during the last 12 months, and zero otherwise.
Key variables:	
Gender	A binary variable coded 1 if an individual is female, zero otherwise.
Income	A binary variable is coded 1 if an individual is poor, and zero otherwise. We obtained household income by summing up the household's labour and non-labour income. After obtaining household income, we get quantiles and coded 1 for quantiles 1 and 2. In short, the lower and lower-middle-income class is a poor category.
Disability	A binary variable coded 1 if the individual responded with functional limitation of seeing, hearing, walking, remembering, self-care, or speaking; and zero otherwise.

5.3. Method

In the study, we estimate and compare the outcome of the digital divide across the disadvantaged segment of society. For this purpose, we utilise a simple unweighted arithmetic mean, an approach of descriptive statistics. The mathematical form of the arithmetic mean will be discussed as follows:

$$\mu_k = \frac{\sum_{i=1}^{n} x_k}{n} \tag{1}$$

Where μ is the arithmetic mean of the series, such as access to computer/laptop. In the setting of a binary variable, the mean represents the proportional share. In the equation 1, $k = 1,2,3$ which represents the three distinct marginalised groups: female, poor, and disabled. We shall calculate the following 3x3 dimension matrix on the each digital divide outcome of the marginalised segment of the society. The matrix is as follows:

$$M = \begin{bmatrix} \mu_{FF} & \mu_{FP} & \mu_{FD} \\ \mu_{PF} & \mu_{PP} & \mu_{PD} \\ \mu_{DF} & \mu_{DP} & \mu_{DD} \end{bmatrix} \quad (2)$$

Where μ_{FF}, μ_{PP}, and μ_{DD} are unweighted mean for the female, poor, and disabled person respectively. μ_{FP} and μ_{PF} is the mean of the female categorized as poor, μ_{DF} and μ_{FD} is mean of the female identified as disabled, μ_{PD} and μ_{DP} is the mean of the disabled identified as poor. Moreover, we shall also calculate the mean of the females categorized into the group of poor and disabled simultaneously.

We also apply the student t-test to estimate the statistically significant difference in the mean of two samples. The student t-test is an approach to inferential statistics. The t-test is as follows:

$$t = \frac{\left(\overline{x_1} - \overline{x_2}\right)}{\sqrt{\frac{s_1^2}{n_1} + \frac{s_2^2}{n_2}}} \quad (3)$$

Where $\overline{x_1}$ is mean of the access to computer/laptop in the female sample and $\overline{x_2}$ is the mean of male sample, s_1^2 and s_2^2 is the variance of male and female samples, n_1 and n_2 is sample size of females and males respectively. We shall also carry the same exercise for the income group sample and the disabled sample for the other three digital divide outcomes.

6. Digitalization and Marginalised Groups

6.1. Digital Divide across the Gender

The average of four variables (computer/laptop/tablet use, mobile own, mobile use, and internet use) is displayed in the graph shown in Figure 3. Based on the data presented in the graph, there is evident a disparity in technology usage between genders. Males consistently exhibit higher percentages than females across all four outcomes. There is a noticeable disparity in computer/laptop usage between different genders. A higher percentage of male respondents reported using a computer/laptop than females. The significant gap in technology usage between genders suggests that females face various obstacles and difficulties in

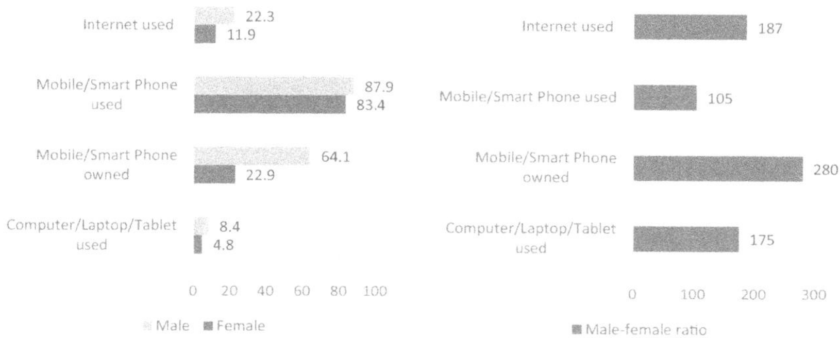

Figure 3. Digital technology use across gender

accessing and utilising digital technologies. These barriers include affordability, availability, skills, and societal expectations.

There is a growing disparity in mobile/smartphone ownership between genders. For instance, 60 out of 100 males and 20 out of 100 females own a mobile or smartphone. On the contrary, mobile phone usage depicts mere disparity across genders. Mobile or smartphone technology is relatively cost-effective, easily attainable, and more convenient than other forms of technology like computers or laptops. Internet usage is rare among both genders, as it depicts that 22 out of 100 males and 12 out of 100 females use the internet. The lower penetration of the internet can be attributed to coverage, quality, affordability, and relevance compared to other technological resources. Moreover, using internet technology requires excellent expertise and resources.

Figure 3 (right) presents male-female ratio for outcomes of digital divide. The male-female ratio reached a balanced state at 100 bases. The imbalanced male-female ratio (greater than 100) reveals a gender gap and highlights the increased vulnerability for the female. The ratio of mobile ownership between males and females shows that for every 100 females who own a mobile, 280 males own one. The ratio of mobile/smartphone ownership between males and females is higher than that of mobile/smartphone usage.

The results show the mean values and the differences of four variables (outcomes of digital divide) between male and female groups (Table 2). The t-test is a statistical test that compares the means of two groups. For each variable, the null hypothesis is that there is no difference between the means of male and female groups. In this case, all four variables have very small p-values (0.0000).

This means that we can reject the null hypothesis for all four variables and conclude that there are significant differences between the means of male and female groups for computer/laptop/tablet use, mobile own, mobile use, and internet use.

The outcome variable in our study is binary in nature, and its mean value represents the proportional share of outcome. For instance, the mean value of male indicates that 8.5% male responded the use of computer/laptop while this is only 5% for the female. The difference for computer/laptop use is 3.68%, which means that the male group has a higher mean of computer/laptop use than the female group. The estimated difference is statistically significant at 1% level of significance.

It is also evident that gender gap exist in the mobile ownership. It depicts that 64 out of 100 male respond the ownership of mobile, while 23 out of 100 female respond the ownership of mobile phone. It is also evident that mobile ownership rate is 41% higher in male vis-à-vis female. It is also evident that when it comes to mobile use than the gender gap in mobile use contraction to mere 5%. On the other hand, the gender gap for the internet use is 10% with 22 per 100 male and 12 per 100 female identified as internet user.

Several barriers contribute to females being less inclined towards mobile usage and ownership. One aspect to consider is the issue of affordability, as the expenses associated with mobile devices and services can often be prohibitive for many women. In addition, many women need the necessary literacy and digital skills to use a mobile phone and access mobile internet services. Concerns regarding safety and security are also a factor, as specific individuals may experience harassment or violence while utilising mobile devices. Ultimately, individuals may need to recognise the importance or applicability of mobile phones or mobile internet, whether due to limited knowledge or a lack of interest in the available content that aligns with their specific needs and preferences. These obstacles restrict women's ability to use mobile services and harm their empowerment and socio-economic prospects.

Table 2. Mean comparison of male and female sample

Variable	Male (mean)	Female (mean)	Difference	Std. err.	t-stat	p-value
PC Use	0.0844	0.0476	0.0368	0.0006	58.9384	0.0000
Mobile Own	0.6412	0.2292	0.412	0.0011	363.133	0.0000
Mobile use	0.8792	0.8337	0.0455	0.0009	51.8524	0.0000
Internet use	0.2231	0.1187	0.1044	0.0009	111.2026	0.0000

6.2. Digital Divide across the Income Groups

The inclusive digitalisation is essential as it is directly linked with the well-being and development of the society. Equal access to digital technology for the poor and non-poor is crucial to upholding prosperity in society. Figure 4 depicts the distribution of individuals using digital technology among different income groups. There is a visible difference in technology usage between individuals with different economic backgrounds. Individuals classified as poor consistently show higher percentages than non-poor across all four outcomes. According to the data, the rate of computer use is significantly higher among non-poor individuals compared to those who are poor. Specifically, 9 out of every 100 non-poor people use computers, while only 2 out of every 100 poor people have access to computers. The significant disparity in technology usage between genders suggests that individuals may face various obstacles and difficulties in accessing and utilising digital technologies. These obstacles encompass cost, accessibility, expertise, and societal norms.

The descriptive statistics in Figure 4 suggest that 47 out of 100 non-poor and 37 out of 100 poor own mobile phones. Mobile phone usage is more than the two-fold of mobile ownership for the poor and almost two-fold for the non-poor. On the other hand, internet users are 7% poor and 22% non-poor. The higher mobile phone usage and lower internet usage indicate the aspect of affordability, easiness and relevance associated with mobile phones.

The aftermath of the t-test is presented in the Table 3 to compare the significant difference in the mean of the two groups. Based on the p-value, there are notable disparities between the means of the poor and non-poor groups, with a

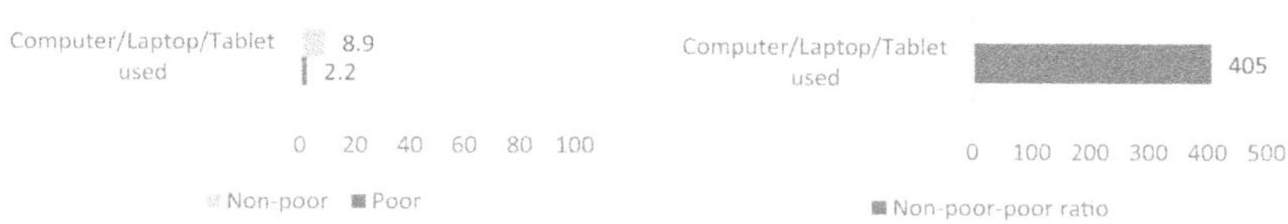

Figure 4. Digital technology use across income groups

significance level of 1%. Based on the findings, a more significant proportion of non-poor individuals use the technology compared to the poor group. The disparity indicates a 16% difference in internet usage, a 10% discrepancy in mobile ownership, and a 7% distinction in mobile and computer/laptop usage. The disparity in internet usage among different income groups has significant implications for inclusivity in terms of access and coverage.

Poor individuals are often less likely to use or own digital resources. This can be attributed to various factors, such as the high cost, inadequate infrastructure, limited education and digital skills, and relevance of digital technology and content catering to their needs and interests. These factors hinder poor individuals' ability to fully utilise the potential benefits of digital technology.

Table 3. Mean comparison of non-poor and poor sample

	Non-poor (Mean)	Poor (Mean)	Difference	Std. err.	t-stat	p-value
PC Use	0.0886	0.0221	0.0665	0.0007	101.1509	0.0000
Mobile Own	0.4734	0.3711	0.1023	0.0013	77.8149	0.0000
Mobile use	0.8805	0.8099	0.0705	0.0009	76.0201	0.0000
Internet use	0.2238	0.0685	0.1553	0.001	157.6343	0.0000

6.3. Digital Divide and Disability Gap

The inclusion of disabled persons in the process of digitalization diffusion is of utmost relevance due to its benefits. The outcomes of the digital divide across persons with and without disabilities are presented in Figure 5. There is a noticeable disparity in technology usage, with higher percentages observed among non-disabled individuals compared to disabled individuals across all four outcomes. It is interesting to note that the percentage of non-disabled individuals who use computers is higher compared to disabled individuals. Specifically, 7 out of every 100 non-disabled people use computers, while only 4 disabled people do. The noticeable difference in technology usage between individuals with different abilities indicates that people may encounter various challenges and difficulties when accessing and using digital technologies.

There is a slight difference in mobile ownership and usage among both disabled and non-disabled individuals. Mobile phones are generally more affordable and convenient to use than other options. There is a disparity in internet usage, with only 18 out of 100 non-disabled individuals and 11 out of 100 disabled

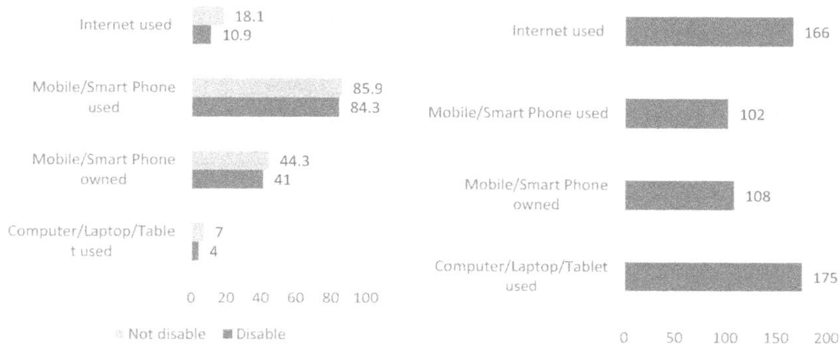

Figure 5. Digital technology use across disable and non-disable

individuals accessing the internet. It appears that mobile/smartphone technology is more cost-effective, accessible, and significant when compared to internet technology. Furthermore, it implies that harnessing internet technology requires more expertise and resources.

We presented the t-test results in Table 4, which compared the significant difference in the mean of disabled and non-disabled persons. It appears that a greater proportion of individuals in the non-disabled group are using the technology compared to the disabled group. The extent of the disparity indicates a 7% difference in internet usage, a 3% discrepancy in mobile ownership, and a 2% distinction in mobile use and 3% in computer/laptop usage.

The digital divide is more pronounced among disabled individuals for several reasons. These include lack of accessibility, affordability, skills, awareness, and support. Moreover, factors that navigate the digital exclusion of disabled persons are social stigma and isolation, limited access to education, and lower digital literacy due to limited opportunities to develop digital skills, employment, healthcare, and social participation. Negative attitudes and misconceptions about the capabilities of disabled individuals also contribute to discrimination and exclusion from digital opportunities.

Table 4. Mean comparison of non-disable and disable sample

	Non-disable	Disable	Difference	Std. err.	t-stat	p-value
PC Use	0.0699	0.0402	0.0297	0.001	30.9413	0.0000
Mobile Own	0.4432	0.4098	0.0335	0.0019	17.4779	0.0000
Mobile use	0.8588	0.8432	0.0156	0.0014	11.5616	0.0000
Internet use	0.1806	0.1085	0.0721	0.0015	49.6109	0.0000

6.4. Digital Divide and Extent of Disparities

The study also explores the digital divide among marginalised groups, including women, individuals living in poverty, and those with disabilities. Our investigation showed that individuals from marginalised groups may belong to multiple marginalised groups simultaneously. For this purpose, we explored and compared the outcomes of digital technology across seven marginalised groups by utilising the Venn diagram (see Figure 6a–d). The percentages in each section of the circles represent the usage of computers by different groups and their overlaps (see Figure 6a). The findings suggest that 5 out of 100 females, 2 out of 100 poor people, and 4 out of 100 disabled people use the computer. From the overlapping perspectives, 1 out of 100 females who are also poor, 2 out of 100 females who are disabled use computers, and 1 out of 100 poor people who are disabled use computers.

On the other hand, less than 1% (precisely 0.89) of females who are poor and disabled use computers. The findings suggest that the gap in digital technology

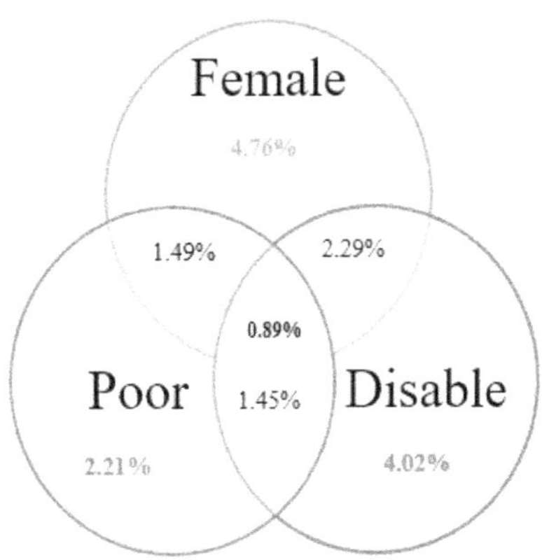

Figure 6a. Computer/laptop usage distribution

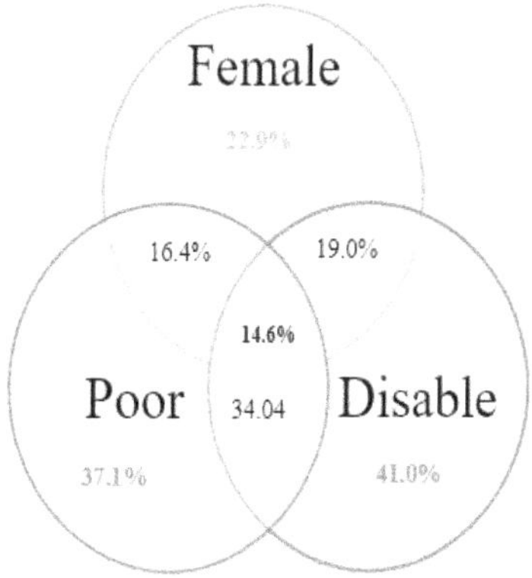

Figure 6b. Mobile ownership distribution

usage also widens as disparities grow. Having multiple disparities heightens the vulnerability of these groups when it comes to accessing, affording, or being aware of computers. Additionally, it indicates the necessity for policies and programmes that are more inclusive and accessible to address the digital divide and empower these specific groups.

Based on Figures 6b and 6c findings, individuals who experience a single disparity tend to have relatively higher rates of mobile ownership or usage. On the other hand, when someone experiences two disparities, the proportion of mobile ownership and usage decreases compared to the case of a single disparity. In the three disparities, there is a significant decrease in the proportion of individuals who own and use mobile devices, dropping to one and a half or below.

It has been noted that among the three marginalised segments of society, the poor are more vulnerable to the digital divide than the other two categories. In a similar vein, when it comes to digital exclusion, disabled persons are more inclined compared to females. The composition of individuals who are poor with female or disabled persons is more vulnerable than the composition of females with disabled persons.

7. Conclusion

This study examines the prevalence of digital technology resources among the marginalized segments of society. The aftermaths of descriptive and inferential statistics provide evidence of a disparity between males and females accessing

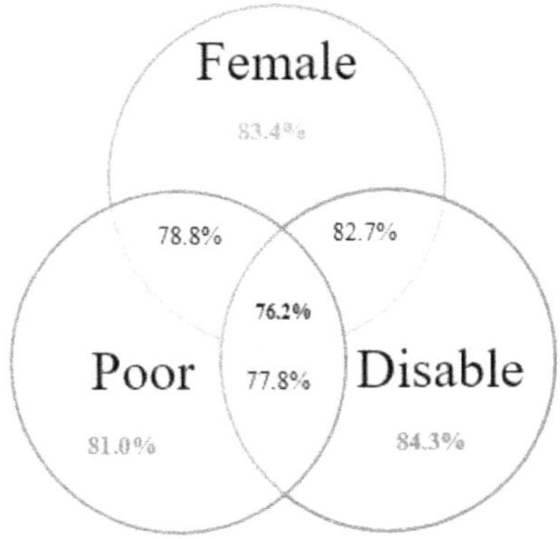

Figure 6c. Mobile usage distribution

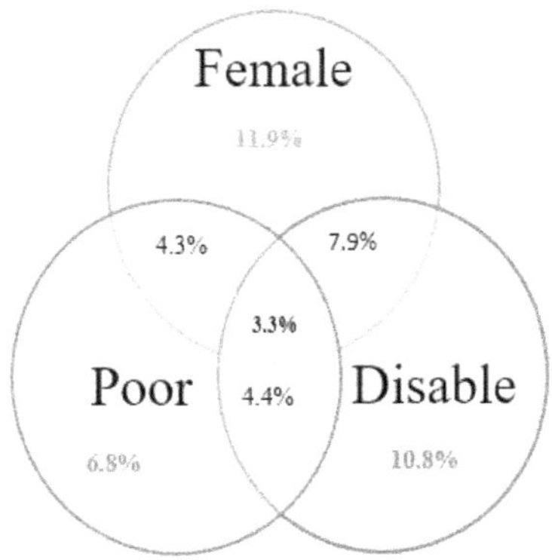

Figure 6d. Internet usage distribution

digital resources. Females have less access to computers, mobile phones, and the internet than males. The study also unveils that poor individuals have less access to digital resources than the non-poor. Moreover, the digital divide is more profound in access to digital resources for the person with disabilities than without disabilities. The disparity in access to digital resources is more profound amongst the poor than the other deprived groups. The proportional share in access to digital resources in a reference group decreases as individuals encounter more disparities.

According to research findings, significant disparities in accessing digital resources are apparent in the context of gender, income groups, and disabled persons. It is essential to acknowledge the policy measures aimed at promoting gender equality, reducing income inequality, and addressing disability issues, which can help bridge the digital divide. To overcome the barriers that impede access to digital technology, it is crucial to focus on affordability, digital infrastructure, digital literacy and inclusive online environments. It is relevant to undertake data monitoring and research to create specific interventions for marginalised communities.

References

Kurniawati, M. A. (2021). Analysis of the impact of information communication technology on economic growth: empirical evidence from Asian countries. *Journal of Asian Business and Economic Studies*, 29(1), 2–18.

Lythreatis, S., Singh, S. K., & El-Kassar, A. N. (2022). The digital divide: A review and future research agenda. *Technological Forecasting and Social Change*, 175, 121359.

Ma, J. K. H., & Cheng, S. (2022). First- and second-level digital divides from 2009 to 2018. In: *Adolescent well-being and ICT use. human well-being research and policy making*. Cham: Springer.

Pakistan Bureau of Statistics. (2020a). *Pakistan social and living standards measurement survey report*. https://www.pbs.gov.pk/sites/default/files//pslm/publications/pslm_district_2019-20/PSLM_2019_20_District_Level.pdf

Sachs, J. D., Modi, V., Figueroa, H., Machado, M., Sanyal, K., Khatun, F., & Reid, K. (2016). How information and communications technology can accelerate action on the sustainable development goals. *The Earth Institute*.

Shair, W., Tayyab, M., Nawaz, S., & Amjad, K. (2023). Digital divide in Pakistan: Barriers to ICT adoption. *Bulletin of Business and Economics*, 12(2), 243–252.

Shair, W., Waheed, A., Kamran, M. M., & Kubra, N. (2022a). Digital divide in Pakistan: Barriers to ICT usage among the individuals of Pakistan. *Journal of Economic Impact*, 4(3), 196–204.

Shair, W., Zahra, T., Tayyab, M., & Kubra, N. (2022b). The impact of the digital divide on wage gaps among individuals in Pakistan. *Journal of Policy Research*, 8(4), 97–107.

Van Deursen, A. J., & Helsper, E. J. (2015). The third-level digital divide: Who benefits most from being online? *Communication and Information Technologies*

Annual (*Studies in Media and Communications* (Vol. 10, pp. 29–52)). Leeds: Emerald Group Publishing Limited.

Verma, A., Dandgawhal, P. S., & Giri, A. K. (2023). Impact of ICT diffusion and financial development on economic growth in developing countries. *Journal of Economics, Finance and Administrative Science.*

Hayati Yusof, Zulnurhaini Zolkaply, Ong Hock Siong,
Yee Chew Fong, Mohamad Fared Mohamad Makmor,
Lee Weng Onn

Being Stateless in Malaysia and Its Implications

1. Introduction

In August 2022, Malaysia was alarmed by the news of a father who threw his three children off an elevated highway – MRR2 (Middle Ring Road 2) before jumping off the highway himself. Three of them died – the father, an eight year old girl and a boy believed to be six or seven years old. The father and the young girl were found with their United Nations High Commissioner for Refugees (UNHCR) cards. The younger boy, aged about five years old survived the ordeal and was treated at the intensive care unit of a local hospital for serious injuries. They were identified as Myanmar nationals (Zack, 2022). Later, it was reported that the father had a mental health issue ("Man who threw children off MRR2 had mental health issues, say cops", 2022).

In a different case, on an island located about 10 km off the coast of Sandakan, Pulau Berhala, is home to about 5,000 sea gypsies or the Bajau Laut ethnic people. The sea gypsies believed to have fled to Sabah in the 1970s to escape the war between the Philippines government and the independent movement by the Moro National Liberation Front. They managed to resettle in many parts of the state such as in Lahat Datu, Semporna and Sandakan. These are the undocumented migrants (and children) working and living illegally on Sabah soil (Amir, 2021).

At the 77th General Assembly of the United Nation 2022, the then Malaysian Prime Minister urged other member nations to get involved by accepting Myanmar refugees (especially the Rohingya) who look for shelter in members' home countries rather than simply criticizing the firm Malaysian decision to return the asylum seekers to their country of origins (United Nation, 2022). Malaysia is not party to the 1951 Refugee Convention or its 1967 protocols and the Malaysian law did not distinguish between refugees and undocumented migrants (Neo, 2023). The followings are the modern cases in the cities.

1.1. Case 1

As a young adult who was born in Penang to a Malaysian father and an Indonesian mother, Mel (not a real name) was still unable to obtain a Malaysian identity card. Without a valid ID (Malaysian identity card due to the carelessness of several parties), Mel could not continue studying and had to start working at a tender age of 14. Despite being registered as a Malaysian upon birth, she had faced difficulties all along as a result of a delay in her parents' marriage registration in Malaysia. Her struggles included giving up her hope and ambition in her dream sport, living without the full support of her parents and not having a valid bank account, driving licence and no access to public hospitals ("No IC at 21", 2023).

1.2. Case 2

Daisy, aged 7, was adopted by her parents. She was not permitted to enrol in any government school due to her status as a non-citizen. Her parents did not have any idea who Daisy's parents are or their whereabouts, thus, they could neither obtain a passport for her nor enrol her into an expensive private school. Thanks to the intervention by the Education Ministry, after her story was made public, now she is able to enjoy going to school like many other children. Similar to Daisy, May, 7, was born in Thailand to a Malaysian father and a Thai mother. She was able to start school in Malaysia with the help or intervention of a local political party. In addition, Tan who is from northern Malaysia also faced similar challenges when he did not have a birth certificate. He was returned to his grandparents by his Myanmar mother who could not trace his Malaysian father. His case prompted the northern state's chief minister to intervene on behalf of all stateless children in allowing them to enter public schools in the state (New, 2018).

According to New (2018), being stateless included those who are abandoned at birth, unable to track down their biological parents and whose parents (one parent is a foreigner) failed to register their marriage before the birth of the stateless children.

2. Implications of Being Stateless in Malaysia

Stateless means someone who is not a citizen of any country in the world. In Malaysia, stateless is a result of gender inequalities when a child was born overseas and out of wedlock to a Malaysian father and/or born overseas to a Malaysian mother (Lim, 2023). There are differences between a stateless person, an undocumented person, a migrant and a refugee. In total, there are 10 categories of being statelessness in Malaysia including the indigenous people ('orang asli' or 'orang asal') who were born in Malaysia but undocumented or unregistered at birth, Malaysia-born children who were abandoned by their real parents or adopted by Malaysians, those with incomplete documents, internally displaced, nomadic Bajau Laut (sea gypsies), multigenerational migrants and refugees (Lim, 2023).

Based on Table 1, the stateless people had no permission to work (Suzarika et al., 2020; Kunapalan et al., 2020; Melati et al., 2020; Norhafiza et al., 2022), they only worked as operational employees (such as restaurant helpers) with low wages and no benefits. Baltazar and Cheong (2021) classified the stateless job as 3D (dirty, dangerous and difficult) with no health or unemployment insurance (especially during the pandemic). Furthermore, stateless children could not get access to education or attend public schools, sometimes they were forced to stop schooling because they could not produce legal documentation or when they lacked identification such as having a passport. The third obstacle is getting access to healthcare services (Suzarika et al., 2020; Kunapalan et al., 2020; Melati et al., 2020). Most of the sea gypsy mothers have never received treatments at the hospitals during their pregnancies (Norhafiza et al., 2022). Moreover, the government's prolonged exclusion of undocumented and stateless people has created a blind spot towards Malaysian response to COVID-19 pandemic, risking non-citizens exposure to infection and undermining the management effort both at national and regional levels (Baltazar & Cheong, 2021).

For the refugees, life is a challenge when they could not speak or understand the local languages (Suzarika et al., 2020), they even looked like illegal immigrants (Suzarika et al., 2020; Kunapalan et al., 2020) and sometimes they were falsely detained by the local authorities due to the lack of self-identification. This opened up opportunities for physical abuse to the stateless (Kunapalan et al., 2020). Often, refugees run away or hide when they bumped into patrol cars. The perception of the public towards the refugees is not always positive as they reminded the locals of the illegal immigrants or PATI (Pendatang Asing Tanpa Izin). It is like a label fixed in the minds of the locals.

Table 1. Preliminary findings from literatures

Author/ Refugee Challenge	**Subject**	**Permission to work**	**Access to Education**	**Access to Healthcare**	**Speak local language fluently**	**Understand local culture**	**Look like Illegal immigrant**	**Physical Abuse**	**Mental Health Issues**	**Temporary Work Permit**
Suzarika et al. (2020)	Refugees	No	No	No	No	–	Yes	–	Yes	–
Kunapalan et al. (2020)	Refugees	No	No	No	–	–	Yes	Yes	Yes	Yes
		Other issues: No basic knowledge of system and local policies; Knowledge sharing to help social integration and remove language gap								
Melati et al. (2020)	Refugees	No	No	No	–	–	–	–	–	–
		Other issues: No freedom to move around								
Norhafiza et al. (2022)	Stateless children	–	No	–	–	–	–	–	–	–
		Other issues: Involve in social problems, freedom without parents' monitoring, inability to speak Malaysian language								
Baltazar & Cheong (2021)	Stateless, undocumented and migrant	–	–	No	–	–	–	–	–	–
		Other issues: No one should be left behind in a robust and inclusive public health infrastructure – as an acknowledgment to stateless' long-term economic contributions to Malaysia								

3. Further Action

Addressing statelessness is crucial for upholding the fundamental human rights and ensuring the well-being of individuals affected by this issue. It calls for comprehensive actions at both a national and global scale, including legislative changes, public education campaigns, and collaboration between governments, non-governmental organizations (NGOs), and international organizations. In Malaysia, the government, NGOs, United Nations High Commissioner for Refugees (UNHCR) and even individuals have kept up their planning and response efforts on the issue. This is evident in some of the government's initiatives to assist stateless individuals in both West and East Malaysia. State government in Sabah for example, provides temporary shelters for stateless children, aiming for sea gypsy (Bajau Laut) children, with or without guardians. Children spend three months acquiring some self-care, community living, and spiritual learning skills before being released to their guardians with conditions (Miwil, 2022).

A local catalyst, Development of Human Resources for Rural Areas (DHRRA) Malaysia, is also extensively working to combat statelessness in Malaysia. One initiative taken by DHRRA with the technical support provided by United Nations High Commissioner for Refugees (UNHCR) resulted in a decrease number of statelessness in West Malaysia from an estimated 40,000 people in 2009 to 12,400 people as of the end of December 2017 (DHRRA Malaysia, 2022). This local NGO had helped 264 stateless children enrolled in elementary and secondary schools. As mentioned earlier, citizens have also taken individual initiatives to assist stateless people. Alternative schools for stateless children in Semporna are a proof of successful individual works which later have gained government's attention. Since then, more alternative schools were developed in Tawau and Kota Kinabalu for which projects received contribution from the state government ("Sekolah Alternatif Terima RM100,000 Daripada Kerajaan Sabah", 2023).

Beyond these, there are still more works to be done, especially for Sabah's stateless and vulnerable people, which primarily consist of sea gypsies, undocumented indigenous and migrant populations who have resided in the state for generations. It is more difficult to establish programmes in East Malaysia than West Malaysia as the number of populations especially in Sabah remains unknown. It might be challenging to develop intervention plans without accurate baseline data and estimates of the impacted populations. A systematic organization of mapping, data collection, and data sharing is necessary for greater predictability and evidence-based domestic policy. It also requires supports and collaboration between the states and agencies for issue mitigation and resolution (StraComm USIM, 2021).

Furthermore, because Malaysia follows a strict dualist philosophy, treaties that have been ratified do not automatically come into effect. The Federal Constitution of Malaysia specifically excludes international law from its definition of "law" (StraComm USIM, 2021). In an interview with Malaysiakini, Bugaya legislators (Sabah state legislative assembly) admitted that statelessness was a problem in their districts but there are no concrete policy views to address it (Halim, 2020). However, there are some progresses at policy level when the former Prime Ministers of Malaysia have announced some changes in terms and standard operating procedures (SOP) for citizenship applications. After all, dealing with statelessness is a complicated and multifaceted issue that may call for co-operations between governmental organizations, non-governmental organizations (NGOs), legal professionals, and impacted populations. Indeed, the precise course of action will be determined according to the specific circumstances at hand and Malaysia's legal system.

4. Conclusion

Statelessness is a serious issue in Malaysia that has an impact on many individuals and different communities. There are about 10 forms of statelessness in Malaysia, including those who are native and were born here without proper documentation or registration, people with insufficient documentation, internally displaced people, nomadic Bajau Laut (sea gypsies), intergenerational migrants, and refugees, as well as foundling and abandoned children born in Malaysia. These stateless people have no legal protection and have entitlements to just a restricted number of options such as getting a job, minimum access to healthcare and education, which could have denied their basic human rights. Even worse, if statelessness issues are not being addressed properly, it is possible for statelessness to be passed down through families, perpetuating the vicious cycle of poverty, illiteracy and legal ambiguity.

Malaysia has made progress in addressing the issue of statelessness, nonetheless, more must be done to guarantee that everyone living as stateless has access to legal recognition and the fundamental freedoms that come with citizenship. Efforts to reduce and ultimately eliminate statelessness involve legal reforms, awareness campaigns, support services and international co-operation. Previous actions taken based on humanitarian principle alone (such as giving permission to stay with no access to education for the stateless children or to the Rohingya refugees) are insufficient. However, it is not easy to end statelessness as this issue is politically sensitive in many affected countries including Malaysia and in fact, Malaysia's legal system will dictate the best course of action in every case. In spite of this, it is nevertheless essential that the government, non-governmental organizations (NGOs) and international organizations continue to collaborate, giving support to those who are stateless while devising a promising future ahead especially for the young stateless generations.

References

Amir, Y. (2021, February 5). *Living in a sea of trash: Sabah's stateless children face bleak future*. Retrieved September 25, 2023 from https://www.channelnewsasia.com/asia/sabah-stateless-children-sea-gypsies-bajau-laut-881736

Baltazar, M. A. K., & Cheong, A. R. (2021). Reaching stateless, undocumented and migrant communities during the Covid-19 pandemic: Lessons from the grassroots humanitarian effort in Sabah, Malaysia. *Statelessness & Citizenship Review*, 3(1), 131–141.

DHRRA Malaysia. (2022). *Report: Statelessness in Malaysia*. Retrieved September 28, 2023 from https://dhrramalaysia.org.my/wp-content/uploads/2022/04/STATELESSNESS-IN-MALAYSIA-REPORT-05042022_compressed.pdf

Halim, M. F. (2020, September 26). *Sekolah Alternatif: A school for Semporna's invisible children*. Malaysiakini. Retrieved September 28, 2023 from https://www.malaysiakini.com/news/544148

Kunapalan, H., Ismail, N. B., & Yatiban, A. B. (2020). The roles of Non-Governmental Organisations (NGOs) in assisting refugees: From Malaysia context. *Malaysian Journal of Social Sciences and Humanities (MJSSH)*, 5(5), 89–94.

Lim, I. (2023, June 30). *'Invisible' in Malaysia: Why are people born here stateless and will the government's citizenship proposals fix or worsen the problem?*. Retrieved September 27, 2023 from https://www.malaymail.com/news/malaysia/2023/06/30/invisible-in-malaysia-why-are-people-born-here-stateless-and-will-the-govts-citizenship-proposals-fix-or-worsen-the-problem/76895

Melati, N., Flanders, S., & Chuah, H. Y. (2020). Poverty and precarious employment: The case of Rohingya refugee construction workers in Peninsular Malaysia. *Humanities and Social Sciences Communications*, 7(1), 1–11.

Miwil, O. (2022, November 28). Sabah to set up temporary shelters to help stateless kids. *New Straits Times*. Retrieved September 28, 2023 form https://www.nst.com.my/news/nation/2022/11/855590/sabah-set-temporary-shelters-help-stateless-kids

Neo, C. C. (February 11, 2023). *Malaysia has become less friendly to Myanmar Refugees. What hope for them now?*. Retrieved September 6, 2023 from https://www.channelnewsasia.com/cna-insider/malaysia-myanmar-refugees-asylum-raids-deportations-hope-safe-haven-3262911

New, J. L. (January 14, 2018). *This seven-year-old from Seremban was not allowed to enrol in a government school at first. Why?* Retrieved September 27, 2023 from https://cilisos.my/this-7-year-old-from-seremban-was-not-allowed-to-enrol-in-a-government-school-at-first-why/

Norhafiza, M. H., Aprina, O. & Norazlan, H. Y. (2022). Stateless issue in Semporna, Sabah: Impact on the stateless children's education (Sea Gypsies): Isu Stateless di Semporna, Sabah: Kesan ke atas Pendidikan Kanak-Kanak Tanpa Negara (Bajau Laut) . *EDUCATUM Journal of Social Sciences*, 8(2), 32–43. https://doi.org/10.37134/ejoss.vol8.2.4.2022

Sekolah Alternatif Terima RM100,000 Daripada Kerajaan Sabah. (2023, April 8). *Sabah Gazette*. Retrieved September 27, 2023 from https://www.sabahgazette.com/sekolah-alternatif-terima-rm100000-daripada-kerajaan-sabah/

StraComm USIM. (2021, July 16). *Addressing statelessness in Malaysia: New hope and remaining challenges*. Universiti Sains Islam Malaysia. Retrieved September 27, 2023 from https://www.usim.edu.my/news/face-of-usim/addressing-statelessness-in-malaysia-new-hope-and-remaining-challenges/

Suzarika, S., Rohaida, N., & Ma Kalthum, I. (2020). The plight of refugees in Malaysia: Malaysia as a transit country in protecting refugees' rights. *Journal of Nusantara Studies (JONUS)*, *5*(1), 378–394.

United Nation. (September 20–26, 2022). *Malaysia – Prime Minister addresses UN General Debate, 77th Session*. Retrieved September 26, 2023 from https://www.youtube.com/watch?v=aqt7JQ8J6Aw

Zack, J. (2022, August 3). *Man throws kids off MRR2*. Retrieved September 25, 2023 from https://www.thestar.com.my/news/nation/2022/08/03/man-throws-kids-off-mrr2

www.ingramcontent.com/pod-product-compliance
Ingram Content Group UK Ltd.
Pitfield, Milton Keynes, MK11 3LW, UK
UKHW021921120926
8556IPUK00042BA/1107

9 783631 919576